Random House
Webster's
Pocket
Computer &
Internet
Dictionary

D0544338

Random House
Webster's
Pocket
Computer &
Internet
Dictionary

RANDOM HOUSE
NEW YORK

Random House Webster's
Pocket Computer & Internet Dictionary

Trademarks

This work is based on *Random House Webster's Computer & Internet Dictionary*, 3rd Edition by Philip Margolis, published in 1998 by Random House, Inc.

Library of Congress Cataloging-in-Publication Number: 99-74253

Visit the Random House Web site at www.randomhouse.com

Typeset by Random House Reference & Information Publishing

Typeset and printed in the United States of America on acid-free paper

0 9 8 7 6 5 4 3 2 1
First Edition
June 1999
ISBN: 0-375-70626-7

New York   Toronto   London   Sydney   Auckland

Contents

Pronunciation Key

The symbol (′), as in **moth′er,** is used to mark primary stress; the syllable preceding it is pronounced with greater prominence than the other syllables in the word. The symbol (′), as in **grand′moth′er,** is used to mark secondary stress; a syllable marked for secondary stress is pronounced with less prominence than one marked (′) but with more prominence than those bearing no stress mark at all.

a	act, bat	o͝o	book, put
ā	able, cape	o͞o	ooze, rule
â	air, dare	ou	out, loud
ä	art, calm		
		p	page, stop
b	back, rub	r	read, cry
ch	chief, beach	s	see, miss
d	do, bed	sh	shoe, push
		t	ten, bit
e	ebb, set	th	thin, path
ē	equal, bee	t͟h	that, other
f	fit, puff	u	up, love
g	give, beg	û	urge, burn
h	hit, hear		
		v	voice, live
i	if, big	w	west, away
ī	ice, bite	y	yes, young
		z	zeal, lazy, those
j	just, edge	zh	vision, measure
k	kept, make		
l	low, all	ə	occurs only in unac-
			cented syllables and
m	my, him		indicates the sound of
n	now, on		a *in* along
ng	sing, England		e *in* system
			i *in* easily
o	box, hot		o *in* gallop
ō	over, no		u *in* circus
ô	order, ball		
oi	oil, joy		

Guide to Computer Terms by Category

Application Programming Interfaces (APIs)

API
ASPI
CGI
DirectX
DMI
HLLAPI
ISAPI
JDBC
MAPI
MCI
MDI
NSAPI
ODBC
ODI
SDK
TAPI
TSAPI

Applications

accounting software
applet
application
autosave
bells and whistles
bloatware
CAD
CAD/CAM
CAE
calculator
calendar
CAM
close
compound document
contact manager
courseware
data processing
document management

e-mail client
end user
ERP
export
feature
handwriting recognition
import
legacy application
open
PIM
PKZIP
quit
run
runtime version
save
scheduler
shareware
spell checker
vanilla

Artificial Intelligence

agent
artificial intelligence
bot
cybernetics
expert system
fuzzy logic
genetic programming
handwriting recognition
language
natural language
neural network
optical character
    recognition
pattern recognition
robot
robotics
voice recognition

Audio

3-D audio

AC-3
AIFF
AU
digital audio
digitize
Dolby Digital
fps
MIDI
MP3
MPEG
RealAudio
sampling
sound card
streaming
WAV
wave table synthesis

Browsers

ActiveX control
bookmark
browse
browser
Internet Explorer
Java
JavaScript
Microsoft
Mosaic
Mozilla
Navigator
Netscape
plug-in
Shockwave
VBScript

Buses

32-bit
Access.bus
ADB
address bus
AGP
AT bus

burst mode
bus
bus mastering
CardBus
EIDE
EISA
expansion bus
external bus
Fibre Channel
HIPPI
hot plugging
I2O
IEEE 1394
Industry Standard
    Architecture (ISA) bus
interface
local bus
Micro Channel
    Architecture (MCA)
NuBus
PCI
PCMCIA
SCSI
USB
VL-Bus
VME bus

Business Presentation

area chart
bar chart
column graph
exploded view
legend
line graph
pie chart
presentation graphics
scatter diagram

Cables

coaxial cable
fiber optics

SLIP
V.22
V.22bis
V.32
V.34
V.35
V.42
V.90
Xmodem
Ymodem
Zmodem

Compiling, Binding and Linking

bind
coff
compile
link
map
object code
source code

Computer Entertainment

3DO
MOO
MUCK
MUD
MUSH

Computer Industry Companies

ISV
OEM
Silicon Valley
VAR

Computer Science

architecture
computer literacy
computer science
computer system
digital

dynamic
ergonomics
IT
logical
meta-
paperless office
physical
proprietary
sampling
stateless
system
transparent
virtual

Configuring Adapters

ASPI
configuration
configure
DIP
DIP switch
hot plugging
IRQ
jumper
plug-and-play
PnP
SCAM
setup
toggle

Connectors, Plugs and Sockets

BNC connector
connector
DIN connector
pinout
plug
RJ-11
RJ-45
slot
Slot 1
socket

Socket 7
Socket 8
Zero Insertion Force
    (ZIF) socket

Convergence
cable modem
CDMA
convergence
DSS
PC/TV
WebTV

Data
analog
attribute
BLOB
browse
comma-delimited
control character
convert
corrupted
data
data dictionary
data entry
data integrity
data mining
data processing
digital
digitize
escape sequence
export
fixed-length
import
integer
ISAM
key
line feed
machine readable
metadata
petabyte

precision
punctuation
purge
random access
raw data
read
read-only
read/write
record
replication
sequential access
sign
variable length
variable-length record
write

Data Compression
ARC
codec
data compression
DCT
disk compression
file compression
lossless compression
lossy compression
LZW
MNP
MP3
MPEG
pack
packed file
PKZIP
sampling
tar
unpack
ZIP

Data Formats
AIFF
alphanumeric
ANSI Character Set

literal
mathematical expression
scientific notation
static variable
subscript
variable

Faxing
digitize
fax
fax machine
fax modem
Group 3 protocol
Group 4 protocol
MFP
optical scanner
telecopy

File Management
alias
directory
document
dot
extension
FAT32
file
file allocation table
file management system
filename
folder
hidden file
ISAM
lock
NFS
NTFS
parent directory
path
pathname
redirection
root directory
slack space

subdirectory
text file
UNC
VSAM
wildcard character
working directory

File Transfer
anonymous FTP
Binary File Transfer
    (BFT)
BinHex
download
FTP
MIME
TFTP
upload
Uuencode
Xmodem
Ymodem

Flat-Panel displays
active-matrix display
backlighting
CSTN
DSTN
dual-scan display
electroluminescent
    display (ELD)
flat technology monitor
flat-panel display
gas-plasma display
LCD
LCD monitor
passive-matrix display
plasma display
supertwist
TFT

Formatting
alignment

bleed
feathering
flow
flush
footer
forced page break
gutter
hanging indent
hard
header
hyphenation
justification
justify
landscape
layout
leader
left justify
margins
MuTeX
odd header
orientation
orphan
overstrike
page break
page layout program
pagination
pica
point
portrait
proportional spacing
ragged
redlining
repaginate
soft
strikeout
style
style sheet
tag
text wrap

thumbnail
vertical justification
widow
word wrap

Formatting Standards

CSS
HTML
LaTeX
MuTeX
PDF
PostScript
rich text format
SGML
TeX
TrueType
XML

Foundation Classes

AFC
JDK
MFC

Graphical User Interfaces (GUIs)

alert box
AWT
branch
button
cascading windows
check box
choose
click
collapse
desktop
dialog box
double click
drag
drag-and-drop
graphical user interface
GUI

resolution
RGB monitor
S-Video
screen
screen flicker
smart terminal
terminal
touch screen
true color
TTL monitor
VDT radiation
VDU
Windows terminal

Motherboards

ATX
backplane
BIOS
daughtercard
form factor
heat sink
LPX
motherboard
NLX
POST
printed circuit board
voltage regulator
VRM

Multimedia

BLOB
digital watermark
HDTV
MCI
MPC
multimedia
multimedia kit
SMIL
streaming
television board
tweening

WebTV

Multiplexing

FDM
multiplex
multiplexor
PCM
TDM
TDMA
WDM

Network Interface Cards (NICs)

3COM
AUI
BNC connector
DLC
IRMA board
MAC address
NDIS
network interface card
ODI
protocol stack
transceiver

Network Management

audit trail
CMIP
DMI
IS
MIB
MIS
network management
remote control
RMON
SMS
sniffer
SNMP
spoof
system management
systems administrator

ZV Port

PowerPC
BeOS
CHRP
PowerPC
PPCP
RISC

**Printer
Manufacturers**
HP
Okidata

Printers
carriage
cartridge
continuous-form paper
cps
daisy-wheel printer
dot-matrix printer
dpi
draft mode
draft-quality
font cartridge
form feed
friction feed
GDI
GDI printer
gppm
host-based printer
HP-compatible printer
HPGL
imagesetter
ImageWriter
impact printer
ink-jet printer
laser printer
LaserWriter
LCD printer
letter-quality (LQ)

line printer
Linotronic
LPT
MFP
near-letter-quality
nonimpact printer
offset printing
overstrike
Page Description Language (PDL)
page printer
paper feed
PCL
pin
plotter
PostScript
ppm
print server
printer
printer driver
printer engine
printout
raster image processor
resident font
resolution enhancement
sheet feeder
smoothing
snapshot printer
soft font
spooler
thermal printer
toner
tractor feed
WYSIWYP

**Procedures, Functions
and Routines**
aggregate function
argument
call

Programming

function
invoke
module
parameter
procedure
recursion
routine
RPC
stub
system call

Programming

ActiveX
algorithm
alpha version
benchmark
beta test
big-endian
bloatware
bomb
bubble sort
bug
bytecode
CICS
code
constant
contiguous
control
data type
debug
declare
delimiter
DLL
dummy
dump
dynamic variable
easter egg
encapsulation
filter
flag

flow control
front end
functional specification
garbage in, garbage out
geek
genetic programming
glitch
hack
hacker
hard coded
hardwired
heap sort
heuristic programming
High Performance
    Computing
interprocess
    communication (IPC)
ISO 9000
iteration
JDBC
kludge
library
line
listing
loop
macro
mask
memory leak
MPP
name
nesting
OCX
optimize
overhead
parse
patch
program
programmer
property

X-Window
Xenix

User Interfaces
active
Apple key
associate
autosave
box
case sensitive
character based
CICS
clipboard
command driven
context sensitive
control
Control key combination
copy
CUA
current
cursor
cursor control keys
cursor position
default
delete
documentation
ergonomics
floating
form
Help
highlight
hot key
insertion point
interactive
keystroke
learn mode
light bar
look-and-feel
modifier key
option

overwrite mode
prompt
Recycle Bin
reverse video
screen font
screen saver
select
shortcut
shortcut key
tear-off menu
undo
user
user interface
user-friendly
wizard

Video
digital video
digitize
fps
genlock
S-Video
sampling
streaming
television board
video
video capture
video editing
video overlay
VoD

Video Adapters
color depth
DDC
genlock
graphics accelerator
graphics coprocessor
graphics mode
PAL
RAMDAC
SGRAM

A a

abort *v.t.* **1.** to stop (a program or function) before it has finished naturally: *to abort a print job; to abort a search.* —*v.i.* **2.** to terminate before completion: *The program aborted because of a bug in the software.*
⇒ See also BOMB; CRASH; HANG; QUIT.

absolute address *n.* a fixed address in memory. Also called **real address, machine address.**
⇒ See also ADDRESS; RELATIVE ADDRESS.

absolute cell reference *n.* in spreadsheet applications, a reference, to a particular cell or group of cells, that never changes.
⇒ See also CONSTANT; RELATIVE CELL REFERENCE; SPREADSHEET.

AC-3 the coding system used by Dolby Digital.
⇒ See also DOLBY DIGITAL.

Accelerated Graphics Port *n.* See AGP.

accelerator board *n.* **1.** GRAPHICS ACCELERATOR. **2.** a type of expansion board that makes a computer faster by adding a faster CPU or FPU.
⇒ See also BUS; COPROCESSOR; CPU; EXPANSION BOARD; FLOATING-POINT NUMBER; FPU; GRAPHICS ACCELERATOR; MAIN MEMORY; MOTHERBOARD; RAM; ZERO INSERTION FORCE (ZIF) SOCKET.

access *v.t.* **1.** to retrieve data from; to use. Programs can read data from or write data to main memory. A user can access files, directories (or folders), databases, computers, or peripheral devices. **2.** to read (data) from or write (data) to a mass storage device. —*n.* **3.** the act of accessing data. **4.** a privilege to use computer information in some manner. For example, a user who is granted only *read access* to a file can read the file but cannot modify or delete it.
⇒ See also ACCESS TIME; MASS STORAGE; MEMORY; RANDOM ACCESS; READ; WRITE.

Access.bus *n.* a serial communications protocol developed by Philips Semiconductors and Digital Equipment (DEC) for connecting relatively low-speed peripheral devices to a computer. Access. bus uses a bus topology, which enables it to support up to 125 devices.

⇒ See also BUS; SERIAL PORT; USB.

access code *n.* PASSWORD.

⇒ See also ACCESS; LOG ON; PASSWORD.

access control *n.* the mechanisms and policies that restrict access to computer resources. An *access control list* specifies which operations different users can perform on specific files and directories.

⇒ See also AUTHORIZATION; SECURITY.

accessory slot *n.* EXPANSION SLOT.

access time *n.* the time required to locate a piece of information and make it available to the computer. Ideally, the access time of memory chips should be fast enough to keep up with the CPU. Access time is also frequently used to describe the speed of disk drives.

⇒ See also ACCESS; CLOCK SPEED; CPU; CYCLE TIME; DATA TRANSFER RATE; DISK CACHE; INTERLEAVE; WAIT STATE.

accounting software *n.* computer programs that perform accounting operations.

⇒ See also PERSONAL FINANCE MANAGER; YEAR 2000 PROBLEM.

ACM Association for Computing Machinery: an organization composed of U.S. computer professionals. The ACM publishes information relating to computer science, holds seminars, and creates and promotes computer standards.

⇒ See also STANDARD.

acoustic coupler *n.* a device onto which a telephone handset is placed to connect a computer with a network. Acoustic couplers are no longer widely used because current modems usually connect via modular telephone connectors. However, acoustic couplers are useful in some situations, as in hotel rooms where the telephone cable is anchored to the wall.

⇒ See also MODEM; NETWORK.

ACPI Advanced Configuration and Power Interface: a power management specification developed by Intel, Microsoft, and Toshiba. ACPI, which is included in Windows 98, enables the operating system to control the amount of power

given to each device attached to the computer, which permits the operating system to turn off peripheral devices when they are not in use.
⇒ See also APM; POWER MANAGEMENT; SLEEP MODE.

Acrobat *n.* a suite of programs developed by Adobe Systems, Inc., for creating and distributing electronic documents. A user can create and distribute the PDF file electronically. People viewing a PDF file (or document) with Acrobat Reader see the document with the exact layout and typography intended by the author.
⇒ See also PDF.

acronym *n.* a word formed by combining some parts (usually the first letters) of other terms. For example, *modem* is an acronym derived from *mod(ulator)/dem(odulator)*. An acronym is pronounced as if it were a word rather than just a series of individual letters.

active *adj.* referring to objects currently displayed or used on a computer. For example, in graphical user interfaces, the *active window* is the window currently receiving mouse and keyboard input. In spreadsheet applications, the *active cell* is the cell, usually highlighted, in which data can be entered or modified. The *active program* is the program currently running.
⇒ See also CELL; GRAPHICAL USER INTERFACE; SPREADSHEET; WINDOW.

active backplane *n.* See under BACKPLANE.

Active Directory *n.* a new directory service from Microsoft; part of Windows NT 5.0.
⇒ See also DIRECTORY SERVICE; LDAP; NDS; WINDOWS NT; X.500.

active matrix *n.* See under ACTIVE-MATRIX DISPLAY.

active-matrix display *n.* a type of flat-panel display in which the screen is refreshed more frequently than in conventional passive-matrix displays and is therefore sharper and brighter. The terms *TFT* and *active-matrix* are often used interchangeably.
⇒ See also FLAT-PANEL DISPLAY; LCD; TFT.

ActiveMovie *n.* a new multimedia streaming technology developed by Microsoft. It is built into the Internet Explorer browser and will be part of future versions of the Windows operating system. Supporting most multimedia formats, ActiveMovie enables users to view multimedia content distributed over the Internet or on CD-ROM.

⇒ See also MULTIMEDIA; QUICKTIME; STREAMING.

Active Server Pages n. a specification for a dynamically created Web page with a .ASP extension that contains either Visual Basic or Jscript code. When a browser requests an ASP page, the Web server generates a page with HTML code and sends it back to the browser.

⇒ See also CGI; VISUAL BASIC.

ActiveX n. a loosely defined set of technologies developed by Microsoft for sharing information among different applications.

⇒ See also ACTIVEX CONTROL; ADO; COMPONENT OBJECT MODEL; DIRECTX; JAVA; MICROSOFT; OLE; WINDOWS DNA.

ActiveX control n. a control using ActiveX technologies. An ActiveX control can be automatically downloaded and executed by a Web browser. Programmers can develop ActiveX controls in a variety of languages, including C, C++, Visual Basic, and Java. An ActiveX control is similar to a Java applet.

⇒ See also ACTIVEX; BROWSER; DYNAMIC HTML; INTERNET EXPLORER; JAVABEANS; OCX; SHOCKWAVE.

ActiveX Data Objects n. See ADO.

Ada n. a high-level, general-purpose programming language developed for the U.S. Defense Department. It incorporates modular techniques that make it easy to build and maintain large systems. Ada is the mandatory development language for most U.S. military applications. It is often the language of choice for large systems that require real-time processing. [named after Augusta Ada Byron (1815–52), Countess of Lovelace and daughter of Lord Byron, who is considered by many to be the world's first programmer]

⇒ See also HIGH-LEVEL LANGUAGE; MODULAR ARCHITECTURE; REAL TIME.

adapter n. **1.** EXPANSION BOARD. **2.** the circuitry required to support a particular device. For example, *video adapters* enable a computer to support graphics monitors, and *network adapters* enable a computer to attach to a network.

⇒ See also CONTROLLER; EXPANSION BOARD; VIDEO ADAPTER.

adaptive differential pulse-code modulation *n.* See ADPCM.

ADB Apple Desktop Bus: a type of communications pathway built into all versions of the Apple Macintosh computer and used to connect low-speed input devices such as the keyboard and mouse.

⇒ See also BUS; MACINTOSH COMPUTER; PORT.

add-in *n.* **1.** a component added to a computer or other device to increase its capabilities. Add-ins can increase memory or add graphics or communications capabilities to a computer. They come in the form of expansion boards, cartridges, or chips. **2.** a software program that extends the capabilities of larger programs.

⇒ See also ADD-ON; CARTRIDGE; EXPANSION BOARD; OLE.

add-on *n.* a product designed to complement another product. Add-ons usually refer to an entire circuit board, cartridge, or software program, although they can also be individual chips that are inserted into boards.

⇒ See also ADD-ON BOARD; ADD-IN; CARTRIDGE; EXPANSION BOARD; EXPANSION SLOT; PRINTED CIRCUIT BOARD.

add-on board *n.* EXPANSION BOARD.

address *n.* **1.** a location of data, usually in main memory or on disk. Computer memory may be thought of as an array of storage boxes, each of which is one byte in length and has a unique number. By specifying an address, programmers can access a particular byte of data. Disks are divided into tracks and sectors, each with a unique address. **2.** a name or token that identifies a network component. In local-area networks (LANs), every node has a unique address. On the Internet, every file has a unique address, called a URL.

⇒ See also ABSOLUTE ADDRESS; ADDRESS BUS; ADDRESS

SPACE; BASE ADDRESS; DISK; E-MAIL ADDRESS; MAC AD-
DRESS; MACHINE ADDRESS; MAIN MEMORY; MEMORY; OFF-
SET; RELATIVE ADDRESS; SECTOR; TRACK; URL.

address bus *n.* a collection of wires connecting
the CPU with main memory that is used to identify particular locations (addresses) in main memory. The width of the address bus (that is, the
number of wires) determines how many unique
memory locations can be addressed.
⇒ See also ADDRESS; BUS; CPU; MAIN MEMORY.

Address Resolution Protocol *n.* See ARP.

address space *n.* the set of all legal addresses
in memory for a given application. The address
space represents the amount of memory available
to a program.
⇒ See also ADDRESS; MAIN MEMORY; MEMORY; THUNK;
VIRTUAL MEMORY.

ADO ActiveX Data Objects: Microsoft's newest
high-level interface for data objects. ADO is designed eventually to replace *Data Access Objects
(DAO)* and *Remote Data Objects (RDO)*. ADO is
more general and can be used to access many
different types of data, including Web pages and
spreadsheets.
⇒ See also ACTIVEX; DAO; ODBC.

Adobe Acrobat *n.* ACROBAT.

Adobe Photoshop *n.* a leading paint program
from Adobe Systems, Inc. Photoshop runs on
both Macintoshes and Windows PCs.
⇒ See also DESKTOP PUBLISHING; IMAGE ENHANCE-
MENT; PAINT PROGRAM.

Adobe PostScript *n.* POSTSCRIPT.

ADPCM Adaptive Differential Pulse-Code Modulation: a form of *pulse-code modulation (PCM)* that
produces a digital signal with a lower bit rate
than standard PCM. ADPCM records only the difference between samples and adjusts the coding
scale dynamically to accommodate large and
small differences.
⇒ See also MODULATE; PCM; SAMPLING.

ADSL asymmetric digital subscriber line: a technology that allows more data to be sent over existing copper telephone lines, known as POTS.
ADSL supports data rates of from 1.5 to 9 Mbps

when receiving data and from 16 to 640 Kbps when sending data. ADSL requires a special ADSL modem. It is not currently available to the general public except in trial areas.

⇒ See also ISDN; POTS; SDSL.

Advanced Differential Pulse-Code Modulation n. See ADPCM.

Advanced Graphics Port n. See AGP.

Advanced Micro Devices n. See AMD.

Advanced Power Management n. See APM.

Advanced SCSI Programming Interface n. See ASPI.

AFC Application Foundation Classes: a set of Microsoft foundation classes written entirely in Java. The AFC sits on top of the Java Development Kit (JDK) and extends Sun's Abstract Windows Toolkit (AWT).

⇒ See also AWT; CLASS; IFC; JAVA; JDK; MFC.

agent n. a program that performs some information-gathering or information-processing task in the background. Typically, an agent is given a very small and well-defined task. Special software, for example, enables a user to configure an agent to search the Internet for certain types of information.

⇒ See also ARTIFICIAL INTELLIGENCE; DAEMON.

aggregate function n. a function that performs a computation on a set of values rather than on a single value. For example, finding the average or mean of a list of numbers is an aggregate function. All database management and spreadsheet systems support a set of aggregate functions that can operate on a set of selected records or cells.

⇒ See also DATABASE MANAGEMENT SYSTEM; FUNCTION; SPREADSHEET.

AGP n. Accelerated Graphics Port: an interface specification developed by Intel Corporation. AGP is based on PCI but is designed especially for the throughput demands of 3-D graphics. AGP introduces a dedicated point-to-point channel so that the graphics controller can directly access main memory.

⇒ See also 3-D GRAPHICS; 3-D SOFTWARE; GRAPHICS ACCELERATOR; NLX; PCI; TEXTURE.

AI ARTIFICIAL INTELLIGENCE.

AIFF Audio Interchange File Format: a common format for storing and transmitting sampled sound. The format was developed by Apple Computer and is the standard audio format for Macintosh computers. It is also used by Silicon Graphics, Incorporated (SGI).

AIX Advanced Interactive eXecutive: a version of UNIX produced by IBM. AIX runs on a variety of computers, including PCs and workstations.
⇒ See also UNIX.

alert box *n.* a small box that appears on the display screen to give information or to warn about a potentially damaging operation. For example, it might warn that the system is deleting one or more files. Unlike dialog boxes, alert boxes do not require any user input. Also called **message box.**
⇒ See also BOX; DIALOG BOX; GRAPHICAL USER INTERFACE; WINDOW.

algorithm *n.* a formula or set of steps for solving a particular problem. The set of rules must be unambiguous and have a clear stopping point. Algorithms can be expressed in any language, from natural languages like English to programming languages like FORTRAN.
⇒ See also ARTIFICIAL INTELLIGENCE; BUBBLE SORT; HEAP SORT; HEURISTIC PROGRAMMING; PROGRAM; PROGRAMMING LANGUAGE; PSEUDOCODE.

alias *n.* an alternative name for an object, such as a variable, file, or device.
⇒ See also DEVICE; FILE; NAME; VARIABLE.

aliasing *n.* **1.** in computer graphics, the process by which smooth curves and other lines become jagged because the resolution of the graphics device or file is not high enough to represent a smooth curve. **2.** in digital sound, a static distortion resulting from a low sampling rate—below 40 kilohertz (Khz).
⇒ See also ANTIALIASING; JAGGIES; RESOLUTION; SMOOTHING.

alignment *n.* **1.** the arrangement of text or

graphics relative to a margin. **2.** the relative positions of graphical objects.

⇒ See also DRAW PROGRAM; JUSTIFICATION; MARGINS.

alpha blending *n.* See under ALPHA CHANNEL.

alpha channel *n.* in graphics, a portion of each pixel's data that is reserved for transparency information. A 32-bit graphics system contains four channels—three 8-bit channels for red, green, and blue (RGB) and one 8-bit alpha channel. The alpha channel specifies how the pixel's colors should be merged with another pixel when the two are overlaid. Rendering overlapping objects that include an alpha value is called *alpha blending.*

⇒ See also ANIMATION; GRAPHICS; MASK; PIXEL; RGB MONITOR.

alphanumeric *adj.* utilizing the combined set of all letters in the alphabet and the numbers 0 through 9. Most operating systems allow the use of any letters or numbers in filenames but prohibit the use of many punctuation characters.

⇒ See also CHARACTER; SPECIAL CHARACTER.

Alpha Processor *n.* a powerful RISC processor developed by Digital Equipment Corporation and used in its line of workstations and servers. It is the only microprocessor, other than x86 microprocessors, that runs Windows NT.

⇒ See also MICROPROCESSOR; RISC; WINDOWS NT; WORKSTATION.

alpha testing *n.* See under ALPHA VERSION.

alpha version *n.* a very early version of a software product. Typically, software goes through two stages of testing. The first stage, called *alpha testing,* is often performed by users within the organization developing the software. The second stage, called *beta testing,* generally involves a limited number of external users.

⇒ See also BETA TEST; DEBUG.

Alta Vista *n.* a software firm associated with Digital Equipment Corporation (DEC) that offers products used to locate and manage information on the Internet or an intranet. The Alta Vista search service contains one of the largest Web indices.

⇒ See also DEC; EXCITE; HOTBOT; INFOSEEK; LYCOS; MAGELLAN; OPEN TEXT; SEARCH ENGINE; SPIDER; WEB-CRAWLER; WORLD WIDE WEB; YAHOO!.

Alt key *n.* Alternate key: a key that is similar to a second Control key. It is held down while pressing another key. The meaning of any Alt key combination depends on which application is running.

⇒ See also CONTROL CHARACTER; KEYBOARD; OPTION KEY.

ALU arithmetic logic unit: the part of a computer that performs all arithmetic computations and all comparison operations. The ALU is one component of the CPU.

⇒ See also CPU.

AMD Advanced Micro Devices: a manufacturer of chips for personal computers. AMD is challenging Intel with a set of Intel-compatible microprocessors.

⇒ See also CYRIX; INTEL; INTEL MICROPROCESSORS; K6; MICROPROCESSOR; MMX; PENTIUM MICROPROCESSOR.

American National Standards Institute *n.* See ANSI.

American Standard Code for Information Interchange *n.* See ASCII.

America Online *n.* a popular online service. *Abbr.:* AOL

⇒ See also COMPUSERVE INFORMATION SERVICE; MSN; ONLINE SERVICE.

Amiga *n.* a family of personal computers originally produced by Commodore Business Machines and built around the Motorola 680x0 line of microprocessors. Amigas are powerful computers that have extra microprocessors to handle graphics and sound generation. Although the Amiga operating system is not compatible with other PC operating systems, emulation programs enable the Amiga to run PC, Macintosh, and even UNIX programs.

⇒ See also GRAPHICS; MICROPROCESSOR; MIDI; PERSONAL COMPUTER.

analog *adj.* of or being a mechanism that represents data by measurement to a continuous physical variable. Early attempts at building computers used analog techniques, but today almost all computers are digital.

⇒ See also DAC; DIGITAL.

analog monitor *n.* the traditional type of color display screen that has been used for years in televisions.

⇒ See also ANALOG; CRT; DIGITAL; DIGITAL MONITOR; FLAT-PANEL DISPLAY; MONITOR; MULTISCANNING MONITOR; VIDEO ADAPTER.

anchor *v.t.* in desktop publishing, to fix (a graphical object) so that its position relative to some other object remains the same during repagination: *to anchor a picture next to a piece of text.*

⇒ See also DESKTOP PUBLISHING.

AND operator *n.* a Boolean operator that returns a value of TRUE if both its operands are TRUE, and FALSE otherwise.

⇒ See also BOOLEAN OPERATOR; OPERAND; OPERATOR.

animated GIF *n.* a type of GIF image that can be animated by combining several images into a single GIF file. Applications that support the animated GIF standard, *GIF89A*, cycle through each image.

⇒ See also ANIMATION; GIF.

animation *n.* a simulation of movement created by displaying a series of pictures, or frames. Many software applications enable the user to create animations that can be displayed on a computer monitor.

⇒ See also VIDEO; 3-D GRAPHICS; 3-D SOFTWARE; ALPHA CHANNEL; ANIMATED GIF; MODELING; MORPHING; MULTIMEDIA; SGI; SPRITE; TWEENING.

annotation *n.* a comment attached to a particular section of a document. Many applications enable the user to enter annotations on text documents, spreadsheets, presentations, and other objects. This is a particularly effective way to use computers to edit and review work in a workgroup environment.

⇒ See also WORKGROUP COMPUTING.

anonymous FTP *n.* a method for downloading public files using the File Transfer Protocol (FTP). The user types the word *anonymous* or the abbreviation *ftp* as a username; the password can be anything, as an e-mail address or simply the word *guest*.

⇒ See also DOWNLOAD; FTP.

ANSI (an'sē), *n.* American National Standards Institute: a voluntary organization that creates standards for the computer industry. In addition to programming languages, ANSI sets standards for a wide range of technical areas, from electrical specifications to communications protocols.

⇒ See also FDDI; PORTABLE; STANDARD.

ANSI Character Set *n.* a collection of special characters (including many foreign characters, special punctuation, and business symbols) and associated codes adopted by the ANSI standards organization.

⇒ See also ASCII; ISO LATIN 1.

ANSI.SYS (an'sē dot'sis'), *n.* a DOS device driver that makes a monitor conform to the ANSI standard, which specifies a series of escape sequences that cause the monitor to behave in various ways.

⇒ See also ANSI; BIOS; CONFIG.SYS; DRIVER; ESCAPE SEQUENCE.

answer-only modem *n.* a modem that can receive messages but cannot send them. Only the most inexpensive modems are answer-only.

⇒ See also MODEM.

antialiasing *n.* in computer graphics, a software technique for diminishing jaggies by surrounding the stairsteps with intermediate shades of gray (for gray-scaling devices) or color (for color devices). Although this reduces the jagged appearance of the lines, it also makes them fuzzier.

⇒ See also JAGGIES; RESOLUTION; SMOOTHING.

antistatic mat *n.* a mat on which one can stand while repairing a computer or adding expansion cards. The mat absorbs static electricity, which might otherwise damage electronic components. Another way to eliminate damage caused by static electricity is to wear an antistatic wristband.

antivirus program *n.* a utility that searches a hard disk and memory for viruses and removes them. Most antivirus programs include an update feature that enables the program to download profiles of new viruses and thereby detect and destroy them.

⇒ See also MACRO VIRUS; VIRUS.

AOL AMERICA ONLINE.

Apache Web server *n.* a public-domain Web server developed by a loosely knit group of programmers. Because it was developed from existing NCSA code plus various patches, it was called *a patchy server* — hence the name *Apache server.* By some estimates, it is used to host more than 50 percent of all Web sites in the world.

⇒ See also LINUX; WEB SERVER.

API application program interface: a set of routines, protocols, and tools for building software applications. A good API makes it easier to develop a program by providing all the building blocks. A programmer puts the blocks together.

⇒ See also APPLICATION; HLLAPI; INTERFACE; OPERATING ENVIRONMENT; ROUTINE; RPC; SDK; TAPI; TSAPI; WIN32.

APM Advanced Power Management: an API developed by Intel and Microsoft that allows developers to include power management in BIOSes. APM defines a layer between the hardware and the operating system that effectively shields the programmer from hardware details.

⇒ See also ACPI; POWER MANAGEMENT.

app *n. Informal.* an application program; application software. A *killer app* is an application that surpasses its competitors.

⇒ See also APPLICATION.

append *v.t.* to add (something) at the end: *to append a field to a record.*

⇒ See also CONCATENATE; INSERT.

Apple Computer *n.* a personal-computer company founded in 1976 by Steven Jobs and Steve Wozniak. In addition to inventing new technologies, Apple has often been the first to bring sophisticated technologies to the personal computer.

⇒ See also GRAPHICAL USER INTERFACE; LOCALTALK;

MACINTOSH COMPUTER; NEXTSTEP; PLUG-AND-PLAY; POWERPC; QUICKTIME; RISC.

Apple Desktop bus n. See ADB.

Apple key n. a special key on Macintosh computers labeled with the Apple logo. On all but the oldest Apple computers the Apple key serves as the Command key.
⇒ See also COMMAND KEY.

Apple Macintosh computer n. MACINTOSH COMPUTER.

AppleScript n. a scripting language developed by Apple Computer that is integrated into the MacOS starting with System 7.5. AppleScript provides an easy way to automate common tasks and is powerful enough to automate complex tasks and customize applications.
⇒ See also MACOS; MACRO; SCRIPT.

applet n. a program designed to be executed from within another application. Applets cannot be executed directly from the operating system. A well-designed applet can be invoked from many different applications.
⇒ See also APPLICATION; COMPONENT; JAVA; OLE; SERVLET.

AppleTalk n. an inexpensive local-area network (LAN) architecture built into all Apple Macintosh computers and laser printers.
⇒ See also LOCAL-AREA NETWORK; LOCALTALK; MACINTOSH COMPUTER; TOPOLOGY.

application n. a program or group of programs designed for end users. Application software includes database programs, word processors, and spreadsheets.
⇒ See also APPLET; APPLICATION SHARING; END USER; LEGACY APPLICATION; SYSTEMS SOFTWARE; UTILITY.

Application Foundation Classes n. See AFC.

Application Program Interface n. See API.

application sharing n. a feature of many videoconferencing applications that enables the conference participants to run the same application simultaneously. The application itself resides on only one of the machines connected to the conference.
⇒ See also APPLICATION; VIDEOCONFERENCING; WHITEBOARD.

application software *n.* See under APPLICATION.

Application Specific Integrated Circuit *n.* See ASIC.

applications software *n.* See under APPLICATION.

ARC (ärk), *n.* a data compression format, popular among bulletin board systems (BBSs), that produces files with names ending in a *.arc* extension.
⇒ See also DATA COMPRESSION; ZIP.

Archie *n.* a program that allows the user to search for files anywhere on the Internet by filename.
⇒ See also FILENAME; GOPHER; INTERNET.

architecture *n.* a fundamental underlying design of hardware, software, or both. The architecture of a system always defines its broad outlines and may also define precise mechanisms.
⇒ See also CLIENT/SERVER ARCHITECTURE; FUNCTIONAL SPECIFICATION; MODULAR ARCHITECTURE; OPEN ARCHITECTURE; STANDARD.

archival backup *n.* a type of backup in which all files are copied to a backup storage device. Also called **full backup**.
⇒ See also ARCHIVE; BACKUP; INCREMENTAL BACKUP.

archive *v.t.* **1.** to copy (files) to a long-term storage medium for backup. Large computer systems often have two layers of backup, the first of which is a disk drive. Periodically, the files on the disk are then archived to a second storage device, usually a tape drive. **2.** to compress (a file). —*n.* **3.** a disk, tape, or directory that contains files that have been backed up. **4.** a file that contains one or more files in a compressed format.
⇒ See also ARC; ARCHIVAL BACKUP; ATTRIBUTE; BACKUP.

ARCnet *n.* Attached Resource Computer network: one of the oldest, simplest, and least expensive types of local-area network.
⇒ See also ETHERNET; LOCAL-AREA NETWORK; TOKEN-RING NETWORK.

area chart *n.* a type of presentation graphic that emphasizes a change in values by filling in the portion of the graph beneath the line connecting various data points.

⇒ See also PRESENTATION GRAPHICS.

areal density *n.* the amount of data that can be packed onto a storage medium. Areal densities are generally measured in gigabits per square inch. The term is useful for comparing different types of media, such as magnetic disks and optical disks.

⇒ See also DENSITY; DISK; OPTICAL DISK.

argument *n.* a variable to which a value will be assigned when a program is run. It is given in parentheses following a function name and used to calculate the function.

⇒ See also OPTION; PARAMETER; ROUTINE.

arithmetic expression *n.* an expression that represents a numeric value. Other types of expressions can represent character or Boolean values.

⇒ See also EXPRESSION.

arithmetic logic unit *n.* See ALU.

arithmetic operator *n.* See under OPERATOR.

ARP Address Resolution Protocol: a TCP/IP protocol used to convert an IP address into a physical address, such as an Ethernet address.

⇒ See also DLC; IP ADDRESS; TCP/IP.

ARPANET *n.* a large wide-area network created by the U.S. Defense Advanced Research Project Agency (ARPA). In 1969 it served as a testbed for new networking technologies, linking many universities and research centers.

⇒ See also INTERNET; NSFNET.

array *n.* in programming, a series of objects that are all of the same size and type, such as a series of integers or characters.

⇒ See also DATA STRUCTURE; DATA TYPE; MATRIX; SUBSCRIPT; VECTOR.

arrow key *n.* one of usually four keys for moving the cursor or insertion point right, left, up, or down. When combined with the Shift, Function, Control, or Alt keys (on PCs), the arrow keys can have different meanings. For example, pressing Ctrl + right arrow might move the cursor to the right one word at a time. On Macintoshes, the arrow keys can be combined with the Shift, Option, and Command keys.

⇒ See also KEYBOARD.

artificial intelligence (AI) *n.* the branch of computer science concerned with making computers behave like humans. The term was coined in 1956 by John McCarthy at the Massachusetts Institute of Technology. The greatest advances in artificial intelligence have occurred in the field of game playing. The best computer chess programs are now capable of beating humans. In the area of robotics, computers are now widely used in assembly plants, but they are capable only of very limited tasks. Natural-language processing offers the greatest potential rewards because it would allow people to interact with computers without specialized knowledge.

⇒ See also COMPUTER SCIENCE; CYBERNETICS; EXPERT SYSTEM; FUZZY LOGIC; GENETIC PROGRAMMING; HEURISTIC PROGRAMMING; LISP; PROLOG; ROBOTICS; VOICE RECOGNITION.

AS/400 Application System/400: a line of IBM minicomputers introduced in 1988 and still popular today.

⇒ See also IBM; MINICOMPUTER.

ascender *n.* in typography, the portion of a lowercase letter that rises above the main body of the letter. For example, the letter *t*'s ascender is the part of the vertical line above the horizontal line.

⇒ See also BASELINE; DESCENDER; X-HEIGHT.

ASCII (as′kē), *n.* American Standard Code for Information Interchange: a code for representing English characters as numbers, with each letter assigned a number from 0 to 127. Most computers use ASCII codes to represent text, which makes it possible to transfer data from one computer to another.

⇒ See also ANSI CHARACTER SET; ASCII FILE; CHARACTER SET; EBCDIC; EXTENDED ASCII; ISO LATIN 1; TEXT FILE; UNICODE.

ASCII file *n.* a text file in which each byte represents one character according to the ASCII code. ASCII characters include spaces and punctuation, but an ASCII, or *plain text*, file will not include the kind of formatting, like bolded text, normally present in a word-processed file.

⇒ See also ASCII; PLAIN TEXT; BINARY FILE.

ASIC (ā′sik), *n.* Application Specific Integrated Circuit: a chip designed for a particular application. ASICs are built by connecting existing circuit building blocks in new ways.

⇒ See also CHIP; INTEGRATED CIRCUIT.

ASP ACTIVE SERVER PAGES.

aspect ratio *n.* in computer graphics, the relative horizontal and vertical sizes. For example, if a graphic has an aspect ratio of 2:1, the width is twice as large as the height. When resizing graphics, it is important to maintain the aspect ratio.

⇒ See also AUTOSIZING; GRAPHICS.

ASPI Advanced SCSI Programming Interface: an interface specification for sending commands to a SCSI host adapter. ASPI has become a de facto standard.

⇒ See also SCSI.

assembler *n.* a program that translates programs from assembly language to machine language.

⇒ See also ASSEMBLY LANGUAGE; MACHINE LANGUAGE.

assembly language *n.* a programming language that is once removed from a computer's machine language. Assembly languages have the same structure and set of commands as machine languages, but they enable a programmer to use names instead of numbers. Most programs are now written in a high-level language, but assembly language is used when speed is essential or an operation is required that is impossible in a high-level language.

⇒ See also ASSEMBLER; COMPILE; LOW-LEVEL LANGUAGE; MACHINE LANGUAGE; PROGRAMMING LANGUAGE.

assign *v.t.* to give (a value) to a variable. In many languages, a value is assigned by using the equal sign (=), as in the statement x = 5.

⇒ See also OPERATOR; STATEMENT; VARIABLE.

associate *v.t.* to link (a certain type of file) to a specific application. In MS-DOS and Microsoft Windows environments, the file's type is speci-

fied by its three-character extension, such as the .DOC extension, which identifies Microsoft Word documents. Once a file type has been associated with an application, selecting any file of that type automatically starts its associated application.
⇒ See also EXTENSION; FILENAME.

Association for Computing Machinery *n.* See ACM.

asterisk *n.* a punctuation mark denoted by a snowflake shape (*). In many operating systems and applications, the asterisk is used as a wildcard symbol to represent any string of characters. It is also used to denote multiplication, as in n * 2.5.
⇒ See also WILDCARD CHARACTER.

asymmetric digital subscriber line *n.* See ADSL.

asymmetric encryption *n.* See under PUBLIC-KEY ENCRYPTION.

async *adj.* ASYNCHRONOUS.

asynchronous *adj.* not synchronized; not occurring at predetermined or regular intervals. This term is usually used to describe communications in which data can be transmitted intermittently rather than in a steady stream. Most communications between computers and devices are asynchronous.
⇒ See also COMMUNICATIONS; FLOW CONTROL; ISOCHRONOUS; START BIT; STOP BIT.

Asynchronous Transfer Mode *n.* See ATM.

AT advanced technology: an IBM PC model that includes an Intel 80286 microprocessor, a 1.2-MB floppy drive, and an 84-key AT keyboard. Today the term is used more generally to refer to any PC with an 80286 processor.
⇒ See also INTEL MICROPROCESSORS; PC.

ATA AT Attachment: a disk drive implementation that integrates the controller on the disk drive itself. There are several versions of ATA.
⇒ See also CONTROLLER; DISK DRIVE; EIDE; IDE INTERFACE; PIO; ULTRA ATA.

AT bus *n.* the expansion bus on the IBM PC/AT and compatible computers. The AT bus, which runs at 8 megahertz and has a 16-bit data path, is the de facto standard for PCs.

⇒ See also BACKWARD COMPATIBLE; BUS; EISA; EXPANSION BOARD; IBM PC; INDUSTRY STANDARD ARCHITECTURE (ISA) BUS; LOCAL BUS; MICRO CHANNEL ARCHITECTURE (MCA); PCI; VL-BUS.

AT command set *n.* the de facto standard language for controlling modems. The AT command set is recognized by virtually all personal computer modems.

⇒ See also HAYES COMPATIBLE; MODEM.

AT keyboard *n.* an 84-key keyboard introduced with the PC/AT. It was later replaced with the 101-key Enhanced Keyboard.

⇒ See also ENHANCED KEYBOARD.

ATM Asynchronous Transfer Mode: a network technology based on transferring data in cells or packets of a fixed size. The small, constant cell size allows ATM equipment to transmit video, audio, and computer data over the same network.

⇒ See also CELL RELAY; ETHERNET; FDDI; FRAME RELAY; INTERNET; IP SWITCHING; QoS; TCP/IP.

Attached Resource Computer Network *n.* ARCNET.

attachment *n.* a file attached to an e-mail message. Many e-mail systems support only text files as e-mail. If the attachment is a binary file or formatted text file, it must be encoded before it is sent and decoded once it is received.

⇒ See also E-MAIL.

Attachment Unit Interface *n.* See AUI.

attribute *n.* **1.** a property or characteristic. In a word processing application, an underlined word is said to have the *underline attribute.* In database systems, a field can have various attributes. **2.** in DOS systems, every file has *file attributes* that indicate, for example, whether the file is read-only, whether it needs to be backed up, and whether it is visible or hidden.

⇒ See also DOS; FIELD; FILE; HIDDEN FILE.

ATX the modern shape and layout of PC motherboards. It improves on the previous standard, the *Baby AT form factor,* by rotating the orientation of the board 90 degrees. This allows for a more efficient design.

⇒ See also ATX; BABY AT; FORM FACTOR; MOTHER-BOARD.

.au See under AU.

AU audio: a common format for sound files on UNIX machines. It is also the standard audio file format for the Java programming language. AU files generally end with a *.au* extension.

⇒ See also DIGITAL AUDIO; MIDI; WAV.

audio card *n.* SOUND CARD.

Audio Interchange File Format *n.* See AIFF.

audit trail *n.* a record showing who has accessed a computer system and what operations he or she has performed during a given period of time. Audit trails are useful both for maintaining security and for recovering lost transactions.

⇒ See also LOG FILE; SECURITY.

AUI Attachment Unit Interface: the portion of the Ethernet standard that specifies how a cable is to be connected to an Ethernet card.

⇒ See also COAXIAL CABLE; ETHERNET; NETWORK IN-TERFACE CARD.

authentication *n.* the process of identifying an individual, usually based on a username and password.

⇒ See also AUTHORIZATION; BIOMETRICS; CHALLENGE-RESPONSE; CHAP; DIGITAL SIGNATURE; KERBEROS; PAP; PASSWORD; RADIUS; USERNAME.

authoring tool *n.* a program used to write hypertext or multimedia applications. Authoring tools usually enable the author to create a final application by linking objects, such as a paragraph of text and an illustration.

⇒ See also HYPERTEXT; MULTIMEDIA; PROGRAMMING LANGUAGE; SCRIPT.

authorization *n.* the process of granting or denying access to a network resource.

⇒ See also ACCESS CONTROL; AUTHENTICATION; EX-TRANET; SECURITY.

authorware *n.* AUTHORING TOOL.

auto-answer *n.* a feature supported by many modems that enables a computer to accept incoming calls even if no one is present. All fax machines are auto-answer.

⇒ See also FAX MACHINE; FAX MODEM; MODEM.

autoexec.bat *n.* automatically executed batch file: the file that DOS automatically executes when a computer boots up.

⇒ See also BATCH FILE; BOOT.

automatic acceleration *n.* DYNAMIC ACCELERATION.

automatic recalculation *n.* in spreadsheets, a mode in which all cells are recalculated whenever a value changes in one. Alternatively, if *manual recalculation* is specified, the user must instruct the application to recalculate.

⇒ See also RECALCULATE; SPREADSHEET.

auto-redial *n.* a feature supported by many modems that allows the modem to continue redialing a number until it makes a connection.

⇒ See also MODEM.

auto-repeat *n.* a feature of some keys on computer keyboards that causes them to repeat as long as they are held down.

⇒ See also KEYBOARD.

autosave *n.* a feature supported by many applications in which the program automatically saves data files at predetermined intervals.

⇒ See also CRASH; SAVE; WORD PROCESSING.

autosizing *n.* a monitor's ability to automatically adjust the raster, depending on the resolution of signals being received.

⇒ See also ASPECT RATIO; MONITOR; RASTER; RESOLUTION; SVGA; VGA; VIDEO ADAPTER.

autosync monitor *n.* MULTISCANNING MONITOR.

autotracing *n.* the process of converting a bit-mapped image (or raster image) into a vector image. In a bit-mapped image, each object is represented by a pattern of dots, whereas in a vector image every object is defined geometrically.

⇒ See also BIT MAP; BIT-MAPPED GRAPHICS; EPS; OPTICAL SCANNER; PCX; POSTSCRIPT; TIFF; VECTOR GRAPHICS.

AUX *n.* Auxiliary port: the logical name in DOS systems for the standard communications port.

⇒ See also COM; PORT.

A/UX (ôks, oks), *n.* Apple's version of UNIX, which runs on some versions of the Macintosh.
⇒ See also UNIX.

auxiliary storage *n.* MASS STORAGE.

avatar *n.* **1.** a graphical icon that represents a real person in a cyberspace system. 3-D avatars even change shape, depending on what they are doing (for example, walking or sitting). **2.** a common name for the superuser account on UNIX systems.
⇒ See also CHAT; CYBERSPACE; MUD; VIRTUAL REALITY.

AVI Audio Video Interleave: the file format for Microsoft's Video for Windows standard.
⇒ See also VIDEO FOR WINDOWS.

awk *n.* an interpreted programming language that is included in most versions of UNIX. The name is derived from the initials of its creators—Alfred A(ho), Peter W(einberger), and Brian K(ernighan).
⇒ See also PERL; PROGRAMMING LANGUAGE.

AWT *n.* Abstract Windows Toolkit: the Java API that enables programmers to develop Java applications with GUI components, such as windows, buttons, and scroll bars. Ideally, the AWT should enable any Java application to appear the same in a Windows, Macintosh, and UNIX environment. In practice, however, most Java applications look slightly different on each platform.
⇒ See also AFC; GRAPHICAL USER INTERFACE; IFC; JAVA; VIRTUAL MACHINE.

B b

Baby AT, *n.* the form factor used by most PC motherboards prior to 1998, replaced by the ATX form factor.

⇒ See also ATX; FORM FACTOR; LPX; NLX.

backbone, *n.* another term for *bus*, the main wire that connects nodes: often used to describe the main network connections composing the Internet.

⇒ See also BUS; HIPPI; MAE; NAP; NETWORK; NODE; NSP; T-3 CARRIER; vBNS.

back end, *n.* See under FRONT END.

background *n.* **1.** in a multitasking computer system, a process that can access data stored on a disk and write data to the video display but that cannot accept interactive output from a user. **2.** the area of a display screen not covered by characters and graphics.

⇒ See also DISPLAY SCREEN; FOREGROUND; MONITOR; MULTITASKING.

backlighting, *n.* a technique used to make flat-panel displays easier to read.

⇒ See also BACKGROUND; FLAT-PANEL DISPLAY; NOTEBOOK COMPUTER; SUPERTWIST.

backplane, *n.* a circuit board containing sockets into which other circuit boards can be plugged. *Active backplanes* contain logical circuitry that performs computing functions. *Passive backplanes* contain almost no computing circuitry.

⇒ See also MOTHERBOARD; PRINTED CIRCUIT BOARD; VME BUS.

backslash, *n.* the *backslash* character is \, as against the simple *slash* or *forward slash* character, which is /. The backslash represents the root directory in DOS and Windows systems and is also used to separate directory names and file-names in a pathname.

⇒ See also PATHNAME; ROOT DIRECTORY.

backspace, *n.* a character that causes the cursor to move backward one character space, possibly deleting the preceding character.

⇒ See also ASCII; Backspace key; cursor; keyboard; pointer.

Backspace key, *n.* a key that moves the cursor or insertion point backward one character space and usually deletes the character to the left of the cursor or insertion point.

⇒ See also arrow keys; backspace; Delete key; keyboard.

back up *v.t.* to copy (files) to a second medium (a disk or tape) as a precaution in case the first medium fails.

⇒ See also 3480, 3490; archival backup; archive; data compression; data integrity; DMA; HSM.

backup *n.* **1.** the act of backing up. **2.** a substitute or alternative: usu. refers to a disk or tape that contains a copy of data.

backward compatible *adj.* **1.** of a program, able to use files and data created with an older version of the same program. **2.** of a computer, able to run the same software as the previous model of the computer. Also called **downward compatible**.

⇒ See also compatible; upward compatible.

bad sector *n.* a portion of a disk that cannot be used because it is flawed.

⇒ See also disk; format; sector.

BAK file *n.* in DOS systems, a file with a .BAK extension, indicating that it is a backup.

⇒ See also autosave; extension.

ballistic tracking *n.* dynamic acceleration.

banding *n.* the presence of extraneous lines in a printed page.

⇒ See also color printer.

bandwidth *n.* the amount of data that can be transmitted in a fixed amount of time: usu. expressed in bits per second (bps) or bytes per second for digital devices and in cycles per second or Hertz (Hz) for analog devices.

⇒ See also bus; CIR; EISA; I/O; latency; PCI.

bar chart *n.* in presentation graphics, a type of graph in which different values are represented by rectangular bars.

⇒ See also presentation graphics.

barrel distortion *n.* See under PINCUSHION DISTORTION.

base address *n.* an address that serves as a reference point for other addresses.
⇒ See also ADDRESS; OFFSET; RELATIVE ADDRESS.

baseband transmission *n.* a type of digital data transmission in which each medium (wire) carries only one signal, or channel, at a time: used for communications from the computer to devices (printers, monitors, and so on), communications via modems, and most networks.
⇒ See also 10BASE-2; BROADBAND ISDN (B-ISDN); BROADBAND TRANSMISSION; CHANNEL; COMMUNICATIONS; ISDN; LOCAL-AREA NETWORK; NETWORK.

baseline *n.* in typography, the imaginary line on which characters sit.
⇒ See also ASCENDER; DESCENDER; FONT; TYPEFACE; X-HEIGHT.

base memory *n.* CONVENTIONAL MEMORY.

BASIC *n.* Beginner's All-purpose Symbolic Instruction Code: one of the earliest and simplest high-level programming languages, used for a wide variety of business applications: developed by John Kemeney and Thomas Kurtz at Dartmouth College.
⇒ See also GW-BASIC; HIGH-LEVEL LANGUAGE; INTERPRETER; MUMPS; PROGRAMMING LANGUAGE; QBASIC; VISUAL BASIC.

basic input/output system *n.* See BIOS.

Basic-Rate Interface *n.* See BRI.

batch file *n.* a file that contains a sequence, or batch, of commands that are always executed together: ends with a .BAT extension in DOS systems. Also called **command file, shell script.**
⇒ See also AUTOEXEC.BAT; BAT FILE; BATCH PROCESSING; DOS.

batch processing *n.* executing a series of noninteractive jobs at one time.
⇒ See also BATCH FILE; INTERACTIVE; TRANSACTION PROCESSING.

BAT file *n.* a batch file, so called because the filename ends with a .BAT extension in DOS systems.

⇒ See also BATCH FILE; EXTENSION; FILENAME.

battery pack *n.* a rechargeable battery used in portable computer devices, such as notebook computers, often containing nickel cadmium (Ni-Cad), nickel metal hydride (NiMH), or lithium-ion batteries.

⇒ See also LITHIUM-ION BATTERY; NiCad BATTERY PACK; NiMH BATTERY PACK; POWER MANAGEMENT.

baud (bôd), *n.* the number of signaling elements or bits that occur each second in transmitting data, as over a phone line. [named after J. M. E. Baudot, the inventor of the Baudot telegraph code]

⇒ See also BPS; MODEM.

baud rate *n.* BAUD.

bay *n.* a site in a personal computer where a hard or floppy disk drive, CD-ROM drive, or tape drive can be installed. Also called **drive bay.**

⇒ See also DISK DRIVE; EXPANSION BOARD; MASS STORAGE; SLOT.

BBS BULLETIN BOARD SYSTEM.

BCD binary-coded decimal: a format for representing decimal numbers (integers) in which each digit is represented by four bits (a nibble).

⇒ See also BINARY; BINARY FORMAT; DECIMAL; HEXADECIMAL; NIBBLE.

B-channel *n.* Bearer-Channel: the main data channel in an ISDN connection.

⇒ See also BRI; CHANNEL; ISDN.

BEDO DRAM *n.* Burst EDO DRAM: a type of EDO DRAM that can process four memory addresses in one burst but stay synchronized with the CPU clock for short periods (bursts) only and cannot keep up with processors whose buses run faster than 66 MHz.

⇒ See also BURST MODE; DRAM; EDO DRAM; PIPELINE BURST CACHE; RDRAM; SDRAM; SLDRAM.

Bell 103 *n.* the de facto standard protocol in the United States for transmitting data over telephone lines at transmission rates of 300 baud.

⇒ See also ASYNCHRONOUS; BAUD; CCITT; COMMUNICATIONS PROTOCOL; FULL DUPLEX; PROTOCOL.

Bell 212A *n.* the de facto standard protocol in

the United States for transmitting data over telephone lines at transmission rates of 1,200 baud.

⇒ See also ASYNCHRONOUS; BAUD; CCITT; COMMUNICATIONS PROTOCOL; FULL DUPLEX; PROTOCOL.

bells and whistles *n.pl.* extra, often unnecessary, features provided by an application.

⇒ See also FEATURE.

benchmark *n.* a test used to compare performance of hardware and/or software.

⇒ See also FLOPS; SPEC.

BeOS *n.* an operating system developed by Be, Inc., that runs on the PowerPC platform and Intel x86 processors and provides a modern graphical user interface (GUI), preemptive multitasking, multithreading, and built-in support for symmetric multiprocessing (SMP).

⇒ See also MAC OS; OPERATING SYSTEM; POWERPC; SMP.

Berkeley Internet Name Domain *n.* See BIND.

Bernoulli disk drive *n.* a special type of floppy disk drive from Iomega Corporation that was faster and had greater storage capacity than traditional floppy drives: no longer being produced.

⇒ See also DISK; HARD DISK DRIVE; MASS STORAGE.

beta *n.* BETA TEST.

beta test *n.* the last stage of testing for a computer product prior to commercial release, usually involving sending the product to various beta test sites outside the company for real-word exposure to situations that would be encountered by users: often preceded by a round of testing called alpha testing, conducted inside the company.

⇒ See also ALPHA VERSION; APPLICATION.

Bézier curve (bez′ē ā′), *n.* curved lines (splines) defined by mathematical formulas. Nearly all draw programs support Bézier curves.

⇒ See also DRAW PROGRAM; GRAPHICS; NURBS; SPLINE; VECTOR GRAPHICS.

BFT BINARY FILE TRANSFER.

BGP Border Gateway Protocol: an Internet protocol that enables groups of routers (called autonomous systems) to share routing information so

that efficient, loop-free routes can be established.
⇒ See also ROUTER; ROUTING.

Big Blue *n.* an informal name for International Business Machines Corporation (IBM). Blue is IBM's corporate color.
⇒ See also IBM PC.

big-endian *adj.* denoting the most significant bytes in multibyte data types. In *big-endian* architectures, the leftmost bytes (those with a lower address) are most significant. In *little-endian* architectures, the rightmost bytes are most significant. Many mainframe computers use a big-endian architecture. Most modern computers, including PCs, use the little-endian system. The PowerPC system, however, is *bi-endian* because it can understand both.
⇒ See also BYTE; DATA TYPE.

bilevel printer *n.* a type of printer that can print only two levels of intensity for each dot—on or off. Shading is created by varying the position of the dots, or dithering.
⇒ See also COLOR PRINTER; CONTINUOUS TONE; CONTONE PRINTER; DITHERING; PRINTER.

binary *adj.* pertaining to a system of numerical rotation to the base 2 in which each place of a number, expressed as 0 or 1, corresponds to a power of 2. Computers are based on a binary number system.
⇒ See also BINARY FORMAT; DECIMAL; HEXADECIMAL; OCTAL.

binary-coded decimal *n.* See BCD.

binary compatible *adj.* having exactly the same data format, down to the binary level. Two files that are binary compatible have the same pattern of zeroes and ones in the data portion of the file and are therefore interchangeable.
⇒ See also BINARY FILE; COMPATIBLE; CROSS-PLATFORM; EXPORT; HETEROGENEOUS NETWORK; IMPORT.

binary digit *n.* BIT.

binary file *n.* a file stored in binary format that is computer-readable but not human-readable.
⇒ See also ASCII FILE; BINARY FORMAT; COFF; EXECUTABLE FILE.

Binary File Transfer *n.* a standard for transmitting data files using fax modems. *Abbr.*: BFT

⇒ See also CCITT.

binary format *n.* a format for representing data used by some applications for executable programs and numeric data.

⇒ See also BCD; BINARY; BINARY FILE.

binary tree *n.* a special type of tree structure in which each node has at most two leaves: often used for sorting data, as in a heap sort.

⇒ See also HEAP; HEAP SORT; TREE STRUCTURE.

BIND *n.* Berkeley Internet Name Domain: a domain name server (DNS) designed for UNIX systems based on BSD, the version of UNIX developed at the University of California's Berkeley campus.

⇒ See also DNS; DOMAIN NAME.

bind *v.t.* to assign a value to (a symbolic placeholder). The moment at which binding occurs is called *bind time* or *link time.*

⇒ See also ADDRESS; COMPILE; LINK.

binder *n.* LINKER.

BinHex *n.* an encoding scheme that can convert binary data from any type of file into ASCII characters. Encoded files generally have a .hqx extension.

⇒ See also E-MAIL; MIME; UUENCODE.

biometrics *n.* **1.** generally, the study of measurable biological characteristics. **2.** in computer security, authentication techniques that rely on measurable physical characteristics that can be automatically checked, such as computer analysis of fingerprints or speech.

⇒ See also AUTHENTICATION; ELECTRONIC COMMERCE; SECURITY.

BIOS (bī′ōs), *n.* basic input/output system: built-in software that determines what a computer can do without accessing programs from a disk: contains all the code required to control the keyboard, display screen, disk drives, etc.

⇒ See also BOOT; CMOS; ESCD; FLASH MEMORY; I/O; PNP; POST; SHADOWING.

B-ISDN BROADBAND ISDN.

bisync *adj.* binary synchronous: referring to a type of synchronous communications used primarily in mainframe networks.

⇒ See also ASYNCHRONOUS; SYNCHRONOUS.

bit *n.* binary digit: the smallest unit of information on a machine. A single bit can hold only one of two values, 0 or 1.

⇒ See also 32-BIT; ADDRESS SPACE; KILOBIT; MEGABIT; NIBBLE; REGISTER.

bit block transfer *n.* a transformation of a rectangular block of pixels, as by changing the color or shade of all pixels or rotating the entire rectangle.

⇒ See also GRAPHICS; PIXEL; VIDEO ADAPTER.

bitblt (bit′blit′), *n.* Short for BIT BLOCK TRANSFER.

bit map *n.* a representation, consisting of rows and columns of dots, of a graphics image in computer memory. The density of the dots, known as the resolution, determines how sharply the image is represented. The computer translates the bit map into pixels to display it on a monitor or ink dots to print it. Bit-mapped graphics are also called **raster graphics**.

⇒ See also BIT-MAPPED GRAPHICS; PIXEL; RESOLUTION; VECTOR GRAPHICS.

bit-mapped font *n.* See under FONT.

bit-mapped graphics *n.* the representation of graphics images as bit maps. Also called **raster graphics**.

⇒ See also BIT MAP; COMPUTER IMAGING; GRAPHICS; PNG; VECTOR GRAPHICS.

BITNET *n.* Because It's Time Network: one of the oldest and largest wide-area networks, used extensively by universities.

⇒ See also INTERNET; NETWORK; WIDE-AREA NETWORK.

bits per second *n.* See BPS.

bitwise operator *n.* an operator that manipulates individual bits rather than bytes or groups of bytes.

⇒ See also OPERATOR.

blank character *n.* the character produced when the space bar is pressed. Also called **space character**.

bleed *n.* **1.** text or graphics extending all the way to the edge of the paper, used for graphical effect and for printed tabs. —*v.i.* **2.** to run to the edge of the paper, thereby producing a bleed.

bloatware *n. Informal.* software that has many features and requires a great deal of disk space and RAM.
⇒ See also VAPORWARE.

BLOB *n.* binary large object: a collection of binary data used primarily to hold multimedia objects as a single entity in a database management system (DBMS).
⇒ See also DATABASE MANAGEMENT SYSTEM; FIELD; OBJECT.

block *n.* **1.** in word processing, a group of characters that has been highlighted for some action, such as deleting or changing the font. **2.** in data management, a group of records on a storage device. **3.** in communications, a fixed-size chunk of data that is transferred as a unit. —*v.t.* **4.** in word processing, to specify or highlight (a section of text). See definition (1) above. Some applications call this *selecting*.
⇒ See also COMMUNICATIONS; SELECT; WORD PROCESSING; XMODEM.

block graphics *n.* graphical images created in character mode.
⇒ See also CHARACTER MODE.

BMP the standard bit-mapped graphics format used in the Windows environment. BMP files, which conventionally have names that end in a . BMP extension, store graphics in a format called *device-independent bit map (DIB)*.
⇒ See also BIT MAP; DIB; GRAPHICS FILE FORMATS.

BNC BNC CONNECTOR.

BNC connector *n.* British Naval Connector or Bayonet Nut Connector or Bayonet Neill Concelman: a type of connector used with coaxial cables and to connect some monitors.
⇒ See also 10BASE-2; COAXIAL CABLE; CONNECTOR;

board *n.* EXPANSION BOARD; PRINTED CIRCUIT BOARD.

boilerplate *n.* phrases, units of text, or graphics elements designed to be used repeatedly.
⇒ See also TEMPLATE.

boldface *n.* thick, heavy type. **This is an exam-**

ple of boldface.

⇒ See also FONT.

bomb *v.i.* (of a program) to hang or end prematurely.

⇒ See also ABORT; BUG; CRASH; HANG.

bookmark *v.t.* **1.** to mark (a document, a place in a document, or the address of a Web page) for later retrieval. —*n.* **2.** a marker or address that identifies a document or a place in a document.

⇒ See also BROWSER.

Boolean expression *n.* an expression that results in a value of either TRUE or FALSE. Also called **comparison expression, conditional expression, relational expression.**

⇒ See also BOOLEAN LOGIC; BOOLEAN OPERATOR; EXPRESSION; RELATIONAL OPERATOR.

Boolean logic *n.* a form of algebra in which all values are reduced to either TRUE or FALSE: important for computer science because it fits with the binary numbering system, in which each bit has a value of either 1 or 0. [named after the 19th-century British mathematician George Boole]

⇒ See also BINARY; BOOLEAN EXPRESSION; BOOLEAN OPERATOR.

Boolean operator *n.* an operator that can be used to manipulate TRUE/FALSE values. There are five Boolean operators: AND, OR, XOR, NOR, NOT. Boolean operators are widely used in programming and in forming database queries.

⇒ See also AND OPERATOR; BOOLEAN EXPRESSION; BOOLEAN LOGIC; OR OPERATOR; NOR OPERATOR; NOT OPERATOR; XOR OPERATOR.

boot *v.t.* **1.** to start (a computer) by loading the operating system, which is essential for running all other programs. —*n.* **2.** the starting up of a computer by loading the operating system and other basic software. Turning the computer on from an off position is a *cold boot.* Resetting a computer that is already on is a *warm boot.*

⇒ See also BIOS; BOOTABLE DISKETTE; BOOTP; CLEAN BOOT; COLD BOOT; MBR; OPERATING SYSTEM; POST; WARM BOOT.

bootable diskette *n.* a diskette from which a computer can be booted if the hard disk is damaged, as by a virus. Also called **bootable floppy, boot disk, startup disk**.

⇒ See also BOOT; MBR; VIRUS.

bootable floppy *n.* BOOTABLE DISKETTE.

boot disk *n.* BOOTABLE DISKETTE.

BOOTP Bootstrap Protocol: an Internet protocol that enables a diskless workstation to boot without requiring a hard or floppy disk drive.

⇒ See also BOOT; DISKLESS WORKSTATION.

boot sector *n.* See under MBR.

Border Gateway Protocol *n.* See BGP.

Borland International *n.* a company in Scotts Valley, Calif., that provides programming and database tools.

⇒ See also C++; PASCAL; RDBMS; SPREADSHEET.

bot *n.* robot: a computer program that runs automatically.

⇒ See also ROBOT.

box *n.* **1.** in graphical user interfaces, an enclosed area, resembling a window, that appears on the screen. A *dialog box*, for example, requests some type of input or information from the user. An *alert box* appears on the screen when it is necessary to give information immediately to the user. **2.** *Informal.* a personal computer or workstation.

⇒ See also ALERT BOX; BUTTON; DIALOG BOX; GRAPHICAL USER INTERFACE; ICON; WINDOW; ZOOM.

bps bits per second: the standard measure of data transmission speeds.

⇒ See also BAUD; CCITT; COMMUNICATIONS; MODEM.

branch *n.* in tree structures, a single line of the tree that ends with a leaf.

⇒ See also DIRECTORY; TREE STRUCTURE.

Break key *n.* a key on computer keyboards that temporarily interrupts the computer's communications line.

⇒ See also KEYBOARD.

BRI Basic-Rate Interface: the basic ISDN configuration.

⇒ See also B-CHANNEL; ISDN.

bridge *n.* a protocol-independent device that connects two local-area networks (LANs) or two segments of the same LAN.

⇒ See also BROUTER; HUB; INTERNETWORKING; LOCAL-AREA NETWORK; REPEATER; ROUTER; WIDE-AREA NETWORK.

British Naval Connector *n.* BNC CONNECTOR.

broadband ISDN (B-ISDN) *n.* a standard for transmitting voice, video, and data at the same time over fiber optic telephone lines. *Abbr.:* B-ISDN

⇒ See also BPS; BROADBAND TRANSMISSION; FIBER OPTICS; ISDN; SONET.

broadband transmission *n.* a type of data transmission in which a single medium (wire) can carry several channels at once.

⇒ See also BASEBAND TRANSMISSION; BROADBAND ISDN (B-ISDN); CHANNEL; COMMUNICATIONS; LOCAL-AREA NETWORK; NETWORK.

broadcast *v.t.* to send (the same message) simultaneously to multiple recipients.

⇒ See also E-MAIL; FAX; MULTICAST; RTSP; WEBCASTING.

brouter (brou′tər), *n.* bridge router: a device that functions as both a router and a bridge.

⇒ See also BRIDGE; ROUTER.

browse *v.i.* **1.** in database systems, to look through data quickly without being able to modify it. Many database systems support a special *browse mode,* in which users can flip through fields and records quickly. Usually, data cannot be modified in browse mode. **2.** in object-oriented programming languages, to examine data structures. **3.** to view formatted documents.

⇒ See also BROWSER; DATA STRUCTURE; DATABASE MANAGEMENT SYSTEM; FIELD; RECORD; SURF.

browser *n.* Web browser: a software application used to locate and display Web pages.

⇒ See also ACTIVEX CONTROL; BROWSE; HTML; INTERNET EXPLORER; MOSAIC; NAVIGATOR; WORLD WIDE WEB; XML.

BSDI Berkeley Software Design, Inc.: a commercial supplier of Internet and networking software based on the BSD (Berkeley) version of UNIX.

⇒ See also UNIX; WEB SERVER.

bubble memory *n.* a type of nonvolatile memory composed of a thin layer of material that can be easily magnetized in only one direction. The application of a magnetic field to a circular area of this substance that is not magnetized in the same direction reduces the area to a smaller circle, or bubble.

⇒ See also EEPROM; NONVOLATILE MEMORY.

bubble sort *n.* a simple but popular sorting algorithm: used frequently as a programming exercise because it is relatively easy to understand.

⇒ See also ALGORITHM; HEAP SORT; PSEUDOCODE.

buffer *n.* **1.** a temporary storage area, usually in RAM, that holds data until the computer is ready to process it. Many programs keep track of data on a buffer and then copy the buffer to disk. —*v.t.* **2.** to move (data) into a temporary storage area.

⇒ See also CACHE; COMMAND BUFFER; DISK CACHE; SAVE; SPOOLING.

bug *n.* an error or defect in software or hardware that causes a program to malfunction.

⇒ See also BOMB; CRASH; GLITCH; HANG; MEMORY LEAK.

built-in font *n.* RESIDENT FONT.

built-in function *n.* a function that is built into an application and can be accessed by end users.

⇒ See also FUNCTION.

bullet *n.* a small graphical element used to highlight or itemize a list.

⇒ See also DINGBAT.

bulletin board system *n.* an electronic facility for collecting and relaying messages.

⇒ See also COMMUNICATIONS SOFTWARE; E-MAIL; ON-LINE SERVICE.

bundled software *n.* software that is sold as part of a package with a computer or other hardware component or with other software.

⇒ See also HARDWARE; SOFTWARE.

burst mode *n.* a transmission mode in which data is sent faster than normal for a limited period of time and under special conditions.

⇒ See also BEDO DRAM; DATA TRANSFER RATE; PIPELINE BURST CACHE; WAIT STATE.

bus *n.* **1.** a collection of wires through which data is transmitted from one part of a computer to another. **2.** in networking, a central cable that connects all devices on a local-area network (LAN). Also called **backbone**.

⇒ See also 32-BIT; ACCESS.BUS; ADB; ADDRESS BUS; BUS MASTERING; CHANNEL; CLOCK SPEED; CONTROLLER; EXPANSION BUS; LOCAL BUS; PCI; USB; VME BUS.

business graphics *n.* PRESENTATION GRAPHICS.

bus mastering *n.* a feature supported by some bus architectures that enables a controller connected to the bus to communicate directly with other devices on the bus without going through the CPU.

⇒ See also BUS; PCI.

bus mouse *n.* an obsolete kind of mouse that connects to a computer via an expansion board.

⇒ See also BUS; MOUSE; SERIAL PORT.

bus network *n.* a network in which all nodes are connected to a single wire (the bus) that has two endpoints.

⇒ See also ETHERNET; RING NETWORK; STAR NETWORK; TOKEN BUS NETWORK; TOPOLOGY.

bus topology *n.* see under TOPOLOGY.

button *n.* **1.** in graphical user interfaces, a small outlined area in a dialog box that the user can click on to select an option or command. **2.** a button on a mouse that the user clicks to perform various functions, such as selecting an object.

⇒ See also CLICK; DIALOG BOX; GRAPHICAL USER INTERFACE; MOUSE; RADIO BUTTONS.

byte *n.* binary term: a unit of storage capable of holding a single character: equal to 8 bits.

⇒ See also BIG-ENDIAN; GIGABYTE; KILOBYTE; MEGABYTE; NIBBLE.

bytecode *n.* the compiled format for Java programs.

⇒ See also COMPILE; JAVA; JIT.

C c

C a programming language developed at Bell Labs in the mid-1970s: used for a variety of applications, from business programs to engineering.
⇒ See also ASSEMBLY LANGUAGE; C++; EIFFEL; HIGH-LEVEL LANGUAGE; MACHINE LANGUAGE; PROGRAMMING LANGUAGE; UNIX; VISUAL C++.

C++ a programming language developed at Bell Labs that adds object-oriented features to its predecessor, C.
⇒ See also C; HIGH-LEVEL LANGUAGE; JAVA; MFC; OBJECT-ORIENTED; PROGRAMMING LANGUAGE; SMALL-TALK; VISUAL C++.

CA CERTIFICATE AUTHORITY.

cable modem *n.* a modem, designed to operate over cable TV lines, that can achieve very fast access to the World Wide Web.
⇒ See also WEBTV.

cache (kash), *n.* a special high-speed storage mechanism, either a reserved section of main memory or an independent high-speed storage area. A *memory cache* is a section of high-speed static ram (SRAM). A *disk cache* uses conventional main memory to speed access to data stored on the hard disk.
⇒ See also BUFFER; DISK CACHE; MAIN MEMORY; PIPE-LINE BURST CACHE; RAM DISK; TAG RAM; WRITE-BACK CACHE.

cache memory *n.* CACHE.

CAD *n.* computer-aided design: a combination of hardware and software that enables an engineer or an architect to view a design from any angle and to zoom in or out for close-ups and long-distance views. The computer also keeps track of design dependencies and changes the values of linked quantities automatically.
⇒ See also CAD/CAM; CAE; CAM; DIGITIZING TAB-LET; GRAPHICS; LIGHT PEN; MONITOR; MOUSE; PLOTTER; WORKSTATION.

CAD/CAM *n.* computer-aided design/computer-aided manufacturing: computer systems that can be used to design a product and to control its manufacture.

⇒ See also 3-D SOFTWARE; CAD; CADD; CAM; MODELING.

CADD computer-aided design and drafting: a CAD system with drafting features, as one that enables an engineer or an architect to insert size annotations and other notes into a design.

⇒ See also CAD; CAD/CAM.

CAE computer-aided engineering: a computer system that analyzes engineering designs. CAE systems can simulate a design under a variety of conditions to see how it works.

⇒ See also CAD; CASE.

calculator *n.* **1.** a small hand-held computer that performs mathematical calculations. **2.** a program on a computer that simulates a hand-held calculator.

⇒ See also DESK ACCESSORY (DA).

calendar *n.* a program that enables the user to record events and appointments on an electronic calendar: part of a more general category of software known as PIMs (personal information managers).

⇒ See also PIM; SCHEDULER; UTILITY.

call *v.t.* **1.** to invoke (a routine). —*n.* **2.** an invocation of a routine.

⇒ See also FUNCTION; ROUTINE.

CAM *n.* computer-aided manufacturing: the use of computer systems to help automate a factory, including real-time control, robotics, or materials requirements.

⇒ See also CAD; CAD/CAM; ROBOTICS.

camera-ready *adj.* in desktop publishing, referring to the final state of a publication before it is printed. The term arises from the old method of making a film image of pages to transfer to printing plates.

⇒ See also DESKTOP PUBLISHING; IMAGESETTER; ISP; OFFSET PRINTING.

caps *n.pl.* capital letters.

⇒ See also CASE SENSITIVE; UPPERCASE.

Caps Lock key *n.* a key on computer keyboards that, when activated, causes all subsequent alphabetic characters to be uppercase but has no effect on other keys.

⇒ See also KEYBOARD; TOGGLE; UPPERCASE.

capture *v.t.* **1.** to save (the output of a program) as the information currently visible on a display screen either to a printer or to a file. **2.** to record (keystrokes during the definition of a macro).

⇒ See also LEARN MODE; SCREEN CAPTURE.

card *n.* **1.** EXPANSION BOARD. **2.** in hypertext systems, a single page of information.

⇒ See also HyperCard; HYPERTEXT.

CardBus *n.* the 32-bit version of the PCMCIA PC Card standard.

⇒ See also PC CARD; PCMCIA.

caret *n.* a wedge-shaped symbol (^) generally found above the 6 on computer keyboards, sometimes used to indicate the Control key. Also called **hat.**

⇒ See also CONTROL KEY.

carpal tunnel syndrome *n.* a common form of repetitive strain injury (RSI) produced by repeating the same small movements many times.

⇒ See also ERGONOMICS.

carriage *n.* the mechanism on a printer that feeds paper.

⇒ See also PAPER FEED; PRINTER.

carriage return *n.* a special code that moves the cursor (or print head) to the beginning of the current line. *Abbr.:* cr

⇒ See also LINE FEED; RETURN.

carrier *n.* CARRIER SIGNAL, CARRIER SYSTEM, CARRIER SERVICE PROVIDER.

⇒ See also FDM; MULTIPLEX; T-1 CARRIER; T-3 CARRIER.

Carrier Sense Multiple Access/Collision Detection *n.* See CSMA/CD.

carrier service provider *n.* a company offering telephone and data communications between points in a state or in one or more countries.

carrier signal *n.* a frequency in a communications channel modulated to carry analog or digital information.

carrier system *n.* a communications system

providing a number of point-to-point channels through some type of multiplexing.

cartridge *n.* **1.** a removable storage medium (tape, disk, or memory chip). **2.** for laser and ink jet printers, a container that holds the toner or ink.

⇒ See also FONT CARTRIDGE; LASER PRINTER; REMOVABLE HARD DISK; SLOT; TONER.

cartridge font *n.* FONT CARTRIDGE.

cascading delete *n.* in relational database management systems, a *referential integrity* rule specifying that when a record is deleted from one table, any linked records in a related table will also be deleted.

Cascading Style Sheets *n.* See CSS.

cascading update *n.* in relational database management systems, a *referential integrity* rule specifying that if a value in a field in one table is modified, all linked records containing that same field, with the same information, in a related table will also be modified accordingly.

cascading windows *n.pl.* windows arranged so that they overlap one another with the title bar always visible. Also called **overlaid windows.**

⇒ See also TILED WINDOWS; WINDOW.

CASE *n.* Computer Aided Software Engineering: a category of software that provides tools to automate, manage, and simplify the development process for programming teams.

⇒ See also CAE; PROGRAM.

case sensitive *adj.* referring to a program that distinguishes between uppercase (capital) and lowercase (small) letters.

⇒ See also LOWERCASE; UPPERCASE.

cathode-ray tube *n.* See CRT.

CAV Constant Angular Velocity: a technique for reading data from rotating disks in which the disk rotates at a constant number of revolutions per second regardless of what area of the disk is being accessed.

⇒ See also CD-ROM; CD-ROM PLAYER; CLV.

CBT computer-based training: a type of education in which the student learns to use computer applications by executing special training programs.

⇒ See also COURSEWARE; DISTANCE LEARNING.

CCD charge-coupled device: a chip containing semiconductor elements connected so that the output of one serves as the input of the next. CCDs are often used as image-detectors.

⇒ See also DIGITAL CAMERA; OPTICAL SCANNER.

CCITT Comité Consultatif International Téléphonique et Télégraphique: an organization that sets international communications standards; now known as ITU (the parent organization).

⇒ See also BAUD; BPS; COMMUNICATIONS PROTOCOL; DATA COMPRESSION; E-MAIL; FAX MACHINE; FAX MODEM; FULL DUPLEX; HALF DUPLEX; ISDN; ITU; MNP; MODEM; PROTOCOL; STANDARD; X.400; X.500.

CD COMPACT DISC.

CD-DA RED BOOK.

CDDI Copper Data Distribution Interface: a network technology capable of carrying data at 100 Mbps over unshielded twisted-pair (UTP) cable.

⇒ See also FDDI; LOCAL-AREA NETWORK; TWISTED-PAIR CABLE; UTP.

cdev (sē′dev′), *n.* control panel device: a type of Macintosh utility that enables the user to adjust basic system parameters. Also called **control panel.**

⇒ See also CONTROL PANEL.

CDF channel definition format: a specification developed by Microsoft that allows Web publishers to *push* content at users. Once a user subscribes to a CDF channel, any software that supports the CDF format will automatically receive new content posted on the channel's Web server.

⇒ See also INTERNET EXPLORER; POINTCAST; PUSH.

CDFS CD-ROM File System: the Windows 95 and 98 driver for CD-ROM players, replacing MSCDEX.

⇒ See also CD-ROM PLAYER; MSCDEX; VCACHE.

CD-I Compact Disc–Interactive: a software and hardware standard developed jointly by Philips International and Sony Corporation for storing video, audio, and binary data on compact optical disks. Also called **Green Book standard.**

⇒ See also CD-ROM; CD-ROM/XA; DVD; DVI; GREEN BOOK; OPTICAL DISK; OS/9.

CDMA Code-Division Multiple Access: a digital cellular technology in which every transmission channel varies its frequency according to a predetermined pattern to avoid interference.

⇒ See also CELLULAR; GSM; MULTIPLEX; PCS; TDM; TDMA.

CDPD Cellular Digital Packet Data: a data transmission technology developed for use on cellular phone frequencies that offers data transfer rates of up to 19.2 Kbps.

⇒ See also CELL; PACKET SWITCHING.

CD-R CD-R DRIVE.

CD-R drive *n.* Compact Disc-Recordable drive: a type of disk drive that can create CD-ROMs and audio CDs allowing users to "master" a CD-ROM or audio CD for publishing.

⇒ See also CD-ROM; CD-ROM PLAYER; CD-RW DISK; ORANGE BOOK.

CD-recordable drive *n.* CD-R DRIVE.

CD-ROM (sē'dē'rom'), *n.* Compact Disc–Read-Only Memory: a type of optical disk capable of storing large amounts of data.

⇒ See also CAV; CD-I (COMPACT DISC-INTERACTIVE); CD-ROM PLAYER; CD-ROM/XA; CD-RW DISK; CLV; COMPACT DISC; DISK; ERASABLE OPTICAL DISK; MASS STORAGE; MULTIMEDIA; OPTICAL DISK; YELLOW BOOK.

CD-ROM drive *n.* CD-ROM PLAYER.

CD-ROM player *n.* an internal or external device in a computer that can read information from a CD-ROM. Also called **CD-ROM drive.**

⇒ See also ACCESS TIME; BAY; CAV; CD-ROM; CDFS; CLV; IDE INTERFACE; MPC; MSCDEX; MULTIMEDIA KIT; MultiRead; parallel port; PhotoCD; SCSI.

CD-ROM/XA *n.* CD-ROM/extended architecture: a specification developed by Sony, Philips, and Microsoft that enables many different types of data—audio, video, compressed video, and graphics—to be stored on a single CD-ROM.

⇒ See also CD-I (COMPACT DISC-INTERACTIVE); CD-ROM; YELLOW BOOK.

CD-RW disk *n.* CD-Rewritable disk: a type of CD disk that can be written, erased, and rewritten.
⇒ See also CD-R DRIVE; CD-ROM; DVD+RW; DVD-RAM; DVI; MULTIREAD.

cell *n.* **1.** in spreadsheet applications, a box in which one can enter a single piece of data, text, a numeric value, or a formula. **2.** in communications and networking, a fixed-size packet of data. **3.** in cellular telephone systems, a geographic area.
⇒ See also CDPD; CELL RELAY; CELLULAR; FIELD; FORMULA; SPREADSHEET.

cell relay *n.* a system that transmits data in small, fixed-size packets or cells containing only basic path information that allows switching devices to route each cell quickly.
⇒ See also ATM; CELL; FRAME RELAY; PACKET; PACKET SWITCHING.

Cells in Frames *n.* a specification that enables ATM cells to be carried in Ethernet packets.
⇒ See also ATM; ETHERNET.

cellular *adj.* referring to communications systems that divide a geographic region into sections, called cells, to make the most use of a limited number of transmission frequencies.
⇒ See also CDMA; CELL; GSM; PCS; TDMA.

cellular digital packet data *n.* See CDPD.

central processing unit *n.* See CPU.

centrex *n.* central office exchange service: a type of PBX service in which switching occurs at a local telephone station instead of at the company premises.
⇒ See also PBX.

Centronics interface *n.* a standard interface for connecting printers and other parallel devices.
⇒ See also ECP; EPP; INTERFACE; PARALLEL INTERFACE; STANDARD.

CERN (sûrn), *n.* European Laboratory for Particle Physics [Conseil Europeen pour la Recherche Nucleaire in French]: a research laboratory headquartered in Geneva, Switzerland, and funded by many different countries.
⇒ See also WEB SERVER; WORLD WIDE WEB.

Certificate Authority *n.* a trusted third-party

organization or company that issues digital certificates used to create digital signatures and public-private key pairs: a critical component in data security and electronic commerce.

⇒ See also DIGITAL CERTIFICATE; DIGITAL SIGNATURE; ELECTRONIC COMMERCE; PKI; PUBLIC-KEY ENCRYPTION.

CGA color/graphics adapter: a graphics system for PCs introduced in 1981 by IBM: superseded by VGA systems.

⇒ See also BACKWARD COMPATIBLE; EGA; GRAPHICS MODE; IBM PC; MCGA; PALETTE; RESOLUTION; SVGA; TEXT MODE; VGA; VIDEO ADAPTER; XGA.

CGI Common Gateway Interface: a specification for transferring information between a World Wide Web server and a program. A CGI program is any program designed to accept and return data that conforms to the CGI specification.

⇒ See also ACTIVE SERVER PAGES; DYNAMIC HTML; FORM; ISAPI; JAVA; NSAPI; PERL; SERVLET; WORLD WIDE WEB.

CGM *n.* Computer Graphics Metafile: a file format designed to be the standard vector graphics file format and supported by a wide variety of software and hardware products.

⇒ See also ANSI; GRAPHICS FILE FORMATS; VECTOR GRAPHICS.

Challenge Handshake Authentication Protocol *n.* See CHAP.

challenge-response *adj.* describing authentication techniques in which an individual is prompted (the challenge) to provide some private information (the response) that depends on the challenge. It is thus resistant to eavesdropping.

⇒ See also AUTHENTICATION; CHAP; SMART CARD.

channel *n.* **1.** in communications, a path between two computers or devices: *TV channels; IRC channels.* **2.** for IBM PS/2 computers, EXPANSION BUS. **3.** in sales and marketing, the way in which a vendor communicates with and sells products to consumers.

⇒ See also B-CHANNEL; BUS; COMMUNICATIONS; IRC.

channel bonding *n.* a technology that combines two telephone lines into a single channel, effectively doubling data transfer speeds.

⇒ See also ISDN; K56FLEX; MODEM; X2.

channel definition format *n.* See CDF.

CHAP *n.* Challenge Handshake Authentication Protocol: a type of authentication in which the authentication agent (typically a network server) sends the client program a key to be used to encrypt the username and password as protection against eavesdropping.

⇒ See also AUTHENTICATION; CHALLENGE-RESPONSE; PAP.

character *n.* in the C language, any symbol that requires one byte of storage.

⇒ See also ALPHANUMERIC; ASCII; CHARACTER BASED; CPI; EXTENDED ASCII; GRAPHICS BASED.

character based *adj.* referring to programs capable of displaying only ASCII and extended ASCII characters. Character-based programs treat a display screen as an array of boxes, each of which can hold one character.

⇒ See also CHARACTER MODE; EXTENDED ASCII; GRAPHICAL USER INTERFACE; GRAPHICS BASED; TEXT MODE.

character mode *n.* a mode of resolution in which the display screen is treated as an array of blocks, each of which can hold one ASCII character. Programs that run entirely in character mode are called *character-based* programs.

⇒ See also ASCII; BLOCK GRAPHICS; CHARACTER BASED; PIXEL; VIDEO ADAPTER.

character recognition *n.* OPTICAL CHARACTER RECOGNITION.

character set *n.* a defined list of characters recognized by computer hardware and software. Each character is represented by a number.

⇒ See also ASCII; CHARACTER; CONTROL CHARACTER; UNICODE.

characters per inch *n.* See CPI.

characters per second *n.* See CPS.

character string *n.* a series of characters manipulated as a group, often specified by enclosing the characters in single or double quotes: 'WASHINGTON' and "WASHINGTON".

⇒ See also DATA TYPE; NAME.

charge-coupled device *n.* See CCD.

chassis *n.* a metal frame that serves as the structural support for electronic components, as circuit boards, wiring, and slots for expansion boards.
⇒ See also DESKTOP MODEL COMPUTER; EXPANSION BOARD; PRINTED CIRCUIT BOARD; SLOT; TOWER MODEL.

chat *n.* real-time communication between two users via computer offered by most networks and online services.
⇒ See also AVATAR; CHAT ROOM; E-MAIL; INSTANT MESSAGING; IRC; NETMEETING; ONLINE SERVICE.

chat room *n.* a virtual room, actually a channel, where a chat session takes place.
⇒ See also ACRONYM; CHAT; IRC; LURK; MUD.

check box *n.* in graphical user interfaces, a box that can be clicked to turn an option on or off. When the option is on, an x or a $\checkmark$ appears in the box.
⇒ See also BOX; DIALOG BOX; GRAPHICAL USER INTERFACE; OPTION.

checksum *n.* a method of error detection in which each transmitted message is accompanied by a numerical value based on the number of "1" or "0" bits in the message.
⇒ See also COMMUNICATIONS; CRC; ECC MEMORY; ERROR DETECTION.

chip *n.* a small piece of semiconducting material (usually silicon) on which an integrated circuit is embedded. A typical chip is less than ¼ square inches and can contain millions of electronic components (transistors).
⇒ See also ASIC; CHIPSET; CONTROLLER; CPU; INTEGRATED CIRCUIT; MICROPROCESSOR; MOORE'S LAW; PGA; PINOUT; PLD; PRINTED CIRCUIT BOARD; SEMICONDUCTOR; SIMM; TRANSISTOR.

chipset *n.* a number of integrated circuits designed to work together to perform one or more related functions. The term is often used to refer to the main chips (other than CPU and memory) on a motherboard.
⇒ See also CHIP; CONTROLLER; MICROPROCESSOR; TRITON.

choose *v.t.* to pick (a command or option), as by clicking on a menu command or command button.

⇒ See also CLICK; COMMAND; COMMAND KEY; GRAPHICAL USER INTERFACE; MENU; OPTION; SELECT.

Chooser *n.* a Macintosh desk accessory (DA) that enables the user to select and configure printers and network devices, such as file servers.

⇒ See also DESK ACCESSORY (DA).

CHRP (chûrp), *n.* Common Hardware Reference Platform: a specification for PowerPC-based machines that can run the MacOS, Windows NT, or AIX. Also called **PowerPC Platform (PPCP)**.

⇒ See also MacOS; MACINTOSH COMPUTER; PowerPC; PPCP.

CICS Customer Information Control System: a mainframe program from IBM that controls the interaction between applications and users and lets programmers develop screen displays without detailed knowledge of the terminals being used.

⇒ See also COBOL; TP MONITOR; TRANSACTION PROCESSING.

CIDR *n.* Classless Inter-Domain Routing: an IP addressing scheme in which a single IP address can be used to designate many unique IP addresses.

⇒ See also IP ADDRESS; ROUTING.

CIE color model *n.* a color model based on human perception developed by the CIE (Commission Internationale de l'Eclairage) committee.

⇒ See also CMYK; COLOR MATCHING; RGB MONITOR.

CIF 1. Cells in Frames. **2.** Common Intermediate Format.

Cinepak *n.* a popular codec (compression/ decompression technology) for computer video developed by SuperMac Inc.

⇒ See also CODEC; INDEO.

cipher text *n.* data that has been encrypted and is therefore unreadable until it has been converted into plain text (decrypted) with a key.

⇒ See also ENCRYPTION; PLAIN TEXT.

CIR *n.* committed information rate: a specified amount of guaranteed bandwidth (measured in bits per second) on a Frame Relay service.

⇒ See also BANDWIDTH; FRAME RELAY; QoS.

circuit board *n.* PRINTED CIRCUIT BOARD.

circuit switching *n.* a type of communications in which a dedicated channel (or circuit) is established for the duration of a transmission. The telephone system is a *circuit-switching network*.
⇒ See also PACKET SWITCHING; PSTN.

CIS *n.* COMPUSERVE INFORMATION SERVICE. See under COMPUSERVE.

CISC (sisk), *n.* complex instruction set computer: an architecture in which the CPU supports many multistep instructions.
⇒ See also ARCHITECTURE; CPU; MACHINE LANGUAGE; RISC.

Cisco Systems *n.* one of the leading manufacturers of network equipment.
⇒ See also 3COM; BRIDGE; INTERNETWORKING; LAYER TWO FORWARDING; ROUTER; SWITCH; VLAN.

class *n.* in object-oriented programming, a category that defines all the common properties of the different objects that belong to it.
⇒ See also AFC; IFC; MFC; OBJECT-ORIENTED PROGRAMMING; OVERLOADING; POLYMORPHISM.

Classless Inter-Domain Routing *n.* See CIDR.

clean boot *n.* starting (booting) a computer in a manner that loads only those files and programs absolutely required.
⇒ See also BOOT; OPERATING SYSTEM.

clear *v.t.* to erase. *Clear the screen*, for example, means to erase everything on the display screen. *Clear a variable* means to remove whatever data is currently stored in the variable. *Clear memory* means to erase all data currently stored in memory.
⇒ See also DISPLAY SCREEN; MEMORY; VARIABLE.

click *v.i.* **1.** to tap on a mouse button, pressing it down and then immediately releasing it. The phrase *to click on* means to select (a screen object) by moving the mouse pointer to the object's position and clicking a mouse button. —*n.* **2.** the pressing down and rapid release of a mouse button. **3.** in the World Wide Web advertising industry, the selection of a banner ad by a user. The effectiveness of Web advertisements is measured by their *click-through rate*—how often people who see the ad click on it.

⇒ See also CHOOSE; DOUBLE CLICK; DRAG; MOUSE; SHIFT CLICKING.

client *n.* an application that runs on a personal computer or workstation and relies on a server to perform some operations. An *e-mail client* is an application that enables the user to send and receive e-mail.

⇒ See also CLIENT-SIDE; CLIENT/SERVER ARCHITECTURE; E-MAIL CLIENT; SERVER; THIN CLIENT.

client/server architecture *n.* a network architecture in which each computer or process on the network is either a client or a server. Also called **two-tier architecture.**

⇒ See also ARCHITECTURE; CLIENT; CLIENT-SIDE; LOCAL-AREA NETWORK; NETWORK; NODE; PEER-TO-PEER ARCHITECTURE; PROCESS; SERVER; SERVER-SIDE; SYBASE; THIN CLIENT; THREE-TIER; TWO-TIER.

client-side *adj.* occurring on the client side of a client-server system, as JavaScript scripts, which are executed by the browser (the client).

⇒ See also CLIENT; CLIENT/SERVER ARCHITECTURE; SERVER-SIDE.

clip *v.t.* in computer graphics, to cut off (a portion of a graphic) at a defined boundary.

⇒ See also CROP; GRAPHICS; WINDOW.

clip art *n.* electronic illustrations that can be inserted into a document.

⇒ See also DESKTOP PUBLISHING.

clipboard *n.* a special memory area (*buffer*) where data is stored temporarily before being copied to another location. Cutting and pasting in word-processing programs is done by means of a clipboard.

⇒ See also COPY; CUT; PASTE.

Clipper chip *n.* an encryption chip designed under the auspices of the U.S. government with the intention of enforcing its use in all devices that might use encryption, including computers, modems, telephones, and televisions. Clipper chips send information with each message that would allow government officials to decrypt it.

⇒ See also CRYPTOGRAPHY; ELECTRONIC FRONTIER FOUNDATION; ENCRYPTION; SECURITY.

clock rate *n.* CLOCK SPEED.

clock speed *n.* the speed, expressed in megahertz, at which a microprocessor executes instructions. Also called **clock rate**.
⇒ See also BUS; CPU; INSTRUCTION; MICROPROCESSOR; OVERCLOCK; SUPERSCALAR; WAIT STATE.

clone *n.* a computer, software product, or device that functions exactly like another, better-known product.
⇒ See also COMPATIBLE; IBM PC; PC.

close *v.t.* **1.** to finish work on (a data file) and save it. **2.** in graphical user interfaces, to remove (a window) from the screen.
⇒ See also GRAPHICAL USER INTERFACE; OPEN; SAVE; WINDOW.

cluster *n.* a group of disk sectors to which the operating system assigns numbers that it uses to keep track of files. DOS and Windows keep track of clusters with the file allocation table (FAT).
⇒ See also FILE ALLOCATION TABLE; FRAGMENTATION; PARTITION; ScanDisk; SECTOR; SLACK SPACE.

clustering *n.* connecting two or more computers together in such a way that they behave like a single computer: used for parallel processing, load balancing, and fault tolerance.
⇒ See also FAULT TOLERANCE; LOAD BALANCING; MSCS; PARALLEL PROCESSING; WOLFPACK.

CLUT *n.* color look-up table: same as PALETTE (def. 1).

CLV Constant Linear Velocity: a method by which CD-ROM players access data.
⇒ See also CAV; CD-ROM; CD-ROM PLAYER.

CMIP (sē′mip′), *n.* Common Management Information Protocol: an OSI standard protocol used with the Common Management Information Services (CMIS) that provides improved security and better reporting of unusual network conditions.
⇒ See also ISO; NETWORK MANAGEMENT.

CMOS (sē′môs′, -mos′), *n.* complementary metal oxide semiconductor: a widely used type of semiconductor that uses both NMOS (negative polarity) and PMOS (positive polarity) circuits and requires less power than chips using just one type of transistor.

⇒ See also BIOS; SEMICONDUCTOR.

CMS COLOR MANAGEMENT SYSTEM.

CMYK Cyan-Magenta-Yellow-Black: a color model in which all colors are described as a mixture of these four process colors: CMYK is the standard color model used in offset printing for full-color documents.

⇒ See also COLOR MATCHING; COLOR SEPARATION; DESKTOP PUBLISHING; INTEL MICROPROCESSORS; OFFSET PRINTING; RGB MONITOR; SPOT COLOR; WYSIWYP.

coaxial cable *n.* a type of wire that consists of a center wire surrounded by insulation and a grounded shield of braided wire that minimizes electrical and radio frequency interference. It is the primary type of cabling used by the cable television industry and widely used for computer networks.

⇒ See also 10BASE-2; 10BASE5; AUI; BNC CONNECTOR; INFORMATION SUPERHIGHWAY; NETWORK; UTP.

COBOL *n.* common business oriented language: a high-level programming language developed in the late 1950s and early 1960s that is very popular for business applications that run on large computers. It is the most widely used programming language in the world.

⇒ See also CICS; CODASYL; HIGH-LEVEL LANGUAGE; PROGRAMMING LANGUAGE.

CODASYL (kō′də sil), *n.* Conference on Data Systems Languages: an organization founded in 1957 by the U.S. Department of Defense to develop computer programming languages. Although the organization no longer exists, the term CODASYL is still used sometimes to refer to COBOL, which it developed.

⇒ See also COBOL.

code *n.* **1.** a set of symbols for representing something: *ASCII code.* **2.** written computer instructions. —*v.i.* **3.** *Informal.* to program; to write source code.

⇒ See also ASCII; COMPILE; EXECUTABLE FILE; MACHINE LANGUAGE; OBJECT CODE; PROGRAM; PSEUDOCODE; SOURCE CODE.

codec 1. compressor/decompressor: any technology for compressing and decompressing data, as MPEG, Indeo, Cinepak. **2.** in telecommunications, a device that encodes or decodes a signal. **3.** the translation of a binary value into a voltage that can be transmitted over a wire.

⇒ See also CINEPAK; INDEO; MPEG; QUICKTIME; VIDEO FOR WINDOWS.

Code Division Multiple Access *n.* See CDMA.

coff *n.* Common Object File Format: a binary file format used in UNIX System V and Windows.

⇒ See also BINARY FILE; UNIX.

cold boot *n.* the start-up of a computer from a powered-down state.

⇒ See also BOOT.

collapse *v.t.* to compress (a view of a hierarchy) so that only the roots of each branch are visible.

⇒ See also BRANCH; HIERARCHICAL; ROOT DIRECTORY.

color depth *n.* the number of distinct colors that can be represented by a piece of hardware or software, expressed in bits. Also called **bit depth.**

⇒ See also OPTICAL SCANNER; TRUE COLOR; VIDEO ADAPTER.

color/graphics adapter *n.* See CGA.

Color Look-Up Table *n.* PALETTE (def. 1).

color management system *n.* a system for ensuring that colors remain the same regardless of the device or medium used to display the colors. *Abbr.:* CMS

⇒ See also CIE COLOR MODEL; CMYK; COLOR MATCHING; PANTONE MATCHING SYSTEM (PMS); PROCESS COLORS; RGB MONITOR; WYSIWYP.

color matching *n.* the process of ensuring that a color displayed in one medium remains the same when converted to another medium.

⇒ See also CIE COLOR MODEL; CMYK; COLOR MANAGEMENT SYSTEM (CMS); RGB MONITOR.

color monitor *n.* a display monitor capable of displaying many colors.

⇒ See also CRT; DEGAUSS; DOT PITCH; LCD MONITOR; MASK PITCH; MONITOR; RGB MONITOR; VIDEO ADAPTER.

color printer *n.* a printer capable of printing more than one color, usually based on the CMYK color model.

⇒ See also BANDING; BILEVEL PRINTER; CMYK; COLOR SEPARATION; CONTONE PRINTER; INK-JET PRINTER; LASER PRINTER; PRINTER; PROCESS COLORS; SNAPSHOT PRINTER.

color separation *n.* the separation of a color graphic or photo into single layers of the four basic ink colors (cyan, magenta, yellow, and black) in order to print the picture on an offset press.

⇒ See also CMYK; COLOR MANAGEMENT SYSTEM (CMS); COLOR PRINTER; DESKTOP PUBLISHING; PROCESS COLORS.

Color Super-Twist Nematic *n.* See CSTN.

column *n.* **1.** (on a display screen in character mode) a vertical line of characters extending from the top to the bottom of the screen. **2.** (in spreadsheets) a vertical row of cells, usu. identified by letters. **3.** (in database management systems) *field*. **4.** (in documents) a vertical area reserved for text.

⇒ See also CELL; CHARACTER MODE; DATABASE MANAGEMENT SYSTEM; DESKTOP PUBLISHING; DISPLAY SCREEN; FIELD; SPREADSHEET; WORD PROCESSING.

column graph *n.* a type of presentation graphic in which numerical values are illustrated with horizontal columns.

⇒ See also PRESENTATION GRAPHICS.

COM *n.* **1.** in DOS systems, the name of a serial communications port. **2.** COMPONENT OBJECT MODEL.

⇒ See also AUX; COMMUNICATIONS; PORT; SERIAL; WINDOWS DNA.

COM file *n.* in DOS environments, an executable command file with a .COM filename extension and a maximum size of 64K.

⇒ See also COMMAND; DOS; EXE FILE; EXECUTABLE FILE; EXTENSION; FILE.

Comité Consultatif International Téléphonique et Télégraphique *n.* See CCITT.

comma-delimited *adj.* referring to a format in which each piece of data is separated by a comma: a popular format for transferring data from one application to another.

⇒ See also EXPORT; IMPORT.

command *n.* an instruction to a computer or device to perform a specific task. Commands can be given by special words (keywords), function keys, choices in a menu, buttons or other graphical objects on the screen. Also called **directive**.

⇒ See also BAT FILE; COM FILE; COMMAND DRIVEN; COMMAND LANGUAGE; COMMAND LINE; DOS; EXE FILE; EXTERNAL COMMAND; FUNCTION KEYS; INSTRUCTION; INTERNAL COMMAND; KEYWORD; MENU; USER INTERFACE.

command buffer *n.* a temporary storage area where commands are kept.

⇒ See also BUFFER; COMMAND; UNDO.

COMMAND.COM *n.* the DOS file that contains the DOS command processor.

⇒ See also COMMAND PROCESSOR; INTERNAL COMMAND.

command driven *adj.* referring to programs and operating systems that accept commands in the form of special words or letters.

⇒ See also COMMAND; MENU DRIVEN; USER INTERFACE.

Command key *n.* on a Macintosh computer, a special command key marked by a four-leaf clover or an apple: similar to a PC's Alt key. Also called **Apple key, Open Apple**.

⇒ See also APPLE KEY; CONTROL KEY; KEYBOARD.

command language *n.* the programming language through which a user communicates with the operating system or an application. The DOS command language includes the commands DIR, COPY, and DEL. With graphical user interfaces, the command language consists of operations performed with a mouse or similar input device.

⇒ See also COMMAND; COMMAND PROCESSOR; GRAPHICAL USER INTERFACE; OPERATING SYSTEM; SHELL.

command line *n.* the line on the display screen where a command is expected.

⇒ See also COMMAND; PROMPT.

command-line interpreter *n.* COMMAND PROCESSOR.

command processor *n.* the part of the operating system that receives and executes operating system commands. In operating systems with a graphical user interface, the command processor interprets mouse operations and executes the appropriate command. Also called **command-line interpreter.**

⇒ See also COMMAND LANGUAGE; OPERATING SYSTEM.

Commodore Amiga *n.* AMIGA.

common carrier *n.* PUBLIC CARRIER.

Common Gateway Interface *n.* See CGI.

Common Hardware Reference Platform *n.* See CHRP.

Common Intermediate Format *n.* a format used in videoconferencing systems that easily supports both NTSC and PAL signals. *Abbr.:* CIF

⇒ See also NTSC; PAL; QCIF; VIDEOCONFERENCING.

Common Management Information Protocol *n.* See CMIP.

Common Object Request Broker Architecture *n.* See CORBA.

Common User Access *n.* See CUA.

communications *n.* the transmission of data from one computer to another, or from one device to another. A *communications device* is any machine that assists data transmission, as a modem, cable, or a port. *Communications software* refers to programs that make it possible to transmit data.

⇒ See also BASEBAND TRANSMISSION; COMMUNICATIONS PROTOCOL; COMMUNICATIONS SOFTWARE; FLOW CONTROL; MODEM; NETWORK; PORT.

communications protocol *n.* the set of rules defining a format for data that is to be transmitted. Protocols also include techniques for detecting and recovering from transmission errors and for encoding and decoding data.

⇒ See also ASYNCHRONOUS; BELL 103; BELL 212A; BPS; CCITT; COMMUNICATIONS; FULL DUPLEX; HALF DUPLEX; HDLC; IPX; PROTOCOL.

communications software *n.* software that makes it possible to send and receive data over telephone lines through modems.

⇒ See also AUTO-ANSWER; BATCH FILE; BULLETIN BOARD SYSTEM; COMMUNICATIONS; COMMUNICATIONS PROTOCOL; EDITOR; EMULATION; KERMIT; LOG ON;

MACRO; MAINFRAME; MODEM; MULTITASKING; QUEUE; SCRIPT.

compact disc *n.* a polycarbonate platter with one or more metal layers capable of storing digital information. *Abbr.:* CD
⇒ See also CD-ROM; DVD; ERASABLE OPTICAL DISK; MASS STORAGE; MultiRead; OPTICAL DISK; RED BOOK; WORM.

Compaq *n.* one of the leading PC manufacturers, based in Houston, Texas, and founded in 1982 by Rod Canion, Bill Murto, and Jim Harris.
⇒ See also DEC; DELL COMPUTER; IBM; PC.

comparison operator *n.* RELATIONAL OPERATOR.

compatible *n.* **1.** a product that can work with or is equivalent to another, better-known product; an IBM-compatible PC. Also called **clone**. —*adj.* **2.** referring to the ability of one device or program to work with another device or program.
⇒ See also BACKWARD COMPATIBLE; BINARY COMPATIBLE; CLONE; COMPATIBLE; dBASE; EMULATION; FONT CARTRIDGE; IBM PC; PC; PLUG COMPATIBLE; STANDARD; UPWARD COMPATIBLE.

compile *v.t.* to transform (a program written in a high-level programming language) from source code into object code so that the program can run.
⇒ See also ASSEMBLY LANGUAGE; BIND; BYTECODE; COMPILER; HIGH-LEVEL LANGUAGE; INTERPRETER; LINK; OBJECT CODE; PARSE; PROGRAMMING LANGUAGE; RUNTIME; SOURCE CODE.

compiler *n.* a program that translates source code into object code.
⇒ See also ASSEMBLY LANGUAGE; COMPILE; INTERPRETER; JIT; LINK; OBJECT CODE; PARSE; PROGRAMMING LANGUAGE; SOURCE CODE.

complementary metal oxide semiconductor *n.* See CMOS.

complex instruction set computer *n.* See CISC.

component *n.* **1.** a small binary object or program that performs a specific function and operates easily with other components and applications. **2.** a part of a device.

⇒ See also APPLET; COMPONENT OBJECT MODEL; COMPONENT SOFTWARE; OCX; VBX.

Component Object Model *n.* a model for binary code developed by Microsoft that enables programmers to develop software objects that can be accessed by any COM-compliant application.

⇒ See also ACTIVEX; COMPONENT; COMPONENT SOFTWARE; DCOM; OLE; OPENDOC; SOM.

component software *n.* software designed to work as a component of a larger application. Also called **componentware**.

⇒ See also COMPONENT; COMPONENT OBJECT MODEL; OBJECT-ORIENTED PROGRAMMING; OLE; OPENDOC; PLUG-IN.

componentware *n.* COMPONENT SOFTWARE.

COM port *n.* See COM.

composite video *n.* a type of video signal in which all information—the red, blue, and green signals (and sometimes audio signals as well)—is mixed together: used by televisions in the United States.

⇒ See also NTSC; RGB MONITOR; S-VIDEO.

compound document *n.* a document that contains elements from a variety of computer applications, such as text from a word processor, graphics from a draw program, and a chart from a spreadsheet application, all stored in such a way that each piece of data can be manipulated by the application that created it.

⇒ See also DOCUMENT; OLE; OPENDOC.

compression *n.* DATA COMPRESSION.

CompuServe Information Service *n.* one of the first and largest online services, CompuServe supports a wide array of *forums* and provides many types of electronic-mail services. In addition, it is connected to hundreds of different database systems. In 1997, the content portion of CompuServe was acquired by America Online and the network service was acquired by World-Com.

⇒ See also AMERICA ONLINE; MSN; ONLINE SERVICE.

computer *n.* a programmable machine that responds to a specific set of instructions in a well-defined manner and can execute a prerecorded list of instructions (a program). The actual machinery—wires, transistors, and circuits—is called *hardware;* the instructions and data are called *software.*

⇒ See also CPU; HARDWARE; MAINFRAME; MICROPROCESSOR; MINICOMPUTER; PERSONAL COMPUTER; SOFTWARE; SUPERCOMPUTER; WORKSTATION.

computer-aided design *n.* See CAD.

computer-aided engineering *n.* See CAE.

computer-aided instruction *n.* COMPUTER-BASED TRAINING. See CBT.

computer-aided manufacturing *n.* See CAM.

Computer-Aided Software Engineering *n.* See CASE.

Computer-Aided Systems Engineering *n.* See CASE.

computer-based training *n.* See CBT.

Computer Graphics Metafile *n.* See CGM.

computer imaging *n.* a field of computer science covering images that can be stored on a computer (digital images). Also called **digital imaging.**

⇒ See also BIT-MAPPED GRAPHICS; DIGITAL PHOTOGRAPHY; OPTICAL SCANNER.

computer literacy *n.* a person's level of expertise and familiarity with computers and his or her ability to use applications.

⇒ See also POWER USER.

computer science *n.* the study of computers, including hardware design, artificial intelligence, and software engineering.

⇒ See also ARTIFICIAL INTELLIGENCE; IT; PROGRAM; SOFTWARE ENGINEERING.

computer system *n.* a complete, working computer including any software and peripheral devices that are necessary to make it function.

⇒ See also COMPUTER; OPERATING SYSTEM.

computer-telephony-integration *n.* See CTI.

computer virus *n.* VIRUS.

concatenate *v.t.* to link together or join (a series

of characters or a group of files).
⇒ See also APPEND; CHARACTER STRING.

concatenation *n.* the act of linking together two or more objects.
⇒ See also CONCATENATE.

concentrator *n.* a device that combines multiple communication channels onto a single transmission medium in such a way that all the individual channels can be simultaneously active.
⇒ See also HUB; MULTIPLEXOR.

conditional *adj.* referring to an action that takes place only if a specific condition is met. Conditional expressions enable a program to act differently each time it is executed, depending on the input.
⇒ See also EXPRESSION; PROGRAMMING LANGUAGE.

conference *n.* an area in a bulletin board or online service in which participants can discuss a topic of common interest. Also called **forum**.
⇒ See also BULLETIN BOARD SYSTEM; FORUM; LURK; ONLINE SERVICE.

CONFIG.SYS *n.* the configuration file for DOS systems.
⇒ See also BOOT; CONFIGURATION; DRIVER; HIMEM. SYS.

configuration *n.* the way a system is set up, or the assortment of components such as main memory, floppy drive, hard disk, monitor, modem, etc., that make up the system. Configuration can refer to either hardware or software, or the combination of both.
⇒ See also CONFIG.SYS; CONFIGURATION FILE; CONTROL PANEL; DIP SWITCH; JUMPER; MIF; PARAMETER; REGISTRY.

configuration file *n.* a file that contains configuration information.
⇒ See also .INI FILE; CONFIG.SYS; CONFIGURATION.

configure *v.t.* to set up (a program or computer system) for a particular application.
⇒ See also CONFIGURATION.

connectionless *adj.* referring to network protocols in which a host can send a message without establishing a connection with the recipient. Ethernet, IPX, and UDP are connectionless protocols.

⇒ See also CONNECTION-ORIENTED; IPX; PROTOCOL; UDP.

connection-oriented *adj.* referring to a protocol that requires a channel to be established between the sender and receiver before any messages are transmitted. The telephone, TCP, and HTTP are connection-oriented protocols.

⇒ See also CONNECTIONLESS.

connectivity *n.* the ability of a program or device to link with other programs and devices. A program that can *import* data from a wide variety of other programs and can *export* data in many different formats is said to have *good connectivity.*

⇒ See also EXPORT; IMPORT.

connector *n.* the part of a cable that plugs into a port or interface to connect one device to another.

⇒ See also BNC CONNECTOR; DIN CONNECTOR; INTERFACE; PINOUT; PORT; RJ-45.

connect time *n.* the amount of time a computer is logged in to a remote computer.

⇒ See also ONLINE SERVICE.

console *n.* **1.** the combination of display monitor and keyboard (or other device that allows input). The term *console* usually refers to a dedicated terminal attached to a minicomputer or mainframe and used to monitor the status of the system. Also called **terminal**. **2.** MONITOR or DISPLAY SCREEN. **3.** a bank of meters and lights indicating a computer's status, with switches that allow an operator to control the computer.

⇒ See also DISPLAY SCREEN; KEYBOARD; TERMINAL.

constant *n.* in programming, a value that never changes, as a number, a character, or a character string.

⇒ See also ABSOLUTE CELL REFERENCE; CHARACTER STRING; FORMULA; LITERAL; VARIABLE.

Constant Linear Velocity *n.* See CLV.

contact manager *n.* an application that enables the user to store and find contact information, such as names, addresses, and telephone numbers.

⇒ See also PIM.

contention *n.* **1.** competition for resources, as in a situation where two or more computers attempt to transmit a message across the same wire at the same time. **2.** a type of network protocol that defines what happens when two or more nodes try to send messages across a network simultaneously.

⇒ See also CSMA/CD; ETHERNET.

context sensitive *adj.* referring to a program feature that changes depending on what the user is doing in the program. *Context-sensitive help* provides documentation for the particular feature that is being used.

⇒ See also HELP.

context switching *n.* TASK SWITCHING.

contiguous *adj.* immediately adjacent, as sectors on a disk that come one after the other.

⇒ See also FRAGMENTATION.

continuous-form paper *n.* a type of printing paper that consists of a single roll of paper, perforated at regular intervals so that sheets can be separated.

⇒ See also PAPER FEED; TRACTOR FEED.

continuous tone *adj.* (of an image) having an almost unlimited range of color or shades of gray, as photographs and television images.

⇒ See also BILEVEL PRINTER; CONTONE PRINTER; DIGITAL; GRAY SCALING; HALFTONE.

contone printer *n.* a type of printer that uses a combination of dithering and printing at different levels of intensity to produce different colors and different shades of light and dark.

⇒ See also BILEVEL PRINTER; COLOR PRINTER; CONTINUOUS TONE; DITHERING.

control *n.* **1.** an object in a window or dialog box, as a push-button, scroll bar, radio button, or pull-down menu. **2.** an OLE or ActiveX object.

⇒ See also ACTIVEX CONTROL; GRAPHICAL USER INTERFACE; OCX; OLE; VBX.

control character *n.* a special, nonprinting character, used to control display monitors, printers, etc.

⇒ See also ASCII; BREAK KEY; CONTROL KEY; KEYBOARD.

Control key *n.* a key on PC keyboards labeled *Ctrl*, used in combination with other characters. Many Apple keyboards have both Ctrl and Cmd keys.

⇒ See also APPLE KEY; COMMAND KEY; CONTROL KEY COMBINATION.

Control key combination *n.* a command issued by pressing a keyboard character in conjunction with the Control key.

⇒ See also COMMAND; CONTROL KEY.

controller *n.* a device that controls the transfer of data between a computer and a peripheral device, as a disk drive, display screen, keyboard, or printer.

⇒ See also ADAPTER; ATA; BUS; CHIP; CPU; DRIVER; EISA; EXPANSION BOARD; MICROCONTROLLER; PCI; PERIPHERAL DEVICE; PRINTED CIRCUIT BOARD; SCSI.

control panel *n.* a utility on both Macintoshes and Windows operating systems that permits the user to set such system parameters as the sensitivity of the mouse.

⇒ See also CDEV.

control panel device *n.* See CDEV.

control program *n.* **1.** a program that enhances an operating system by creating an environment in which other programs can be run. **2.** OPERATING SYSTEM.

⇒ See also GRAPHICAL USER INTERFACE; MICROSOFT WINDOWS; OPERATING ENVIRONMENT; OPERATING SYSTEM.

conventional memory *n.* on DOS systems, the portion of memory that is available to standard DOS programs.

⇒ See also EXPANDED MEMORY; EXTENDED MEMORY; MAIN MEMORY.

convergence *n.* **1.** the coming together of two or more disparate disciplines or technologies. **2.** in graphics, the degree of sharpness of an individual color pixel on a monitor.

⇒ See also GRAPHICS; MONITOR; PIXEL; RGB MONITOR.

convert *v.t.* to change (data) from one format to

another.

⇒ See also EXPORT; IMPORT.

cookie *n.* a message to identify users that is given to a Web browser by a Web server.

⇒ See also BROWSER; DYNAMIC HTML; LOG FILE; STATELESS; WEB SERVER; WORLD WIDE WEB.

CoolTalk *n.* an Internet telephone (Voice on the Net) tool built into Netscape Navigator 3.0 that supports audio conferencing, a whiteboard, and a chat tool.

⇒ See also INTERNET TELEPHONY; NETMEETING.

cooperative multitasking *n.* a type of multitasking in which the process currently controlling the CPU must offer control to other processes: all programs must cooperate for it to work.

⇒ See also MICROSOFT WINDOWS; MULTITASKING; UNIX.

Copper Distributed Data Interface *n.* See CDDI.

coprocessor *n.* a special-purpose processing unit that assists the CPU in performing certain types of operations. A *math* (or *numeric*) coprocessor performs mathematical computations, particularly floating-point operations. A *graphics coprocessor* is specially designed for handling graphics computations.

⇒ See also ACCELERATOR BOARD; CPU; FLOATING-POINT NUMBER.

copy *v.t.* **1.** to copy (a piece of data) to a temporary location, as to duplicate a section of a document and place it in a *buffer* (sometimes called a *clipboard*) from which it can be retrieved and pasted somewhere else. **2.** in file management, to make a duplicate of (a file). —*n.* **3.** a duplicate of a piece of data, such as a file or a directory.

⇒ See also BUFFER; CLIPBOARD; CUT; FILE MANAGEMENT SYSTEM; PASTE.

copy protection *n.* any of the programming techniques used to prevent the unauthorized copying of software.

⇒ See also DIGITAL WATERMARK; DONGLE; DVD-VIDEO; SHAREWARE; SOFTWARE LICENSING; SOFTWARE PIRACY; WAREZ.

CORBA *n.* Common Object Request Broker Architecture: an architecture that enables objects written in different programming languages and running on different systems to communicate with one another; developed by the Object Management Group (OMG).

⇒ See also DCOM; DISTRIBUTED COMPUTING; IIOP; OBJECT; OMG; ORB; RMI; RPC; SOM.

core memory *n.* an obsolete term for RAM, which was composed of doughnut-shaped magnets called *cores*.

⇒ See also MAIN MEMORY.

corrupted *adj.* referring to data that have been damaged in some way.

Courier font *n.* a common monospaced (fixed-pitch) font, supported by most printers and most word-processing software.

⇒ See also FIXED PITCH; FONT; MONOSPACING.

courseware *n.* software designed to be used in an educational program.

⇒ See also CBT.

cpi characters per inch: a typographic measurement specifying the number of characters that can fit on a printed line one inch long.

⇒ See also CHARACTER; FIXED PITCH; FONT; MONOSPACING; PITCH; PROPORTIONAL SPACING.

CP/M Control Program for Microprocessors: an obsolete operating system for personal computers created by Digital Research Corporation.

⇒ See also DOS; OPERATING SYSTEM.

cps characters per second: a unit of measure used to describe the speed of dot-matrix and daisy-wheel printers.

⇒ See also PRINTER.

CPU central processing unit: the most important element of a computer system. It includes an arithmetic-logic unit for calculations and a control unit for sequencing operations and transferring data between the CPU and memory. The CPU also issues instructions to I/O devices.

⇒ See also ALU; CHIP; CISC; CLOCK SPEED; CO-PROCESSOR; INTEL MICROPROCESSORS; MICROPROCESSOR; MMU; POWERPC; RISC.

CPU time *n.* the amount of time the CPU is actually executing instructions, used to compare the speed of two different processors, to gauge how CPU-intensive a program is, and to measure the amount of processing time being allocated to different programs in a multitasking environment.

⇒ See also CPU; MULTITASKING.

crack *v.t.* **1.** to break into (a computer system). **2.** to copy (commercial software) illegally by breaking protection techniques.

⇒ See also HACKER; PHREAKING; SMURF.

cracker *n.* a person who cracks computer systems or software.

crash *n.* **1.** a serious computer failure in which a computer stops working or a program suddenly aborts as the result of a hardware malfunction or software bug. —*v.i.* **2.** to fail or break.

⇒ See also ABORT; BOMB; BUG; FATAL ERROR; GPF; HANG; HEAD CRASH; INVALID PAGE FAULT; SMART.

CRC cyclic redundancy check: a common technique for detecting data transmission errors.

⇒ See also CHECKSUM; COMMUNICATIONS PROTOCOL; ERROR DETECTION; ZMODEM.

crippled version *n.* a demonstration version of a piece of software that has one or more critical features disabled.

⇒ See also BETA TEST.

crop *v.t.* in computer graphics, to cut off the edges of (an image) to make it the proper size or to remove unwanted parts.

⇒ See also CLIP.

crop marks *n.pl.* printed or drawn lines indicating where the paper on which a composed page has been printed should be cut to produce the correct page size.

⇒ See also CAMERA-READY; DESKTOP PUBLISHING; OFFSET PRINTING.

cross-platform *adj.* referring to the capability of software or hardware to run identically on different platforms, as Windows and Macintosh.

⇒ See also BINARY COMPATIBLE; LOCAL-AREA NETWORK; PLATFORM.

CRT cathode-ray tube: the technology used in most televisions and computer display screens.

⇒ See also COLOR MONITOR; DEGAUSS; DISPLAY

SCREEN; LCD MONITOR; MONITOR; PINCUSHION DISTORTION; REFRESH.

cryptography *n.* the art of protecting information by transforming or encrypting it into an unreadable format called *cyphertext.*
⇒ See also CLIPPER CHIP; DES; PRETTY GOOD PRIVACY; PUBLIC-KEY ENCRYPTION; SECURITY; SYMMETRIC-KEY CRYPTOGRAPHY.

CSMA/CD Carrier Sense Multiple Access/Collision Detection: a set of rules determining how to avoid network deadlock when two devices attempt to use a data channel simultaneously: a type of contention protocol.
⇒ See also 100BASE-T; CONTENTION; ETHERNET.

CSS Cascading Style Sheets: a feature added to HTML that enables both Web site developers and users to create style sheets that define how different elements, such as headers and links, appear. These style sheets can then be applied to any Web page.
⇒ See also HTML; STYLE SHEET.

CSTN color super-twist nematic: an LCD technology developed by Sharp Electronics Corporation. It is based on a passive matrix, which is less expensive to produce than an active-matrix (TFT) display.
⇒ See also DSTN; LCD; PASSIVE-MATRIX DISPLAY; SUPER-TWIST; TFT.

CSU See under CSU/DSU.

CSU/DSU Channel Service Unit/Data Service Unit: a device that performs protective and diagnostic functions for a telecommunications line.
⇒ See also SMDS; T-1 CARRIER; T-3 CARRIER; V.35.

CTI computer-telephony-integration: systems that enable a computer to accept incoming calls and route them to the appropriate device or person.
⇒ See also TELEPHONY.

Ctrl CONTROL KEY.

CUA Common User Access: a set of standards for user interfaces developed by IBM: one component of the *System Application Architecture (SAA)* standards introduced in 1987.
⇒ See also SAA; USER INTERFACE.

current *adj.* referring to an object that is active

or acting as a reference point: *current directory; current drive; current cell.*

⇒ See also ACTIVE; DEFAULT; WORKING DIRECTORY.

cursor *n.* **1.** a special symbol, usually a solid rectangle or a blinking underline character, that signifies where the next character will be displayed on the screen. **2.** Also called **puck.** a device, similar in appearance to a mouse, that is used to sketch lines on a digitizing tablet. **3.** in some database languages, short for *cur(rent) s(et) o(f) r(ecords),* the currently selected set of records.

⇒ See also ARROW KEYS; DIGITIZING TABLET; MOUSE; POINTER.

cursor control keys *n.pl.* special keys on computer keyboards that move the cursor, such as arrow keys, *End, Home, Page Up, Page Down,* and *Backspace* keys.

⇒ See also ARROW KEYS; CURSOR; KEYBOARD.

cursor position *n.* the position of the cursor on the display screen.

⇒ See also CURSOR; DISPLAY SCREEN; TEXT MODE.

CU-SeeMe *n.* a videoconferencing program that uses the Internet to transmit audio and video signals.

⇒ See also VIDEOCONFERENCING.

Customer Information Control System *n.* See CICS.

customer support *n.* service that computer and software manufacturers, and third-party software companies offer to customers, as mail-in or carry-in service, on-site contract, etc. Also called **technical support**.

⇒ See also BULLETIN BOARD SYSTEM; DOWNLOAD.

cut *v.t.* in word processing, to remove (a section of text) from a document to a temporary buffer, from which it can be moved to another place.

⇒ See also BUFFER; CLIPBOARD; COPY; DELETE; PASTE.

cut-sheet feeder *n.* SHEET FEEDER.

cyber- a prefix used to describe new things that are being made possible by the spread of computers: *cyberphobia; cyberpunk; cyberspace.*

⇒ See also CYBERSPACE; VIRTUAL REALITY.

cybernetics *n.* originally the study of biological and artificial control systems, now concerned with discovering what mechanisms control systems and, in particular, how systems regulate themselves.

⇒ See also ARTIFICIAL INTELLIGENCE; ROBOTICS.

cyberspace *n.* a metaphor for describing the non-physical terrain created by computer systems, within which people can communicate with one another.

⇒ See also AVATAR; INFORMATION SUPERHIGHWAY; MUD; ONLINE SERVICE; VIRTUAL REALITY; VRML.

cycle time *n.* a measurement of how quickly two successive pieces of data can be fetched from a memory chip.

⇒ See also ACCESS TIME; DRAM; SRAM.

cyclic redundancy check *n.* See CRC.

cylinder *n.* a single track location on all the platters making up a hard disk.

⇒ See also HARD DISK; PLATTER; TRACK.

Cyrix *n.* a U.S. corporation founded in 1988 that manufactures Intel-compatible microprocessors: acquired by National Semiconductor in 1997.

⇒ See also AMD; INTEL; INTEL MICROPROCESSORS; MICROPROCESSOR; PENTIUM MICROPROCESSOR.

D d

D3D Direct3D.

DA desk accessory.

DAC digital-to-analog converter: a device (usually a single chip) that converts digital data into analog signals that can be carried by telephone signals or processed by a monitor.
⇒ See also ANALOG; DIGITAL; RAMDAC.

daemon (dē′mən, dā′-), *n.* a process, such as a print spooler or an e-mail handler, that runs in the background and performs a specified operation at predefined times or in response to certain events. Also called **System Agent; service.**
⇒ See also AGENT; PROCESS; UNIX.

daisy chain *n.* **1.** a hardware configuration in which devices are connected in a series. —*v.t.* **2.** to connect (devices) in a daisy chain pattern.
⇒ See also SCSI.

daisy-wheel printer *n.* an obsolete type of printer in which letters are mounted on spokes, rotated into position, and struck by a hammer to produce text.
⇒ See also IMPACT PRINTER; PRINTER.

DAO 1. data access objects: software objects that work with Microsoft's Jet database engine, generally created with Visual Basic and including all of the applications in Microsoft Office, such as MS-Word, MS-Access, and Excel. **2.** disk at once: a method of recording to CD-R disks in which all data are written in a single session.
⇒ See also ADO; JET; VISUAL BASIC.

DASD (daz′də), *n.* Direct Access Storage Device: another name for disk drive in the world of mainframes.
⇒ See also DISK DRIVE; RANDOM ACCESS.

DAT *n.* digital audio tape: a type of magnetic tape that uses helical scan to record data and can hold from 2 to 24 GB of data in a cartridge about the size of a credit card.
⇒ See also DDS; GIGABYTE; HELICAL-SCAN CARTRIDGE; MASS STORAGE; MEGABYTE; SEQUENTIAL ACCESS; TAPE.

data *n.pl.* or *n.* **1.** distinct pieces of information, usually formatted in a special way. Strictly speaking, data is the plural of *datum*, a single piece of information. When used as a singular noun, it means "information." **2.** binary machine-readable information as distinguished from textual human-readable information. —*adj.* **3.** in database management systems, referring to the files that store the database information, as opposed to index files and data dictionaries, which store administrative information.

⇒ See also ASCII; BINARY; DATA DICTIONARY; DATA INTEGRITY; DATABASE MANAGEMENT SYSTEM; METADATA; PROGRAM; SOFTWARE.

database *n.* **1.** a collection of information in electronic form that is organized in such a way that a computer program can quickly select desired pieces of data. Traditional databases are organized by *fields, records,* and *files.* A field is a single piece of information; a record is one complete set of fields; and a file is a collection of records. For example, a telephone book is analogous to a file. It contains a list of records, each of which consists of three fields: name, address, and telephone number. An alternative concept in database design is known as *Hypertext.* In a Hypertext database, any object, whether it be a piece of text, a picture, or a film, can be linked to any other object. Hypertext databases are particularly useful for organizing large amounts of disparate information, but they are not designed for numerical analysis. **2.** DATABASE MANAGEMENT SYSTEM.

⇒ See also DATA MINING; DATA WAREHOUSE; DATABASE MANAGEMENT SYSTEM; DISTRIBUTED DATABASE; FIELD; FILE; Hypertext; METADATA; OLAP; RDBMS; RECORD; REPLICATION.

DATABASE 2 *n.* See DB2.

database management system *n.* a collection of programs for storing, modifying, and extracting information from a database, as a computerized library system, an automated teller machine, a flight reservation system, or a computerized parts inventory system.

⇒ See also BLOB; DATA DICTIONARY; DATA MART;

DATABASE; DB2; DISTRIBUTED DATABASE; FLAT-FILE DATABASE; FOURTH-GENERATION LANGUAGE; HYPERTEXT; Informix; ISAM; MULTIDIMENSIONAL DBMS; OLAP; Oracle; PROGRESS SOFTWARE; QUERY; RDBMS; REPORT WRITER; SQL; STORED PROCEDURE.

data bus *n.* BUS.

data communications *n.* COMMUNICATIONS.

data compression *n.* the storage of data in a format that requires less space than usual: used esp. in backup utilities, spreadsheet applications, and database management systems.
⇒ See also ARC; CCITT; DCT; DISK COMPRESSION; DSP; JPEG; LOSSLESS COMPRESSION; LOSSY COMPRESSION; LZW; MNP; MP3; MPEG; ZIP.

data dictionary *n.* in database management systems, a file that defines the basic organization of a database, containing a list of all files in the database, the number of records in each file, and the names and types of each field.
⇒ See also DATABASE MANAGEMENT SYSTEM.

data encryption *n.* ENCRYPTION.

Data Encryption Standard *n.* See DES.

data entry *n.* the process of entering data into a computerized database or spreadsheet, either by an individual typing at a keyboard or by a machine entering data electronically.
⇒ See also DATABASE; SPREADSHEET.

datagram *n.* PACKET.

data integrity *n.* the validity of data. ⇒ See also BACKUP; DATA; ERROR DETECTION.

data mart *n.* a database, or collection of databases, focused on a particular subject and designed to help managers make decisions about their business.
⇒ See also DATA WAREHOUSE; DATABASE MANAGEMENT SYSTEM.

data mining *adj.* referring to a class of database applications that look for hidden patterns in a collection of data.
⇒ See also DATABASE.

data processing *n.* **1.** the organization and manipulation of data, usu. large amounts of numeric data. **2.** INFORMATION TECHNOLOGY (IT).

⇒ See also ACCOUNTING SOFTWARE; APPLICATION.

data rate *n.* DATA TRANSFER RATE.

data recovery *n.* salvaging data stored on damaged media, such as magnetic disks and tapes.

⇒ See also HEAD CRASH; VIRUS.

data structure *n.* in programming, a scheme for organizing related pieces of information.

⇒ See also ARRAY; FILE; HEAP; LIST; RECORD; STACK; TREE STRUCTURE.

data transfer rate *n.* the speed with which data can be transmitted from one device to another, typically measured in megabits (million bits) or megabytes (million bytes) per second. Also called **throughput**.

⇒ See also ACCESS TIME; BURST MODE; KBPS; MBPS; MBPS; STREAMING.

data type *n.* in programming, the classification of a particular piece of information, as integer, string, and so forth.

⇒ See also BIG-ENDIAN; CHARACTER; DATABASE; DECLARE; FIELD; FLOATING-POINT NUMBER; INTEGER; OVERLOADING; POLYMORPHISM; VARIABLE.

data warehouse *n.* a combination of many databases across an entire enterprise that presents a coherent picture of business conditions at a single point in time and is designed to support management decision-making.

⇒ See also DATA MART; DATABASE; METADATA.

data warehousing *n.* DATA WAREHOUSE.

daughtercard *n.* a printed circuit board that plugs into another circuit board (usu. the motherboard) and accesses motherboard components (memory and CPU) directly instead of sending data through the slower expansion bus. Also called **daughterboard.**

⇒ See also EXPANSION BOARD; MOTHERBOARD; PRINTED CIRCUIT BOARD.

DB2 Database 2: a group of relational database products offered by IBM that provides an open database environment that runs on a wide variety of computing platforms.

⇒ See also DATABASE MANAGEMENT SYSTEM; RDBMS.

dBASE *n.* a database management system produced by Ashton-Tate Corporation: a de facto standard supported by nearly all database management and spreadsheet systems.

⇒ See also DATABASE MANAGEMENT SYSTEM; EXPORT; IMPORT.

DBMS DATABASE MANAGEMENT SYSTEM.

DCC Direct Cable Connection: a Windows 95 feature that enables two computers to be connected via a serial or parallel cable and to access each other's files, functioning as if they were on a local-area network (LAN).

⇒ See also ECP; LOCAL-AREA NETWORK; NETWORK NEIGHBORHOOD; NULL-MODEM CABLE.

DCE 1. Distributed Computing Environment: a suite of technology services developed by The Open Group for creating distributed applications that run on different platforms. **2.** Data Communications Equipment: a device that communicates with a Data Terminal Equipment (DTE) device in RS-232C communications.

⇒ See also DISTRIBUTED PROCESSING; DTE; FAULT TOLERANCE; MIDDLEWARE; MODEM; OSF; THE OPEN GROUP.

DCI DIRECTDRAW.

DCOM *n.* Distributed Component Object Model: an extension of the Component Object Model (COM) to support objects distributed across a network.

⇒ See also COMPONENT OBJECT MODEL; CORBA; DISTRIBUTED COMPUTING; DSOM; RMI.

DCT Discrete Cosine Transform: a technique used for data compression.

⇒ See also DATA COMPRESSION; JPEG; LOSSY COMPRESSION.

DDC Display Data Channel: a VESA standard for communication between a monitor and a video adapter.

⇒ See also MONITOR; VESA; VIDEO ADAPTER.

DDE Dynamic Data Exchange: an older interprocess communication (IPC) system built into the Macintosh, Windows, and OS/2 operating systems, replaced by OLE, which provides greater control over shared data.

⇒ See also INTERPROCESS COMMUNICATION (IPC); OLE.

DDR-SDRAM *n.* Double Data Rate-Synchronous **DRAM**: a type of SDRAM that supports data transfers on both edges of each clock cycle, effectively doubling the memory chip's data throughput. Also called **SDRAM II.**
⇒ See also SDRAM.

DDS Digital Data Storage: the industry standard for digital audio tape (DAT) formats.
⇒ See also DAT.

deadlock *n.* a condition that occurs in multitasking and client/server environments when two processes are each waiting for the other to proceed, with the result that neither process responds to input. Also called **deadly embrace.**
⇒ See also HANG.

deadly embrace *n.* DEADLOCK.

debug *v.t.* to find and remove errors, or bugs, from (a program or design).
⇒ See also ALPHA VERSION; BUG; TWEAK.

debugger *n.* a special program used to find errors, or bugs, in other programs by allowing a programmer to stop a program at any point and examine and change the values of variables.
⇒ See also BUG.

DEC (dek), *n.* Digital Equipment Corporation: one of the leading producers of workstations, servers, and high-end PCs and also the developer of Alta Vista. It was acquired by Compaq in 1998.
⇒ See also ALTA VISTA; COMPAQ; IBM; SERVER; SGI; SUN MICROSYSTEMS; VAX; WORKSTATION.

decimal *n.* any number in base 10 (the numbers used in everyday life).
⇒ See also BCD; BINARY; FLOATING-POINT NUMBER; HEXADECIMAL; INTEGER; OCTAL.

declare *v.t.* in programming, to define the name and data type of (a variable or other programming construct).
⇒ See also DATA TYPE; PROGRAMMING LANGUAGE; VARIABLE.

decrement *n.* **1.** the act or process of decreasing. **2.** the amount lost by decreasing. —*v.t.* **3.** to decrease (the value of a variable).

⇒ See also INCREMENT.

decryption n. the process of decoding data, which has previously been encrypted into a secret format, by means of a secret *key* or password.

⇒ See also CRYPTOGRAPHY; ENCRYPTION; SECURITY.

dedicated adj. reserved for a specific use: *dedicated channel; dedicated server.*

⇒ See also CHANNEL; EXPANSION SLOT; NETWORK; SERVER.

de facto standard n. a format, language, or protocol that has become a standard as a result of its wide use and recognition by the industry, as Kermit communications protocol or PostScript page description language.

⇒ See also HAYES COMPATIBLE; KERMIT; PCL; POSTSCRIPT; STANDARD; XMODEM.

default n. a preset value or setting that a device or program automatically selects if no substitute is specified: *default margins, default directory.* For example, word processors have default margins and default page lengths that the user can override or reset. The *default drive* is the disk drive the computer accesses unless a different one is specified. Likewise, the *default directory* (or *folder*) is the directory the operating system searches unless a different one is specified. The default can also be an action that a device or program will take. For example, some word processors generate backup files *by default.*

⇒ See also MODE.

Defrag n. a DOS and Windows utility for defragmenting the hard disk.

⇒ See also DISK OPTIMIZER; FRAGMENTATION; SCANDISK.

defragment v.t. to optimize (a disk) by unfragmenting files—that is, by putting scattered pieces of a file together in a contiguous sequence.

⇒ See also FRAGMENTATION.

defragmentation n. See under DEFRAGMENT.

degauss v.t. to remove magnetism from (a device). The term is usually used in reference to color monitors and other display devices that use a cathode-ray tube (CRT).

⇒ See also COLOR MONITOR; CRT; MONITOR; PIN-CUSHION DISTORTION.

degausser *n.* a device for degaussing magnetic tape, disks, or other objects.

delete *v.t.* to remove or erase (data or images), as from a file, a display screen, or a disk.

⇒ See also CUT; RECYCLE BIN.

Delete key *n.* a key used to remove characters and other objects.

⇒ See also BACKSPACE; Backspace key; INSERTION POINT; KEYBOARD.

delimiter *n.* a punctuation character, as a backslash, comma, semicolon, or quotation mark, that separates two names or two pieces of data or marks the beginning or end of a programming construct.

⇒ See also PATHNAME.

Dell Computer *n.* the world's largest mail-order computer vendor, founded by Michael Dell in 1984.

⇒ See also COMPAQ; PC.

Delphi *n.* a rapid application development (RAD) system, based on Pascal, developed by Borland International, Inc.

⇒ See also PASCAL; RAPID APPLICATION DEVELOPMENT; VISUAL BASIC.

demand paging *n.* in virtual memory systems, a type of swapping in which pages of data are not copied from disk to RAM until they are needed, as opposed to anticipatory paging, in which the operating system attempts to anticipate which piece of data will be needed next and copies it to RAM before it is actually required.

⇒ See also PAGING; RAM; SWAP; VIRTUAL MEMORY.

demodulate *v.t.* to convert (received modulated carrier signals) into a form that can be used by a computer.

⇒ See also MODULATE.

demodulation *n.* the act or process, performed by a modem, of demodulating received carrier signals.

⇒ See also MODULATE.

density *n.* a measure of how much data can be

stored in a given amount of space on a disk or tape: *double density; high density.*

⇒ See also AREAL DENSITY; DISK; DISK DRIVE; DOUBLE-DENSITY DISK; FDHD; FLOPPY DISK; HIGH-DENSITY DISK.

DES Data Encryption Standard: a popular symmetric-key encryption method, developed in 1975 and standardized by ANSI in 1981 as ANSI X. 3.92. It uses a 56-bit key and may not be exported from the U.S. or Canada.

⇒ See also CRYPTOGRAPHY; SYMMETRIC-KEY CRYPTOGRAPHY.

descender *n.* in typography, the portion of a lowercase letter that falls below the baseline.

⇒ See also ASCENDER; BASELINE; X-HEIGHT.

Deschutes *n.* one of Intel's Pentium II microprocessors having transistor sizes of 0.25 microns.

⇒ See also PENTIUM II; PENTIUM MICROPROCESSOR.

desk accessory (DA) *n.* on Apple Macintoshes, a small, stand-alone program designed to perform a single task.

⇒ See also UTILITY.

desktop *n.* **1.** in graphical user interfaces, the primary display screen, consisting of icons representing files, folders, programs, etc. **2.** DESKTOP MODEL COMPUTER.

⇒ See also GRAPHICAL USER INTERFACE; SHORTCUT.

Desktop Management Interface *n.* See DMI.

desktop model computer *n.* a computer designed to fit comfortably on top of a desk, typically with the monitor sitting on top of the computer.

⇒ See also CHASSIS; PERSONAL COMPUTER; TOWER MODEL.

desktop publishing *n.* the use of a personal computer or workstation to produce high-quality printed documents, using different typefaces and creating or inserting illustrations.

⇒ See also ADOBE PHOTOSHOP; COLOR SEPARATION; ISP; OFFSET PRINTING; PAGE LAYOUT PROGRAM.

desktop system *n.* DESKTOP MODEL COMPUTER.

destination *n.* **1.** the file storage device to which data is moved from the source. —*adj.* **2.**

indicating the file or device to which data is moved.

⇒ See also SOURCE.

device *n.* any machine or component, as a disk driver, printer, or modem, that attaches to a computer.

⇒ See also COMPUTER; CONFIG.SYS; DRIVER; INPUT DEVICE.

Device Bay *n.* a specification developed by Intel, Compaq, and Microsoft to standardize the size, shape, and connection of computer components, such as disk drives, modems, and audio devices.

⇒ See also IEEE 1394; PCMCIA; USB.

device dependent *adj.* referring to programs that can run only on a certain type of hardware.

⇒ See also MACHINE DEPENDENT.

device driver *n.* DRIVER.

DHCP Dynamic Host Configuration Protocol: a protocol for assigning IP addresses to devices on a network and keeping track of such addresses.

⇒ See also WINS.

DHTML DYNAMIC HTML.

dialog box *n.* in a graphical user interface, a box that appears on a display screen to present information or request input.

⇒ See also BOX; GRAPHICAL USER INTERFACE; POP-UP WINDOW; WINDOW.

dial-up access *n.* the connection of a device to a computer network via a modem and a telephone.

⇒ See also DIAL-UP NETWORKING; FRACTIONAL T-1; INTERNET; ISP; L2TP; LEASED LINE; MODEM; POP; RADIUS.

Dial-Up Networking *n.* a component in Windows 98 that allows a computer to be connected to a network via a modem. *Abbr.:* DUN

⇒ See also DIAL-UP ACCESS; POP; RAS; WINDOWS 95.

DIB *n.* **1.** Dual Independent Bus: a bus architecture that is part of Intel's Pentium Pro and Pentium II microprocessors and enables the processor to access cache and main memory simultaneously, which increases throughput. **2.** device-independent bitmap: the bit-mapped graphics format used by Windows in which colors are represented in a format independent of the final output device.

⇒ See also BIT-MAPPED GRAPHICS; BMP; GRAPHICS FILE FORMATS; NETWORK MANAGEMENT; PENTIUM PRO; RMON.

digital *adj.* describing any system based on discontinuous data or events. Computers are digital machines because at their most basic level they can distinguish between just two values, 0 and 1, or off and on.

⇒ See also ANALOG; DAC; DIGITAL AUDIO; DIGITIZE; MODEM.

digital audio *n.* the reproduction and transmission of sound stored in a digital format: includes CDs and any sound files stored on a computer.

⇒ See also AU; DIGITAL; DIGITAL VIDEO; DOLBY DIGITAL; MIDI; MP3; WAV.

digital audio tape *n.* See DAT.

digital camera *n.* a camera that stores images digitally rather than recording them on film. Pictures may then be downloaded to a computer system and manipulated with a graphics program.

⇒ See also DIGITAL; DIGITAL PHOTOGRAPHY; FLASH-PIX; OPTICAL RESOLUTION; PHOTOCD.

digital cash *n.* a system that permits people to pay for goods or services by means of encrypted serial numbers that are transferred from one computer to another.

⇒ See also ELECTRONIC COMMERCE; INTERNET; SMART CARD.

digital certificate *n.* an attachment to an electronic message that verifies the identity of the user sending the message and enables the receiver to encode a reply: used for security purposes.

⇒ See also CERTIFICATE AUTHORITY; ENCRYPTION; PUBLIC-KEY ENCRYPTION; SSL; X.509.

Digital Data Storage *n.* See DDS.

digital envelope *n.* a type of security that uses a fast but less-secure code to encrypt a message, and then a slow but highly-secure code to protect the encryption key.

⇒ See also ENCRYPTION; PUBLIC-KEY ENCRYPTION; SYMMETRIC ENCRYPTION.

Digital Equipment Corporation *n*. See DEC.

digital imaging *n*. COMPUTER IMAGING.

Digital Light Processing *n*. See DLP.

digital monitor *n*. a monitor that accepts digital rather than analog signals.

⇒ See also ANALOG; ANALOG MONITOR; DIGITAL; MONITOR; VIDEO ADAPTER.

digital nervous system *n*. See DNS.

digital photography *n*. the art and science of producing and manipulating photographs that are represented as bit maps. They are produced directly with a digital camera, by capturing a frame from a video, or by scanning a conventional photograph.

⇒ See also COMPUTER IMAGING; DIGITAL CAMERA; FlashPix; IMAGE ENHANCEMENT; IMAGE PROCESSING; SNAPSHOT PRINTER.

Digital Service Unit/Channel Service Unit *n*. See CSU/DSU.

digital signal processing *n*. See DSP.

digital signature *n*. a digital code that can be attached to a message to identify the sender.

⇒ See also AUTHENTICATION; CERTIFICATE AUTHORITY; ELECTRONIC COMMERCE; SSL.

Digital Simultaneous Voice and Data *n*. See DSVD.

digital-to-analog converter *n*. See DAC.

digital versatile disk *n*. See DVD.

digital video *n*. the capturing, manipulation, and storage of video in digital formats.

⇒ See also DIGITAL AUDIO; DIGITAL PHOTOGRAPHY; DOLBY DIGITAL; MOTION-JPEG; VIDEO CAPTURE; VIDEO EDITING.

Digital Video Interactive *n*. See DVI.

digital watermark *n*. a pattern of bits inserted into a digital image or an audio or video file that identifies the file's copyright information (author, rights, etc.).

⇒ See also COPY PROTECTION; FlashPix; SOFTWARE PIRACY.

digitize *v.t.* to convert (data) into a digital form.

⇒ See also BIT MAP; DIGITAL; OPTICAL SCANNER; PCM; SAMPLING.

digitizing tablet *n.* an input device, consisting of an electronic tablet and a special cursor or pen, that enables the user to enter drawings and sketches into a computer. The tablet is able to detect movement of the cursor or pen and translate the movements into digital signals.

⇒ See also CURSOR; INPUT DEVICE; MOUSE.

DIMM *n.* dual in-line memory module: a small circuit board that holds memory chips.

⇒ See also DRAM; SIMM.

DIN connector *n.* a connector, as the keyboard connector for PCs, that conforms to one of the many standards defined by the Deutsche Industrienorm, the standards-setting organization for Germany.

⇒ See also CONNECTOR.

dingbat *n.* a small picture, such as a star or a pointing finger, that can be inserted into a document.

⇒ See also BULLET; FONT.

DIP *n.* dual in-line package: a type of chip housed in a rectangular casing with two rows of connecting pins on either side.

⇒ See also CHIP; PGA.

DIP switch *n.* any in a series of tiny toggle switches built into a *DIP* on a circuit board.

⇒ See also CHIP; CONFIGURATION; EXPANSION BOARD; PRINTED CIRCUIT BOARD; TOGGLE.

DirecPC *n.* a service offered by Hughes Network Systems that provides Internet access through private satellite dishes.

⇒ See also ISDN; ISP.

Direct3D *n.* an Application Programming Interface (API) developed by Microsoft for manipulating and displaying three-dimensional objects.

⇒ See also 3-D SOFTWARE; DIRECTDRAW; DIRECTX; GRAPHICS ACCELERATOR; OPENGL.

direct access *n.* RANDOM ACCESS.

Direct Access Storage Device *n.* See DASD.

Direct Cable Connection *n.* See DCC.

direct-connect modem *n.* a modem that connects directly to a telephone line via modular connectors rather than requiring an acoustic coupler.

⇒ See also ACOUSTIC COUPLER; MODEM.

DirectDraw *n.* a software interface standard for transferring video processing from a PC's CPU to the video adapter.

⇒ See also DIRECT3D; GDI; GRAPHICS ACCELERATOR; VIDEO ADAPTER.

directive *n.* COMMAND.

direct memory access *n.* See DMA.

directory *n.* **1.** a special kind of file used to organize other files into a hierarchical structure. To access a file, you may need to specify the names of all the directories above it. You do this by specifying a path containing these names in order, separated from each other by a delimiter. The topmost directory in any file is called the *root directory*. A directory that is below another directory is called a *subdirectory*. A directory above a subdirectory is called the *parent directory*. Under UNIX, the root directory is represented by a forward slash (/); under DOS and Windows by a backslash (\). Some graphical user interfaces use the term *folder* instead of *directory*. **2.** in networks, a database of network resources, such as e-mail addresses. See under DIRECTORY SERVICE.

⇒ See also FILE; FILE MANAGEMENT SYSTEM; FOLDER; HIERARCHICAL; PATH; ROOT DIRECTORY; TREE STRUCTURE.

directory service *n.* a network service that identifies all resources, as e-mail addresses, computers, and peripheral devices, on a network and makes them accessible to users and applications.

⇒ See also ACTIVE DIRECTORY; LDAP; NDS; UNC; X.500.

DirectX *n.* a set of APIs developed by Microsoft that enables programmers to write programs that access hardware features of a computer without knowing exactly what hardware will be installed on the machine on which the program eventually runs.

⇒ See also ACTIVEX; DIRECT3D; GRAPHICS ACCELERA-
TOR.

disc *n.* DISK. The spelling *disc* is often used for optical discs, whereas *disk* generally refers to magnetic disks, but there is no real rule.
⇒ See also DISK; OPTICAL DISK.

discretionary hyphen *n.* a hyphen that is inserted automatically by a hyphenation utility to
split a word that would otherwise extend beyond
the right margin. If the document is edited so
that the word no longer requires hyphenating,
the hyphen disappears.
⇒ See also HARD HYPHEN.

disk *n.* a round plate of plastic or metal, coated
with magnetically or optically active material, on
which data can be encoded.
⇒ See also AREAL DENSITY; CD-ROM; DISK DRIVE;
ERASABLE OPTICAL DISK; FLOPPY DISK; FORMAT; HARD
DISK; HEAD; MASS STORAGE; OPTICAL DISK; REMOVABLE
HARD DISK.

disk cache *n.* a portion of RAM used to speed up
access to data on a disk.
⇒ See also ACCESS TIME; BUFFER; CACHE; DISK DRIVE;
RAM; SMARTDRIVE; VCACHE.

disk compression *n.* a type of data compression utility that works by storing compressed versions of files on the hard disk.
⇒ See also DATA COMPRESSION; HARD DISK DRIVE;
PACKED FILE.

disk controller *n.* a chip and associated circuitry that is responsible for controlling a disk
drive.
⇒ See also CONTROLLER; DISK DRIVE; EISA; IDE IN-
TERFACE; SCSI.

disk crash *n.* HEAD CRASH.

disk drive *n.* a machine that reads data from
and writes data onto a disk. A disk drive rotates
the disk very fast and has one or more heads that
read and write data.
⇒ See also ATA; DISK; DISK STRIPING; FLOPPY DISK;
HARD DISK; MASS STORAGE; OPTICAL DISK; RAID;
SMART.

diskette *n.* FLOPPY DISK.

diskless workstation *n.* a workstation or PC

on a local-area network (LAN) that stores files on a network file server instead of having its own disk.

⇒ See also BOOTP; DISK DRIVE; LOCAL-AREA NETWORK; NET PC; NETWORK COMPUTER; SERVER; WORKSTATION.

disk mirroring n. a technique in which data is written to two duplicate disks simultaneously so that the system can instantly switch to the other disk without any loss of data or service if one of the disk drives fails.

⇒ See also FAULT TOLERANCE; RAID; SERVER MIRRORING.

disk operating system n. See DOS.

disk optimizer n. a program that uses a variety of techniques to make a disk more efficient.

⇒ See also DEFRAG; FRAGMENTATION.

disk pack n. a stack of removable hard disks for a mainframe, encased in a metal or plastic container.

⇒ See also HARD DISK; REMOVABLE HARD DISK.

disk striping n. a technique for spreading data over multiple disk drives to speed up operations that retrieve data from disk storage.

⇒ See also RAID.

dispatch table n. INTERRUPT VECTOR TABLE.

display v.t. **1.** to make (data or images) appear on a monitor. —n. **2.** DISPLAY SCREEN or MONITOR.

display adapter n. VIDEO ADAPTER.

Display Control Interface n. DIRECTDRAW.

Display Data Channel n. See DDC.

display screen n. the part of a monitor on which information is displayed.

⇒ See also CAD/CAM; DESKTOP PUBLISHING; FLAT-PANEL DISPLAY; GRAPHICS; MONITOR; NOTEBOOK COMPUTER; PINCUSHION DISTORTION; RASTER; RESOLUTION.

distance learning n. a type of education in which students work on their own at home or at the office and communicate with faculty and other students via computer.

⇒ See also CBT; FORUM; VIDEOCONFERENCING.

Distributed Component Object Model n. See DCOM.

distributed computing *n.* a type of computing in which different components and objects constituting an application can be located on different computers connected to a network.

⇒ See also CORBA; DCOM; OBJECT-ORIENTED PROGRAMMING; OMG.

Distributed Computing Environment *n.* See DCE.

distributed database *n.* a database that consists of two or more data files located at different sites on a computer network.

⇒ See also DATABASE; DATABASE MANAGEMENT SYSTEM; DISTRIBUTED PROCESSING; NETWORK; TWO-PHASE COMMIT.

distributed processing *n.* any of a variety of computer systems that use more than one computer, or processor, to run an application.

⇒ See also DATABASE MANAGEMENT SYSTEM; DCE; DISTRIBUTED DATABASE; LOCAL-AREA NETWORK; PARALLEL PROCESSING.

Distributed System Object Model *n.* See DSOM.

dithering *n.* creating the illusion of new colors and shades by varying the pattern of dots. Newspaper photographs, for example, are dithered; different shades of gray are produced by varying the patterns of black and white dots.

⇒ See also BILEVEL PRINTER; CONTONE PRINTER; GRAY SCALING; HALFTONE.

Divx (div′iks), *n.* Digital video express: a DVD-ROM format being promoted by several large Hollywood companies, including Disney, Dreamworks SKG, Paramount, and Universal, in which a movie (or other data) loaded onto a DVD-ROM is playable only during a specific time frame.

⇒ See also DVD; DVD-ROM.

DLC Data Link Control: the second lowest layer in the OSI Reference Model.

⇒ See also ARP; IEEE 802 STANDARDS; MAC ADDRESS; NETWORK INTERFACE CARD; NODE; OSI.

DLL Dynamic Link Library: a library of executable functions or data that can be used by a Windows application.

⇒ See also LIBRARY; LINK; OLE; VBX.

DLP Digital Light Processing: a technology developed by Texas Instruments, used for projecting images from a monitor onto a large screen for presentations.
⇒ See also LCD; MONITOR; TEXAS INSTRUMENTS.

DLT Digital Linear Tape: a type of magnetic tape storage device that is faster than most other types of tape drives, achieving transfer rates of 2.5 MBps.
⇒ See also TAPE; TAPE DRIVE.

DMA direct memory access: a technique for transferring data from main memory to a device without passing it through the CPU.
⇒ See also BACKUP; CHANNEL; CPU; DIP SWITCH; EXPANSION BOARD; JUMPER; MAIN MEMORY; REAL TIME.

DMI Desktop Management Interface: an API to enable software to collect information about a computer environment, such as what software and expansion boards are installed.
⇒ See also MIF.

DNA WINDOWS DNA.

DNS 1. Domain Name System (or Service): an Internet service that translates domain names, which are alphabetic, into IP addresses, which are composed of numbers. **2.** digital nervous system: a term coined by Bill Gates to describe a network of personal computers that make it easier to obtain and understand information.
⇒ See also BIND; DOMAIN; DOMAIN NAME; IAHC; INTERPROCESS COMMUNICATION (IPC); WINS.

docking station *n.* a platform into which a portable computer can be installed, usu. containing slots for expansion cards, bays for storage devices, and connectors for peripheral devices, such as printers and monitors.
⇒ See also BAY; DESKTOP MODEL COMPUTER; EXPANSION BOARD; NOTEBOOK COMPUTER; PORT REPLICATOR; PORTABLE; SLOT.

document *n.* **1.** a file created with a word processor that can contain graphics, charts, and other objects in addition to text. —*v.t.* **2.** to enter written explanations into (a program's source code or a similarly opaque text).

⇒ See also COMPOUND DOCUMENT; DOCUMENTATION; FILE.

documentation *n.* instructions for using a computer device or program.
⇒ See also HELP; MAN PAGE; README FILE.

document management *n.* the computerized management of electronic as well as paper-based documents. A document-management system generally includes an optical scanner and OCR system, a database system, and a search mechanism.
⇒ See also OPTICAL CHARACTER RECOGNITION; PAPERLESS OFFICE.

Document Object Model *n.* See DOM.

Dolby Digital *n.* a standard for high-quality digital audio that is used for the sound portion of video stored in digital format, especially videos stored on DVD-ROMs.
⇒ See also AC-3; DIGITAL AUDIO; DIGITAL VIDEO; DVD.

DOM *n.* Document Object Model: the specification for the representation of the objects in a Web page (text, images, headers, links, etc.) that defines what attributes are associated with each object and how the objects and attributes can be manipulated.
⇒ See also DYNAMIC HTML; HTML; JAVASCRIPT; WEB PAGE; XML.

domain *n.* a group of computers and devices on a network that are administered as a unit with common rules and procedures: defined within the Internet by the *IP address*.
⇒ See also DNS; DOMAIN NAME; INTERNET.

domain name *n.* a name that identifies one or more IP addresses and is used in a URL, usually along with the name of a particular host computer, to identify a particular Web page. Every domain name has a suffix that indicates which top-level domain (TLD) it belongs to, as *gov* for government agencies, *edu* for educational institutions, and *org* for organizations.
⇒ See also DNS; DOMAIN; IAHC; INTERNIC; IP ADDRESS; TLD; WHOIS.

Domain Name Server *n.* See DNS.

Domain Name Service n. See DNS.

dongle n. a device that attaches to a computer to control access to a particular application as a means of copy protection.
⇒ See also COPY PROTECTION.

DOS (dôs *or* dos *or as initials*), n. disk operating system: any operating system, but most often MS-DOS (Microsoft disk operating system). Originally developed by Microsoft for IBM, MS-DOS was the standard operating system for IBM-compatible personal computers.
⇒ See also MICROSOFT; MICROSOFT WINDOWS; OPERATING SYSTEM; OS/2; PC; PIF FILE.

dot n. **1.** same as the period character (.): used in DOS, Windows, and OS/2 systems to separate a filename from its extension or in URLs to separate the parts of a host name. **2.** in bit-mapped representations, a single point, the smallest identifiable part of an image.
⇒ See also BIT MAP; DPI; EXTENSION; FILENAME; RESOLUTION.

dot-matrix printer n. a type of printer that produces characters and illustrations by striking pins against an ink ribbon to print closely spaced dots in the appropriate shape.
⇒ See also IMPACT PRINTER; OKIDATA; PRINTER.

dot pitch n. a measurement that indicates the distance between like-colored phosphor dots on a display screen, measured in millimeters.
⇒ See also COLOR MONITOR; MASK PITCH; MONITOR; PIXEL.

dots per inch n. See DPI.

double click v.i. to tap a mouse button twice in rapid succession, as to open a file.
⇒ See also CLICK; MOUSE.

double-density disk n. an obsolete kind of floppy disk that has twice the storage capacity of a single-density floppy.
⇒ See also DENSITY; FLOPPY DISK.

double precision adj. referring to a type of floating-point number that has more precision (that is, more digits to the right of the decimal point) than a single-precision number. It uses twice as many bits as a regular floating-point number.

⇒ See also FLOATING-POINT NUMBER; IEEE.

double-scan display *n.* DUAL-SCAN DISPLAY.

double-sided disk *n.* a floppy disk with both sides prepared for recording data.

⇒ See also DISK DRIVE; FLOPPY DISK.

double-speed CD-ROM *n.* a CD-ROM drive that transfers data at about 300Kbp/sec.

double supertwist *n.* See DSTN.

down *adj.* of a computer system, not working or not available to users, either because it has crashed or because routine servicing is taking place.

⇒ See also CRASH.

download *v.t.* to copy (data or software) from a main source to a peripheral device, as from an online service to one's own computer, or from a computer into a laser printer.

⇒ See also ANONYMOUS FTP; BULLETIN BOARD SYSTEM; FONT; ONLINE SERVICE; UPLOAD.

downloadable font *n.* SOFT FONT.

downward compatible *adj.* BACKWARD COMPATIBLE.

DP DATA PROCESSING.

dpi dots per inch: a measure of resolution used for images. The more dots per inch, the higher the resolution. A resolution of 600 dots per inch means 600 dots across and 600 dots down, or 360,000 dots per square inch.

⇒ See also DOT; LASER PRINTER; RESOLUTION.

draft mode *n.* a printing mode in which the printer prints text as fast as possible without regard to print quality.

⇒ See also DOT-MATRIX PRINTER; LETTER QUALITY (LQ); NEAR LETTER QUALITY.

draft-quality *adj.* referring to or producing print whose quality is less than near-letter-quality.

⇒ See also DOT-MATRIX PRINTER; DRAFT MODE; LETTER QUALITY (LQ); NEAR LETTER QUALITY.

drag *v.t.* **1.** in graphical user interfaces, to move (an icon or other image) on a display screen, esp. by using a mouse. More generally, to perform any operation, such as moving a block of text from one part of a document to another, in which the mouse button is held down while the mouse is moved. **2.** to move (the mouse) while holding down the button, as to select a block of text.

⇒ See also DRAG-AND-DROP; GRAPHICAL USER INTERFACE; MOUSE; SELECT.

drag-and-drop *adj.* describing an application that allows the user to drag objects to specific locations on the screen to perform actions on them.

⇒ See also DRAG; GRAPHICAL USER INTERFACE.

drag-n-drop *adj.* DRAG-AND-DROP.

DRAM (dē′ram′), *n.* dynamic random access memory: a type of memory used in most personal computers.

⇒ See also BEDO DRAM; DIMM; DYNAMIC RAM; EDO DRAM; MDRAM; PIPELINE BURST CACHE; RDRAM; SDRAM; SGRAM; SLDRAM.

drawing tablet *n.* DIGITIZING TABLET.

draw program *n.* a graphics program that uses vector graphics and enables the user to draw pictures, then store the images in files, merge them into documents, and print them.

⇒ See also GRAPHICS; PAINT PROGRAM; VECTOR GRAPHICS.

drive *n.* DISK DRIVE.

drive bay *n.* an area of reserved space in a personal computer case where hard or floppy disk drives (or tape drives) can be installed.

⇒ See also BAY; DISK DRIVE; MASS STORAGE.

driver *n.* a program that controls a device, as a printer, disk drive, or keyboard.

⇒ See also CONFIG.SYS; CONTROLLER; DEVICE; ODI; VIRTUAL DEVICE DRIVER.

drop cap *n.* in desktop publishing, the first letter of a paragraph that is enlarged to "drop" down two or more lines.

⇒ See also DESKTOP PUBLISHING.

drop-down menu *n.* PULL-DOWN MENU.

DS-1 See T-1.

DS-3 See T-3.

DSL See xDSL.

DSOM *n.* Distributed System Object Model: a version of **SOM** that supports sharing binary objects across networks.

⇒ See also CORBA; DCOM; SOM.

DSP 1. digital signal processing: the process of using a data compression technique to manipulate analog information, such as sound or photographs, that has been converted into a digital form. **2.** digital signal processor: a special type of coprocessor designed for performing the mathematics involved in DSP. Most DSPs are programmable, which means that they can be used for manipulating different types of information, including sound, images, and video.

⇒ See also COPROCESSOR; DATA COMPRESSION; DIGITIZE; GRAPHICS ACCELERATOR; MMX; SOUND CARD.

DSS digital satellite system: a network of satellites that broadcast digital data.

⇒ See also HDTV.

DSTN double-layer supertwist nematic: a passive-matrix LCD technology that uses two display layers to counteract the color shifting that occurs with conventional supertwist displays.

⇒ See also CSTN; LCD; PASSIVE-MATRIX DISPLAY; SUPERTWIST.

DSU See CSU/DSU.

DSVD Digital Simultaneous Voice and Data: an all-digital technology for concurrent voice and data (SVD) transmission over a single analog telephone line.

⇒ See also ITU; MODEM; POTS.

DTE Data Terminal Equipment: a device that controls data flowing to or from a computer.

⇒ See also DCE; RS-232C; UART.

DTMF Dual Tone Multi-Frequency: the signaling system used by touchtone telephones. Each key produces a sound consisting of two specific frequencies (tones).

⇒ See also TELEPHONY.

DTP DESKTOP PUBLISHING.

dual in-line memory module n. See DIMM.

dual in-line package n. See DIP.

dual-scan display n. a type of passive-matrix LCD display that provides faster refresh rates than conventional passive-matrix displays by dividing the screen into two sections that are refreshed simultaneously.

⇒ See also ACTIVE-MATRIX DISPLAY; FLAT-PANEL DISPLAY; LCD; PASSIVE-MATRIX DISPLAY.

dual supertwist *n.* See under SUPERTWIST.

Dual Tone Multi-Frequency *n.* See DTMF.

dumb terminal *n.* a display monitor and keyboard with no processing capabilities.

⇒ See also DISPLAY SCREEN; INTELLIGENT TERMINAL; SMART TERMINAL; TERMINAL; WINDOWS TERMINAL.

dummy *adj.* referring to a placeholder. A *dummy variable* is a variable that does not contain any useful data, but does reserve space that a real variable will use later.

⇒ See also VARIABLE.

dump *v.t.* **1.** to output (computer data), esp. in order to diagnose a failure. —*n.* **2.** the result of copying raw data from one place to another with little or no formatting for readability.

DUN DIAL-UP NETWORKING.

duplex *n.* FULL DUPLEX.

DV DIGITAL VIDEO.

DVD digital versatile disc or digital video disc: a type of CD-ROM that holds a minimum of 4.7GB, enough for a full-length movie.

⇒ See also CD-I (COMPACT DISC–INTERACTIVE); CD-ROM; COMPACT DISC; DIVX; DOLBY DIGITAL; DVD+RW; DVD-RAM; DVD-ROM; DVD-VIDEO; DVI; MPEG; MULTIMEDIA.

DVD-RAM *n.* a type of rewritable DVD disc.

⇒ See also CD-RW DISK; DVD; DVD+RW; DVD-ROM; DVD-VIDEO.

DVD-ROM *n.* a type of read-only DVD disc.

⇒ See also DIVX; DVD; DVD-RAM; MPEG.

DVD+RW a standard for rewritable DVD disks being promoted by Hewlett-Packard, Philips, and Sony. It is competing with another standard, called DVD-RAM, developed by the DVD Consortium. The two standards are incompatible.

⇒ See also CD-RW DISK; DVD; DVD-RAM.

DVD-Video *n.* a video format for displaying full-length digital movies on a player that attaches to a television like a videocassette player.

⇒ See also COPY PROTECTION; DVD; DVD-ROM.

DVI 1. Digital Video Interactive: a technology developed by General Electric that enables a computer to store and display moving video images like those on television by using specialized processors to compress and decompress the data. **2.** Device Independent: a file format used by the TeX typography system.

⇒ See also CD-I (COMPACT DISC–INTERACTIVE); CD-RW DISK; CODEC; DVD; INDEO; INTEL; MPEG.

Dvorak keyboard *n.* a keyboard on which the middle row of keys includes the most common letters, and common letter combinations are positioned in such a way that they can be typed quickly. [named after August Dvorak, who invented it with his brother-in-law, William Dealy]

⇒ See also KEYBOARD; MACRO; QWERTY KEYBOARD.

DW DATA WAREHOUSING.

DXF Data Exchange File: a two-dimensional graphics file format supported by most PC-based CAD products.

⇒ See also CAD; GRAPHICS; GRAPHICS FILE FORMATS.

dynamic *adj.* referring to actions that take place at the moment they are needed rather than in advance: *dynamic memory allocation.*

⇒ See also DYNAMIC VARIABLE; STATIC VARIABLE.

dynamic acceleration *n.* a feature that causes the mouse resolution to depend on how fast the mouse is moved. When it is moved fast, the cursor moves proportionally farther. Also called **ballistic tracking, automatic acceleration, variable acceleration.**

⇒ See also MOUSE; RESOLUTION.

Dynamic Data Exchange *n.* See DDE.

Dynamic Host Configuration Protocol *n.* See DHCP.

dynamic HTML *n.* **1.** in contrast to static HTML pages, Web content that changes each time it is viewed, depending on such factors as time of day and profile of the reader. **2.** Dynamic HTML, extensions that enable a Web page to react to user input without sending requests to the Web server.

⇒ See also ACTIVEX CONTROL; CGI; COOKIE; DOM; JAVA; JAVASCRIPT; SSI; W3C; WINDOWS DNA.

dynamic link library *n.* See DLL.

dynamic RAM *n.* a type of physical memory that must be constantly refreshed to avoid losing its contents: used in most personal computers.

⇒ See also MAIN MEMORY; RAM; REFRESH; SRAM.

dynamic variable *n.* in programming, a variable whose storage is allocated when the program is run.

⇒ See also STATIC VARIABLE; VARIABLE.

E e

easter egg *n.* a secret message or screen buried in an application, made visible only through an elaborate sequence of keystrokes not revealed in the documentation. Usually easter eggs are used to display the credits for the development team, or a humorous message.
⇒ See also APPLICATION; PROGRAM.

EBCDIC (eb′si dik), *n.* Extended Binary-Coded Decimal Interchange Code: an IBM code for representing characters as numbers. Although it is widely used on large IBM computers, most other computers, including PCs and Macintoshes, use ASCII codes.
⇒ See also ASCII.

ECC Error-Correcting Code: a technique for adding redundant bits to detect and correct errors in blocks of binary data.
⇒ See also PARITY.

ECC memory *n.* Error-Correcting Code memory: a type of memory that includes special circuitry for ensuring the accuracy of data as it passes in and out of memory.
⇒ See also CHECKSUM; MEMORY.

e-commerce *n.* ELECTRONIC COMMERCE.

ECP Extended Capabilities Port: a parallel-port standard for PCs that supports bi-directional communication between the PC and peripheral devices such as a printer.
⇒ See also CENTRONICS INTERFACE; DCC; EPP; PARALLEL PORT.

edge connector *n.* the part of a printed circuit board that plugs into a computer or device. The edge connector usually has a row of metallic tracks that provide the electrical connection.
⇒ See also PRINTED CIRCUIT BOARD.

EDI Electronic Data Interchange: the transfer of data between different companies through the use of networks, such as the Internet. EDI is becoming increasingly important as a way for companies to buy, sell, and trade information.
⇒ See also ELECTRONIC COMMERCE.

editor *n.* a program used to create and edit text files. A *line editor* is a primitive form of editor that requires the user to specify a particular line of text before making changes to it. A *screen-oriented editor* lets the user modify any text that appears on the display screen by moving the cursor to the desired location. In general, editors provide fewer formatting features than word processors. The term *editor* usually refers to source code editors.
⇒ See also SOURCE CODE; WORD PROCESSING.

EDO DRAM *n.* Extended Data Output Dynamic Random Access Memory: a type of DRAM that is faster than conventional DRAM. EDO DRAM can start accessing the next block of memory at the same time that it sends the previous block to the CPU.
⇒ See also ACCESS TIME; BEDO DRAM; CYCLE TIME; DRAM; FPM RAM; RDRAM; SDRAM; SLDRAM.

EEMS Enhanced Expanded Memory Specification: an enhanced version of the original EMS, which enables DOS applications to use more than 1MB (megabyte) of memory.
⇒ See also EXPANDED MEMORY; LIM MEMORY.

EEPROM (dub'əl ē'prom', ē'ē'prom'), *n.* electrically erasable programmable read-only memory: a special type of PROM that can be erased by exposing it to an electrical charge. EEPROM retains its contents even when the power is turned off.
⇒ See also EPROM; FLASH MEMORY; MEMORY; NVRAM; PROM; RAM; ROM.

EGA enhanced graphics adapter: a now obsolete graphics display system for PCs introduced by IBM in 1984. EGA supports 16 colors from a palette of 64 and provides a resolution of 640 by 350.
⇒ See also CGA; VGA; VIDEO ADAPTER.

EIA ELECTRONIC INDUSTRIES ASSOCIATION.

EIA (Electronic Industries Association) interface *n.* See RS-232C.

EIDE enhanced IDE: a newer version of the IDE mass storage device interface standard. It supports data rates up to at least 16.6 MBps. EIDE has replaced SCSI in many areas. For historical

reasons it is also known as Fast ATA or Fast IDE.
⇒ See also ATA; ESDI; IDE INTERFACE; SCSI.

Eiffel *n.* an advanced programming language introduced in 1986. A basic Windows compiler is available at no charge. Eiffel encourages object-oriented program development and supports a systematic approach to software development.
⇒ See also C; OBJECT-ORIENTED PROGRAMMING.

8088 an early Intel microprocessor, used in the original IBM PC and PC/XT.

8086 an early Intel microprocessor.

8514/A a high-resolution video standard for PCs developed by IBM in 1987. It is designed to extend the capabilities of VGA. The 8514/A standard provides a resolution of 1,024 by 768 pixels, and a palette of 262,000 colors.
⇒ See also INTERLACING; MONOCHROME; PALETTE; RESOLUTION; SVGA; VIDEO ADAPTER; XGA.

80486 an early Intel microprocessor, faster than an 80386 but slower than a Pentium.

80386 an early Intel microprocessor, faster than an 80286 but slower than an 80486.

80286 an early Intel microprocessor, faster than an 8086 but slower than an 80386.

EISA *n.* Extended Industry Standard Architecture: a bus architecture designed for PCs using an Intel 80386, 80486, or Pentium microprocessor. EISA buses are 32 bits wide and support multiprocessing. Computers with an EISA bus can use new EISA expansion cards as well as old AT expansion cards. EISA and MCA are not compatible with each other.
⇒ See also BUS; EXPANSION BOARD; INDUSTRY STANDARD ARCHITECTURE (ISA) BUS; LOCAL BUS; MICRO CHANNEL ARCHITECTURE (MCA); MULTIPROCESSING; PCI.

ELD ELECTROLUMINESCENT DISPLAY.

electrically erasable programmable read-only memory *n.* See EEPROM.

electroluminescent display (ELD) *n.* a technology used in some notebook computers to produce a flat-panel display. It works by sandwiching a thin film of phosphorescent substance between two plates coated with wire at right angles. When an electrical current is passed through wire on each plate, the phosphorescent film at the intersection glows, creating a pixel.

⇒ See also ACTIVE-MATRIX DISPLAY; FLAT-PANEL DISPLAY; GAS-PLASMA DISPLAY; LCD; NOTEBOOK COMPUTER.

electronic commerce *n.* the conducting of business on-line. This includes, for example, buying and selling products with digital cash and via Electronic Data Interchange (EDI).

⇒ See also BIOMETRICS; CERTIFICATE AUTHORITY; DIGITAL CASH; DIGITAL SIGNATURE; EDI; ESD; PKI; SET.

Electronic Data Interchange *n.* See EDI.

Electronic Frontier Foundation *n.* a nonprofit organization dedicated to protecting civil liberties in the modern communications age.

⇒ See also CLIPPER CHIP.

Electronic Industries Association *n.* a trade association representing the U.S. high technology community. It began in 1924 as the Radio Manufacturers Association.

⇒ See also RS-232C; RS-422 AND RS-423; RS-485; STANDARD.

electronic mail *n.* E-MAIL.

electronic publishing *n.* the publishing of information in an electronic form. This includes publishing CD-ROMs as well as making information available through online services.

⇒ See also CD-ROM; MULTIMEDIA; ONLINE SERVICE.

electrostatic discharge *n.* See ESD.

elevator *n.* a scroll box. See under SCROLL BAR.

ELF emission *n.* extremely low frequency emission: a magnetic field generated by common electrical appliances, such as computer monitors.

⇒ See also MPR II; MONITOR.

e-mail or email *n.* **1.** the transmission of messages over communications networks. Some e-mail systems are confined to a single computer system or network, but others have gateways to other computer systems. **2.** a message sent by such a system. Messages can be notes entered from the keyboard or files stored on disk. Sent messages are stored in electronic mailboxes.

⇒ See also ACRONYM; ATTACHMENT; BROADCASTING;

BINHEX; CCITT; E-MAIL ADDRESS; FINGER; GATEWAY; IMAP; INSTANT MESSAGING; MAILBOX; MAILING LIST; MAPI; MIME; NETWORK; ONLINE SERVICE; POP; SNAIL-MAIL; SNMP; SPAM; USERNAME; UUENCODE; WORK-GROUP COMPUTING.

e-mail address *n.* a name that identifies an electronic post office box on a network where e-mail can be sent. Different types of networks have different formats for e-mail addresses. Every user on the Internet has a unique e-mail address.
⇒ See also ADDRESS; E-MAIL; X.400.

e-mail client *n.* an application that runs on a personal computer or workstation and enables the user to send, receive, and organize e-mail. E-mail is sent from many clients to a server, which re-routes the mail to its intended destination.
⇒ See also CLIENT; EUDORA; FINGER; MAILING LIST; PINE; TNEF.

embedded command *n.* in word processing, a sequence of special characters inserted into a document that affects the formatting of the document when it is printed. Embedded commands are usually invisible when the file is being edited.
⇒ See also COMMAND; FONT; WORD PROCESSING.

embedded computer *n.* EMBEDDED SYSTEM.

embedded object *n.* a reference to an object created by one application, embedded (rather than just inserted or pasted) in a document created by another application in such a way that changes made to the object by the first application automatically appear in the embedded version.
⇒ See also DOCUMENT; OLE.

embedded system *n.* a specialized computer system that is part of a larger system or machine. Virtually all appliances that have a digital interface, such as watches, microwaves, VCRs, and cars, contain embedded systems.
⇒ See also MICROCONTROLLER; SYSTEM.

emoticon *n.* a small symbol formed with punctuation characters: used to communicate humor, sarcasm, etc., within an e-mail message. For example, a :-) emoticon indicates that the previous statement is meant as a joke and should not be taken seriously.

⇒ See also E-MAIL; SMILEY.

EMS EXPANDED MEMORY SPECIFICATION.

⇒ See also EXPANDED MEMORY.

emulation *n.* the ability of a program or device to imitate another program or device. Emulation can make one printer accept formatting codes meant for a printer of some other type. It is also possible for a computer to emulate another type of computer.

⇒ See also COMMUNICATIONS SOFTWARE; COMPATIBLE; LOG ON; MAINFRAME; TERMINAL.

Encapsulated PostScript *n.* See EPS.

encapsulation *n.* **1.** (in programming) the process of combining elements to create a new entity. For example, a complex data type such as a record or structure encapsulates a collection of simpler pieces of data. **2.** (in networking) TUNNELING.

encryption *n.* the translation of data into a secret code. To read an encrypted file, one must have access to a secret key or password. Encryption is the most effective way to achieve data security.

⇒ See also CIPHER TEXT; CLIPPER CHIP; CRYPTOGRAPHY; DECRYPTION; DIGITAL CERTIFICATE; DIGITAL ENVELOPE; PASSWORD; PLAIN TEXT; PUBLIC-KEY ENCRYPTION; RSA; SECURITY; SYMMETRIC ENCRYPTION.

endian *n.* See under BIG-ENDIAN.

End key *n.* a special cursor control key on PC keyboards and Macintosh extended keyboards. The End key might move the cursor to the end of the line, the end of the page, or the end of the file, depending on which program is running.

⇒ See also KEYBOARD.

end of file *n.* EOF MARK.

end of line *n.* EOL MARK.

end user *n.* the final or ultimate user of a computer system. The end user is the individual who uses the product after it has been fully developed and marketed.

⇒ See also EULA; USER.

Energy Star *n.* a voluntary labeling program of the U.S. Environmental Protection Agency (EPA) and the U.S. Department of Energy that identifies energy efficient products.

⇒ See also GREEN PC.

Enhanced Data Output DRAM *n.* EDO DRAM.

Enhanced Expanded Memory Specification *n.* See EEMS.

enhanced graphics adapter *n.* See EGA.

Enhanced IDE *n.* See EIDE.

Enhanced Keyboard *n.* a 101- or 102-key keyboard from IBM that supersedes the keyboard for the PC/AT computer. The Enhanced Keyboard has a row of 12 function keys at the top instead of 10 function keys grouped on the left side of the keyboard.

⇒ See also EXTENDED KEYBOARD; FUNCTION KEYS; KEYBOARD.

Enhanced Small Device Interface *n.* See ESDI.

Enter key *n.* a key that informs the currently running program that the user has finished with a line of input. In some programs, the Enter key causes whatever option or action has been selected to be executed.

⇒ See also RETURN KEY.

enterprise *n.* in the computer field, any large organization. An intranet is an example of an enterprise computing system.

⇒ See also ERP; INTRANET.

enterprise resource planning *n.* See ERP.

environment *n.* **1.** the state of a computer, usually determined by which programs are running and basic hardware and software characteristics. One ingredient of an environment is the operating system. **2.** in DOS and UNIX systems, an area in memory that the operating system and other programs use to store various types of miscellaneous information.

⇒ See also DOS; OPERATING SYSTEM; PLATFORM.

EO ERASABLE OPTICAL DISK.

EOF mark *n.* end-of-file mark: a special character or sequence of characters that marks the end of a file. Operating systems need to keep track of where every file ends.

⇒ See also EOL MARK.

EOL mark *n.* end-of-line mark: a special character or sequence of characters that marks the end of a line.

⇒ See also EOF MARK.

EPOC *n.* an operating system from Psion Software, designed specifically for mobile, ROM-based computing devices.

⇒ See also HAND-HELD COMPUTER; OPERATING SYSTEM; PDA; WINDOWS CE.

EPP *n.* Enhanced Parallel Port: a parallel port standard for PCs that supports bi-directional communication between the PC and attached devices, such as a printer.

⇒ See also CENTRONICS INTERFACE; ECP; PARALLEL PORT.

EPROM (ē′prom′), *n.* erasable programmable read-only memory: a special type of memory that retains its contents until it is exposed to ultraviolet light. The ultraviolet light clears its contents, making it possible to reprogram the memory. A special device called a *PROM programmer* or *PROM burner* is needed to write to and erase an EPROM. EPROMs are used widely in personal computers because they enable the manufacturer to update the contents of the memory until the computer is shipped.

⇒ See also EEPROM; MEMORY; PROM.

EPS Encapsulated PostScript: the graphics file format used by the PostScript language. EPS files can be either binary or ASCII.

⇒ See also GRAPHICS; GRAPHICS FILE FORMATS; POSTSCRIPT.

erasable optical disk *n.* a type of optical disk that can be erased and loaded with new data. In contrast, most optical disks, called CD-ROMs, are read-only.

⇒ See also ACCESS TIME; CD-ROM; DISK; FLOPPY DISK; MASS STORAGE; OPTICAL DISK.

erasable programmable read-only memory *n.* See EPROM.

ergonomics *n.* the science concerned with designing safe and comfortable machines for use by humans. In the computer field, ergonomics plays an important role in the design of monitors and keyboards.

⇒ See also CARPAL TUNNEL SYNDROME.

ERP enterprise resource planning: a business management system that integrates all facets of the business, including planning, manufacturing, sales, and marketing. Software applications are available to help business managers implement ERP.

⇒ See also ENTERPRISE.

error checking and correcting *n.* See ECC.

Error-Correcting Code memory *n.* ECC MEMORY.

error detection *n.* in communications, a class of techniques for detecting garbled messages.

⇒ See also CCITT; CHECKSUM; CRC; DATA INTEGRITY; KERMIT; MNP; XMODEM.

ESC *n.* ESCAPE KEY.

⇒ See also ESCAPE CHARACTER.

escape character *n.* a special character that can have many different functions. It is often used to abort the current command and return to a previous place in the program. It is also used to send special instructions to printers and other devices. An escape character is generated with the *Escape key*.

⇒ See also ESCAPE SEQUENCE; KEYBOARD.

Escape key *n.* a key on computer keyboards, usually labeled *Esc*. In DOS and Windows environments, pressing the Escape key usually cancels or aborts the current operation.

⇒ See also ABORT; ESC; KEYBOARD.

escape sequence *n.* a sequence of special characters that sends a command to a device or program. Typically, an escape sequence begins with an *escape character*, but this is not universally true.

⇒ See also ESCAPE CHARACTER.

ESCD Extended System Configuration Data: a format for storing information about Plug-and-Play (PnP) devices in the BIOS.

⇒ See also BIOS; PLUG-AND-PLAY; PNP.

ESD 1. Electronic Software Distribution: a system

for selling software over a network. ESD systems provide secure communications that customers use to download and pay for software. **2.** electrostatic discharge: the rapid discharge of static electricity from one object to another of a different potential. An electrostatic discharge can damage integrated circuits in computer and communications equipment.

⇒ See also ELECTRONIC COMMERCE; UPGRADE.

ESDI (ez′dē *or as initials*), *n.* Enhanced Small Device Interface: an obsolete interface standard developed by a consortium of the leading personal-computer manufacturers for connecting disk drives to PCs.

⇒ See also DISK DRIVE; EIDE; IDE INTERFACE; SCSI; ST-506 INTERFACE.

Ethernet *n.* a local-area network (LAN) protocol developed by Xerox Corporation in cooperation with DEC and Intel in 1976. Ethernet uses a bus or star topology and supports data transfer rates of 10 Mbps or 100 Mbps. It is one of the most widely implemented LAN standards.

⇒ See also 100BASE-T; 10BASE-2; 10BASE5; 10BASE T; ATM; AUI; BUS NETWORK; CSMA/CD; GIGABIT ETHERNET; IEEE; IEEE 802 STANDARDS; LOCAL-AREA NETWORK; NETWORK; PROTOCOL; SHARED ETHERNET; SWITCHED ETHERNET; TOPOLOGY.

Eudora *n.* a popular e-mail client now owned by QUALCOMM, Inc.

⇒ See also E-MAIL CLIENT.

EULA End-User License Agreement: the type of license used for most software.

⇒ See also END USER; SOFTWARE LICENSING.

even header *n.* in word processing, a header that appears only on even-numbered pages.

⇒ See also HEADER.

even parity *n.* the parity-checking mode in which each set of transmitted bits must have an even number of set bits. The parity-checking system on the sending side ensures even parity by setting the extra *parity bit* if necessary.

⇒ See also PARITY CHECKING.

event *n.* an action or occurrence detected by a

program. Events can be user actions, such as clicking a mouse button or pressing a key, or system occurrences, such as running out of memory.
⇒ See also INTERRUPT.

exabyte *n.* 2^{60} (1,152,921,504,606,846,976) bytes. An exabyte is equal to 1,024 petabytes.
⇒ See also PETABYTE; TERABYTE; YOTTABYTE; ZETTABYTE.

Excite *n.* a World Wide Web search engine developed by Excite, Inc. It provides a full-text index of approximately 50 million Web pages.
⇒ See also ALTA VISTA; HOTBOT; INFOSEEK; LYCOS; MAGELLAN; OPEN TEXT; SEARCH ENGINE; WEBCRAWLER; YAHOO!.

exclusive OR *n.* a Boolean operator that returns a value of TRUE only if both its operands have different values. Conversely, an *inclusive OR operator* returns a value of TRUE if *either* of its operands is TRUE. Whereas an inclusive OR can be translated "this, that, or both," an exclusive OR means "this or that, but not both." An exclusive OR is often called an *XOR* or *EOR*.
⇒ See also BOOLEAN OPERATOR.

executable file *n.* a file in a format that the computer can directly execute. Unlike source files, executable files cannot be read by humans.
⇒ See also ASSEMBLER; BINARY FILE; BINARY FORMAT; COM FILE; COMPILER; EXE FILE; FILE; SOURCE CODE.

execute *v.t.* to run (a program) or perform (a command).
⇒ See also LAUNCH.

EXE file (ē′eks/ē′) *n.* in DOS and Windows systems, an executable file with a .EXE extension.
⇒ See also COM FILE; EXECUTABLE FILE; EXTENSION; PROGRAM.

expanded memory *n.* a technique for utilizing more than 1MB (megabyte) of main memory in DOS-based computers. Also called **EMS (Expanded Memory Specification)**.
⇒ See also CONVENTIONAL MEMORY; EEMS; EXTENDED MEMORY; LOW MEMORY; MAIN MEMORY; RAM DISK.

expansion board *n.* a printed circuit board that can be inserted into a computer to give it added capabilities. Sound cards and graphics accelerators are examples of expansion boards.

⇒ See also ACCELERATOR BOARD; ADAPTER; ADD-IN; ADD-ON; CPU; DAUGHTERCARD; EXPANSION SLOT; GRAPHICS ACCELERATOR; PCI; PRINTED CIRCUIT BOARD; SOUND CARD; TELEVISION BOARD; VIDEO ADAPTER.

expansion bus *n.* a collection of wires and protocols that allows the expansion of a computer by the insertion of printed circuit boards. Nearly all new PCs have a PCI bus for performance as well as an ISA bus for backward compatibility.

⇒ See also BUS; EISA; EXPANSION BOARD; EXPANSION SLOT; LOCAL BUS; PCI; PROTOCOL; VL-Bus.

expansion card *n.* EXPANSION BOARD.

expansion slot *n.* an opening in a computer where an expansion board can be inserted to add new capabilities to the computer.

⇒ See also EXPANSION BOARD; LOCAL BUS; PRINTED CIRCUIT BOARD.

expert system *n.* a computer application that performs a task that would otherwise be performed by a human expert. Expert systems are part of a general category of computer applications known as *artificial intelligence.*

⇒ See also ARTIFICIAL INTELLIGENCE; HEURISTIC PROGRAMMING; Prolog.

exploded view *n.* a picture or diagram that shows the components of an object slightly separated, as if there had been a neat explosion in the middle of the object. Many spreadsheet applications can automatically create simple exploded diagrams such as exploded pie charts.

⇒ See also SPREADSHEET.

export *v.t.* to format (data) in such a way that it can be used by another application. An application that can export data can create a file in a format that another application understands, enabling the two programs to share the same data.

⇒ See also EXPORT; COMMA-DELIMITED; CONVERT; FILTER; IMPORT; MIDDLEWARE.

expression *n.* in programming, an expression is any legal combination of symbols that represents a value. Each programming language and application has its own rules for what is legal and illegal.

⇒ See also ARITHMETIC EXPRESSION; BOOLEAN EXPRESSION; CHARACTER STRING; DATA TYPE; FLOATING-POINT NUMBER; FORMULA; INTEGER; OPERAND; OPERATOR; QUERY.

extended ASCII *n.* a set of codes that extends the basic ASCII set. The basic ASCII set uses 7 bits for each character, giving it a total of 128 unique symbols. The extended ASCII character set uses 8 bits, which gives it an additional 128 characters. The extra characters can represent characters from foreign languages and special symbols for drawing pictures.

⇒ See also ASCII; CHARACTER BASED; ISO LATIN 1.

Extended Binary-Coded Decimal Interchange Code *n.* See EBCDIC.

Extended Capabilities Port *n.* See ECP.

extended graphics array *n.* See XGA.

Extended Industry Standard Architecture *n.* See EISA.

extended keyboard *n.* a keyboard for Macintosh computers that contains up to 15 function keys above the alphanumeric keys, and a numeric keypad.

⇒ See also ENHANCED KEYBOARD.

extended memory *n.* memory above and beyond the standard 1MB (megabyte) of main memory that DOS supports. Extended memory is generally only usable with the Windows and OS-2 operating systems.

⇒ See also CONVENTIONAL MEMORY; EXPANDED MEMORY; HIGH MEMORY AREA; LOW MEMORY; PROTECTED MODE; RAM DISK; VCPI; XMS.

Extended Memory Specification *n.* See XMS.

extended VGA *n.* See SVGA.

eXtensible Markup Language *n.* See XML.

extension *n.* **1.** an extra feature added to a standard programming language or operating system. **2.** in DOS and some other operating systems, one or several letters at the end of a filename. Filename extensions usually follow a period (dot) and indicate the type of information stored in the file. **3.** in Macintosh environments, a program that extends the system's capabilities. **4.** PLUG-IN.

⇒ See also ASSOCIATE; DOT; FTS FILE; GID FILE; INIT; MEMORY RESIDENT.

external bus *n.* a bus that connects a computer to peripheral devices.

⇒ See also IEEE 1394; PERIPHERAL DEVICE.

external cache *n.* L2 CACHE.

external command *n.* in DOS systems, any command that does not reside in the COMMAND. COM file. This includes all other COM files, as well as EXE and BAT files.

⇒ See also COMMAND; COMMAND.COM; INTERNAL COMMAND.

external modem *n.* a modem that resides in a self-contained box outside the computer system.

⇒ See also INTERNAL MODEM; MODEM.

extranet *n.* an intranet that is partially accessible to authorized persons outside of a company or organization.

⇒ See also AUTHORIZATION; FIREWALL; INTRANET.

extremely low-frequency (ELF) emission *n.* ELF EMISSION.

e-zine *n.* electronic magazine: a Web site that is modeled after a print magazine. Some e-zines are simply electronic versions of existing print magazines, whereas others exist only in their digital form.

⇒ See also WEB SITE.

F f

F1, F2 . . . F15 *n.* the names of the function keys. See under FUNCTION KEYS.

facsimile machine *n.* FAX MACHINE.

FAQ (ef′ā′kyōō′ *or* fak), *n.* frequently asked questions: an electronic document that contains answers to the most commonly asked questions about some topic, often a technical one.
⇒ See also HELP.

Fast ATA *n.* See EIDE.

Fast Ethernet *n.* See 100BASE-T.

fast IDE *n.* See EIDE.

Fast Page Mode RAM *n.* See FPM RAM.

FAT *n.* FILE ALLOCATION TABLE.

fatal error *n.* an error that causes a program to abort. When a fatal error occurs, whatever data the program was currently processing may be lost.
⇒ See also ABORT; CRASH; GPF; RUNTIME ERROR.

FAT32 *n.* a new version of the file allocation table (FAT) available in Windows 95 OSR 2 and in Windows 98. It can support larger disks (up to 2 terabytes) and stores files with less wasted space.
⇒ See also CLUSTER; FILE ALLOCATION TABLE; FILE MANAGEMENT SYSTEM; OSR 2; SLACK SPACE.

fault tolerance *n.* the ability of a system to respond to an unexpected hardware or software failure. There are many levels of fault tolerance, the lowest being the ability to continue operation in the event of a power failure.
⇒ See also CLUSTERING; DISK MIRRORING; RAID; SERVER MIRRORING.

fax *v.t.* **1.** to send (a document) by fax machine or fax modem. —*n.* **2.** a document that has been faxed or is about to be faxed. **3.** FAX MACHINE.

fax board *n.* FAX MODEM.

fax machine *n.* a device that can send or receive documents, drawings, photographs, etc., over a telephone line. Fax machines work by digitizing an image—dividing it into a grid of dots. Electronically, each dot is represented by a bit that has a value of either 0 (off) or 1 (on), depending on whether it is black or white. In this way, the fax machine translates a picture into a bit map that can be transmitted like computer data. The receiving fax machine reads the data, translates the zeros and ones back into dots, and reprints the picture.

⇒ See also BPS; DIGITIZE; FAX MODEM; MFP; OPTICAL SCANNER; THERMAL PRINTER.

fax modem *n.* a device that can be attached to a personal computer to transmit and receive electronic documents as faxes. A fax modem is designed to transmit documents to a fax machine or to another fax modem. Documents sent through a fax modem must already be in an electronic form (that is, in a disk file). The principle disadvantage of fax modems is that a separate optical scanner is needed if a user wants to fax paper documents.

⇒ See also BROADCAST; FAX MACHINE; MODEM; OPTICAL SCANNER.

FC-AL Fibre Channel Arbitrated Loop: a standard for high-speed optical communication.

⇒ See also FIBRE CHANNEL.

FCC Federal Communications Commission: a U.S. government agency that regulates interstate and foreign communications. Among other duties, the FCC is responsible for rating personal computers according to how much radiation they emit.

FCIF Full Common Intermediate Format: same as COMMON INTERMEDIATE FORMAT.

FDC floppy disk controller: a chip and associated circuitry for controlling a floppy disk drive.

FDD FLOPPY DISK DRIVE.

FDDI Fiber Distributed Data Interface: a set of ANSI standards for sending digital data over fiber optic cable. FDDI networks are token-passing networks and support data rates of up to 100 Mbps (100 million bits) per second. They are typically used as backbones for wide-area networks.

⇒ See also ATM; CDDI; FIBER OPTICS; NETWORK.

FDHD (fud/hud/), *n.* floppy drive, high density: a 3½-inch disk drive for Macintosh computers that can accept double-density or high-density 3½-

inch floppy disks. FDHDs can also read DOS-formatted floppy disks, which enables Macintosh computers and PCs to share data.

⇒ See also DENSITY; DOS; FLOPPY DISK; MACINTOSH COMPUTER; SUPERDRIVE.

fdisk *n.* a DOS and Windows utility that prepares a hard disk for formatting by creating one or more partitions on the disk.

⇒ See also FORMAT; PARTITION.

FDM Frequency Division Multiplexing: a multiplexing technique that uses different frequencies to combine multiple streams of data for transmission over a communications medium.

⇒ See also CARRIER; MULTIPLEX; TDM; WDM.

feathering *n.* in desktop publishing, the process of adding space between all lines on a page or in a column to force vertical justification.

⇒ See also JUSTIFICATION; VERTICAL JUSTIFICATION.

feature *n.* a notable property of a device or software application.

⇒ See also BELLS AND WHISTLES; BLOATWARE; OVERHEAD; VANILLA.

Federal Communications Commission *n.* See FCC.

female connector *n.* a connector, as at the end of a cable or on a port, containing holes into which a male connector can be inserted.

FF FORM FEED.

Fiber Distributed Data Interface *n.* See FDDI.

fiber optics *n.* a technology that uses glass or plastic fibers to transmit data, video and voice signals, etc. A fiber optic cable consists of a bundle of glass threads, each of which is capable of transmitting messages modulated onto light waves.

⇒ See also FDDI; ISDN; LOCAL AREA NETWORK; SDH; SONET; UTP; WDM.

Fibre Channel *n.* a high-speed serial data transfer architecture for optical fibers, developed by a consortium of computer and mass storage device manufacturers and now being standardized by ANSI.

⇒ See also BUS; HIPPI; SCSI.

field *n.* a unit of information, such as a person's name, that combines with related fields, such as an official title or company name, to form one complete record in a computerized database.
⇒ See also ATTRIBUTE; BLOB; CELL; DATA TYPE; DATABASE; DATABASE MANAGEMENT SYSTEM; FORM; RECORD.

file *n.* a collection of data or information that has a name. Different types of files store different types of information. For example, program files store programs, whereas text files store text.
⇒ See also DIRECTORY; DOCUMENT; EXECUTABLE FILE; FILENAME; FOLDER; LIBRARY.

file allocation table *n.* a table that the operating system uses to locate files on a disk. Because of fragmentation, a file may be divided into many sections that are scattered around the disk. *Abbr.:* FAT
⇒ See also CLUSTER; DISK; FAT32; FILE; FILE MANAGEMENT SYSTEM; FRAGMENTATION; PARTITION; SLACK SPACE; VFAT.

file attribute *n.* See under ATTRIBUTE (def. 2).

file compression *n.* storing a file in a standard format, such as ARC or ZIP, that takes up less space than the file's native format. File compression is useful for conserving storage space and for facilitating electronic transmission.
⇒ See also PACKED FILE.

file defragmentation *n.* the automated process of taking scattered parts of a file and placing them in contiguous locations on a disk.

file extension *n.* EXTENSION.

file format *n.* a format for encoding information in a file. Each type of file has a different file format. It specifies first whether the file is a binary or ASCII file, and second, how the information is organized.
⇒ See also FILE; FORMAT; GRAPHICS FILE FORMATS; PDF.

file fragmentation *n.* FRAGMENTATION.

file locking *n.* See under LOCK.

file management system *n.* FILE SYSTEM.

filename *n.* the name of a file. Most operating

systems prohibit the use of certain characters in a filename and impose a limit on its length. In addition, many systems allow a filename extension that consists of one or more characters following the proper filename.

⇒ See also ALIAS; DIRECTORY; EXTENSION; FILE; WILDCARD CHARACTER.

filename extension *n.* EXTENSION.

file server *n.* See under SERVER.

file system *n.* the system that an operating system or program uses to organize and keep track of files. For example, a *hierarchical file system* is one that uses directories to organize files into a tree structure.

⇒ See also DIRECTORY; FAT32; FILE ALLOCATION TABLE; HIERARCHICAL; NFS; NTFS; VFAT; VSAM.

File Transfer Protocol *n.* See FTP.

File Transport Protocol *n.* See FTP.

fill *v.t.* **1.** in graphics applications, to paint the inside of (an enclosed object) with a single color or texture. **2.** in spreadsheet applications, to copy the contents of one cell to (an entire range of cells).

⇒ See also GRAPHICS; SPREADSHEET.

filter *n.* **1.** a program that accepts a certain type of data as input, transforms it, and then outputs the transformed data. For example, a program that sorts names is a filter. **2.** a pattern through which data is passed. Only data that match the pattern are allowed to pass through the filter. **3.** in paint programs and image editors, an effect that can be applied to a bit map. Some filters mimic conventional photographic filters, but others transform images in unusual ways.

⇒ See also EXPORT; IMAGE EDITOR; IMAGE ENHANCEMENT; IMPORT; PHOTO ILLUSTRATION.

Finder *n.* the desktop management system for Macintosh computers.

⇒ See also CLIPBOARD; DESKTOP; FILE MANAGEMENT SYSTEM; MACOS; MULTIFINDER; MULTITASKING.

finger *n.* a UNIX program that takes an e-mail address as input and returns information about the user who owns that e-mail address.

⇒ See also E-MAIL; E-MAIL CLIENT; INSTANT MESSAGING; WHOIS.

firewall *n.* a system designed to prevent unauthorized access to or from a private network, esp. an intranet connected to the Internet. A firewall is considered a first line of defense in protecting private information. For greater security, data can be encrypted.
⇒ See also EXTRANET; INTRANET; IP SPOOFING; NAT; NETWORK; PROXY SERVER; SECURITY.

FireWire *n.* See IEEE 1394.

firmware *n.* software (programs or data) that has been written onto read-only memory (ROM, EPROM, EEPROM, etc.).
⇒ See also HARDWARE; PROM; ROM; SOFTWARE.

fixed disk *n.* HARD DISK.

fixed-frequency monitor *n.* a monitor that can accept signals in only one frequency range.
⇒ See also MONITOR; MULTISCANNING MONITOR.

fixed-length *adj.* having a set length that never varies. In database systems, a fixed-length field is one whose length is the same in each record. A fixed-length record is one in which every field has a fixed length.
⇒ See also DATABASE MANAGEMENT SYSTEM; FIELD; RECORD; VARIABLE LENGTH.

fixed-pitch *adj.* referring to fonts in which every character has the same width. Most typewriters and inexpensive printers use fixed-pitch fonts.
⇒ See also COURIER FONT; CPI; FONT; MONOSPACING; PITCH; PROPORTIONAL SPACING.

fixed-width *adj.* FIXED-PITCH.

flag *n.* **1.** a software or hardware mark that signals a particular condition or status. The flag is said to be *set* when it is turned on. **2.** a special mark indicating that a piece of data is unusual. For example, a record might contain an *error flag* to indicate that the record consists of unusual, probably incorrect, data. —*v.t.* **3.** to mark (an object) to indicate that a particular event has occurred or that the object marked is unusual in some way.
⇒ See also SEMAPHORE.

flame *n.* **1.** an e-mail or newsgroup message in

which the writer attacks another participant in overly harsh, and often personal, terms. —*v.i.* **2.** to post a flame. —*v.t.* **3.** to attack (a person) online.

⇒ See also CONFERENCE; E-MAIL; FORUM; MODERATED NEWSGROUP; ONLINE SERVICE.

flash BIOS *n.* BIOS that has been recorded on an updatable flash memory chip.

flash EEPROM *n.* FLASH MEMORY.

flash memory *n.* a special type of *EEPROM* that can be erased and reprogrammed in blocks instead of one byte at a time. Many modern PCs have their BIOS stored on a flash memory chip so that it can easily be updated if necessary. Flash memory is also used by modem manufacturers.

⇒ See also BIOS; EEPROM.

FlashPix *n.* a format for storing digital images, especially digital photographs, developed by Eastman Kodak Company.

⇒ See also COMPUTER IMAGING; DIGITAL CAMERA; DIGITAL PHOTOGRAPHY; DIGITAL WATERMARK.

flash ROM *n.* FLASH MEMORY.

flatbed scanner *n.* a type of optical scanner that consists of a flat surface on which documents are placed.

⇒ See also OPTICAL SCANNER.

flat-file database *n.* a relatively simple database system in which each database is contained in a single file. Flat databases are adequate for many small applications.

⇒ See also RELATIONAL DATABASE; DATABASE MANAGEMENT SYSTEM; RDBMS.

flat-panel display *n.* a very thin display screen used in portable computers and increasingly as a replacement for a CRT with desktop computers. Nearly all flat-panel displays use LCD technologies.

⇒ See also ACTIVE-MATRIX DISPLAY; BACKLIGHTING; DISPLAY SCREEN; DUAL-SCAN DISPLAY; ELECTROLUMINESCENT DISPLAY (ELD); GAS-PLASMA DISPLAY; LCD; LCD MONITOR; NOTEBOOK COMPUTER; TFT; VIRTUAL DESKTOP.

flat screen *n.* FLAT-PANEL DISPLAY.

flat technology monitor *n.* a monitor that

has a flat display screen to reduce glare. Conventional display screens are curved, which makes them more susceptible to reflections from external light sources.

⇒ See also CRT; FLAT-PANEL DISPLAY; MONITOR.

flicker n. SCREEN FLICKER.

floating adj. (in graphical user interfaces) referring to an element that can be moved to different places. Many applications support *floating toolbars*, which are collections of icons that represent tools. They can be moved on the screen to create a customized working environment.

⇒ See also PALETTE.

floating point n. See under FLOATING-POINT NUMBER.

floating-point number n. a number with no fixed number of digits before and after the decimal point (hence the term *floating point*). Such numbers are used in most computer calculations.

⇒ See also DATA TYPE; DOUBLE PRECISION; FPU; NORMALIZATION; PRECISION; SCIENTIFIC NOTATION.

floating-point unit n. See FPU.

floppy n. FLOPPY DISK.

floppy disk n. a soft magnetic disk. It comes in two basic sizes: 3½-inch disks (encased in a rigid envelope) and 5¼-inch disks (a common size for PCs made before 1987). Floppy disks are slower to access than hard disks and have less storage capacity, but they are portable and much less expensive.

⇒ See also DENSITY; DISK; FDHD; FLOPPY DRIVE; HiFD; SuperDisk; Zip drive.

floppy disk drive n. FLOPPY DRIVE.

floppy drive n. short for floppy disk drive (FDD), a disk drive that can read and write to floppy disks.

⇒ See also DISK DRIVE; FLOPPY DISK; HiFD; ZIP DRIVE.

FLOPS n. floating point operations per second: a common benchmark measurement for rating the speed of computers.

⇒ See also MEGAFLOPS; GIGAFLOPS; BENCHMARK; FLOATING-POINT NUMBER; FPU; MIPS; SPEC.

floptical *adj.* designating a type of disk drive technology that uses a combination of magnetic and optical techniques to achieve greater storage capacity than normal floppy disks.
⇒ See also OPTICAL DISK.

flow *v.t.* in desktop publishing, to insert (a body of text) into a document such that it wraps (or *flows*) around any objects on the page.
⇒ See also DESKTOP PUBLISHING.

flow control *n.* in communications, the process of adjusting the speed of transmission to ensure that the receiving device can handle all of the incoming data. This is particularly important where the sending device is capable of sending data much faster than the receiving device can receive it.
⇒ See also ASYNCHRONOUS; COMMUNICATIONS; LOOP; PROGRAM; PROGRAMMING LANGUAGE.

flush *adj.* **1.** aligned along a margin. For example, text that is *flush left* is aligned along the left margin. *Flush-right* text is aligned along the right margin. —*v.t.* **2.** to move (data) from a temporary storage area such as RAM to a more permanent storage medium such as a disk.
⇒ See also JUSTIFY; MARGINS; RAGGED.

folder *n.* in graphical user interfaces such as Windows and the Macintosh environment, an object that can contain multiple documents or other folders. Folders are used to organize information.
⇒ See also DESKTOP; DIRECTORY; FILE; GRAPHICAL USER INTERFACE.

font *n.* a design for a set of characters. A font is the combination of typeface and other qualities, such as size, pitch, and spacing. For example, within Times Roman, there are many fonts to choose from. More loosely, a font can refer to a typeface. In this sense, computers and display or output devices use two methods to represent fonts. In a *bit-mapped font,* every character is represented by an arrangement of dots. A font of a different size requires a different set of bit maps. In the other method, a *vector graphics system,* the outline of each character is defined geometrically. Such fonts are *scalable* and the same outline can be any size.

⇒ See also BIT-MAPPED GRAPHICS; CPI; FIXED PITCH; FONT CARTRIDGE; FONT FAMILY; KERNING; PAGE DESCRIPTION LANGUAGE (PDL); PITCH; POINT; POSTSCRIPT; PROPORTIONAL SPACING; SCALABLE FONT; SOFT FONT; TRUETYPE; TYPEFACE; VECTOR GRAPHICS.

font card *n.* FONT CARTRIDGE.

font cartridge *n.* a ROM cartridge that contains one or more fonts. The cartridge is inserted into a printer to give the printer the ability to print different fonts. Another way to load fonts into a printer is to download them from the computer's storage device.

⇒ See also CARTRIDGE; DOWNLOAD; FONT; LASER PRINTER; SOFT FONT.

font family *n.* a set of fonts all with the same typeface, but with different sizes, weights, and slants.

⇒ See also FONT; TYPEFACE.

footer *n.* one or more lines of information repeated at the bottom of every page of a document. Once the user specifies what text should appear in the footer, the application automatically inserts it. Most applications allow the use of special symbols in the footer that represent changing values. For example, if a symbol is entered for the page number, the application will replace the symbol with the correct number on each page.

⇒ See also HEADER.

footprint *n.* the amount of floor or desk space occupied by a device. A *small-footprint* computer is one whose width and depth are relatively small.

⇒ See also DESKTOP MODEL COMPUTER; TOWER MODEL.

forced page break *n.* a special code that directs an application to start a new page when printing, regardless of whether or not it has reached the bottom of the current page.

⇒ See also HARD; PAGE BREAK; SOFT.

foreground *n.* **1.** in multiprocessing systems, the process that is currently accepting input from the keyboard or other input device is sometimes called the *foreground process.* **2.** on display screens, the characters and pictures that appear on the screen. The background is the uniform canvas behind the characters and pictures.

⇒ See also BACKGROUND; MULTIPROCESSING.

foreign key *n.* See under KEY.

form *n.* a formatted document containing blank fields that users can fill in with data. The form appears on the display screen and the user fills it in by selecting options with a pointing device or typing in text from the keyboard. The data is then sent directly to a forms processing application, which enters the information into a database.

⇒ See also CGI; FIELD; OPTICAL CHARACTER RECOGNITION.

format *v.t.* **1.** to prepare (a storage medium, usually a disk) for reading and writing. The operating system erases all existing information on the disk, tests the disk to make sure all sectors are reliable, marks bad sectors, and creates internal address tables that it later uses to locate information. —*n.* **2.** a particular arrangement. Almost everything associated with computers has a format.

⇒ See also CONTROLLER; DISK; FDISK; HARD DISK; INITIALIZE; INTERLEAVE; LOW-LEVEL FORMAT; MFM; RLL; SECTOR; TAG.

form factor *n.* the physical size and shape of a device. It is often used to describe the size of circuit boards.

⇒ See also ATX; BABY AT; LPX; NLX; PRINTED CIRCUIT BOARD.

form feed *n.* **1.** the process that advances the paper in a printer to the beginning of the next page. **2.** a special character that causes the printer to advance one page length or to the top of the next page.

⇒ See also ASCII.

forms software *n.* a type of program used for designing and filling in forms on a computer. Most forms software packages contain a number of sample forms that can be modified.

formula *n.* **1.** an equation or expression. **2.** in spreadsheet applications, an expression that defines how one cell relates to other cells.

⇒ See also CELL; CONSTANT; EXPRESSION; SPREAD-SHEET.

FORTRAN *n.* the oldest high-level programming language. Designed for IBM in the late 1950s, it is still popular today, particularly for scientific applications that require extensive mathematical computations.

⇒ See also HIGH-LEVEL LANGUAGE; PROGRAMMING LANGUAGE.

forum *n.* an online discussion group. Online services and bulletin board services (BBSs) provide a variety of forums, in which participants with common interests can exchange open messages.

⇒ See also BULLETIN BOARD SYSTEM; CONFERENCE; DISTANCE LEARNING; NEWSGROUP; ONLINE SERVICE; USENET.

486 short for the *Intel 80486 microprocessor.*

⇒ See also INTEL MICROPROCESSORS.

4GL FOURTH-GENERATION LANGUAGE.

fourth-generation language *n.* a programming language that is closer to human languages than typical high-level programming languages. Most fourth-generation languages are used to access databases. The other three generations of computer languages are: *first generation* (machine language); *second generation* (assembly language); and *third generation* (high-level programming language).

⇒ See also DATABASE MANAGEMENT SYSTEM; NATURAL LANGUAGE; PROGRAMMING LANGUAGE; QUERY; QUERY LANGUAGE.

FPM RAM *n.* Fast Page Mode RAM: a type of Dynamic RAM (DRAM) that allows faster access to data in the same row or page.

⇒ See also CPU; EDO DRAM; INTERLEAVED MEMORY; MEMORY; RAM; RDRAM; SLDRAM; WAIT STATE.

fps frames per second: a measure of how much information is used to store and display motion video. The term applies equally to film video and digital video. The more frames per second (fps), the smoother the motion appears.

⇒ See also AVI; NTSC.

FPU floating-point unit: a specially designed chip that performs *floating-point* calculations. Computers equipped with an FPU perform certain types of applications much faster than computers that lack one. In particular, graphics applications are faster with an FPU.

⇒ See also COPROCESSOR; FLOATING-POINT NUMBER; FLOPS.

fractal *n.* a shape that is "self-similar", that is, a shape that looks the same at different magnifications. Many of the computer-generated images that appear in science fiction films utilize fractals.

⇒ See also GRAPHICS.

fractional T-1 *n.* one or more channels of a T-1 long-distance data transmission line. A full T-1 contains 24 channels of 64 Kbps each.

⇒ See also DIAL-UP ACCESS; LEASED LINE; T-1 CARRIER.

FRAD *n.* Frame Relay Assembler/Disassembler: a communications device that breaks a data stream into frames for transmission over a Frame Relay network and recreates a data stream from incoming frames.

fragmentation *n.* **1.** the condition of a disk in which files are divided into pieces scattered around the disk, slowing access to them. Fragmentation occurs naturally when a disk is used frequently; at some point, the layout of available space will force the operating system to store parts of a file in noncontiguous locations. **2.** a similar condition for RAM. *External fragmentation* occurs when RAM has small, unused regions scattered throughout it. *Internal fragmentation*, which is more common, arises when memory is allocated in frames of fixed size, but the frame size is larger than the amount that programs request.

⇒ See also CLUSTER; DEFRAG; DISK OPTIMIZER; FILE ALLOCATION TABLE.

frame *n.* **1.** in graphics and desktop publishing applications, a rectangular area in which text or graphics can appear. **2.** in communications, a packet of transmitted information. **3.** in video and animation, a single image in a sequence of images. **4.** in HTML, a subdivision of a Web browser's display area. See FRAMES.

⇒ See also FPS.

Frame Relay *n.* a packet-switching protocol for connecting devices on a Wide-Area Network (WAN).

⇒ See also ATM; CELL RELAY; CIR; FRAD; PACKET SWITCHING; PVC.

Frame Relay Assembler/Dissassembler *n.* See FRAD.

frames *n.pl.* a feature supported by most modern Web browsers that enables the Web author to divide the browser display area into two or more sections (frames). The contents of each frame are taken from a different Web page.

⇒ See also HTML.

frames per second *n.pl.* See FPS.

FreeBSD *n.* a popular and free version of UNIX that runs on Intel microprocessors.

⇒ See also LINUX; UNIX.

freeware *n.* software given away by the author, for use by others, although the author retains the copyright.

⇒ See also PUBLIC-DOMAIN SOFTWARE; SHAREWARE; WAREZ.

Frequency Division Multiplexing *n.* See FDM.

friction feed *n.* a method of feeding paper through a printer. Friction-feed printers use plastic or rubber rollers to squeeze a sheet of paper and pull it through the printer.

⇒ See also PRINTER; SHEET FEEDER; TRACTOR FEED.

front end *n.* **1.** for software applications, the user interface. **2.** in client/server applications, the client part of the program. The server part is called the *back end*. **3.** for compilers, the part responsible for checking syntax and detecting errors. The *back end* performs the actual translation into object code.

⇒ See also CLIENT/SERVER ARCHITECTURE; COMPILER; DISTRIBUTED PROCESSING; USER INTERFACE.

frozen *adj.* unresponsive. The term is used to describe a monitor, keyboard, or the entire computer system when it no longer reacts to input because of a malfunction.

⇒ See also CRASH.

FTM FLAT TECHNOLOGY MONITOR.

FTP File Transfer Protocol or File Transport Protocol: the protocol used on the Internet for sending files.

⇒ See also ANONYMOUS FTP; COMMUNICATIONS; INTERNET; TFTP; UUCP.

.fts extension n. FTS FILE.

FTS file n. a hidden index file ending in a .FTS (full-text search) extension used by the Windows 95 and NT Help system.

⇒ See also EXTENSION; GID FILE; HELP.

full duplex n. the transmission of data in two directions simultaneously. When a terminal is used in full-duplex mode, a user's keystrokes do not appear on the screen until they have been received and sent back by the computer at the other end of the line.

⇒ See also COMMUNICATIONS; HALF DUPLEX; MODEM; SIMPLEX.

full-length adj. referring to full-sized, 16-bit expansion boards, such as video adapters and graphics accelerators, that can be inserted into a computer and to the full-length expansion slots that can accept them.

function n. **1.** in programming, a named section of a program that performs a specific task. **2.** an operation or command.

⇒ See also COMMAND; LIBRARY; PROCEDURE; PROGRAM; ROUTINE.

functional spec n. FUNCTIONAL SPECIFICATION.

functional specification n. a formal description of a software system that is used as a blueprint for implementing the program. At minimum, a functional specification should precisely state the purpose or function of the software.

⇒ See also ARCHITECTURE; SOFTWARE ENGINEERING; USER INTERFACE.

function keys n.pl. special keys on the keyboard that have different meanings depending on which program is running. Function keys are normally labeled F1 to F10 or F12 (or F15 on Macintoshes).

⇒ See also ALT KEY; ENHANCED KEYBOARD; F1, F2... F15; KEYBOARD.

fuzzy logic *n.* a type of logic that recognizes more than simple true and false values. Fuzzy logic has proved to be particularly useful in expert system and other artificial intelligence applications. It is also used in some spell checkers to suggest a list of probable words to replace a misspelled one.

⇒ See also ARTIFICIAL INTELLIGENCE; BOOLEAN LOGIC; EXPERT SYSTEM; SPELL CHECKER.

G g

G GIGA; GIGABYTE.

garbage in, garbage out a well-known computer axiom meaning that if invalid data is entered into a system, the resulting output will be invalid regardless of the sophistication with which it is processed. *Abbr.:* GIGO

gas-plasma display *n.* a type of thin display screen, called a *flat-panel display*, used in some older portable computers. It works by sandwiching neon gas between two plates.
⇒ See also FLAT-PANEL DISPLAY; LCD; NOTEBOOK COMPUTER.

gateway *n.* in networking, a combination of hardware and software that links two different types of networks.
⇒ See also NETWORK.

GB GIGABYTE.

Gbps gigabits per second: a data transfer speed measurement for high-speed networks such as Gigabit Ethernet.
⇒ See also GIGABIT; GIGABIT ETHERNET; MBPS.

GDI Graphical Device Interface: a Windows standard for representing graphical objects and transmitting them to output devices, such as monitors and printers.
⇒ See also DIRECTDRAW; GDI PRINTER; HOST-BASED PRINTER.

GDI printer *n.* a printer that has built-in support for Windows Graphical Device Interface (GDI), which is used by most Windows applications to display images on a monitor. Also called **host-based printer.**
⇒ See also GDI; HOST-BASED PRINTER; PCL; POST-SCRIPT; PRINTER; WINDOWS.

geek *n.* computer geek: an individual with a passion for computers, to the exclusion of other human interests.
⇒ See also HACKER.

GEM *n.* **1.** a graphical user interface developed by Digital Research. It is built into personal computers made by Atari and is also used as an interface for some DOS programs. **2.** a special graphics file format used in GEM-based applications.

⇒ See also GRAPHICAL USER INTERFACE; MACINTOSH COMPUTER; MICROSOFT WINDOWS.

general protection fault *n.* See GPF.

genetic programming *n.* a type of programming that utilizes the same properties of natural selection found in biological evolution.

⇒ See also ARTIFICIAL INTELLIGENCE; LISP.

genlock *n.* generator locking device: a device that enables a composite video machine, such as a TV, to accept two signals simultaneously by locking their vertical and horizontal synchronization signals together.

⇒ See also COMPOSITE VIDEO.

Geoport *n.* a serial port for Apple computers, now obsolete, that provides an interface between a telephone line and the computer.

⇒ See also SERIAL PORT; VIDEOCONFERENCING.

GFLOPS *n.* GigaFLOPS.

⇒ See also FLOPS.

.gid extension *n.* See under GID FILE.

GID file *n.* a hidden Windows 95 configuration file, ending with a .GID extension, used by the Windows Help system to speed up access to help file topics.

⇒ See also EXTENSION; FTS FILE; HELP.

GIF (jif, gif), *n.* graphics interchange format: a bit-mapped graphics file format used by the World Wide Web, CompuServe, and many BBSs. It supports color and various resolutions and includes data compression.

⇒ See also ANIMATED GIF; DATA COMPRESSION; GRAPHICS FILE FORMATS; IMAGE MAP; LZW; PNG.

giga *n.* **1.** in decimal notation, 10^9. For example, a *gigavolt* is 1,000,000,000 volts. **2.** in referring to computers, which use the binary notation system, 2^{30} or 1,073,741,824, a little more than 1 billion.

⇒ See also BINARY; MASS STORAGE; MEGABYTE.

gigabit *n.* **1.** in describing data storage, 1,024 megabits. **2.** in describing data transfer rates, one 10^9 (1,000,000,000) bits.

⇒ See also GBPS; GIGABYTE; MEGABIT.

Gigabit Ethernet *n.* a version of Ethernet that supports data transfer rates of 1 gigabit (1,000 megabits) per second.
⇒ See also 100Base-T; Ethernet; HIPPI; IEEE.

gigabyte *n.* 2^{30} (1,073,741,824) bytes: equal to 1,024 megabytes. *Abbr.:* G, GB.
⇒ See also BYTE; GIGA; GIGABIT; MEGABYTE; PETABYTE.

GigaFLOPS *n.* one billion *FLOPS*.

GIGO (gī′gō *or as separate letters*), *n.* GARBAGE IN, GARBAGE OUT.

glitch *n.* a malfunction, as of hardware.
⇒ See also BUG.

GNU (nōō *or as separate letters*), *n.* GNU's not UNIX: a non-proprietary UNIX-compatible software system developed by the Free Software Foundation (FSF).
⇒ See also LINUX; UNIX.

Gopher *n.* a system that predates the World Wide Web for organizing and displaying files on Internet servers. [named after the mascot of the University of Minnesota, where it was developed]
⇒ See also ARCHIE; INTERNET; JUGHEAD; VERONICA; WORLD WIDE WEB.

GPF General Protection Fault: a computer condition that causes a Windows application to crash, as when one application tries to use memory assigned to another.
⇒ See also CRASH; FATAL ERROR; INVALID PAGE FAULT; RUNTIME ERROR.

gppm graphics pages per minute: the speed with which laser printers can print nontext pages.
⇒ See also LASER PRINTER; PPM.

grabber *n.* **1.** a device that captures data, as one that can capture full-motion video from a television or video camera and convert it to digital form for storage on a computer's disk. **2.** in some applications, a special tool or cursor that enables the user to grab objects on the screen and move them or manipulate them: often represented by a hand icon.
⇒ See also CURSOR.

Graphical Device Interface *n.* See GDI.

graphical user interface n. a program interface, as Microsoft Windows and that used by the Apple Macintosh, that takes advantage of the computer's graphics capabilities to free the user from having to learn complex command languages. It makes the computer easier to use. Also called **GUI**.

⇒ See also AWT; CHARACTER BASED; DESKTOP; DRAG-AND-DROP; ICON; MACINTOSH COMPUTER; MDI; MICROSOFT WINDOWS; POINTER; POINTING DEVICE; USER INTERFACE; XEROX.

graphics n. **1.** pictorial computer output. —adj. **2.** pertaining to any computer device or program that makes a computer capable of displaying and manipulating pictures: *graphics applications; a graphics monitor.* Software applications that include graphics are said to *support* graphics. For example, certain word processors let the user draw or import pictures. All CAD/CAM systems support graphics. Some database management systems and spreadsheet programs support graphics because they let users display data in the form of graphs and charts. Such simple displays are often referred to as *business graphics*.

⇒ See also ALPHA CHANNEL; BIT MAP; BIT-MAPPED GRAPHICS; CAD; CAD/CAM; CHARACTER BASED; CLIP ART; CPU; DESKTOP PUBLISHING; DISPLAY SCREEN; GRAPHICS FILE FORMAT; IMAGE PROCESSING; LASER PRINTER; MICROSOFT WINDOWS; MONITOR; PERSONAL COMPUTER; PLOTTER; 3-D GRAPHICS.

graphics accelerator n. a type of video adapter that contains its own processor. A graphics accelerator is specialized for computing graphical transformations and therefore achieves better results than the general-purpose CPU used by the computer. It also has its own memory for storing screen images.

⇒ See also 3-D GRAPHICS; ACCELERATOR BOARD; AGP; CPU; DIRECT3D; DIRECTDRAW; DIRECTX; DRAM; GRAPHICS; MDRAM; MULTIMEDIA; PCI; SGRAM; VIDEO ADAPTER; VIDEO MEMORY; VRAM.

graphics adapter n. VIDEO ADAPTER.

graphics based adj. referring to software and hardware that treat objects on a display screen as bit maps or geometrical shapes rather than as characters.

⇒ See also CHARACTER BASED.

graphics card *n*. VIDEO ADAPTER.

graphics character *n*. a character whose displayed image is a shape rather than a letter, number, or punctuation mark.

⇒ See also BLOCK GRAPHICS; CHARACTER MODE; EXTENDED ASCII.

graphics coprocessor *n*. See under COPROCESSOR.

⇒ See also GRAPHICS ACCELERATOR.

graphics display system *n*. the combination of monitor and video adapter that makes a computer capable of displaying graphics.

⇒ See also GRAPHICS; MONITOR; VIDEO ADAPTER.

graphics file format *n*. a file format, either bit-mapped or vector, that is designed specifically for representing graphical images.

⇒ See also BMP; CGM; DIB; DXF; EPS; GEM; GIF; GRAPHICS; HPGL; IGES; PCX; PIC; PICT FILE FORMAT; TIFF; WMF.

graphics mode *n*. a sophisticated mode of resolution in which the display screen is treated as an array of pixels, and characters and other shapes are formed by turning on combinations of pixels. Programs that run entirely in graphics mode are called *graphics-based* programs.

⇒ See also CHARACTER BASED; GRAPHICS BASED; PIXEL; VIDEO ADAPTER.

graphics monitor *n*. a monitor capable of displaying graphics.

⇒ See also GRAPHICS; MONITOR.

graphics pages per minute *n*. See GPPM.

graphics tablet *n*. DIGITIZING TABLET.

gray scaling *n*. the use of many shades of gray to represent an image.

⇒ See also CONTINUOUS TONE; DATA COMPRESSION; DITHERING; MONITOR; OPTICAL SCANNER.

greeking *n*. **1.** the approximation of text characters on a screen display to show what a document will look like when printed: used by word processors that support a preview function. **2.** nonsense text inserted in a document to allow a layout artist to concentrate on the overall appearance of a page without being concerned about the text to be inserted later.

⇒ See also LAYOUT; PREVIEW.

Green Book *n.* the specification covering CD-I.

⇒ See also CD-I (COMPACT DISC–INTERACTIVE); ORANGE BOOK; RED BOOK; WHITE BOOK; YELLOW BOOK.

green PC *n.* a PC specially designed to minimize power consumption.

⇒ See also ENERGY STAR; SLEEP MODE.

Group 3 protocol *n.* the universal protocol defined by the CCITT for sending faxes.

⇒ See also CCITT; FAX MACHINE.

Group 4 protocol *n.* a protocol defined by CCITT for sending faxes over ISDN networks.

⇒ See also CCITT; FAX MACHINE; ISDN.

groupware *n.* a class of software that helps colleagues (workgroups) attached to a network organize their activities by supporting such operations as telephone utilities, e-mail, and file distribution. Also called **workgroup productivity software.**

⇒ See also E-MAIL; LOTUS NOTES; SCHEDULER; TEAMWARE; WORKGROUP COMPUTING.

GSM Global System for Mobile Communications: one of the leading digital cellular systems, and the de facto standard in Europe and Asia.

⇒ See also CDMA; CELLULAR; PCS; TDMA.

GUI (gōō′ē), *n.* GRAPHICAL USER INTERFACE.

gutter *n.* in desktop publishing, the space between columns in a multiple-column document.

⇒ See also DESKTOP PUBLISHING.

GW-BASIC *n.* a dialect of the BASIC programming language that comes with many versions of the DOS operating system.

⇒ See also BASIC; QBASIC.

H h

H.323 a standard approved by the International Telecommunication Union (ITU) that defines how audiovisual conferencing data is transmitted across networks.
⇒ See also H.324; ITU; RTSP; VIDEOCONFERENCING.

H.324 a suite of standards approved by the International Telecommunications Union (ITU) that defines videoconferencing over analog telephone lines.
⇒ See also H.323; ITU; STREAMING; VIDEOCONFERENCING.

hack *n.* **1.** an inelegant and usually temporary solution to a problem. —*v.t.* **2.** to modify (a program), often in an unauthorized manner. —*v.i.* **3.** to write or explore software systems.
⇒ See also HACKER; KLUDGE.

hacker *n.* *Slang.* **1.** a computer enthusiast, esp. an amateur or a programmer who lacks formal training. **2.** an individual who gains unauthorized access to computer systems.
⇒ See also CRACK; GEEK; IP SPOOFING; PHREAKING; PROGRAMMER; SNIFFER.

half duplex *adj.* referring to the transmission of data in just one direction at a time, as on a walkie-talkie.
⇒ See also COMMUNICATIONS; FULL DUPLEX; MODEM; SIMPLEX.

half height *adj.* referring to a type of bay for disk drives and other mass storage devices.
⇒ See also BAY.

halftone *n.* in printing, a continuous-tone image, such as a photograph, that has been converted into a black-and-white image. Halftones are created through a process in which the density and pattern of black-and-white dots are varied to simulate different shades of gray. In conventional printing, halftones are created by photographing an image through a *screen*. Modern desktop publishing systems can create halftones by simulating this process.

⇒ See also CONTINUOUS TONE; DESKTOP PUBLISHING; DITHERING; MOIRÉ.

hand-held computer *n.* a portable computer that is small enough to be held in one's hand, as one designed to provide personal information manager (PIM) functions such as a calendar and address book.

⇒ See also HANDWRITING RECOGNITION; NOTEBOOK COMPUTER; PALMTOP; PDA; PIM; WINDOWS CE.

Handheld PC *n.* See HPC.

handle *n.* **1.** any of the small boxes that appear with a selected graphical object and that can be dragged to change the size and shape of the object. **2.** in programming, an address datum that enables the program to access a resource, such as a library function. **3.** in an online service, the name employed by a user to identify him or herself.

⇒ See also CHAT; GRAPHICS; ONLINE SERVICE; POINTER.

handshaking *n.* the process by which two devices initiate communications.

⇒ See also COMMUNICATIONS; PROTOCOL.

handwriting recognition *n.* the technique by which a computer system can recognize characters and other symbols written by hand.

⇒ See also HAND-HELD COMPUTER; PDA; PEN COMPUTER.

hang *v.i.* to crash in such a way that the computer does not respond to input from the keyboard or mouse.

⇒ See also ABORT; BOMB; BUG; CRASH; DEADLOCK.

hanging indent *n.* in word processing, a paragraph that has all lines but the first indented.

⇒ See also WORD PROCESSING.

hanging paragraph *n.* HANGING INDENT.

hard *adj.* referring to anything that is permanent or that physically exists, as opposed to "soft" concepts, symbols, and other intangible and changeable objects.

⇒ See also HARDWARE; HARDWIRED; SOFTWARE.

hard card *n.* a hard disk drive and controller on an expansion card.

⇒ See also BAY; CONTROLLER; EXPANSION BOARD; EXPANSION SLOT; HARD DISK.

hard coded *adj.* unchangeable, such as features built into hardware or software in such a way that they cannot be modified.
⇒ See also HARD.

hard copy *n.* a printout of data stored in a computer.
⇒ See also HARD; SOFT.

hard disk (HD) *n.* a rigid magnetic disk on which computer data can be stored, usu. consisting of several platters with read/write heads.
⇒ See also CACHE; CYLINDER; DISK DRIVE; DISK PACK; EIDE; FLOPPY DISK; HARD CARD; HARD DISK TYPE; IDE INTERFACE; INTERLEAVE; MASS STORAGE; PLATTER; REMOVABLE HARD DISK; ScanDisk; SMART; TRACK.

hard disk drive *n.* the mechanism that reads and writes data on a hard disk.
⇒ See also DISK COMPRESSION; DISK DRIVE; HARD DISK.

hard disk type *n.* a number that indicates important features of a hard disk, such as the number of platters and cylinders.
⇒ See also BIOS; HARD DISK.

hard drive *n.* HARD DISK DRIVE.

hard hyphen *n.* a hyphen, usually part of the spelling, that is deliberately inserted in data and that will appear regardless of whether or not it occurs at the end of a line.
⇒ See also DISCRETIONARY HYPHEN.

hard return *n.* a return that causes the word processor to start a new line regardless of how margins are set.
⇒ See also RETURN; SOFT RETURN.

hardware *n.* objects that can be touched, such as disks, disk drives, display screens, keyboards, printers, boards, and chips.
⇒ See also FIRMWARE; HARD; SOFTWARE.

hardwired *adj.* referring to elements of a program or device that cannot be changed.
⇒ See also CONSTANT; HARD.

hash *n.* **1.** HASH VALUE. —*v.t.* **2.** to engage in hashing of (a particular input).

hashing *n.* producing hash values for accessing data or for security.
⇒ See also INDEX; KEY.

hash search *n.* the process of searching a hash table.

hash table *n.* an index of records to which hash values have been assigned.

hash value *n.* a number generated from a string of text in such a way that it is unlikely that some other text will produce the same number: used in security systems and in accessing data. Also called **hash.**

Hayes compatible *adj.* referring to any modem that recognizes modem commands in the AT command set developed by Hayes Microcomputer Products.
⇒ See also AT COMMAND SET; COMMUNICATIONS; DE FACTO STANDARD; MODEM.

HD HARD DISK.

HDC hard disk controller: a chip and associated circuitry for controlling a hard disk drive.

HDD HARD DISK DRIVE.

HDLC High-level Data Link Control: a transmission protocol that is used at the data link layer (layer 2) of the OSI seven-layer model for data communications and that embeds information in a data frame that allows devices to control data flow and correct errors.
⇒ See also COMMUNICATIONS PROTOCOL; FRAME; OSI.

HDTV High-Definition Television: a type of television that provides much better resolution than televisions based on the NTSC standard by compressing images before they are transmitted and decompressing them when they reach the TV.
⇒ See also DSS; NTSC.

head *n.* the mechanism that reads data from or writes data to a magnetic disk or tape. Also called **read/write head.**
⇒ See also DISK DRIVE; HEAD CRASH; PLATTER.

head crash *n.* a serious disk drive malfunction, usu. caused when the head has scratched or burned the disk as the result of a misalignment or the presence of dust particles. Also called **disk**

crash.

⇒ See also CRASH; DATA RECOVERY; DISK; DISK DRIVE; HEAD.

header *n.* **1.** Also called **running head.** in word processing, one or more lines of text set up to appear at the top of each page of a document and automatically inserted by the program. **2.** in many disciplines of computer science, a unit of information that precedes a data object.

⇒ See also FOOTER; WORD PROCESSING.

head-mounted display *n.* See HMD.

heap *n.* **1.** in programming, an area of memory reserved for data that is created when a program actually executes. **2.** a special type of binary tree in which the value at each node is greater than the values at its leaves.

⇒ See also BINARY TREE; DATA STRUCTURE; STACK.

heap sort *n.* a sorting algorithm that works by first organizing the data to be sorted into a special type of binary tree called a *heap* that has the largest value at the top of the tree.

⇒ See also ALGORITHM; BINARY TREE; BUBBLE SORT.

heat sink *n.* a component, usu. made of a zinc alloy, that is designed to lower the temperature of an electronic device by dissipating heat into the surrounding air. A heat sink without a fan is called a *passive heat sink;* a heat sink with a fan is called an *active heat sink.*

⇒ See also MOTHERBOARD; VOLTAGE REGULATOR.

helical-scan cartridge *n.* a type of magnetic tape that uses the same technology as VCR tapes.

⇒ See also DAT; MASS STORAGE; TAPE.

Help *n.* online documentation, accessed by pressing a designated key, as F1 in Windows, or entering a "Help" command.

⇒ See also CONTEXT SENSITIVE; DOCUMENTATION; FAQ; FTS FILE; GID FILE; HELP DESK; MAN PAGE.

help desk *n.* a department within a company that responds to user's technical questions by telephone, e-mail, BBS, or fax.

⇒ See also HELP.

Hercules graphics *n.* an obsolete graphics display system for PCs developed by Van Suwannukul, founder of Hercules Computer Technology, in 1982.

⇒ See also MDA; VIDEO ADAPTER.

heterogeneous network *n.* a network that includes computers and other devices from different manufacturers, as local-area networks (LANs) that connect PCs with Apple Macintosh computers.

⇒ See also LOCAL-AREA NETWORK; NETWORK.

heuristic programming *n.* a branch of artificial intelligence that uses heuristics, or common-sense rules drawn from experience, to solve problems.

⇒ See also ALGORITHM; ARTIFICIAL INTELLIGENCE; EXPERT SYSTEM.

Hewlett-Packard *n.* See HP.

Hewlett-Packard Graphics Language *n.* See HPGL.

hex *adj.* HEXADECIMAL.

hexadecimal *adj.* referring to the base-16 number system, which consists of 16 unique symbols: the numbers 0 to 9 and the letters A to F.

⇒ See also BCD; BINARY; DECIMAL; NIBBLE; OCTAL.

hidden file *n.* a file with a special hidden attribute turned on, so that the file is not normally visible to users.

⇒ See also ATTRIBUTE; FILE MANAGEMENT SYSTEM.

hierarchical *adj.* referring to systems that are organized so that each row of objects is linked to objects directly beneath it.

⇒ See also DIRECTORY; FILE MANAGEMENT SYSTEM; TREE STRUCTURE.

Hierarchical Storage Management *n.* See HSM.

HiFD *n.* High Floppy Disk: a type of high-density floppy disk developed by Sony that can hold 200 MB of data.

⇒ See also FLOPPY DISK; FLOPPY DRIVE; SUPERDISK; ZIP DRIVE.

high ASCII *n.* EXTENDED ASCII.

High Definition Television *n.* See HDTV.

high-density disk *n.* a high-quality floppy disk capable of holding more data than a double-density disk.

⇒ See also DENSITY; FLOPPY DISK.

High-level Data Link Control n. See HDLC.

high-level language n. a programming language such as C, FORTRAN, or Pascal that enables a programmer to write programs that are more or less independent of a particular type of computer. High-level languages are closer to human language and easier to read, write, and maintain than low-level languages.

⇒ See also ADA; ASSEMBLY LANGUAGE; BASIC; C; C++; COBOL; COMPILE; FORTRAN; LISP; LOW-LEVEL LANGUAGE; MACHINE LANGUAGE; OBJECT-ORIENTED PROGRAMMING; PASCAL; PROGRAMMING LANGUAGE.

High Level Language Application Program Interface n. See HLLAPI.

highlight v.t. to make (an object on a display screen) stand out by displaying it in a different mode from that of other objects.

⇒ See also SELECT.

high memory n. in DOS-based systems, the memory area between the first 640K and 1 megabyte. Also called **upper memory area (UMA)**.

⇒ See also CONVENTIONAL MEMORY; DOS; EXPANDED MEMORY; EXTENDED MEMORY; LOW MEMORY; TSR.

high memory area n. in DOS-based systems, the first 64K of extended memory.

⇒ See also EXTENDED MEMORY.

High Performance Computing n. a branch of computer science that concentrates on developing supercomputers and software to run on them.

⇒ See also HPCC; PARALLEL PROCESSING; SUPERCOMPUTER.

High Performance Computing and Communications n. See HPCC.

high resolution n. See under RESOLUTION.

himem.sys n. an extended memory (XMS) driver included with DOS, Windows 3.1, Windows for Workgroups, Windows 95, and Windows 98, loaded automatically during start-up by the newer version of Windows.

⇒ See also CONFIG.SYS; EXTENDED MEMORY; XMS.

HIPPI *n.* High Performance Parallel Interface: a standard technology for connecting devices at short distances and high speeds: an official ANSI standard since 1990 and used primarily to connect supercomputers and to provide high-speed backbones for local-area networks (LANs).

⇒ See also BACKBONE; FIBRE CHANNEL; GIGABIT ETHERNET; SUPERCOMPUTER.

HLLAPI *n.* High Level Language Application Program Interface: an IBM API that allows a PC application to communicate with a mainframe computer.

⇒ See also API; MAINFRAME; TERMINAL; TERMINAL EMULATION.

HMD *n.* head-mounted display: a headset, either a pair of goggles or a full helmet, used with virtual reality systems.

⇒ See also VIRTUAL REALITY.

home computer *n.* a personal computer specially configured for use in a home rather than an office, usu. having medium-power microprocessors and equipped with a full complement of multimedia devices.

⇒ See also MULTIMEDIA; PERSONAL COMPUTER.

Home key *n.* a key on PC and newer Macintosh keyboards that controls cursor movement.

⇒ See also KEYBOARD.

home page *n.* the main page of a Web site usu. serving as an index or table of contents for other documents at the site.

⇒ See also WEB SITE.

home PC *n.* HOME COMPUTER.

hop *n.* an intermediate connection in a string of connections linking two network devices. The more hops, the longer it takes for data to go from source to destination.

⇒ See also PING; ROUTER; TRACEROUTE; TTL.

host *n.* **1.** a computer system that is accessed by a user working at a remote location. **2.** a computer that is connected to a TCP/IP network, including the Internet. —*v.t.* **3.** to provide the infrastructure for (a computer service).

⇒ See also HOST-BASED; REMOTE CONTROL; REMOTE CONTROL SOFTWARE; TELNET.

host-based *adj.* referring to any device that relies on the host computer (the computer the device is attached to) to handle some operations.
⇒ See also HOST; HOST-BASED MODEM; HOST-BASED PRINTER.

host-based modem *n.* a modem that uses the computer's processor to handle some operations. Also called **Win-modem**.
⇒ See also HOST-BASED; MODEM; SOFTWARE MODEM.

host-based printer *n.* a printer that relies on the host computer's processor to generate printable pages.
⇒ See also GDI; GDI PRINTER; HOST-BASED; PRINTER.

HotBot *n.* a World Wide Web search engine developed collaboratively by Inktomi Corporation and HotWired, Inc.
⇒ See also ALTA VISTA; EXCITE; INFOSEEK; LYCOS; SEARCH ENGINE; YAHOO!.

HotJava *n.* a set of products developed by Sun Microsystems that utilize Java technology.
⇒ See also BROWSER; JAVA.

hot key *n.* a user-defined key sequence that executes a command or causes the operating system to switch to another program.
⇒ See also CONTROL CHARACTER; FUNCTION KEYS; MEMORY RESIDENT; TSR.

hot link *n.* **1.** a link between two applications such that changes in one affect the other. —*v.t.* **2.** to establish a link between (two applications).
⇒ See also DATABASE; LINK; OLE; SPREADSHEET.

hot plugging *n.* the ability to add to and remove devices from a computer while the computer is running and have the operating system automatically recognize the change. Also called **hot swapping**.
⇒ See also IEEE 1394; PCMCIA; PLUG-AND-PLAY; USB.

hot spot *n.* an area of a graphics object, or a section of text, that activates a function when selected.
⇒ See also IMAGE MAP; MULTIMEDIA.

hot swap *n.* the act of hot swapping.

hot swapping *n.* HOT PLUGGING.

HP Hewlett-Packard: one of the world's largest computer and electronics companies, founded in 1939 by William Hewlett and David Packard.
⇒ See also HP-COMPATIBLE PRINTER; PCL; PRINTER.

HPC 1. HIGH PERFORMANCE COMPUTING. **2.** Handheld PC: Microsoft's name for a personal digital assistant (PDA).
⇒ See also PDA; WINDOWS CE.

HPCC the U.S. government's term for HIGH PERFORMANCE COMPUTING.

HP-compatible printer *n.* a laser printer that understands the printer control language (PCL) used by Hewlett-Packard Printers.
⇒ See also COMPATIBLE; DRIVER; EMULATION; FONT CARTRIDGE; HP; LASER PRINTER; PCL; POSTSCRIPT.

HPGL Hewlett-Packard Graphics Language: a set of commands for controlling plotters and printers.
⇒ See also PCL; PLOTTER.

.hqx See under BINHEX.

hqx See under BINHEX.

HSM Hierarchical Storage Management: a data storage system that automatically moves data between high-cost and low-cost storage media, effectively turning fast disk drives into caches for slower mass storage devices.
⇒ See also BACKUP; MASS STORAGE; STORAGE; STORAGE DEVICE.

HTML HyperText Markup Language: the authoring language used to create documents on the World Wide Web.
⇒ See also BROWSER; CSS; DOM; FRAMES; HTTP; HYPERTEXT; JAVASCRIPT; SGML; SSI; TAG; VRML; W3C; WORLD WIDE WEB; XML.

HTTP HyperText Transfer Protocol: the underlying protocol used by the World Wide Web that defines how messages are formatted and transmitted, and what actions Web servers and browsers should take in response to various commands.
⇒ See also HTML; S-HTTP; W3C; WORLD WIDE WEB.

hub *n.* a common connection point for devices in a network, commonly used to connect segments of a LAN.

⇒ See also 10BaseT; 3COM; bridge; concentrator; MAU; repeater; star network; switching hub.

human engineering *n.* ergonomics.

HyperCard *n.* a hypertext programming environment for the Macintosh, introduced by Apple in 1987.

⇒ See also authoring tool; hypertext.

hyperlink *n.* an element in an electronic document that links to another place in the same document or in an entirely different one.

⇒ See also hypermedia; hypertext.

hypermedia *n.* an extension to hypertext that supports linking graphics, sound, and video elements in addition to text elements.

⇒ See also hyperlink; hypertext; multimedia; World Wide Web.

Hypertext *n.* a special type of database system, invented by Ted Nelson in the 1960s, in which objects (text, pictures, music, programs, and so on) can be creatively linked to each other.

⇒ See also authoring tool; Help; HTML; HyperCard; hyperlink; hypermedia; multimedia; SGML.

Hypertext Markup Language *n.* See HTML.

HyperText Transfer Protocol *n.* See HTTP.

HyperText Transport Protocol *n.* See HTTP.

hyphenation *n.* in word processing, splitting a word that would otherwise extend beyond the right margin.

⇒ See also word processing; word wrap.

I i

I2 Internet 2: a global network being developed cooperatively by about 100 universities. It will support high bandwidths required by such applications as live video and is expected to be 100 to 1,000 times faster than the current Internet.
⇒ See also INTERNET; NGI INITIATIVE; vBNS.

I2O I/O architecture being developed by a consortium of computer companies called the I2O Special Interest Group (SIG). It is designed to eliminate I/O bottlenecks by utilizing special I/O processors (IOPs) that handle the details of interrupt handling, buffering, and data transfer. Also called **Intelligent I/O.**
⇒ See also I/O; PCI.

IA-64 See under MERCED.

IAB INTERNET ARCHITECTURE BOARD.

IAC Internet Access Coalition: a consortium of companies involved in the Internet—including AT&T, Microsoft, and MCI—whose stated purpose is to maintain the affordability of Internet access over telephone lines and accelerate the availability of inexpensive digital telephone network connections to the Internet.
⇒ See also INTERNET.

IAHC Internet International Ad Hoc Committee: the international organization responsible for managing the Internet's domain name system (DNS).
⇒ See also DNS; DOMAIN NAME.

IANA Internet Assigned Numbers Authority: an organization working under the auspices of the Internet Architecture Board (IAB) that is responsible for assigning new Internet-wide Internet Protocol (IP) addresses.
⇒ See also INTERNET ARCHITECTURE BOARD; IP ADDRESS.

I-beam pointer *n.* a pointer shaped like a capital I, used in graphics-based text-processing applications.
⇒ See also INSERTION POINT; POINTER.

IBM International Business Machines: the largest

computer company in the world. IBM started in 1911 as a producer of punch card tabulating machines, introduced its first computer in 1953, dominated the field of mainframe and minicomputers in the 1960s and 1970s, and launched its first personal computer in 1981.

⇒ See also AS/400; IBM PC; MAINFRAME.

IBM compatible *n.* IBM PC.

IBM PC *n.* **1.** one of a family of personal computers produced by IBM. **2.** Also called **IBM clone, IBM compatible**. a computer that conforms to a set of loosely controlled industry standards that originally reflected those of IBM but are now somewhat more independent.

⇒ See also COMPATIBLE; IBM; PC.

ICC See under SMART CARD.

ICMP Internet Control Message Protocol: an extension to the Internet Protocol (IP) defined by RFC 792. It supports packets containing error, control, and informational messages.

⇒ See also IP; PING.

icon *n.* a small picture that represents an object or program: a principal feature of graphical user interfaces.

⇒ See also GRAPHICAL USER INTERFACE.

IDE 1. See under IDE INTERFACE. **2.** See under INTEGRATED DEVELOPMENT ENVIRONMENT.

⇒ See also IDE INTERFACE; INTEGRATED; VISUAL C++.

IDE interface *n.* Intelligent Drive Electronics or Integrated Drive Electronics: an interface for mass storage devices in which the controller is integrated into the disk or CD-ROM drive.

⇒ See also ATA; EIDE; INTERFACE; SCSI; ST-506 INTERFACE.

identifier *n.* NAME.

⇒ See also VARIABLE.

IE INTERNET EXPLORER.

IEEE (ī′ trip′əl ē′), *n.* Institute of Electrical and Electronics Engineers: an organization of engineers, scientists, and students founded in 1884 and best known for developing standards for the computer and electronics industry.

⇒ See also ETHERNET; GIGABIT ETHERNET; IEEE 802 STANDARDS; TOKEN-RING NETWORK.

IEEE 1394 *n.* a very fast external bus standard that supports data transfer rates of up to 400 Mbps (400 million bits per second).
⇒ See also DEVICE BAY; HOT PLUGGING; PCMCIA; PLUG-AND-PLAY; USB.

IEEE 802 IEEE 802 STANDARDS.

IEEE 802 standards *n.pl.* a set of network standards developed by the IEEE.
⇒ See also DLC; ETHERNET; IEEE; LOCAL-AREA NETWORK; MAN; TOKEN BUS NETWORK; TOKEN-RING NETWORK.

IETF Internet Engineering Task Force: the main standards organization for the Internet, open to any interested individual.
⇒ See also INTERNET; INTERNET ARCHITECTURE BOARD; INTERNET SOCIETY; RFC; SSL; STANDARD.

IFC Internet Foundation Classes: a set of Java classes developed by Netscape that enables programmers to easily add GUI elements, such as windows, menus, and buttons.
⇒ See also AFC; AWT; CLASS; JAVA; JDK.

IGES Initial Graphics Exchange Specification: an ANSI graphics file format for three-dimensional wire frame models.
⇒ See also ANSI; GRAPHICS FILE FORMATS.

IIOP Internet Inter-ORB Protocol: a protocol developed by the Object Management Group (OMG) to implement CORBA solutions over the World Wide Web, enabling browsers and servers to exchange integers, arrays, and more complex objects.
⇒ See also CORBA; OMG.

IIS Internet Information Server: Microsoft's Web server that runs on Windows NT platforms.
⇒ See also ISAPI; WEB SERVER.

illegal page fault *n.* See under PAGING.

image editor *n.* a graphics program that provides a variety of special features for altering bit-mapped images, such as filters and image transformation algorithms, and the ability to create and superimpose layers.

⇒ See also IMAGE ENHANCEMENT; PAINT PROGRAM; PHOTO ILLUSTRATION.

image enhancement *n.* in computer graphics, the process of improving the quality of a digitally stored image by manipulating the image with software.

⇒ See also ADOBE PHOTOSHOP; DIGITAL PHOTOGRAPHY; IMAGE EDITOR; IMAGE PROCESSING; PHOTO ILLUSTRATION; PHOTO SCANNER.

image map or **imagemap** *n.* a single graphic image containing more than one hot spot: used extensively on the World Wide Web.

⇒ See also GIF; HOT SPOT.

image processing *n.* analysis and manipulation of images with a computer.

⇒ See also DIGITAL PHOTOGRAPHY; GRAPHICS; IMAGE ENHANCEMENT; PHOTO SCANNER.

imagesetter *n.* a typesetting device that produces very-high-resolution output on paper or film.

⇒ See also DESKTOP PUBLISHING; ISP; LaTeX; LINOTRONIC; POSTSCRIPT.

ImageWriter *n.* any in a family of dot-matrix printers that Apple offers for the Macintosh computer.

⇒ See also DOT-MATRIX PRINTER; LASERWRITER; MACINTOSH COMPUTER; PRINTER.

IMAP *n.* Internet Message Access Protocol: a protocol for retrieving e-mail messages, developed at Stanford University in 1986.

⇒ See also POP; SMTP.

impact printer *n.* a class of printers, as dot-matrix printers, daisy-wheel printers, and line printers, that work by striking a hammer or pin against an ink ribbon, or against an object that in turn strikes the ink ribbon, to make a mark on the paper.

⇒ See also DAISY-WHEEL PRINTER; DOT-MATRIX PRINTER; INK-JET PRINTER; LINE PRINTER; PRINTER.

import *v.t.* to bring (documents, data, etc.) into one application program from another.

⇒ See also COMMA-DELIMITED; CONVERT; EXPORT; FILTER; MIDDLEWARE.

in-betweening *n.* TWEENING.

inclusive OR operator *n.* a Boolean operator that returns a value of TRUE if either or both of its operands is TRUE.
⇒ See also BOOLEAN OPERATOR.

increment *n.* **1.** the act or process of increasing. **2.** the amount added by increasing.
⇒ See also DECREMENT; LOOP.

incremental backup *n.* a procedure that backs up only those files that have been modified since the previous backup.
⇒ See also ARCHIVAL BACKUP; BACKUP.

Indeo *n.* a codec (compression/decompression technology) for computer video developed by Intel Corporation.
⇒ See also CINEPAK; CODEC; DVI; MPEG.

index *n.* **1.** in database design, a list of keys (or keywords), each of which identifies a unique record. —*v.i.* **2.** to create an index for a database, or to find records using an index.
⇒ See also HASHING; ISAM; KEY; KEYWORD.

Indexed Sequential Access Method *n.* See ISAM.

Industry Standard Architecture (ISA) bus *n.* the bus architecture used in the IBM PC/XT and PC/AT. *Abbr.:* ISA bus
⇒ See also AT BUS; BUS; EISA; LOCAL BUS; PCI; PLUG-AND-PLAY.

Information Services *n.* See IS.

information superhighway *n.* a term used to describe the Internet, bulletin board services, online services, and other services that enable people to obtain information from telecommunications networks.
⇒ See also BULLETIN BOARD SYSTEM; ONLINE SERVICE; TELECOMMUNICATIONS.

Information Systems *n.* See IS.

Information Technology *n.* See IT.

Informix *n.* one of the fastest-growing DBMS software companies.
⇒ See also DATABASE MANAGEMENT SYSTEM; ORACLE; SYBASE.

Infoseek *n.* a World Wide Web search engine developed by Infoseek Corporation that provides categorized lists of Web sites.

⇒ See also ALTA VISTA; EXCITE; HOTBOT; LYCOS; OPEN TEXT; SEARCH ENGINE; WEBCRAWLER; YAHOO!.

Infrared Data Association *n.* See IRDA.

INI *n.* See under .INI FILE.

.INI file (dot′ in′ē fīl′), *n.* a file that has a .INI extension and contains configuration information for MS-Windows.

⇒ See also EXTENSION.

init *n.* **1.** on Macintoshes, an old term for SYSTEM EXTENSIONS. —*v.t.* **2.** INITIALIZE.

⇒ See also EXTENSION.

Initial Graphics Exchange Specification *n.* See IGES.

initialize *v.t.* **1.** on Apple Macintosh computers, to format (a disk). **2.** in programming, to assign a starting value to (a variable). **3.** to start up (a program or system).

⇒ See also ASSIGN; FORMAT; VARIABLE.

ink-jet printer *n.* a type of printer that has magnetized plates that direct a spray of ionized ink onto the paper in the desired shapes.

⇒ See also COLOR PRINTER; FONT; FONT CARTRIDGE; LASER PRINTER; PRINTER; SOLID INK-JET PRINTER.

input *n.* **1.** whatever goes into the computer, as commands entered from the keyboard or data from another computer or device. —*v.t.* **2.** to enter (data) into a computer.

⇒ See also I/O; OUTPUT.

input device *n.* any instrument that feeds data into a computer, as a keyboard, a mouse, or a trackball.

⇒ See also DEVICE; I/O; LIGHT PEN; MOUSE; OUTPUT; TRACKBALL.

input/output *n.* See I/O.

insert *v.t.* to place (an object) between two other objects.

⇒ See also APPEND; INS KEY; INSERT MODE.

insertion point *n.* in graphics-based programs, the point where the next characters typed from the keyboard will appear on the display screen, usually represented by a blinking vertical line.

⇒ See also I-BEAM POINTER; INSERT MODE; POINTER.

Insert key *n.* a key on computer keyboards that turns insert mode on and off.
⇒ See also INSERT MODE.

insert mode *n.* a text-entry mode in the editor that inserts all characters typed at the cursor position (or to the right of the insertion point).
⇒ See also INSERT KEY; INSERTION POINT; OVERSTRIKE.

Ins key *n.* INSERT KEY.

instant messaging *n.* a type of communications service that enables the user to create a private chat room with another individual.
⇒ See also CHAT; E-MAIL; FINGER.

Institute of Electrical and Electronics Engineers *n.* See IEEE.

instruction *n.* a basic command.
⇒ See also CISC; COMMAND; MACHINE LANGUAGE; MICROCODE; RISC; SUPERSCALAR.

integer *n.* a whole number.
⇒ See also CHARACTER STRING; DATA TYPE; FLOATING-POINT NUMBER.

integrated *adj.* **1.** referring to two or more components merged together into a single system. **2.** referring to applications that combine word processing, database management, spreadsheet functions, and communications into a single package.
⇒ See also IDE; MIDDLEWARE.

integrated circuit *n.* a small electronic device made out of a semiconductor material, used in microprocessors, audio and video equipment, automobiles, etc. Also called **chip.**
⇒ See also ASIC; CHIP; PLD; SEMICONDUCTOR; TRANSISTOR.

integrated development environment (IDE) *n.* a programming environment integrated into an application.
⇒ See also POWERBUILDER.

Integrated Drive Electronics *n.* See IDE.

integrated services digital network *n.* See ISDN.

Intel *n.* the world's largest manufacturer of computer chips.
⇒ See also AMD; CYRIX; DVI; INTEL MICROPROCESSORS; NEC; PCI; WINTEL.

Intellifont *n.* a scalable font technology that is part of Hewlett-Packard's PCL 5 page description language (PDL).
⇒ See also PAGE DESCRIPTION LANGUAGE (PDL); PCL; SCALABLE FONT.

Intelligent Drive Electronics *n.* See IDE.

Intelligent I/O *n.* See I2O.

intelligent terminal *n.* a terminal (monitor and keyboard) with processing power.
⇒ See also DUMB TERMINAL; SMART TERMINAL; TERMINAL.

Intel microprocessor *n.* a microprocessor made by Intel Corporation: the basic chip in all PCs.
⇒ See also ALPHA PROCESSOR; MICROPROCESSOR; MULTITASKING; PENTIUM II; PENTIUM MICROPROCESSOR; PENTIUM PRO; REGISTER; RISC.

interactive *adj.* accepting input from a human; allowing users to enter data or commands. Most popular programs, such as word processors, are interactive.

interface *n.* **1.** something that connects two separate entities, as a user interface that connects the computer with a human operator (user). —*v.i.* **2.** to communicate, as two devices that transmit data between each other.
⇒ See also USER INTERFACE.

interlacing *n.* **1.** a display technique in which the electron guns draw only half the horizontal lines on each pass, enabling a monitor to provide more resolution inexpensively but resulting in a slower reaction time. **2.** preparing a graphic image so that alternating rows are displayed in separate passes: esp. prevalent on the World Wide Web.
⇒ See also CRT; MONITOR; REFRESH; RESOLUTION.

interleave *v.t.* to arrange (data) in a noncontiguous way, as on a disk drive to make the drive more efficient and thus increase performance, or as in memory.
⇒ See also DISK; DISK DRIVE; INTERLEAVED MEMORY; SECTOR; TRACK.

interleaved memory *n.* main memory divided into two or more sections so that the CPU can ac-

cess alternate sections immediately, without waiting for memory to catch up (through wait states).
⇒ See also ACCESS TIME; CACHE; CLOCK SPEED; DYNAMIC RAM; FPM RAM; MEMORY; WAIT STATE.

internal bus *n.* EXPANSION BUS.

internal cache *n.* L1 CACHE.

internal command *n.* in DOS systems, any command that resides in the COMMAND.COM file, such as COPY and DIR.
⇒ See also COMMAND; DOS; EXTERNAL COMMAND.

internal font *n.* RESIDENT FONT.

internal modem *n.* a modem on an expansion board that plugs into a computer.
⇒ See also EXPANSION BOARD; EXTERNAL MODEM; MODEM.

International Business Machines *n.* See IBM.

International Standards Organization *n.* See ISO.

International Telecommunication Union *n.* See ITU.

Internet *n.* a decentralized global network connecting millions of computers worldwide.
⇒ See also ARPANET; ATM; DIAL-UP ACCESS; FTP; GOPHER; I2; IAC; IETF; InterNIC; INTRANET; IP ADDRESS; MBONE; MOSAIC; NAP; NGI INITIATIVE; ONLINE SERVICE; USENET; vBNS; WORLD WIDE WEB.

Internet2 *n.* See I2.

Internet Access Coalition *n.* See IAC.

Internet Ad Hoc Committee *n.* See IAHC.

Internet appliance *n.* NETWORK COMPUTER.

Internet Architecture Board *n.* a technical advisory group of the Internet Society.
⇒ See also IANA; IETF; INTERNET SOCIETY; RFC.

Internet Assigned Numbers Authority *n.* See IANA.

Internet box *n.* NETWORK COMPUTER.

Internet Engineering Task Force *n.* See IETF.

Internet Explorer *n.* Microsoft's Web browser.
⇒ See also ACTIVEX CONTROL; BROWSER; CDF; NAVIGATOR; VBSCRIPT; WINDOWS 98.

Internet Foundation Classes *n.* See IFC.

Internet Information Server *n.* See IIS.

Internet Inter-ORB Protocol *n.* See IIOP.

Internet Message Access Protocol *n.* See IMAP.

Internet Phone *n.* either of two popular Voice on the Net products, one produced by Intel and the other developed by VocalTec Ltd.
⇒ See also INTERNET TELEPHONY; NETMEETING; TELEPHONY.

Internet Protocol *n.* See IP.

Internet Relay Chat *n.* See IRC.

Internet Service Provider *n.* See ISP.

Internet Society *n.* a nongovernmental, non-profit organization dedicated to maintaining and enhancing the Internet by means of committees such as the Internet Advisory Board and the Internet Engineering Task Force.
⇒ See also IETF; INTERNET ARCHITECTURE BOARD; STANDARD.

Internet telephony *n.* a category of hardware and software that enables people to use the Internet as the transmission medium for telephone calls.
⇒ See also COOLTALK; INTERNET; INTERNET PHONE; TELEPHONY.

internetworking *n.* the art and science of connecting individual local-area networks (LANs) to create wide-area networks (WANs), and connecting WANs to form even larger WANs, accomplished by means of routers, bridges, and gateways.
⇒ See also BRIDGE; CISCO SYSTEMS; LOCAL-AREA NETWORK; ROUTER; WIDE-AREA NETWORK.

Internetwork Packet eXchange *n.* See IPX.

InterNIC *n.* a collaborative project between AT&T and Network Solutions, Inc. (NSI), supported by the National Science Foundation, that offers services to users of the Internet.
⇒ See also DOMAIN NAME; INTERNET; IP ADDRESS.

interpolated resolution *n.* See under OPTICAL RESOLUTION.

interpreter *n.* a program that translates high-level instructions into an intermediate form, which it then executes.

⇒ See also BASIC; BYTECODE; COMPILE; COMPILER; JAVA; LISP; PAGE DESCRIPTION LANGUAGE (PDL); PERL; POSTSCRIPT; PROGRAMMING LANGUAGE; TCL.

interprocess communication *n.* a capability supported by some operating systems that allows one process to communicate with another process. The processes can be running on the same computer or on different computers connected through a network. *Abbr.:* IPC

⇒ See also DDE; MULTIPROCESSING; NAMED PIPES; NETWORK; OPERATING SYSTEM; PROCESS; SEMAPHORE.

interrupt *n.* **1.** a signal, as one generated by a keystroke or by a printer, informing a program that an event has occurred. —*v.i.* **2.** to send an interrupt signal.

⇒ See also EVENT; INTERRUPT VECTOR TABLE; IRQ.

interrupt request line *n.* See IRQ.

interrupt vector table *n.* a table of *interrupt vectors* (pointers to routines that handle interrupts). Also called **dispatch table.**

⇒ See also INTERRUPT; IRQ.

intranet *n.* a network, based on TCP/IP protocols developed for the Internet, belonging to an organization, usually a corporation, accessible only to the organization's members, employees, or others with authorization. An intranet's Web sites look and act just like other Web sites, but the firewall surrounding an intranet prevents unauthorized access.

⇒ See also ENTERPRISE; EXTRANET; FIREWALL; INTERNET; LOTUS NOTES; NETWORK.

invalid page fault *n.* a page fault that produces an error, as instability of the virtual memory system due to shortage of RAM or of free disk space. Also called **page fault error (PFE).**

⇒ See also CRASH; GPF; PAGE FAULT.

inverse video *n.* REVERSE VIDEO.

inverted tree *n.* See under TREE STRUCTURE.

invisible file *n.* HIDDEN FILE.

invocation *n.* the execution of a program or function.

⇒ See also INVOKE.

invoke *v.t.* to activate (a function or routine) in a program.
⇒ See also CALL; FUNCTION; ROUTINE.

I/O (ī/ō/), input/output: any operation, program, or device whose purpose is to enter data into a computer or to extract data from a computer.
⇒ See also I2O; INPUT; OUTPUT.

IP Internet Protocol: a set of rules that specifies the format of packets (also called **datagrams**) and the addressing scheme.
⇒ See also ICMP; IPNG; IPSEC; PACKET; TCP; TCP/IP; UDP.

IP address *n.* an identifier for a computer or device on a TCP/IP network. The format of an IP address is a 32-bit numeric address written as four numbers separated by periods. Each number can be from 0 to 255.
⇒ See also ARP; CIDR; DNS; DOMAIN NAME; IANA; INTERNET; InterNIC; IP SPOOFING; NAT; PING; ROUTING; SUBNET; TCP/IP; TLD; WHOIS; WINS.

IPC *n.* INTERPROCESS COMMUNICATION.

IP Multicast *n.* sending out data to distributed servers on the MBone (Multicast Backbone): more efficient than normal Internet transmissions because the server can broadcast a message to many recipients simultaneously.
⇒ See also MBONE; MULTICAST; REALVIDEO.

IPng *n.* Internet Protocol next generation: a version of the Internet Protocol (IP) currently being reviewed in IETF standards committees.
⇒ See also IP.

IPsec *n.* IP Security: a set of protocols being developed by the IETF to support secure exchange of packets at the IP layer.
⇒ See also IP; L2TP; SSL.

IP spoofing *n.* a technique used to gain unauthorized access to computers, whereby the intruder sends messages to a computer with an IP address indicating that the message is coming from a trusted source.
⇒ See also FIREWALL; HACKER; IP ADDRESS; ROUTER; SMURF; SPOOF.

IP switch *n.* See under IP SWITCHING.

IP switching *n.* a type of IP routing, developed

by Ipsilon Networks, Inc., that uses ATM hardware to speed packets through networks.
⇒ See also ATM; ROUTER; ROUTING; ROUTING SWITCH.

IPX Internetwork Packet Exchange: a networking protocol used by the Novell NetWare operating systems.
⇒ See also COMMUNICATIONS PROTOCOL; CONNECTIONLESS; NETWARE; SPX; UDP.

IPX/SPX See under SPX.

IRC Internet Relay Chat: a chat system developed by Jarkko Oikarinen in Finland in the late 1980s that enables people connected anywhere on the Internet to join in live discussions.
⇒ See also CHANNEL; CHAT; CHAT ROOM; INTERNET.

IrDA Infrared Data Association: a group of device manufacturers that developed a standard for transmitting data from one device to another via infrared light waves rather than cables.
⇒ See also PARALLEL PORT.

IRMA board *n.* an expansion board for PCs and Macintoshes that enables them to emulate IBM 3278 and 3279 mainframe terminals.
⇒ See also EMULATION; EXPANSION BOARD; STANDALONE; TERMINAL.

IRQ (*pronounced as separate letters*), interrupt request line: a hardware line over which devices can send interrupt signals to the microprocessor.
⇒ See also DIP SWITCH; EXPANSION BUS; INDUSTRY STANDARD ARCHITECTURE (ISA) BUS; INTERRUPT; INTERRUPT VECTOR TABLE.

IS (*pronounced as separate letters*), Information Systems *or* Information Services: the name of the department responsible for computers, networking, and data management. Also called **IT (Information Technology)**, **MIS (Management Information Services)**.
⇒ See also IT; MIS; SYSTEM MANAGEMENT.

ISA (ī′sə), *n.* Industry Standard Architecture. See INDUSTRY STANDARD ARCHITECTURE (ISA) BUS.

ISA bus *n.* INDUSTRY STANDARD ARCHITECTURE (ISA) BUS.

ISAM (ī′sam) *n.* Indexed Sequential Access Method: a method for managing the way a computer accesses records and files stored on a hard disk.

⇒ See also DATABASE MANAGEMENT SYSTEM; INDEX; RANDOM ACCESS; SEQUENTIAL ACCESS.

ISAPI *n.* Internet Server API: an API for Microsoft's IIS (Internet Information Server) Web server that enables programmers to develop Web-based applications that run much faster than conventional CGI programs because they are more tightly integrated with the Web server.

⇒ See also CGI; IIS; NSAPI; STATELESS.

ISDN integrated services digital network: an international communications standard for sending voice, video, and data over digital telephone lines.

⇒ See also ADSL; B-CHANNEL; BRI; BROADBAND ISDN (B-ISDN); CHANNEL BONDING; DirecPC; FDDI; FIBER OPTICS; GROUP 4 PROTOCOL; NDIS; SDSL; SPID; TERMINAL ADAPTER; xDSL.

ISO *n.* International Organization for Standardization: an international organization composed of national standards bodies from more than 75 countries. It has defined important computer standards, as OSI (Open Systems Interconnection), a standardized architecture for designing networks. [< Gk *ísos* equal]

⇒ See also ANSI; CMIP; ISO 9000; NETWORK; OSI; STANDARD.

ISO 9000 *n.* a family of standards approved by the International Organization for Standardization (ISO) that define a quality assurance program.

⇒ See also ISO; STANDARD.

ISOC INTERNET SOCIETY.

isochronous (ī sok′rə nəs), *adj.* time dependent: referring to processes where data must be delivered within certain time constraints.

⇒ See also ASYNCHRONOUS; ATM; IEEE 1394; REAL TIME; SYNCHRONOUS; THROUGHPUT.

ISO Latin 1 *n.* officially named ISO-8859-1, a standard character set developed by the International Organization for Standardization (ISO).

⇒ See also ANSI CHARACTER SET; ASCII; EXTENDED ASCII.

ISP Internet Service Provider: a company that provides access to the Internet for a monthly fee. Also called **IAP (Internet Access Provider)**.

⇒ See also DIAL-UP ACCESS; DirecPC; E-MAIL; INTERNET; MAE; NAP; NSP; RADIUS; T-1 CARRIER; T-3 CARRIER; USENET; WORLD WIDE WEB.

ISV Independent Software Vendor: a company that produces software.

⇒ See also SOFTWARE.

IT (*pronounced as separate letters*), Information Technology: the broad subject concerned with all aspects of managing and processing information, especially within a large organization or company. Also called **IS (Information Services), MIS (Management Information Services)**.

⇒ See also COMPUTER SCIENCE; IS; MIS; SYSTEM MANAGEMENT.

italic *adj.* in typography, referring to fonts with characters slanted to the right.

⇒ See also FONT.

iteration *n.* a single pass through a group of instructions.

⇒ See also LOOP.

ITU International Telecommunication Union: an intergovernmental organization through which public and private organizations develop telecommunications: founded in 1865, United Nations agency since 1947.

⇒ See also CCITT; DSVD; H.323; STANDARD; TELECOMMUNICATIONS; V.35; V.90; X.500.

IVT INTERRUPT VECTOR TABLE.

J j

jaggies *n.pl.* stairlike lines that appear on a display monitor or on printed output where there should be smooth curves or smooth, straight diagonal lines.
⇒ See also ANTIALIASING; SMOOTHING.

Java *n.* a high-level general purpose programming language developed by Sun Microsystems and used to create interactive applications that can run over the Internet.
⇒ See also ACTIVEX; APPLET; AWT; BYTECODE; C++; CGI; DYNAMIC HTML; HOTJAVA; IFC; INTERPRETER; JAVABEANS; JAVASCRIPT; JDBC; JIT; OBJECT-ORIENTED PROGRAMMING; PROGRAMMING LANGUAGE; RMI; SMALLTALK; SUN MICROSYSTEMS; THIN CLIENT; VIRTUAL MACHINE.

JavaBeans *n.* a specification developed by Sun Microsystems that defines how Java objects interact. Java program fragments that conform to it can work together on any platform.
⇒ See also ACTIVEX CONTROL; JAVA; JDK.

Java Database Connectivity *n.* See JDBC.

Java Development Kit *n.* See JDK.

JavaScript *n.* a scripting language for Netscape's Web browser that helps Web authors design interactive sites.
⇒ See also DOM; DYNAMIC HTML; HTML; JAVA; JSCRIPT; SCRIPT; VBSCRIPT.

JavaSoft *n.* the business unit of Sun Microsystems that is responsible for Java technology.
⇒ See also HOTJAVA; JAVA; JDBC; JDK; SUN MICROSYSTEMS.

Java VM *n.* See under VIRTUAL MACHINE.

Jaz drive *n.* a removable disk drive developed by Iomega Corporation, that has a 12-ms average seek time and a transfer rate of 5.5 Mbps.
⇒ See also REMOVABLE HARD DISK.

JDBC Java Database Connectivity: a Java API that enables Java programs to interact with any SQL-compliant database.
⇒ See also JAVA; JAVASOFT; JDK; ODBC; SQL.

JDK Java Development Kit: a software development kit (SDK) for producing Java programs.

⇒ See also AFC; IFC; JAVA; JAVABEANS; JAVASOFT; JDBC; SDK.

Jet *n.* Joint engine technology: the database engine used by Microsoft Office and Visual Basic.

⇒ See also DAO; VISUAL BASIC.

JIT just-in-time compiler: a code generator that converts Java bytecode into machine language instructions.

⇒ See also BYTECODE; COMPILER; JAVA; VIRTUAL MACHINE.

job *n.* a task performed by a computer system, as printing a file.

⇒ See also PROGRAM; TASK.

join *v.t.* in relational databases, to match (tables that have a common field, called a *join field*). The process is called a *join operation*.

⇒ See also DATABASE; FIELD; QUERY; RDBMS.

Joint Photographic Experts Group *n.* See JPEG.

joystick *n.* a lever that moves in all directions and controls the movement of a pointer or some other display symbol, as for use in computer games, CAD/CAM systems, etc.

⇒ See also MOUSE; POINTER.

JPEG (jā′peg′), *n.* Joint Photographic Experts Group: a lossy compression technique for color images that can reduce files to about 5 percent of their normal size.

⇒ See also DATA COMPRESSION; DCT; MOTION-JPEG; MPEG.

.jpg the file extension for a JPEG-encoded image.

JScript *n.* Microsoft's version of NetScape's JavaScript, which is built into Internet Explorer (IE) browsers: not fully compatible with JavaScript.

⇒ See also JAVASCRIPT; VBSCRIPT.

Jughead *n.* a search engine for Gopher sites.

⇒ See also GOPHER; SEARCH ENGINE; VERONICA.

jumper *n.* a metal bridge that closes an electrical circuit to enable a hardware option, usu. consisting of a plastic plug that fits over a pair of protruding pins.

⇒ See also CONFIGURATION; CONFIGURE; EXPANSION BOARD.

justification *n.* alignment of text along a margin.

⇒ See also ALIGNMENT; FEATHERING; LEADING; MICROSPACING; VERTICAL JUSTIFICATION.

justify *v.t.* in word processing, to align (text) along the left and right margins.

⇒ See also FLUSH; JUSTIFICATION.

just-in-time compiler *n.* See JIT.

K k

K kilo: 1,000 for communications purposes, as 56 Kbps (56,000 bits per second); 1,024 when discussing memory and file sizes, as 64 KB (65,536 bytes).
⇒ See also CHANNEL BONDING; MODEM; V.90; X2.

K56flex *n.* a technology developed by Lucent Technologies and Rockwell International for delivering data rates up to 56 Kbps over plain old telephone service (POTS) by taking advantage of high-speed digital lines by which most phone switching stations are connected.
⇒ See also CHANNEL BONDING; MODEM; V.90; X2.

K6 a microprocessor from AMD that supports the MMX instruction set and is completely compatible with Intel's Pentium processors.
⇒ See also AMD; MMX; PENTIUM MICROPROCESSOR; SOCKET 7.

KB kilobyte: in reference to data storage, 1,024 bytes; In reference to data transfer rates, 1,000 bytes.
⇒ See also KILOBYTE.

Kbps kilobits per second: a measure of data transfer speed, as by a modem. One Kbps is 1000 bits per second.
⇒ See also DATA TRANSFER RATE; KILOBIT; MODEM.

Kerberos (kûr′bə ros′), *n.* an authentication system developed at the Massachusetts Institute of Technology (MIT) that is designed to enable two parties to exchange private information across an otherwise open network by means of a unique key, called a *ticket*.
⇒ See also AUTHENTICATION; SECURITY.

Kermit *n.* a communications protocol and set of associated software utilities developed at Columbia University that can be used to transfer files or for terminal emulation. It is frequently used with modem connections but also supports communications via other transport mechanisms. ⇒ See also CCITT; COMMUNICATIONS; COMMUNICATIONS SOFTWARE; FTP; FULL DUPLEX; MNP; MODEM; PROTOCOL; TERMINAL EMULATION; XMODEM; ZMODEM.

kernel *n.* the central module of an operating system, responsible for memory management, process and task management, and disk management.
⇒ See also OPERATING SYSTEM.

kerning *n.* in typography, adjusting the space between characters, esp. by placing two characters closer together than normal, so as to make them look better.
⇒ See also DESKTOP PUBLISHING; FONT; WORD PROCESSING.

key *n.* **1.** a button on a keyboard. **2.** Also called **key field, sort key, index, keyword.** in database management systems, a field used to sort data, as an age field, a data field, or the like. **3.** a password or table needed to decipher encoded data.
⇒ See also DATABASE MANAGEMENT SYSTEM; ENCRYPTION; FIELD; HASHING; INDEX; NORMALIZATION; PASSWORD; REFERENTIAL INTEGRITY; SYMMETRIC-KEY CRYPTOGRAPHY.

keyboard *n.* the set of typewriter-like keys used to enter data into a computer: includes alphanumeric keys, punctuation keys, and special keys that perform a variety of functions.
⇒ See also ADB; ALPHANUMERIC; ALT KEY; ARROW KEYS; BACKSPACE KEY; BREAK KEY; CAPS LOCK KEY; CONTROL KEY; CURSOR; DELETE KEY; DVORAK KEYBOARD; END KEY; ENHANCED KEYBOARD; ENTER KEY.

keyboard buffer *n.* a memory area where data about which keys have been pressed is stored prior to processing.

keyboard template *n.* TEMPLATE (def. 1).

key field *n.* KEY (def. 1).

keypad *n.* NUMERIC KEYPAD.

keystroke *n.* the pressing of a key on a keyboard or keypad.
⇒ See also KEY; KEYBOARD.

keyword *n.* **1.** in text editing and database management systems, an index entry that identifies a specific record or document. **2.** in programming, a word that has a special meaning in a particular programming language, as for a command or parameter, and is therefore reserved by the program. Also called **reserved name.**

⇒ See also COMMAND; INDEX; PARAMETER; VARIABLE.

killer app *n.* See under APP.

⇒ See also APPLICATION.

kilobit *n.* 1,024 bits for data storage; 1,000 bits for data transmission.

⇒ See also BIT; KBPS; MEGABIT.

kilobyte *n.* **1.** 1,024 bytes. **2.** loosely, 1,000 bytes: a computer that has 256K main memory can store approximately 256,000 bytes (or characters).

⇒ See also BINARY; BYTE; GIGA (G); MEGABYTE; MEMORY.

kiosk *n.* a booth providing a computer-related service, as an automated teller machine (ATM).

⇒ See also TOUCH SCREEN.

kludge (klo͞oj), *n.* a derogatory term for a poor design.

⇒ See also HACK.

L1 cache *n.* Level 1 cache: a memory cache generally built into the microprocessor. Also called **primary cache**.
⇒ See also CACHE.

L2 cache *n.* Level 2 cache: cache memory that is generally external to the microprocessor. Also called **secondary cache**.
⇒ See also CACHE; L1 CACHE; PENTIUM MICROPROCESSOR; PENTIUM PRO; TAG RAM.

L2F LAYER TWO FORWARDING.

L2TP Layer Two Tunneling Protocol: an extension to the PPP protocol that enables ISPs to operate Virtual Private Networks (VPNs).
⇒ See also DIAL-UP ACCESS; IPSEC; LAYER TWO FORWARDING; PPTP; TUNNELING; VPN.

label *n.* **1.** a name. **2.** for mass storage devices, the name of a storage volume. **3.** in spreadsheet programs, any descriptive text placed in a cell. **4.** in programming languages, a particular location in a program, usu. a particular line of source code. **5.** a small, sticky piece of paper placed on an object to identify it.
⇒ See also CELL; DISK; MASS STORAGE; NAME; SPREADSHEET; VOLUME.

LAN *n.* LOCAL-AREA NETWORK.

landscape *adj.* in word processing and desktop publishing, pertaining to or producing output with lines of data parallel to the two longer sides of a page.
⇒ See also MONITOR; PORTRAIT; PRINTER; WORD PROCESSING.

language *n.* a set of characters and syntactic rules for their combination and use, by means of which a computer can be given directions: *machine language; programming language; fourth-generation language.*
⇒ See also ARTIFICIAL INTELLIGENCE; FOURTH-GENERATION LANGUAGE; MACHINE LANGUAGE; NATURAL LANGUAGE; PROGRAMMING LANGUAGE; SYNTAX.

laptop computer *n.* a small, flat portable computer, shaped like a briefcase and typically

weighing around 7 pounds. Also called **notebook computer**.
⇒ See also NOTEBOOK COMPUTER; PORTABLE.

large-scale integration *n.* the placement of thousands of electronic components on a single integrated circuit. *Abbr.:* LSI
⇒ See also CHIP; INTEGRATED CIRCUIT; VLSI.

laser printer *n.* a high-speed, high-resolution printer that utilizes a laser beam to form dot-matrix patterns and an electrostatic process to print a page at a time.
⇒ See also COLOR PRINTER; INK-JET PRINTER; LCD PRINTER; OFFSET PRINTING; OKIDATA; PAGE DESCRIPTION LANGUAGE (PDL); PCL; POSTSCRIPT; PRINTER; RESIDENT FONT; RESOLUTION ENHANCEMENT; SMOOTHING; SOFT FONT; TONER.

LaserWriter *n.* a family of Apple laser printers designed to run with a Macintosh computer.
⇒ See also IMAGEWRITER; LASER PRINTER; MACINTOSH COMPUTER; POSTSCRIPT; PRINTER; QUICKDRAW.

latency *n.* **1.** in general, the period of time that one component in a system must wait after requesting a particular action or piece of information from another component. **2.** in networking, the amount of time it takes a packet to travel from source to destination.
⇒ See also BANDWIDTH; QOS; WAIT STATE.

LaTeX *n.* a typesetting system based on the TeX text-formatting language that provides high-level macros.
⇒ See also MACRO; MUTEX; TEX.

launch *v.t.* to start (an application or a program).
⇒ See also EXECUTE; LOAD; RUN.

LAWN *n.* LOCAL-AREA WIRELESS NETWORK.

layer-3 switch *n.* ROUTING SWITCH.

Layer Two Forwarding *n.* a tunneling protocol developed by Cisco Systems that enables organizations to set up virtual private networks (VPNs) that use the Internet backbone to move packets.
⇒ See also CISCO SYSTEMS; L2TP; PPTP; TUNNELING; VPN.

layout *n.* **1.** in word processing and desktop publishing, the arrangement of text and graphics, as on a page or display screen. **2.** in database management systems, the way information is displayed.

⇒ See also DATABASE MANAGEMENT SYSTEM; DESKTOP PUBLISHING; FIELD; REPORT WRITER; WORD PROCESSING; WYSIWYG.

LBA logical block addressing: a method used in DOS and Windows to translate the cylinder, head, and sector specifications of a SCSI or IDE disk drive that is larger than 528 MB into addresses that can be used by an enhanced BIOS.

⇒ See also CYLINDER; DISK DRIVE; HEAD; SECTOR.

LCD liquid crystal display: an information display, as on digital watches, calculators, and portable computers, that uses a liquid-crystal film that changes its optical properties when a voltage is applied.

⇒ See also ACTIVE-MATRIX DISPLAY; BACKLIGHTING; CSTN; DLP; DSTN; ELECTROLUMINESCENT DISPLAY (ELD); FLAT-PANEL DISPLAY; GAS-PLASMA DISPLAY; LCD MONITOR; LCD PRINTER; LED; NOTEBOOK COMPUTER; SUPERTWIST; TFT.

LCD monitor *n.* a monitor that uses LCD technologies rather than the conventional CRT technologies used by most desktop monitors.

⇒ See also COLOR MONITOR; CRT; FLAT-PANEL DISPLAY; LCD; MONITOR.

LCD printer *n.* a type of printer, similar to a laser printer, that shines a light through a liquid crystal panel to form dot-matrix patterns.

⇒ See also LASER PRINTER; LCD; PIXEL.

LDAP *n.* Lightweight Directory Access Protocol: a set of protocols for accessing information directories.

⇒ See also ACTIVE DIRECTORY; DIRECTORY SERVICE; NDS; PUBLIC-KEY ENCRYPTION; TCP/IP.

leader *n.* a row of dots, dashes, or other characters that leads the eye from one text element to another, as in a table of contents.

leading (led′ing), *n.* a typographical term that refers to the vertical space between lines of text. Also called **line spacing.**

⇒ See also FONT; JUSTIFICATION; POINT; VERTICAL JUSTIFICATION.

leading zero (lē′ding), *n.* a zero that appears in the leftmost digit(s) of a number.

leaf *n.* an item, as a file, at the very bottom of a hierarchical tree structure.
⇒ See also HIERARCHICAL; NODE; TREE STRUCTURE.

learn mode *n.* a mode in which a program records a user's keystrokes and other actions, as when defining a macro.
⇒ See also MACRO.

leased line *n.* a permanent telephone or data connection between two points set up by a telecommunications common carrier and used by businesses to connect geographically distant offices.
⇒ See also DIAL-UP ACCESS; FRACTIONAL T-1; T-1 CARRIER; T-3 CARRIER; TDM; TELECOMMUNICATIONS.

LED light emitting diode: an electronic device that lights up when electricity is passed through it: used for displaying readings on digital watches, calculators, etc.
⇒ See also LASER PRINTER; LCD.

LED printer *n.* a type of printer, similar to a laser printer, that uses an array of LEDs to form patterns on the page.

left justify *v.t.* to align (text) along the left margin.
⇒ See also FLUSH; JUSTIFY.

legacy application *n.* an application in which a company or organization has already invested considerable time and money, as a database management system running on a mainframe or minicomputer. It is important that new software products be compatible with a company's legacy applications because these programs can be very difficult to modify or replace.
⇒ See also APPLICATION; MAINFRAME; MINICOMPUTER.

legend *n.* in presentation graphics, text that describes the meaning of colors and patterns used in the chart.
⇒ See also PRESENTATION GRAPHICS.

letter-quality *adj.* referring to or producing print that has the same quality as that produced by a typewriter.
⇒ See also DAISY-WHEEL PRINTER; DOT-MATRIX

PRINTER; DRAFT QUALITY; INK-JET PRINTER; LASER PRINTER; NEAR LETTER QUALITY; PRINTER.

Level 2 cache *n*. L2 CACHE.

library *n*. **1.** a collection of files. **2.** in programming, a collection of precompiled routines, or modules, that a program can use.

⇒ See also DLL; LINKER; MODULE; OBJECT CODE; ROUTINE; RUNTIME.

light bar *n*. on a display screen, a highlighted region that indicates a selected component in a menu.

⇒ See also HIGHLIGHT; MENU; REVERSE VIDEO.

light-emitting diode *n*. See LED.

light pen *n*. an input device analogous to a mouse that utilizes a light-sensitive detector to select objects on a display screen.

⇒ See also CAD/CAM; DISPLAY SCREEN; INPUT DEVICE; MOUSE; PIXEL; POINTER.

Lightweight Directory Access Protocol *n*. See LDAP.

Li-ion *n*. LITHIUM-ION (BATTERY).

LIM *n*. LIM MEMORY.

LIM memory *n*. an obsolete technique for adding memory to DOS systems: superseded by extended memory.

⇒ See also EEMS; EXPANDED MEMORY; EXTENDED MEMORY.

line *n*. **1.** a hardware circuit connecting two devices. **2.** in programming, a single program statement. **3.** in caches, a single data entry.

⇒ See also CHANNEL.

line art *n*. a type of graphic without any shading.

⇒ See also GRAPHICS.

line editor *n*. a primitive type of editor that allows only one line of a file to be edited at a time.

⇒ See also EDITOR.

line feed *n*. **1.** a code that moves the cursor on a display screen down one line. **2.** on a printer, a code that advances the paper one line. *Abbr.*: LF

⇒ See also ASCII; CARRIAGE RETURN.

line graph *n*. a type of graph that highlights trends by drawing connecting lines between data points.

⇒ See also BAR CHART; PIE CHART; PRESENTATION GRAPHICS.

line-interactive UPS *n.* a type of UPS that switches a computer to battery power when it detects a power problem, sometimes leaving the computer without power for several milliseconds before the switch can be effected. Also called **standby power system.**

line printer *n.* a high-speed printer capable of printing an entire line at one time but not capable of printing graphics.

⇒ See also IMPACT PRINTER; PRINTER.

line spacing *n.* LEADING.

lines per inch *n.* a measurement of the fineness of a halftone image.

⇒ See also HALFTONE.

link *v.t.* **1.** to bind (software or hardware objects) together. **2.** to paste (a copy of an object) into a document in such a way that it retains its connection with the original object. **3.** in spreadsheet programs, to take (data for particular cells) from another worksheet. —*v.i.* **4.** to execute a linker. —*n.* **5.** in communications, a line or channel over which data is transmitted. **6.** in data management systems, a pointer to another record. **7.** in some operating systems, such as UNIX, a pointer to a file. **8.** in hypertext systems, such as the World Wide Web, a reference to another document.

⇒ See also CHANNEL; COMMUNICATIONS; COMPILE; DATABASE MANAGEMENT SYSTEM; DLL; FILENAME; HOT LINK; LINKER; OLE; PATH; SPREADSHEET.

link edit *v.i.* to run a linker.

⇒ See also LINKER.

linker *n.* a program that combines object modules to form an executable program. Also called **link editor; binder.**

⇒ See also ADDRESS; COMPILE; EXECUTABLE FILE; MODULE; OBJECT CODE.

Lino *n.* LINOTRONIC.

⇒ See also IMAGESETTER; LINOTRONIC.

Linotronic *n.* a type of high-quality printer, also called an imagesetter, capable of printing at resolutions of up to 2,540 dots per inch.

⇒ See also IMAGESETTER.

Linux (lin′əks, lē′nəks), *n.* a freely distributable implementation of UNIX that runs on a number of hardware platforms, including Intel and Motorola microprocessors.
⇒ See also APACHE WEB SERVER; FREEBSD; GNU; UNIX.

liquid crystal display *n.* See LCD.

liquid crystal shutter printer *n.* LCD PRINTER.

LISP (lisp), *n.* list processor: a high-level programming language especially popular for artificial intelligence applications, developed in the early 1960s at MIT.
⇒ See also ARTIFICIAL INTELLIGENCE; GENETIC PROGRAMMING; HIGH-LEVEL LANGUAGE; PROGRAMMING LANGUAGE; PROLOG.

list *v.t.* to display (data) in an ordered format. —*n.* **2.** any ordered set of data.
⇒ See also DATA; DATA STRUCTURE.

listing *n.* a printout of text, usually a source program.
⇒ See also PRINTOUT; SOURCE CODE.

LISTSERV *n.* an automatic mailing list server developed by Eric Thomas for BITNET in 1986.
⇒ See also MAILING LIST SERVER; MAJORDOMO.

list server *n.* MAILING LIST SERVER.

literal *n.* in programming, a value, such as a number, a character, or a string, written exactly as it is meant to be interpreted.
⇒ See also CONSTANT; NAME; VARIABLE.

Lithium-Ion battery *n.* a type of battery containing Lithium: used for portable devices such as notebook computers.
⇒ See also BATTERY PACK; NiCad BATTERY PACK; NiMH BATTERY PACK.

little-endian *n.* See under BIG-ENDIAN.

load *v.t.* **1.** to install (software). **2.** to copy (a program) from a storage device into memory. **3.** in programming, to copy (data) from main memory into a data register. —*n.* **4.** in networking, the amount of traffic—that is, the data being carried by the network.
⇒ See also MAIN MEMORY; OPERATING SYSTEM; PROGRAM; REGISTER; TRAFFIC.

load balancing *n.* distributing processing and communications activity evenly across a computer network so that no single device is overwhelmed.

⇒ See also CLUSTERING; SERVER; THREE-TIER; TP MONITOR.

loader *n.* a component of an operating system that copies programs from a storage device to main memory, and also replaces the addresses where they can be executed.

⇒ See also LOAD; MAIN MEMORY; PROGRAM; VIRTUAL MEMORY.

local *adj.* in networks, referring to files, devices, and other resources at the user's workstation.

⇒ See also LOCAL-AREA NETWORK; NETWORK; REMOTE; WORKSTATION.

local-area network *n.* a computer network confined to a limited area, as a single building or group of buildings, linking workstations and personal computers so that data and devices such as printers can be shared.

⇒ See also APPLETALK; ARCNET; BRIDGE; CLIENT/SERVER ARCHITECTURE; DCC; E-MAIL; ETHERNET; IEEE 802 STANDARDS; INTERNETWORKING; MAN; NETWARE; NETWORK; NETWORK INTERFACE CARD; NETWORK OPERATING SYSTEM; NODE; NOVELL; PEER-TO-PEER ARCHITECTURE; PERSONAL COMPUTER; SNMP; SWITCHING HUB; TOKEN BUS NETWORK; TOKEN-RING NETWORK; TOPOLOGY; TOPS; VLAN; WIDE-AREA NETWORK.

local-area wireless network *n.* a type of local-area network that uses radio waves or infrared transmissions rather than wires to communicate between nodes. *Abbr.:* LAWN

⇒ See also LOCAL-AREA NETWORK.

local bus *n.* a data bus that connects directly, or almost directly, to the microprocessor.

⇒ See also BUS; EXPANSION BUS; PCI; VL-BUS.

local echo *n.* HALF DUPLEX.

LocalTalk *n.* the cabling scheme supported by the AppleTalk network protocol for Macintosh computers.

⇒ See also APPLETALK; ETHERNET; LOCAL-AREA NETWORK; MACINTOSH COMPUTER.

lock *v.t.* **1.** to make (a file, a database record, or other piece of data) inaccessible for writing so that two or more users do not attempt to modify the same file simultaneously. **2.** in Macintosh environments, to write-protect (a diskette).

⇒ See also DATABASE MANAGEMENT SYSTEM; FILE; LOCAL-AREA NETWORK; MULTI-USER; OPERATING SYSTEM; RECORD; WRITE-PROTECT.

log *v.t.* **1.** to record (an action), as to enter a record into a log file. —*n.* **2.** LOG FILE.

log file *n.* a file that lists actions that have occurred, as requests made to a Web server.

⇒ See also AUDIT TRAIL; COOKIE; LOG.

logical *adj.* **1.** referring to a user's view of the way data or systems are organized, as opposed to the physical, or actual, organization of a system. **2.** referring to any Boolean logic operation.

⇒ See also BOOLEAN LOGIC; PHYSICAL.

logical block address *n.* See LBA.

logical operator *n.* BOOLEAN OPERATOR.

log in *v.i.* LOG ON.

login *v.i.* LOG ON.

log off *v.i.* LOG OUT.

log on *v.i.* to gain access to a computer system or on-line service by entering some kind of personal identifier. Also, **log in, login.**

⇒ See also ACCESS CODE; LOG OUT; PASSWORD; USERNAME.

log out *v.i.* to terminate a session on a computer or on-line service. Also, **log off.**

⇒ See also LOG ON.

look-and-feel *n.* the general appearance and operation of a user interface.

⇒ See also USER INTERFACE.

loop *n.* in programming, a series of instructions that is repeated until a certain condition is met. Each pass through the loop is called an *iteration*.

⇒ See also FLOW CONTROL; ITERATION.

lossless compression *n.* any of the data compression techniques in which the original data can be recovered exactly. Lossless compression generally saves less space than lossy compression.

⇒ See also DATA COMPRESSION; LOSSY COMPRESSION; PKZIP.

lossy compression *n.* any of the data compression techniques, such as those used for video, in which some amount of data is lost because unnecessary information is eliminated.

⇒ See also DATA COMPRESSION; DCT; JPEG; LOSSLESS COMPRESSION.

Lotus 1-2-3 *n.* a spreadsheet program designed for IBM-compatible personal computers by Lotus Corporation in 1982: combines graphics, spreadsheet functions, and data management.

⇒ See also SPREADSHEET; VISICALC.

Lotus Notes *n.* a groupware application developed by Lotus (now part of IBM) that enables users to work with local copies of documents and have their modifications propagated throughout an entire Notes network.

⇒ See also GROUPWARE; INTRANET; REPLICATION.

lowercase *adj.* referring to small letters, as opposed to capital letters.

⇒ See also CASE SENSITIVE; UPPERCASE.

low-level format *n.* the first format of a hard disk, usu. performed at the factory, that sets the interleave factor and prepares the disk for a particular type of disk controller. Also called **physical format**.

⇒ See also CONTROLLER; FORMAT; INTERLEAVE.

low-level language *n.* a machine language or an assembly language.

⇒ See also ASSEMBLY LANGUAGE; HIGH-LEVEL LANGUAGE; LANGUAGE; MACHINE LANGUAGE; PROGRAMMING LANGUAGE.

low memory *n.* in DOS systems, the first 640K of memory, reserved for applications, device drivers, and memory-resident programs (TSRs). Also called **conventional memory**.

⇒ See also EXPANDED MEMORY; EXTENDED MEMORY; HIGH MEMORY; TSR.

low resolution *n.* See under RESOLUTION.

LPT a name frequently used by operating systems to identify a printer: an abbreviation for line printer terminal, now used to identify any type of printer.

⇒ See also PRINTER.

LPX a kind of motherboard used in some desktop model PCs in which expansion boards are inserted into a riser that contains several slots.

⇒ See also ATX; BABY AT; FORM FACTOR; MOTHERBOARD; NLX.

LQ LETTER-QUALITY.

LS-120 SUPERDISK.

LSI LARGE-SCALE INTEGRATION.

luggable *adj.* TRANSPORTABLE.

lurk *v.i.* to read messages in a chat room, newsgroup, or other on-line forum without posting messages in public.

⇒ See also CHAT ROOM; CONFERENCE; NEWSGROUP; SURF.

Lycos *n.* a popular World Wide Web search engine and directory.

⇒ See also ALTA VISTA; EXCITE; HOTBOT; INFOSEEK; OPEN TEXT; SEARCH ENGINE; WEBCRAWLER; YAHOO!.

LZW Lempel-Ziv-Welsh: a popular data compression technique developed in 1977 by J. Ziv and A. Lempel, and later refined by T. Welsh. It is the compression algorithm used in the GIF graphics file format, one of the standard graphics formats used by CompuServe and the World Wide Web.

⇒ See also DATA COMPRESSION; GIF; PNG; ZIP.

M m

M 1. mega or megabyte. **2.** MUMPS.
⇒ See also K; MEGABYTE.

Mac *n.* MACINTOSH COMPUTER.

MAC address *n.* Media Access Control address: a hardware address that uniquely identifies each node of a network.
⇒ See also ADDRESS; DLC; NETWORK INTERFACE CARD; NODE.

machine address *n.* ABSOLUTE ADDRESS.
⇒ See also ADDRESS.

machine code *n.* MACHINE LANGUAGE.

machine dependent *adj.* referring to a software application that runs only on a particular type of computer.
⇒ See also APPLICATION.

machine independent *adj.* able to run on a variety of computers.

machine language *n.* the lowest-level programming language (except for computers that utilize programmable microcode), consisting entirely of numbers. Machine language is the only language computers understand and is almost impossible for humans to use for programming. Therefore, programmers use either a high-level programming language or an assembly language; their programs are then translated into machine language.
⇒ See also ASSEMBLY LANGUAGE; INSTRUCTION; LOW-LEVEL LANGUAGE; MICROCODE.

machine readable *adj.* presented in a form that a computer can accept, as files stored on disk or tape, or data that comes from a device connected to a computer.
⇒ See also OPTICAL CHARACTER RECOGNITION.

Macintosh computer *n.* a computer made by Apple Computer, introduced in 1984 and featuring a graphical user interface (GUI) that utilizes windows, icons, and a mouse.
⇒ See also APPLE COMPUTER; CHRP; GRAPHICAL USER INTERFACE; PowerPC.

MacOS *n.* the official name of the Macintosh operating system.

⇒ See also APPLESCRIPT; BEOS; CHRP; FINDER; MULTIFINDER; OPERATING SYSTEM; SYSTEM.

macro *n.* **1.** a symbol, name, or key that represents a list of commands, actions, or keystrokes. **2.** in dBASE programs, a variable that points to another variable where the data is actually stored.

⇒ See also APPLESCRIPT; BATCH FILE; COMMAND; DBASE; LINK; LOOP; MACRO VIRUS; PROGRAM.

macro virus *n.* a type of computer virus that is encoded as a macro embedded in a document.

⇒ See also ANTIVIRUS PROGRAM; MACRO; VIRUS.

MAE *n.* Metropolitan Area Ethernet: a Network Access Point (NAP) where Internet Service Providers (ISPs) can connect with each other.

⇒ See also BACKBONE; ISP; NAP.

Magellan *n.* a Web directory published by the McKinley Group, now owned by Excite, Inc. [named after the explorer Ferdinand Magellan]

⇒ See also ALTA VISTA; EXCITE; YAHOO!

magic cookie *n.* a UNIX object; any of a group of tokens that are attached to files belonging to a user or program and change depending on the areas entered by the user or program.

magnetic disk *n.* a disk on which data is encoded as microscopic magnetized needles on the disk's surface, allowing the data to be erased and recorded any number of times.

magnetic tape *n.* TAPE.

magneto-optical (MO) drive *n.* a type of disk drive that combines magnetic disk technologies with CD-ROM technologies and that has a storage capacity of more than 200 megabytes.

⇒ See also CD-ROM; HARD DISK; MASS STORAGE; PHASE CHANGE DISK.

mail *n.* E-MAIL.

mailbox *n.* an area in memory or on a storage device where e-mail is placed.

mail client *n.* E-MAIL CLIENT.

mailing list *n.* a list of e-mail addresses identified by a single name, so that an e-mail message sent to the mailing list name is automatically forwarded to all the addresses in the list.

⇒ See also E-MAIL; E-MAIL CLIENT; MAILING LIST SERVER.

mailing list server *n.* a server that manages mailing lists for groups of users.

⇒ See also LISTSERV; MAILING LIST; MAJORDOMO.

mail merge *n.* a feature supported by many word processors that permits the user to personalize form letters by extracting specific information, such as a person's name, from a separate file of data. Also called **print merge.**

⇒ See also MERGE.

mainboard *n.* MOTHERBOARD.

mainframe *n.* a very large and expensive computer capable of supporting hundreds, or even thousands, of users simultaneously.

⇒ See also COMPUTER; HLLAPI; IBM; LEGACY APPLICATION; MICROPROCESSOR; MINICOMPUTER; MVS; SNA; SUPERCOMPUTER; VSAM.

main memory *n.* physical memory that is internal to the computer, as opposed to memory available on external mass storage devices such as disk drives. Also called **RAM.**

⇒ See also ADDRESS SPACE; CACHE; CHIP; CONVENTIONAL MEMORY; EXPANSION BOARD; EXTENDED MEMORY; LOADER; MEMORY; RAM; SWAP.

Majordomo *n.* a free mailing list server that runs under UNIX.

⇒ See also LISTSERV; MAILING LIST SERVER.

male connector *n.* a connector, as at the end of a cable or on a port, containing one or more exposed pins for inserting into a female connector.

MAN *n.* Metropolitan Area Network: a data network designed for a town or city usu. characterized by very-high-speed connections using fiber optical cable or other digital media.

⇒ See also IEEE 802 STANDARDS; LOCAL-AREA NETWORK; NETWORK; WIDE-AREA NETWORK.

Management Information Base *n.* See MIB.

management information system *n.* See MIS.

man page *n.* manual page: a page of on-line

documentation in UNIX systems.

⇒ See also DOCUMENTATION; HELP.

manual recalculation *n.* in spreadsheet programs, a mode in which formulas are not recalculated until the user explicitly (manually) runs the recalculation function.

⇒ See also AUTOMATIC RECALCULATION; RECALCULATE.

map *n.* **1.** a file that shows the structure of a program after it has been compiled and lists every variable in the program along with its memory address. —*v.t.* **2.** to make logical connections between (two entities). **3.** to copy (a set of objects) from one place to another while preserving the objects' organization.

⇒ See also COMPILE; DEBUG; PROGRAMMING LANGUAGE.

map file *n.* MAP (def. 1).

MAPI *n.* Messaging Application Programming Interface: a system built into Microsoft Windows that enables different e-mail applications to work together to distribute mail.

⇒ See also API; E-MAIL.

margins *n.pl.* in word processing, the strips of white space around the edge of the paper and the analogous strips of space shown on screen.

⇒ See also FLUSH; WORD PROCESSING; WORD WRAP.

marquee *n.* **1.** on Web pages, a scrolling area of text. **2.** in graphics software, a sizable and movable frame that identifies a selected portion of a bit-mapped image.

⇒ See also PAINT PROGRAM; SCROLL; SELECT; TAG.

mask *n.* a filter that selectively includes or excludes certain values, as in defining a database field.

⇒ See also FIELD; SUBNET MASK.

mask pitch *n.* in color monitors, the distance between holes in the shadow mask, usu. about .30 millimeters (mm). The tighter the mask pitch, the sharper the image.

⇒ See also COLOR MONITOR; DOT PITCH; RGB MONITOR.

massively parallel processing *n.* See MPP.

mass storage *n.* various techniques and devices, as floppy disks, hard disks, optical disks, and tapes, for storing large amounts of data. Unlike main memory, mass storage devices retain data even when the computer is turned off. Also called **auxiliary storage.**

⇒ See also DAT; ERASABLE OPTICAL DISK; FLOPPY DISK; HARD DISK; HSM; MAGNETO-OPTICAL (MO) DRIVE; MEMORY; OPTICAL DISK; RANDOM ACCESS; STORAGE DEVICE; TAPE.

Master Boot Record *n.* See MBR.

master/slave *adj.* referring to an architecture in which one device (the master) controls one or more other devices (the slaves).

math coprocessor *n.* See under COPROCESSOR.

mathematical expression *n.* any expression that represents a numeric value.

⇒ See also EXPRESSION.

matrix *n.* **1.** a two-dimensional array; that is, an array of rows and columns. **2.** the background area of color display.

⇒ See also ARRAY; BACKGROUND.

MAU *n.* **1.** Media Access Unit: an Ethernet transceiver. **2.** Also, **MSAU.** Multistation Access Unit: a token-ring network device that connects network computers in a star topology while retaining the logical ring structure.

⇒ See also HUB; TOKEN-RING NETWORK; TRANSCEIVER.

maximize *v.t.* in graphical user interfaces, to enlarge (a window) to maximum size.

⇒ See also GRAPHICAL USER INTERFACE; WINDOW; ZOOM.

MB *n.* megabyte (1,000,000 or 1,048,576 bytes, depending on the context).

⇒ See also MEGABYTE.

Mbone (em′bōn′), *n.* Multicast Backbone: an extension to the Internet to support IP multicasting—two-way transmission of data between multiple sites.

⇒ See also INTERNET; IP MULTICAST; MULTIMEDIA.

MBps megabytes per second: a measure of data transfer speed. Mass storage devices are generally measured in MBps.

⇒ See also DATA TRANSFER RATE.

Mbps megabits per second: a measure of data

transfer speed. Networks, for example, are generally measured in Mbps.

⇒ See also DATA TRANSFER RATE; GBPS; MEGABIT.

MBR Master Boot Record: a small program that resides on the first sector of the hard disk and is executed when a computer boots up.

⇒ See also BOOT; BOOTABLE DISKETTE; PARTITION; VIRUS.

Mbyte *n.* MEGABYTE.

MCA MICRO CHANNEL ARCHITECTURE.

MCGA multicolor/graphics array *or* memory controller gate array: the graphics system built into some older PCs.

⇒ See also CGA; EGA; GRAPHICS; MDA; MONITOR; VGA; VIDEO STANDARDS.

MCI 1. Media Control Interface: a high-level API developed by Microsoft and IBM for controlling multimedia devices, such as CD-ROM players and audio controllers, and supported by both OS/2 and Windows. **2.** a large telecommunications company.

⇒ See also API; MULTIMEDIA.

MDA monochrome display adapter: an old monochrome video standard for PCs that supports high-resolution monochrome text but does not support graphics or colors.

⇒ See also GRAPHICS; HERCULES GRAPHICS; MONITOR; MONOCHROME; PIXEL; RESOLUTION; VGA; VIDEO STANDARDS.

MDI Multiple Document Interface: a Windows API that enables programmers to easily create applications with multiple windows.

⇒ See also GRAPHICAL USER INTERFACE; WINDOW.

MDRAM (em′dē′ram′), *n.* Multibank DRAM: a memory technology developed by MoSys, Inc., that utilizes small banks of DRAM (32 KB each) in an array, where each bank has its own I/O port that feeds into a common internal bus. Because of this design, data can be read or written to multiple banks simultaneously, which makes it much faster than conventional DRAM.

⇒ See also DRAM; GRAPHICS ACCELERATOR; MEMORY; SDRAM; VIDEO ADAPTER; VRAM.

mean time between failures *n.* See MTBF.

media *n.pl.* **1.** objects on which data can be stored, as hard disks, floppy disks, CD-ROMs, and tapes. **2.** in computer networks, the cables linking workstations together, as twisted-pair wire (normal electrical wire), coaxial cable (the type of cable used for cable television), and fiber optic cable (glass cables). **3.** the form and technology used to communicate information, as sound, pictures, and videos.

⇒ See also DISK; FIBER OPTICS; LOCAL-AREA NETWORK; MASS STORAGE; MULTIMEDIA; NETWORK.

Media Control Interface *n.* See MCI.

meg *n.* MEGABYTE.

mega *n.* **1.** in decimal systems, one million. **2.** in binary systems, 2^{20}, or 1,048,576.

⇒ See also GIGA (G); KILOBYTE; MEGABYTE.

megabit *n.* **1.** when used to describe data storage, 1,024 kilobits. **2.** when used to described data transfer rates, one million bits.

⇒ See also BIT; GIGABIT; KILOBIT; Mbps.

megabyte *n.* **1.** when used to describe data storage, 1,048,576 (2^{20}) bytes. *Abbr.:* M; MB **2.** when used to describe data transfer rates, one million bytes.

⇒ See also BYTE; GIGABYTE; KILOBYTE.

megaflop *n.* See MFLOP.

megaFLOPS *n.* one million *FLOPS*.

megahertz *n.* See MHz.

membrane keyboard *n.* a type of keyboard in which the keys are covered by a transparent, plastic shell so that they have very little movement but are sensitive to pressure.

memory *n.* **1.** internal storage areas in the computer. **2.** physical memory, or the actual chips capable of holding data.

⇒ See also ADDRESS; CHIP; EEPROM; EPROM; MAIN MEMORY; MEMORY LEAK; NVRAM; PROM; RAM; RDRAM; ROM; VIRTUAL MEMORY; VRAM.

memory cache *n.* See under CACHE.

memory controller gate array *n.* See MCGA.

memory dump *n.* See under DUMP.

memory effect *n.* the property of nickel-cadmium (NiCad) batteries that causes them to lose their capacity for full recharging if they are discharged repeatedly the same amount and then recharged without overcharge before they have fully drained. The term derives from the fact that the battery appears to have a *memory* for the amount of charging it can sustain.

⇒ See also NiCAD BATTERY PACK.

memory leak *n.* a bug in a program that prevents it from freeing up memory it no longer needs and finally causes it to crash because it is out of memory.

⇒ See also BUG; MEMORY.

memory management unit *n.* See MMU.

memory resident *adj.* permanently in memory. Also called **RAM resident.**

⇒ See also MEMORY; OPERATING SYSTEM; SWAP; TSR.

menu *n.* a list of commands or options from which one can choose by highlighting the item and then pressing the Enter or Return key, or by simply pointing to the item with a mouse and clicking one of the mouse buttons.

⇒ See also CHOOSE; COMMAND DRIVEN; GRAPHICAL USER INTERFACE; MOVING-BAR MENU; POP-UP MENU, PULL-DOWN MENU; TEAR-OFF MENU; USER INTERFACE.

menu bar *n.* a horizontal menu that appears on top of a window. Usually, each option in a menu bar is associated with a pull-down menu.

⇒ See also MENU; WINDOW.

menu driven *adj.* referring to programs whose user interface employs menus.

⇒ See also COMMAND DRIVEN; MENU; USER INTERFACE.

Merced (mər sed′), *n.* the code name for a 64-bit microprocessor developed jointly by Intel and Hewlett-Packard that is designed primarily for use in servers and workstations. It uses a new architecture, officially known as *Intel Architecture-64 (IA-64)*, that employs cutting-edge microprocessor techniques.

⇒ See also INTEL MICROPROCESSORS; MICROPROCESSOR; PENTIUM MICROPROCESSOR.

merge *v.t.* **1.** to combine (two files) in such a way that the resulting file has the same organization as the two individual files. **2.** in word processing, to generate form letters by combining one file containing a list of names, addresses, and other information with a second file containing the text of the letter.

⇒ See also MAIL MERGE.

message box *n.* ALERT BOX.

Messaging Application Programming Interface *n.* See MAPI.

meta- in computer science, a prefix that means "about": *metadata; metalanguage; metafile.*

⇒ See also META TAG; METADATA.

metadata *n.* data about data. Metadata describes how and when and by whom a particular set of data was collected, and how the data is formatted.

⇒ See also DATA; DATA WAREHOUSE; DATABASE; META.

meta tag *n.* a special HTML tag that provides information about a Web page, such as who created the page, how often it is updated, what the page is about, and which keywords represent the page's content.

⇒ See also META; SEARCH ENGINE; TAG.

MFC Microsoft Foundation Classes: a large library of C + + classes developed by Microsoft.

⇒ See also AFC; C++; CLASS; VISUAL C++.

MFLOP *n.* mega floating-point operations per second: a common measure of the speed of computers used to perform floating-point calculations.

⇒ See also FLOATING-POINT NUMBER; MIPS.

MFLOPS *n.* See under FLOPS.

MFM modified frequency modulation: an encoding scheme used by PC floppy disk drives and older hard drives.

⇒ See also CONTROLLER; DISK DRIVE; MODULATE; RLL; ST-506 INTERFACE.

MFP multifunction peripheral: a single device that serves as a printer, a scanner, a fax machine, and a photocopier. Also called **multifunction printer.**

⇒ See also FAX MACHINE; OPTICAL SCANNER; PRINTER; SOHO.

MHz megahertz: one million cycles per second. The speed of microprocessors, called the clock speed, is measured in megahertz. For example, a microprocessor that runs at 200 MHz executes 200 million cycles per second.

⇒ See also BUS; CLOCK SPEED; OVERCLOCK.

MIB Management Information Base: a database of objects that can be monitored by a network management system.

⇒ See also NETWORK MANAGEMENT; SNMP.

micro *n.* **1.** MICROPROCESSOR. **2.** PERSONAL COMPUTER. **3.** a prefix meaning *one millionth*. **4.** a prefix meaning something very small: *microfloppy*.

⇒ See also MICROFLOPPY DISK.

Micro Channel Architecture *n.* a bus architecture for older PCs. *Abbr.:* MCA

⇒ See also AT BUS; BUS; LOCAL BUS.

microcode *n.* **1.** the lowest-level instructions that directly control a microprocessor. A single machine-language instruction typically translates into several microcode instructions. **2.** FIRMWARE.

⇒ See also INSTRUCTION; MACHINE LANGUAGE; MICROPROCESSOR.

Microcom Networking Protocol *n.* See MNP.

microcomputer *n.* PERSONAL COMPUTER.

microcontroller *n.* a highly integrated chip that contains all the components making up a controller, a CPU, RAM, some form of ROM, I/O ports, and timers.

⇒ See also CONTROLLER; EMBEDDED SYSTEM; MICROPROCESSOR.

microfloppy disk *n.* an old name for the small, 3.5-inch floppy disks.

⇒ See also DENSITY; DISK; FLOPPY DISK.

microjustification *n.* the use of microspacing to justify text.

⇒ See also MICROSPACING.

microprocessor *n.* a silicon chip that contains a CPU.

⇒ See also ALPHA PROCESSOR; BANDWIDTH; CHIP; CISC; CLOCK SPEED; CPU; CYRIX; MOORE'S LAW; OVERCLOCK; PENTIUM MICROPROCESSOR; POWERPC; SUPERSCALAR.

Microsoft *n.* the largest company in the personal computer industry, founded in 1975 by Paul Allen and Bill Gates. In addition to developing the de facto standard operating systems—DOS and Windows—Microsoft has a strong presence in almost every area of computer software, from programming tools to end-user applications.

⇒ See also ACTIVEX; DOS; INTERNET EXPLORER; MICROSOFT WORD; NETSCAPE; ODBC; WINDOWS; WINDOWS NT; WINTEL.

Microsoft Cluster Server n. See MSCS.

Microsoft Foundation Classes n. See MFC.

Microsoft Internet Explorer n. INTERNET EXPLORER.

Microsoft Network n. See MSN.

Microsoft Windows n. a family of operating systems for personal computers that provides a graphical user interface (GUI), virtual memory management, multitasking, and support for many peripheral devices.

⇒ See also DOS; INTEL MICROPROCESSORS; OPERATING SYSTEM; OS/2; WINDOWS 98; WINDOWS NT.

Microsoft Word n. a popular word processor from Microsoft.

⇒ See also MICROSOFT; WORD PROCESSING.

microspacing n. the insertion of variable-sized spaces between letters to justify text.

⇒ See also JUSTIFICATION; PRINTER.

middleware n. software that connects two otherwise separate applications, as a database system and a Web server. This allows users to request data from the database using forms displayed on a Web browser, and it enables the Web server to return dynamic Web pages based on the user's requests and profile.

⇒ See also DCE; EXPORT; IMPORT; INTEGRATED; ORB; RPC; THREE-TIER; TP MONITOR.

MIDI (mid′ē), n. musical instrument digital interface: a standard adopted by the electronic music industry for controlling devices, such as synthesizers and sound cards, that emit music.

⇒ See also AMIGA; AU; MACINTOSH COMPUTER; SOUND CARD; WAVE TABLE SYNTHESIS.

MIF Management Information Format: a format used to describe a hardware or software component. MIF files are used by DMI to report system configuration information. Although MIF is a system-independent format, it is used primarily by Windows systems. To install a new device in a Windows 95 system, the corresponding MIF file is needed.

⇒ See also CONFIGURATION; DMI.

millennium bug n. YEAR 2000 PROBLEM.

million instructions per second n. See MIPS.

millisecond n. one thousandth of a second. *Abbr.*: ms ⇒ See also ACCESS TIME.

MIME (mīm), n. Multipurpose Internet Mail Extensions: a specification for formatting non-ASCII messages so that they can be sent over the Internet.

⇒ See also BINHEX; E-MAIL; S/MIME; UUENCODE.

mini n. MINICOMPUTER.

minicomputer n. a midsized computer, usu. capable of supporting from 4 to about 200 users simultaneously.

⇒ See also AS/400; COMPUTER; LEGACY APPLICATION; MAINFRAME; MULTI-USER; VAX; WORKSTATION.

minifloppy n. a 5¼-inch floppy disk.
⇒ See also FLOPPY DISK.

minimize v.t. in graphical user interfaces, to convert (a window) into an icon.
⇒ See also GRAPHICAL USER INTERFACE; ICON; WINDOW.

minitower n. a type of computer somewhat smaller than a *tower model* but with the same sort of configuration, including vertically stacked power supply, motherboard, and mass storage devices.

MIPS n. million instructions per second: an old measure of a computer's speed and power.
⇒ See also CPU; FLOPS; MFLOP; SPEC.

MIS management information system *or* management information services: a class of software that provides managers with tools for organizing and evaluating their department. Typically, MIS systems are written in COBOL and run on mainframes or minicomputers. Also called **IS (Information Services; IT (Information Technology).**

⇒ See also COBOL; IS; IT; MAINFRAME; MINICOMPUTER; SYSTEM ADMINISTRATOR; SYSTEM MANAGEMENT.

M-JPEG MOTION-JPEG.

MMU memory management unit: the hardware component that manages virtual memory systems and includes a small amount of memory that holds a table matching virtual addresses to physical addresses.

⇒ See also CPU; PAGE FAULT; VIRTUAL MEMORY.

MMX a set of 57 multimedia instructions built into Intel's newest microprocessors and other x86-compatible microprocessors.

⇒ See also AMD; DSP; INTEL MICROPROCESSORS; K6.

MMX processor n. See MMX.

MMX Technology n. See MMX.

MNP Microcom Networking Protocol: a communications protocol developed by Microcom, Inc., that is used by many high-speed modems and that supports several different classes of communication, with each higher class providing additional features.

⇒ See also COMMUNICATIONS PROTOCOL; DATA COMPRESSION; ERROR DETECTION; KERMIT; MODEM; XMODEM.

mode n. the state or setting of a program or device: *insert mode; overstrike mode.*

⇒ See also INSERT MODE; OVERSTRIKE.

modeling n. **1.** the process of representing a real-world object or phenomenon as a set of mathematical equations. **2.** the process of representing three-dimensional objects in a computer.

⇒ See also 3-D SOFTWARE; ANIMATION; CAD/CAM; NURBS; RENDER; TEXTURE; VRML.

modem n. modulator-demodulator: a device or program that enables a computer to transmit data over telephone lines. Computer information is stored digitally, whereas information transmitted over telephone lines is in the form of analog waves. A modem converts between these two forms.

⇒ See also BPS; CCITT; CHANNEL BONDING; COMMUNICATIONS; COMMUNICATIONS PROTOCOL; COMMUNICATIONS SOFTWARE; DATA COMPRESSION; DIAL-UP ACCESS; DSVD; FLASH MEMORY; HOST-BASED MODEM; K56FLEX; MNP; MODULATE; RJ-11; RS-232C; SOFT-

WARE MODEM; TERMINAL ADAPTER; V.90; WIRELESS MO-
DEM; X2.

moderated newsgroup *n.* a newsgroup monitored by an individual or group (the moderator)
who has the authority to block messages deemed
inappropriate.
⇒ See also FLAME; NEWSGROUP; SPAM.

moderator *n.* See under MODERATED NEWSGROUP.

modified frequency modulation *n.* See
MFM.

modifier key *n.* a key on a keyboard that has a
meaning only when combined with another key,
as the Shift, Control, and Alt keys.

MO drive *n.* MAGNETO-OPTICAL (MO) DRIVE.

Modula-2 *n.* a programming language designed
by Niklaus Wirth, the author of Pascal, that
addresses Pascal's lack of support for separate
compilation of modules and multitasking.
⇒ See also COMPILE; MULTITASKING; PASCAL; PRO-
GRAMMING LANGUAGE.

modular architecture *n.* the design of any system composed of separate components that can
be connected so that any one component (module) can be added or replaced without affecting
the rest of the system.
⇒ See also ARCHITECTURE; INTEGRATED; MODULE.

modulate *v.t.* to blend (data) into a carrier signal.
⇒ See also ADPCM; MFM; MODEM; PCM; TDM.

module *n.* **1.** in software, a part of a program. **2.**
in hardware, a self-contained component.
⇒ See also LINK; MODULAR ARCHITECTURE; PROGRAM;
ROUTINE.

moiré *n.* an undesirable pattern that appears
when a graphic image is displayed or printed
with an inappropriate resolution.
⇒ See also HALFTONE.

monitor *n.* **1.** a display screen. **2.** the entire box
of which the display screen is a part. **3.** a program that observes a computer. For example,
some monitor programs report how often another
program accesses a disk drive or how much CPU
time it uses.

⇒ See also ANALOG MONITOR; BANDWIDTH; COLOR MONITOR; CONVERGENCE; DDC; DIGITAL MONITOR; DLP; DOT PITCH; DPI; ELF EMISSION; FIXED-FREQUENCY MONITOR; FLAT TECHNOLOGY MONITOR; GRAY SCALING; INTERLACING; LCD MONITOR; MULTISCANNING MONITOR; PINCUSHION DISTORTION; PIXEL; RAMDAC; RASTER; REFRESH.

monochrome *adj.* referring to monitors or printers that display the foreground in one color or shades of one color and the background in a second color.

⇒ See also BACKGROUND; FOREGROUND; GRAPHICS; GRAY SCALING; MONITOR.

monochrome display adapter *n.* See MDA.

monospacing *n.* the use of the same width for different characters. In a monospaced font, *W* has the same width as the letter *I*. Courier is an example of a monospaced font.

⇒ See also COURIER FONT; CPI; FONT; PROPORTIONAL SPACING.

MOO (mōō), *n.* Mud, Object Oriented: a specific implementation of a MUD system developed by Stephen White. MOO is in the public domain and can be freely downloaded and executed.

⇒ See also MUD; OBJECT ORIENTED.

Moore's Law *n.* the observation made in 1965 by Gordon Moore, cofounder of Intel, that the number of transistors per square inch on integrated circuits had doubled every year since the integrated circuit was invented. Moore's law has been updated to reflect the fact that data density now doubles approximately every 18 months.

⇒ See also CHIP; INTEGRATED CIRCUIT; MICROPROCESSOR; NANOTECHNOLOGY; TRANSISTOR.

morphing *n.* metamorphosing: an animation technique in which one image is gradually turned into another.

⇒ See also ANIMATION.

Mosaic *n.* an application that simplifies accessing documents on the World Wide Web.

⇒ See also BROWSER; INTERNET; WORLD WIDE WEB.

motherboard *n.* the main circuit board of a microcomputer containing the CPU, BIOS, memory, mass storage interfaces, serial and parallel ports,

expansion slots, and all the controllers required to control standard peripheral devices, such as the display screen, keyboard, and disk drive.
⇒ See also ADD-ON; ATX; BACKPLANE; BIOS; BUS; CONTROLLER; CPU; DAUGHTERCARD; EXPANSION BOARD; EXPANSION SLOT; HEAT SINK; LPX; NLX; OVERCLOCK; PORT; PRINTED CIRCUIT BOARD; VOLTAGE REGULATOR.

motion-JPEG *n.* Joint Photographic Experts Group standard: a standard for storing and compressing digital images.
⇒ See also JPEG; MPEG.

Motorola microprocessors *n.pl.* the microprocessors used in all Apple Macintosh computers and in many workstations until the early 1990s. In 1993, Motorola joined Apple Computer and IBM in designing a new RISC architecture, an effort that culminated in the introduction of the PowerPC architecture in 1994.
⇒ See also CISC; MICROPROCESSOR; POWERPC; RISC.

mount *v.t.* **1.** to make (a mass storage device) available. **2.** to install (a device).
⇒ See also MASS STORAGE.

mouse *n.* a small object that is connected to the CPU by a wire and is rolled along a hard, flat surface to control the movement of the cursor or pointer on a display screen.
⇒ See also ADB; BUS; BUS MOUSE; CLICK; CURSOR; DOUBLE CLICK; EXPANSION BOARD; GRAPHICAL USER INTERFACE; MENU DRIVEN; POINTER; SERIAL PORT; TRACKBALL.

mousepad *n.* a pad over which a mouse can be moved. Mousepads provide more traction than smooth surfaces such as glass and wood, so they make it easier to move a mouse accurately.
⇒ See also MOUSE.

mouse pointer *n.* POINTER (def. 1).

mouse port *n.* PS/2 PORT.

moving-bar menu *n.* a common type of menu in which options are selected by moving a highlighted bar over them by means of a mouse, arrow keys, or the Tab key.
⇒ See also MENU.

Moving Picture Experts Group *n.* See MPEG.

Mozilla *n.* the original name for Netscape's browser, now called Navigator.

MP3 MPEG Layer 3: a type of audio data compression that can reduce digital sound files by a 12:1 ratio with virtually no loss in quality.

⇒ See also DATA COMPRESSION; DIGITAL AUDIO; MPEG.

MPC Multimedia Personal Computer: a software and hardware standard developed by a consortium of computer firms led by Microsoft.

⇒ See also CD-ROM; CD-ROM PLAYER; INTEL MICROPROCESSORS; MULTIMEDIA.

MPEG (em′peg′), *n.* **1.** Moving Picture Experts Group: a working group of ISO. **2.** the family of digital video compression standards and file formats developed by the group.

⇒ See also CODEC; DATA COMPRESSION; DVD; DVD-ROM; DVI; FPS; INDEO; JPEG; MP3; QUICKTIME; VIDEO EDITING.

MPP massively parallel processing: a type of computing that uses many separate CPUs, each having its own memory, running in parallel to execute a single program.

⇒ See also NUMA; SMP.

ms millisecond: one thousandth of a second. Access times of mass storage devices are often measured in milliseconds.

⇒ See also MASS STORAGE.

MSAU See MAU.

MSCDEX Microsoft CD-ROM Extension: a driver that enables DOS and Windows 3.x systems to recognize and control CD-ROM players.

⇒ See also CD-ROM PLAYER; CDFS.

MSCS Microsoft Cluster Server: a clustering technology built into Windows NT 4.0 and later versions that supports clustering of two NT servers to provide a single fault-tolerant server.

⇒ See also CLUSTERING; WINDOWS NT.

MS-DOS (em′es dôs′, -dos′), *n.* See under DOS.

MSN Microsoft Network: Microsoft's online service.

⇒ See also AMERICA ONLINE; COMPUSERVE INFORMATION SERVICE; ONLINE SERVICE.

MS-TNEF See TNEF.

MS-Windows (em'es win'dōz), *n.* Microsoft Windows.

MS-Word (em'es wûrd'), *n.* Microsoft Word.

MTBF mean time between failures: a rating that is measured in hours and indicates the sturdiness of hard disk drives and printers.

⇒ See also DISK DRIVE; SMART.

MTU Maximum Transmission Unit: the largest physical packet size, measured in bytes, that a network can transmit. Any messages larger than the MTU are divided into smaller packets before being sent.

⇒ See also PACKET; WINSOCK.

MUCK (muk), *n.* Multi-User Chat Kingdom: a text-based MUD system. MUCK is similar to MUSH, though it uses different software.

⇒ See also MUD; MUSH.

MUD (mud), *n.* Multi-User Dungeon *or* Multi-User Dimension: a cyberspace where users can take on an identity in the form of an avatar and interact with one another. Also called **3-d world; chat world.**

⇒ See also AVATAR; CHAT ROOM; CYBERSPACE; MOO; MUCK; MUSH; VIRTUAL REALITY.

multicast *v.i.* to transmit a message to a select group of recipients, as to send an e-mail message to a mailing list.

⇒ See also BROADCAST; IP MULTICAST; RTSP; TELECONFERENCE.

Multicast Backbone *n.* See MBONE.

multicolor/graphics array *n.* See MCGA.

multidimensional DBMS *n.* a database management system (DBMS) organized around large groups of records that share a common field value.

⇒ See also DATABASE MANAGEMENT SYSTEM; OLAP; RDBMS.

MultiFinder *n.* the multitasking version of Finder for Apple Macintosh computers. This is the part of the operating system responsible for managing the desktop—locating documents and folders and handling the Clipboard and Scrapbook.

⇒ See also CLIPBOARD; DESKTOP; FINDER; MACOS; MACINTOSH COMPUTER; MULTITASKING; OPERATING SYSTEM.

multifrequency monitor *n.* a type of video monitor capable of accepting signals at more than one frequency range, which enables the monitor to support several different resolutions.

⇒ See also MONITOR; MULTISCANNING MONITOR; VIDEO ADAPTER.

multifunction peripheral *n.* See MFP.

multifunction printer *n.* MULTIFUNCTION PERIPHERAL (MFP).

multilevel printer *n.* CONTONE PRINTER.

multimedia *n.* the use of computers to present text, graphics, video, animation, and sound in an integrated way.

⇒ See also 3DO; ACTIVEMOVIE; ANIMATION; AUTHORING TOOL; CD-ROM; HYPERMEDIA; HYPERTEXT; MBONE; MEDIA; MMX; MPC; SHOCKWAVE; STREAMING; WAV.

multimedia kit *n.* a package of hardware and software that adds multimedia capabilities to a computer, usu. including a CD-ROM or DVD player, a sound card, speakers, and a bundle of CD-ROMs.

⇒ See also CD-ROM; MULTIMEDIA.

Multimedia Personal Computer *n.* See MPC.

Multiple Document Interface *n.* See MDI.

multiplex *v.t.* to combine (multiple analog or digital signals) for transmission over a single line or medium. A common type of multiplexing combines several low-speed signals for transmission over a single high-speed connection.

⇒ See also CARRIER; CDMA; FDM; MULTIPLEXOR; TDM; WDM.

multiplexor *n.* a communications device that multiplexes (combines) several signals for transmission over a single medium. A demultiplexor completes the process by separating multiplexed signals from a transmission line. Also called **mux.**

⇒ See also CONCENTRATOR; MULTIPLEX.

multiprocessing *n.* **1.** a computer system's ability to support more than one process (program) at the same time, as UNIX or OS/2. **2.** the utilization of multiple CPUs in a single computer system. Also called **parallel processing.**

⇒ See also CPU; DISTRIBUTED PROCESSING; INTERPROCESS COMMUNICATION (IPC); MULTITASKING; OS/2; PARALLEL PROCESSING; PROCESS; SMP; UNIX.

Multipurpose Internet Mail Extensions *n.* See MIME.

MultiRead *n.* a specification for CD-ROM and compact disc players that enables them to read discs created by CD-RW drives, developed jointly by Philips Electronics and Hewlett-Packard.

⇒ See also CD-ROM PLAYER; CD-RW DISK; COMPACT DISC.

multiscanning monitor *n.* a type of monitor that automatically adjusts to the signal frequency of the video display board to which it is connected and that can display images based on almost any graphics display system, including MDA, Hercules, EGA, VGA, and SVGA.

⇒ See also ANALOG MONITOR; DIGITAL MONITOR; FIXED-FREQUENCY MONITOR; MULTIFREQUENCY MONITOR; VIDEO ADAPTER; VIDEO STANDARDS.

Multi-station Access Unit *n.* See MAU.

Multistation Access Unit *n.* See MAU.

multisync monitor *n.* MULTISCANNING MONITOR.

multitasking *n.* the ability of a computer to execute more than one task, or program, at the same time.

⇒ See also COOPERATIVE MULTITASKING; MULTIFINDER; MULTIPROCESSING; OPERATING SYSTEM; OS/2; UNIX.

multithreading *n.* the ability of an operating system to execute different parts of a program, called threads, simultaneously.

⇒ See also MULTITASKING; SMP.

multi-user *adj.* referring to computer systems that support two or more simultaneous users, as mainframes and minicomputers.

⇒ See also MAINFRAME; MINICOMPUTER; TIME SHARING.

MUMPS (mumps), *n.* Massachusetts General Hospital Utility Multi Programming System: a general-purpose programming language developed in the late 1960s.

⇒ See also BASIC; FORTRAN.

MUSH (mush), *n*. Multi-User Shared Hallucination: a text-based MUD system.

⇒ See also MUCK; MUD.

musical instrument digital interface *n*. See MIDI.

MuTeX *n*. a package of macros for the TeX typesetting system that supports musical notation.

⇒ See also LaTeX; MACRO; TeX.

mux *n*. MULTIPLEXOR.

MVS Multiple Virtual Storage: the operating system for older IBM mainframes. It has been largely superseded by IBM's newer operating system, *OS/390*.

⇒ See also MAINFRAME; OPERATING SYSTEM; VSAM.

N n

name *n.* a sequence of one or more characters that uniquely identifies a file, variable, account, or other entity.
⇒ See also ALIAS; DOMAIN NAME; EXTENSION; FILENAME; IDENTIFIER; LABEL; LITERAL; VARIABLE.

Named Pipes *n.* an interprocess control (IPC) protocol for exchanging information between two applications, possibly running on different computers in a network.
⇒ See also INTERPROCESS COMMUNICATION (IPC).

name server *n.* a program that translates names from one form to another, such as domain name servers (DNSs) that translate domain names into IP addresses.
⇒ See also DNS; SERVER.

nanosecond *n.* a billionth of a second. Many computer operations, such as the speed of memory chips, are measured in nanoseconds. *Abbr.:* ns
⇒ See also ACCESS TIME.

nanotechnology *n.* a field of science whose goal is to control individual atoms and molecules to create computer chips and other devices that are thousands of times smaller than current technologies permit.
⇒ See also INTEGRATED CIRCUIT; MOORE'S LAW.

NAP Network Access Point: a public network exchange facility where Internet service providers (ISPs) can connect with one another in *peering* arrangements.
⇒ See also BACKBONE; INTERNET; ISP; MAE; NSP.

NAT Network Address Translation: an Internet standard that enables a local-area network (LAN) to use one set of IP addresses for internal traffic and a second set of addresses for external traffic. A NAT provides a type of firewall by hiding internal IP addresses and allows a company to use more internal IP addresses.
⇒ See also FIREWALL; IP ADDRESS.

National Television Standards Committee *n.* See NTSC.

native *adj.* referring to an original form. For example, an application's *native file format* is the one it uses internally. For all other formats, the application must first convert the file to its native format.

⇒ See also EXPORT; IMPORT.

natural language *n.* a human language. Probably the single most challenging problem in computer science is to develop computers that can understand natural languages.

⇒ See also ARTIFICIAL INTELLIGENCE; FOURTH-GENERATION LANGUAGE; LANGUAGE.

navigation keys *n.pl.* CURSOR CONTROL KEYS.

Navigator *n.* Netscape Communication's Web browser. There are many versions of Navigator, and it runs on all the major platforms.

⇒ See also BROWSER; INTERNET EXPLORER; NETSCAPE.

NC a type of network computer designed to execute Java programs locally. NCs must be connected to a network server that holds the data to be processed.

⇒ See also NET PC; NETWORK COMPUTER; THIN CLIENT; WINDOWS TERMINAL.

NDIS Network Device Interface Specification: a Windows device driver interface that enables a single network interface card (NIC) to support multiple network protocols.

⇒ See also ISDN; NETWORK INTERFACE CARD; PROTOCOL.

NDS Novell Directory Services: the directory services for Novell NetWare networks. NDS provides a logical tree-structure view of all resources on the network.

⇒ See also ACTIVE DIRECTORY; DIRECTORY SERVICE; LDAP; NETWARE; X.500.

near-letter-quality *adj.* referring to or producing print that is not quite letter quality but is better than draft quality. Many dot-matrix printers produce near-letter-quality print.

⇒ See also DOT-MATRIX PRINTER; DRAFT MODE; DRAFT QUALITY; LETTER QUALITY (LQ); PRINTER.

NEC one of the world's largest computer and electronics manufacturers.

⇒ See also INTEL; MONITOR; SEMICONDUCTOR.

nesting *n.* the embedding of one object in another object of the same type. Many word processing applications allow users to embed (nest) one document inside another.

Net *n.* the Internet.

Netbeui (net′boo′ē), *n.* NetBios Enhanced User Interface: an enhanced version of the NetBIOS protocol used by network operating systems such as LAN Manager, Windows 95, Windows 98, and Windows NT.
⇒ See also NETBIOS.

NetBIOS *n.* Network Basic Input/Output System: an application programming interface (API) that augments the DOS BIOS by adding special functions for local-area networks (LANs).
⇒ See also API; BIOS; LOCAL-AREA NETWORK; NETBEUI; SMB.

netiquette *n.* the etiquette guidelines for posting messages to on-line services, particularly Internet newsgroups. Netiquette covers not only rules to maintain civility in discussions but also guidelines unique to the electronic nature of forum messages.
⇒ See also FORUM; INTERNET.

NetMeeting *n.* a product developed by Microsoft Corporation that enables groups to teleconference using the Internet as the transmission medium.
⇒ See also CHAT; COOLTALK; INTERNET PHONE; TELECONFERENCE.

Net PC *n.* a type of network computer designed cooperatively by Microsoft and Intel.
⇒ See also DISKLESS WORKSTATION; NC; NETWORK COMPUTER; SMS; WINDOWS TERMINAL; ZAW.

Netscape *n.* officially called *Netscape Communications Corporation*, Netscape was founded in 1994. In addition to its Web browsers, Netscape produces Web servers and tools for building intranets.
⇒ See also MICROSOFT; NAVIGATOR; SUN MICROSYSTEMS.

Netscape Navigator *n.* NAVIGATOR.

Netscape Server API *n.* See NSAPI.

NetShow *n.* a specification developed by Microsoft for streaming multimedia content over the World Wide Web.

⇒ See also RTSP; STREAMING.

NetWare n. a popular local-area network (LAN) operating system developed by Novell Corporation.

⇒ See also ETHERNET; IPX; LOCAL-AREA NETWORK; NDS; NOVELL; OPERATING SYSTEM; SAP; SPX; TOKEN-RING NETWORK.

NetWare Loadable Module n. software that enhances or provides additional functions in a NetWare 3.x or higher server. *Abbr.:* NLM

network n. a group of two or more computer systems linked together. There are many types of computer networks, including local-area networks (LANs) and wide-area networks (WANs).

⇒ See also BACKBONE; CLIENT/SERVER ARCHITECTURE; COMMUNICATIONS; ETHERNET; FIREWALL; HETEROGENEOUS NETWORK; INTRANET; LOCAL-AREA NETWORK; MAN; NETWORK MANAGEMENT; SNA; SNMP; TOKEN-RING NETWORK; WIDE-AREA NETWORK.

network adapter n. NETWORK INTERFACE CARD.

Network Address Translation n. See NAT.

Network Basic Input/Output System n. See NETBIOS.

network card n. NETWORK INTERFACE CARD.

network computer n. a computer with minimal memory, disk storage, and processor power designed to connect to a network, especially the Internet. Network computers rely on the power of the network servers.

⇒ See also DISKLESS WORKSTATION; INTERNET; NC; NET PC; ORACLE; SMS; SUN MICROSYSTEMS; TCO; THIN CLIENT; WINDOWS TERMINAL; WORKSTATION; ZAW.

Network Device Interface Specification n. See NDIS.

Network Directory Services n. See NDS.

Network File System n. See NFS.

network interface card n. an expansion board inserted into a computer so the computer can be connected to a network. *Abbr.:* NIC

⇒ See also AUI; BNC CONNECTOR; DLC; EXPANSION

BOARD; LOCAL-AREA NETWORK; MAC ADDRESS; NDIS; NETWORK; ODI; PROTOCOL; PROTOCOL STACK; TRANSCEIVER.

network management n. the management of computer networks.
⇒ See also CMIP; DIB; MIB; NETWORK; RMON; SECURITY; SNIFFER; SNMP; SPOOF.

Network Neighborhood n. a Windows 95 and 98 folder that lists computers, printers, and other resources connected to a user's local-area network (LAN).
⇒ See also DCC; LOCAL-AREA NETWORK; WINDOWS 95.

Network News Transfer Protocol n. See NNTP.

network operating system (NOS) n. an operating system that includes special functions for connecting computers and devices into a local-area network (LAN). For example, some popular NOSs for DOS and Windows systems include Novell Netware, Artisoft's LANtastic, Microsoft LAN Manager, and Windows NT.
⇒ See also LOCAL-AREA NETWORK; OPERATING SYSTEM.

network PC n. NETWORK COMPUTER.

Network Service Provider n. See NSP.

network topology n. TOPOLOGY.

neural network n. a type of artificial intelligence that attempts to imitate the way a human brain works. A neural network works by creating connections between *processing elements*, the computer equivalent of neurons.
⇒ See also ARTIFICIAL INTELLIGENCE; DIGITAL; VOICE RECOGNITION.

newbie n. Slang. someone who is a new user on an online service, particularly the Internet.
⇒ See also ONLINE SERVICE.

newsgroup n. an on-line discussion group. On the Internet, there are literally thousands of newsgroups covering every conceivable interest.
⇒ See also ACRONYM; FORUM; LURK; MODERATED NEWSGROUP; NEWS READER.

news reader n. an application for reading messages from and posting messages to Internet newsgroups.

⇒ See also NEWSGROUP; NNTP.

Next Generation Internet Initiative n. NGI INITIATIVE.

NEXTSTEP n. an object-oriented operating system developed by Next, Inc. In 1997, Apple Computer acquired Next with the idea of making NEXTSTEP the foundation of its new Macintosh operating system.

⇒ See also APPLE COMPUTER; OBJECT ORIENTED; OPERATING SYSTEM.

NFS Network File System: an open operating system designed by Sun Microsystems that allows all network users to access shared files stored on computers of different types.

⇒ See also FILE MANAGEMENT SYSTEM; UNIX.

NGI Initiative Next Generation Internet Initiative: a U.S. program designed to fund and coordinate federal agencies and academia to design and build the next generation of Internet services.

⇒ See also I2; INTERNET; vBNS.

nibble n. half a byte; four bits. Nibbles are important in hexadecimal and BCD representations.

⇒ See also BCD; BIT; BYTE; HEXADECIMAL.

NIC NETWORK INTERFACE CARD.

NiCad battery pack n. the battery pack for many notebook computers. Nickel-cadmium batteries can provide considerable power, but they need to be recharged every three or four hours.

⇒ See also BATTERY PACK; LITHIUM-ION BATTERY; MEMORY EFFECT; NiMH BATTERY PACK; NOTEBOOK COMPUTER.

NiMH battery pack n. a type of battery pack that is made of nickel-metal hydroxide and can store up to 50 percent more power than NiCad batteries.

⇒ See also BATTERY PACK; LITHIUM-ION BATTERY; MEMORY EFFECT; NiCad BATTERY PACK.

NLM NETWARE LOADABLE MODULE.

NLQ NEAR-LETTER-QUALITY.

NLX a form factor designed by Intel for PC motherboards. It features a number of improvements over the current LPX form factor.

⇒ See also AGP; BABY AT; FORM FACTOR; MOTHER-BOARD; LPX.

NNTP Network News Transfer Protocol: the protocol used to post, distribute, and retrieve USENET messages.

⇒ See also NEWS READER; USENET.

node *n.* **1.** in networks, a processing location. A node can be a computer or some other device, such as a printer. **2.** in tree structures, a point where two or more lines meet.

⇒ See also DLC; LEAF; MAC ADDRESS; NETWORK; TREE STRUCTURE.

noise *n.* **1.** in communications, interference (static) that destroys the integrity of signals on a line. Noise can come from radio waves, nearby electrical wires, lightning, and bad connections. **2.** anything that prevents a clear signal or message from being transmitted.

⇒ See also COMMUNICATIONS; FIBER OPTICS.

nonimpact printer *n.* a type of printer that does not operate by striking a head against a ribbon. Examples of nonimpact printers include laser and ink-jet printers.

⇒ See also IMPACT PRINTER; INK-JET PRINTER; LASER PRINTER; PRINTER.

noninterlaced *adj.* referring to monitors and video standards that do not use interlacing techniques to improve resolution. Although interlacing increases resolution, it also increases screen flicker and reduces reaction time.

⇒ See also INTERLACING; MONITOR; SCREEN FLICKER.

Non-Uniform Memory Access *n.* See NUMA.

nonvolatile memory *n.* any of various types of memory that retain their contents when power is turned off. ROM is nonvolatile.

⇒ See also BUBBLE MEMORY; MEMORY; NVRAM; RAM; ROM.

normalization *n.* **1.** in relational database design, the process of organizing data to minimize duplication. Normalization usually involves dividing a database into two or more tables and defining relationships between the tables. **2.** in data processing, a process applied to all data in a set that produces a specific statistical property. **3.** in programming, changing the format of a floating-point number so the left-most digit in the mantissa is not a zero.

⇒ See also FLOATING-POINT NUMBER; KEY; RDBMS; REFERENTIAL INTEGRITY.

NOR operator *n.* a Boolean operator that returns a value of TRUE only if both operands are FALSE.

⇒ See also BOOLEAN OPERATOR.

NOS NETWORK OPERATING SYSTEM.

notebook computer *n.* an extremely light-weight personal computer weighing typically less than 6 pounds and small enough to fit easily in a briefcase. Many notebook display screens are limited to VGA resolution. Active-matrix screens produce very sharp images but do not refresh as rapidly as full-size monitors. In terms of computing power, modern notebook computers are nearly equivalent to personal computers.

⇒ See also ACTIVE-MATRIX DISPLAY; BACKLIGHTING; BATTERY PACK; HAND-HELD COMPUTER; LAPTOP COMPUTER; PDA; PORT REPLICATOR; SLATE PC; SUBNOTEBOOK COMPUTER; VGA; VIRTUAL DESKTOP; ZV PORT.

Notes *n.* Short for LOTUS NOTES.

NOT operator *n.* a Boolean operator that returns TRUE if its operand is FALSE, and FALSE if its operand is TRUE.

⇒ See also BOOLEAN OPERATOR.

Novell *n.* the world's largest network software company.

⇒ See also LOCAL-AREA NETWORK; NETWARE.

Novell NetWare *n.* NETWARE.

ns nanosecond.

NSAPI Netscape Server API: an API for Netscape's Web servers. NSAPI enables programmers to create sophisticated Web-based applications.

⇒ See also CGI; ISAPI; STATELESS.

NSFnet *n.* a wide-area network developed as the main government network linking universities and research facilities. In 1995 NSFnet was dismantled and replaced with a commercial Internet backbone.

⇒ See also ARPANET; NETWORK; WIDE-AREA NETWORK.

NSP Network Service Provider: a company that provides Internet access to ISPs.

⇒ See also BACKBONE; ISP; NAP.

NT *n.* Short for WINDOWS NT.

NT File System *n.* See NTFS.

NTFS NT file system: one of the file systems for the Windows NT operating system.

⇒ See also FILE MANAGEMENT SYSTEM; UNICODE; VOLUME; WINDOWS NT.

NTSC National Television Standards Committee: an organization responsible for setting television and video standards in the United States.

⇒ See also COMMON INTERMEDIATE FORMAT; COMPOSITE VIDEO; HDTV; INTERLACING; PAL; QCIF; RGB MONITOR; S-VIDEO; SAP; TELEVISION BOARD; VIDEO ADAPTER; VIDEO OVERLAY.

NuBus *n.* the expansion bus for versions of Macintosh computers starting with the Macintosh II and ending with the Performa. Current Macs use the PCI bus.

⇒ See also EXPANSION BUS; MACINTOSH COMPUTER; PCI.

null character *n.* a character that has all its bits set to 0. A null character has a numeric value of 0. In some programming languages, a null character is used to mark the end of a character string. In database and spreadsheet applications, null characters are often used as padding.

⇒ See also CHARACTER STRING; PADDING.

null modem *n.* NULL-MODEM CABLE.

null-modem cable *n.* a specially designed cable that connects two computers directly to each other via their communications ports. Null modems are particularly useful with portable computers.

⇒ See also DCC; MODEM; PORT; RS-232C.

NUMA Non-Uniform Memory Access: a type of parallel processing architecture in which each processor has its own local memory but can also access memory owned by other processors.

⇒ See also MPP; PARALLEL PROCESSING; SMP.

number cruncher *n.* **1.** a computer whose dominant characteristic is its ability to perform large amounts of numerical computations quickly. **2.** a program whose main task is to perform mathematical calculations. **3.** an individual who uses a computer primarily for analyzing numbers.

⇒ See also SUPERCOMPUTER; WORKSTATION.

numeric coprocessor *n.* See under COPROCESSOR.

numeric keypad *n.* a separate set of keys on some keyboards that contains the numbers 0 through 9 and a decimal point arranged as on an adding machine. Numeric keypads make it easier to enter large amounts of numeric data.

⇒ See also ARROW KEYS; KEYBOARD; MODE; NUM LOCK KEY.

Num Lock key *n.* a key that switches the numeric keypad from numeric mode to cursor control mode, and vice versa. In numeric mode, the keys represent numbers even when they are combined with the Shift key, Function key, or Control key.

⇒ See also CURSOR CONTROL KEYS; NUMERIC KEYPAD; TOGGLE.

NURBS Non-Uniform Rational B-Spline: a mathematical representation of a three-dimensional object. Most CAD/CAM applications support NURBS, which can be used to represent analytic shapes, such as cones, as well as free-form shapes, such as car bodies.

⇒ See also 3-D SOFTWARE; BÉZIER CURVE; MODELING; SPLINE.

NVRAM *n.* Non-Volatile Random Access Memory: a type of memory that retains its contents when power is turned off.

⇒ See also EEPROM; MEMORY; NONVOLATILE MEMORY; RAM; SRAM.

O o

OA OFFICE AUTOMATION.

object *n.* any item that can be individually selected and manipulated. This can include pictures on a display screen as well as software entities. In object-oriented programming, an object is a self-contained entity that consists of both data and procedures to manipulate the data.

⇒ See also BLOB; CORBA; OBJECT ORIENTED; OBJECT-ORIENTED GRAPHICS; OBJECT-ORIENTED PROGRAMMING; OLE; OMG.

object code *n.* the code produced by a compiler. Programmers write programs in a form called source code. To get from source code to machine language, the programs must be transformed by a compiler. The compiler produces an intermediary form called object code.

⇒ See also ASSEMBLER; ASSEMBLY LANGUAGE; CODE; COMPILE; LIBRARY; LINK; LOAD; MACHINE LANGUAGE.

Object Linking and Embedding *n.* See OLE.

Object Management Group *n.* See OMG.

object-oriented *adj.* **1.** referring to a special type of programming that combines data structures with functions to create reusable objects. **2.** describing a system that deals with different types of objects and in which actions depend on the type of object being manipulated.

⇒ See also OBJECT-ORIENTED PROGRAMMING; SMALLTALK; VECTOR GRAPHICS.

object-oriented graphics *n.* the representation of graphical objects, such as lines, circles, and rectangles, with mathematical formulas. This enables the system to manipulate the objects more freely. Also, object-oriented images profit from high-quality output devices. One of the most widely used formats for object-oriented graphics is PostScript.

⇒ See also BIT-MAPPED GRAPHICS; GRAPHICS; POSTSCRIPT; SCALABLE FONT; VECTOR GRAPHICS.

object-oriented programming *n.* a type of programming in which programmers define the data type of a data structure and the types of operations (functions) that can be applied to the data structure. The data structure becomes an *object* that includes both data and functions. Programmers can create relationships between one object and another. When a new type of object is added, it inherits many of its features from existing objects. This makes object-oriented programs easier to modify.

⇒ See also C++; CLASS; COMPONENT SOFTWARE; DISTRIBUTED COMPUTING; EIFFEL; ENCAPSULATION; JAVA; OBJECT ORIENTED; OMG; OVERLOADING; POLYMORPHISM; SMALLTALK; UML; VISUAL C++.

Object Request Broker *n.* See ORB.

OC Optical Carrier: used to specify the speed of fiber-optic networks conforming to the SONET standard.

⇒ See also SDH; SONET; T-1 CARRIER; T-3 CARRIER.

OCR OPTICAL CHARACTER RECOGNITION.

octal *adj.* referring to the base-8 number system, which uses just eight unique symbols (0, 1, 2, 3, 4, 5, 6, and 7). Programs often display data in octal format because it is relatively easy for humans to read and can easily be translated into binary format.

⇒ See also BINARY; DECIMAL; HEXADECIMAL.

OCX OLE Custom control: an independent program module that can be accessed by other programs in a Windows environment. OCX controls have now been superseded by ActiveX controls. However, ActiveX is backward compatible with OCX controls.

⇒ See also ACTIVEX CONTROL; COMPONENT; CONTROL; OLE; VBX.

ODBC Open Data Base Connectivity: a standard database access method developed by Microsoft Corporation. The goal of ODBC is to make it possible to access any data from any application, regardless of which database management system (DBMS) is handling the data.

⇒ See also ADO; DATABASE MANAGEMENT SYSTEM; DRIVER; JDBC; QUERY; SQL.

odd header *n.* in word processing, a header that

appears only on odd-numbered pages.

⇒ See also HEADER.

odd parity *n.* the mode of parity checking in which each 9-bit combination of a data byte plus a parity bit contains an odd number of set bits.

⇒ See also PARITY CHECKING.

ODI Open Data-link Interface: an application programming interface (API) developed by Novell for writing network drivers.

⇒ See also API; DRIVER; NETWORK INTERFACE CARD; OSI.

OEM original equipment manufacturer: a company that has a special relationship with computer producers. OEMs buy computers in bulk and customize them for a particular application. They then sell the customized computer under their own name.

⇒ See also VAR.

office automation *n.* the use of computer systems to execute a variety of office operations, such as word processing, accounting, and e-mail. Office automation almost always implies a network of computers with a variety of available programs.

⇒ See also E-MAIL; NETWORK; WORD PROCESSING.

off-line *adj.* **1.** not connected. For example, when a printer is off-line, it can advance the paper (*form feed*) but cannot print documents sent from the computer. **2.** describing events that occur outside of a standard procedure. For example, if someone says, "Let's continue this discussion off-line," it means, "Let's discuss it informally at another time."

⇒ See also FORM FEED; ON-LINE.

offset *n.* **1.** a value added to a base address to produce a second address. Specifying addresses using an offset is called *relative addressing* because the resulting address is relative to some other point. **2.** in desktop publishing, the amount of space along the edge of the paper. Its purpose is to allow room for the binding.

⇒ See also ADDRESS; BASE ADDRESS; DESKTOP PUBLISHING; GUTTER; RELATIVE ADDRESS.

offset printing *n.* a printing technique whereby

ink is spread on a metal plate with etched images, then transferred to an intermediary surface such as a rubber blanket, and finally applied to paper by pressing the paper against the intermediary surface.

⇒ See also DESKTOP PUBLISHING; POSTSCRIPT.

Okidata *n.* one of the leading producers of printers, especially dot-matrix and LED printers.

⇒ See also DOT-MATRIX PRINTER; LASER PRINTER.

OLAP Online Analytical Processing: a category of software tools for analyzing data stored in a database. OLAP tools enable users to study different dimensions of multidimensional data.

⇒ See also DATABASE; DATABASE MANAGEMENT SYSTEM; MULTIDIMENSIONAL DBMS; OLTP.

OLE (ō lā′ *or as separate letters*), *n.* Object Linking and Embedding: a compound document standard that enables the user to create objects with one application and link or embed them in a second application.

⇒ See also ACTIVEX; APPLET; COMPONENT OBJECT MODEL; COMPONENT SOFTWARE; DDE; DLL; EMBEDDED OBJECT; HOT LINK; LINK; OBJECT ORIENTED; OCX; OPEN-DOC.

OLTP On-Line Transaction Processing. See TRANSACTION PROCESSING.

⇒ See also OLAP.

OMG Object Management Group: a consortium of companies that provide a common framework for developing applications using object-oriented programming techniques.

⇒ See also CORBA; DISTRIBUTED COMPUTING; IIOP; OBJECT; OBJECT-ORIENTED PROGRAMMING.

on-board *adj.* literally, on a circuit board. *On-board memory*, for example, refers to memory chips on the motherboard. *On-board modems* are modems that are on expansion boards.

⇒ See also EXPANSION BOARD; MOTHERBOARD; ON-BOARD MODEM; PRINTED CIRCUIT BOARD.

on-board modem *n.* a modem that comes as an expansion board that can be inserted into a computer. Also called **internal modem.**

⇒ See also MODEM.

100Base-T *n.* a networking standard that supports data transfer rates up to 100 Mbps (100 megabits per second). 100Base-T is based on the older Ethernet standard. Because it is 10 times faster than Ethernet, it is often referred to as *Fast Ethernet.*

⇒ See also 10BASET; CSMA/CD; ETHERNET; GIGABIT ETHERNET; SWITCHED ETHERNET.

on-line or **online** *adj.* **1.** turned on and connected. For example, printers are on-line when they are ready to receive data from the computer. **2.** (of a user) connected to a host computer through a modem.

⇒ See also OFF-LINE; PRINTER.

OnLine Analytical Processing *n.* See OLAP.

online help *n.* See under HELP.

online service *n.* a business that provides its subscribers with a wide variety of data transmitted over telecommunications lines. Online services provide an infrastructure in which subscribers can communicate with one another by exchanging e-mail messages or by participating in online conferences (forums). In addition, the service can connect users with an almost unlimited number of third-party information providers. Three of the largest online services are America Online, CompuServe, and MSN.

⇒ See also AMERICA ONLINE; BULLETIN BOARD SYSTEM; CHAT; COMPUSERVE INFORMATION SERVICE; FORUM; INTERNET; MSN.

On-Line Transaction Processing *n.* See OLTP.

OOP OBJECT-ORIENTED PROGRAMMING.

OOPL object-oriented programming language.

open *v.t.* **1.** to make (an object) accessible. Whenever the user accesses a file, the operating system opens the file. In a multiprocessing operating system, the operating system must decide whether the file can be accessed simultaneously by more than one user, and, if so, it must ensure that different users do not try to modify the file's contents at the same time. *—adj.* **2.** (of designs or architectures) accessible; public. See under OPEN ARCHITECTURE.

⇒ See also CLOSE; FILE; OPERATING SYSTEM.

open architecture *n.* an architecture whose specifications are public. This includes officially approved standards as well as privately designed architectures whose specifications are made public.
⇒ See also ADD-ON; ARCHITECTURE; CLONE; PROPRIETARY; STANDARD; THE OPEN GROUP.

Open Data-Link Interface *n.* See ODI.

OpenDoc *n.* a standard application programming interface (API) that makes it possible to design independent programs (components) that can work together on a single document.
⇒ See also COMPONENT OBJECT MODEL; COMPONENT SOFTWARE; COMPOUND DOCUMENT; OLE.

OpenGL *n.* a 3-D graphics language developed by Silicon Graphics. There are two main implementations: Microsoft OpenGL is built into Windows NT and is designed to improve performance on hardware that supports the OpenGL standard; Cosmo OpenGL is a software-only implementation specifically designed for machines that do not have a graphics accelerator.
⇒ See also 3-D SOFTWARE; DIRECT3D; SGI.

Open Graphics Language *n.* OPENGL.

Open Shortest Path First *n.* See OSPF.

Open Software Foundation (OSF) *n.* See under THE OPEN GROUP.

Open System Interconnection *n.* See OSI.

Open Text *n.* a popular Internet search engine developed by Open Text Corporation. Open Text provides powerful ways to fine-tune a query.
⇒ See also ALTA VISTA; EXCITE; INFOSEEK; LYCOS; SEARCH ENGINE; WEBCRAWLER.

operand *n.* in all computer languages, an object that is manipulated.
⇒ See also EXPRESSION; OPERATOR; OVERLOADING.

operating environment *n.* the environment in which users run programs. For example, the DOS environment consists of all the DOS commands available to users. The Macintosh environment, on the other hand, is a graphical user interface that uses icons and menus instead of commands.
⇒ See also CONTROL PROGRAM; ENVIRONMENT; GRAPH-

ICAL USER INTERFACE; MICROSOFT WINDOWS; OPERAT-
ING SYSTEM; SHELL; VIRTUAL MACHINE.

operating system *n.* the program that performs such basic tasks as recognizing input from
the keyboard, sending output to the display
screen, keeping track of files and directories on
the disk, and controlling peripheral devices such
as disk drives and printers. This is the most important program that runs on computers. For
large systems, the operating system makes sure
that different programs and users running at the
same time do not interfere with each other. The
operating system is also responsible for security.
⇒ See also APPLICATION; BeOS; BIOS; COMMAND
PROCESSOR; DOS; FILE MANAGEMENT SYSTEM; KERNEL;
MacOS; MICROSOFT WINDOWS; MULTI-USER; MULTI-
PROCESSING; MULTITASKING; MULTITHREADING; MVS;
OS/2; UNIX; VMS; WINDOWS CE.

operator *n.* **1.** a symbol that represents a specific action. For example, a plus sign (+) is an
arithmetic operator that represents addition. **2.** an
individual responsible for mounting tapes and
disks, making backups, and generally ensuring
that a computer runs properly.
⇒ See also BITWISE OPERATOR; BOOLEAN OPERATOR;
EXPRESSION; OPERAND; OVERLOADING; PRECEDENCE; RE-
LATIONAL OPERATOR.

optical character recognition (OCR) *n.* the
branch of computer science that involves reading
text from paper and translating the images into a
form that the computer can manipulate, such as
ASCII codes. For example, images from pages of
a book or a magazine article can be fed directly
into an electronic computer file, translated by an
OCR system, and then edited with a word processor. All OCR systems include an optical scanner
for reading text, and sophisticated software for
analyzing images.
⇒ See also ASCII; DOCUMENT MANAGEMENT; FONT;
FORM; OPTICAL SCANNER; PRINTED CIRCUIT BOARD.

optical disk *n.* a storage medium from which
data is read and to which it is written by lasers.
Optical disks can store much more data—up to 6
gigabytes (6 billion bytes)—than most portable
magnetic media. The three basic types of optical

disks are: **CD-ROM, WORM,** and **erasable.**

⇒ See also AREAL DENSITY; CD-I (COMPACT DISC-INTERACTIVE); CD-ROM; COMPACT DISC; DISK; ERASABLE OPTICAL DISK; MASS STORAGE; PHASE CHANGE DISK; ROM; WORM.

optical fiber *n.* See under FIBER OPTICS.

optical resolution *n.* the degree of detail with which a device can capture an image. The term is used most frequently with reference to optical scanners and digital cameras. In contrast, the *interpolated resolution* indicates the resolution that the device can yield through *interpolation* —the process of generating intermediate values based on known values.

⇒ See also DIGITAL CAMERA; OPTICAL SCANNER; RESOLUTION.

optical scanner *n.* a device that can read text or illustrations printed on paper and translate the information into a form the computer can use. A scanner digitizes the image—dividing it into a grid of boxes and representing each box with either a zero or a one, depending on whether the box is filled in. The resulting bit map can be stored in a file, displayed on a screen, and manipulated by programs. Some scanners are small, hand-held devices that are moved across the paper. Larger scanners include machines into which sheets of paper are fed. These are called *sheet-fed* scanners. A second type of large scanner, called a *flatbed scanner,* is like a photocopy machine. It consists of a board on which books, magazines, and other documents are placed.

⇒ See also BIT MAP; CCD; COLOR DEPTH; COMPUTER IMAGING; FAX MACHINE; FLATBED SCANNER; FONT; GRAY SCALING; MFP; OPTICAL CHARACTER RECOGNITION; OPTICAL RESOLUTION; PHOTO SCANNER; RESOLUTION; TWAIN.

optimize *v.t.* **1.** in programming, to fine-tune (a program) so that it runs more quickly or takes up less space. **2.** (of a disk) to defragment. **3.** to configure (a device or application) so that it performs better.

⇒ See also DEFRAGMENT; FRAGMENTATION; PROGRAM.

option *n.* **1.** in command-driven interfaces, an

addition to a command that changes or refines the command in a specified manner. **2.** in graphical user interfaces, a choice in a menu or dialog box.

⇒ See also COMMAND; COMMAND DRIVEN; DIALOG BOX; GRAPHICAL USER INTERFACE; MENU.

Option key *n.* a key on Macintosh keyboards used with other keys to generate special characters and commands.

⇒ See also ALT KEY; KEYBOARD; MACINTOSH COMPUTER.

Oracle *n.* the largest software company whose primary business is database products.

⇒ See also DATABASE MANAGEMENT SYSTEM; INFORMIX; NETWORK COMPUTER; SQL; SYBASE.

Orange Book *n.* the specification covering writable CDs, including CD-R.

⇒ See also CD-R DRIVE; GREEN BOOK; RED BOOK; WHITE BOOK; YELLOW BOOK.

ORB Object Request Broker: a component in the CORBA programming model that acts as the middleware between clients and servers. The various ORBs receive the requests, forward them to the appropriate servers, and then hand the results back to the client.

⇒ See also CORBA; MIDDLEWARE.

orientation *n.* See under LANDSCAPE and PORTRAIT.

original equipment manufacturer *n.* See OEM.

OR operator *n.* a Boolean operator that returns a value of TRUE if either (or both) of its operands is TRUE. This is called an *inclusive OR operator*. There is also an *exclusive OR operator* (often abbreviated *XOR*) that returns a value of TRUE only if just one of the operands is TRUE.

⇒ See also BOOLEAN OPERATOR.

orphan *n.* in word processing, the first line of a paragraph that appears as the last line of a page, or the last line of a paragraph that appears as the first line of a page (this is sometimes called a *widow*). Orphans are considered bad form in page layout.

⇒ See also PAGINATION; WIDOW; WORD PROCESSING.

OS OPERATING SYSTEM.

OS/2 *n.* an operating system for PCs developed originally by Microsoft Corporation and IBM but sold and managed solely by IBM. OS/2 is compatible with DOS and Windows programs. However, programs written specifically to run under OS/2 will not run under DOS or Windows.
⇒ See also DOS; GRAPHICAL USER INTERFACE; MICROSOFT WINDOWS; MULTITASKING; OPERATING SYSTEM; PC.

OS-9 *n.* a real-time, multi-user, multitasking operating system developed by Microware Systems Corporation.
⇒ See also CD-I (COMPACT DISC–INTERACTIVE); REAL TIME; WEBTV.

OSF Open Software Foundation: now part of *The Open Group.*
⇒ See also DCE.

OSI Open System Interconnection: an ISO standard for worldwide communications that defines a networking framework for implementing protocols in seven layers. Control is passed from one layer to the next.
⇒ See also DLC; ISO; PROTOCOL STACK.

OSI Reference Model *n.* See OSI.

OSPF Open Shortest Path First: a protocol that defines how routers share routing information. OSPF transfers only routing information that has changed since the previous transfer.
⇒ See also ROUTER; ROUTING; ROUTING INFORMATION PROTOCOL.

OSR 2 OEM Service Release 2: a version of Windows 95 released at the end of 1996. Also called **Windows 95b.**
⇒ See also FAT32; WINDOWS 95.

outline font *n.* a scalable font in which the outlines of each character are geometrically defined. The most popular languages for defining outline fonts are *PostScript* and *TrueType.*
⇒ See also BIT MAP; FONT; POSTSCRIPT; RESOLUTION; SCALABLE FONT; TRUETYPE; TYPEFACE; VECTOR GRAPHICS.

output *n.* **1.** anything that comes out of a computer. Output can be meaningful information or gibberish, and it can appear in a variety of forms—as binary numbers, as characters, as pictures, and as printed pages. Output devices include display screens, loudspeakers, and printers. —*v.t.* **2.** to give out. For example, display screens output images and printers output print.

⇒ See also I/O.

output device *n.* any machine capable of representing information from a computer. This includes display screens, printers, plotters, and synthesizers.

⇒ See also DEVICE; OUTPUT.

overclock *v.t.* to run (a microprocessor) faster than the speed for which it has been tested and approved. Overclocking is a popular technique for eking out a little more performance from a system.

⇒ See also CLOCK SPEED; MHz; MICROPROCESSOR; MOTHERBOARD.

OverDrive *n.* a user-installable microprocessor from Intel for the 486 microprocessor.

⇒ See also INTEL MICROPROCESSORS.

overflow error *n.* an error that occurs when the computer attempts to handle a number that is too large for it.

⇒ See also FLOATING-POINT NUMBER.

overhead *n.* the use of computer resources for performing a specific feature. Typically, the term is used to describe a function that is optional, or an enhancement to an existing application. Programmers often need to weigh the overhead of new features before implementing them.

⇒ See also FEATURE.

overlaid windows *n.pl.* CASCADING WINDOWS.

overloading *n.* in programming languages, a feature that allows an object to have different meanings, depending on its context. It is a feature of most object-oriented languages.

⇒ See also CLASS; DATA TYPE; OBJECT-ORIENTED PROGRAMMING; OPERAND; OPERATOR; POLYMORPHISM.

oversampling *n.* ANTIALIASING.

overstrike *v.t.* to print (one character) directly on top of another. In older printers, this was one way to create unusual characters or bold characters, but it is not necessary with modern printers.

overwrite mode *n.* one of two modes in word processors and text editors. In overwrite mode, every character typed is displayed at the cursor position. If a character is already at that position, it is replaced.

⇒ See also INSERT MODE.

P p

pack *v.t.* to compress (data).
⇒ See also DATA COMPRESSION; PACKED FILE.

packed file *n.* a file in a compressed format. Many operating systems and applications contain commands used to pack a file so that it takes up less memory.
⇒ See also DATA COMPRESSION; DISK COMPRESSION; MODEM.

packet *n.* a piece of a message transmitted over a packet-switching network. A packet contains the destination address in addition to the data.
⇒ See also CELL RELAY; IP; MTU; PACKET SWITCHING; ROUTER; ROUTING; TRACEROUTE.

packet switching *n.* protocols in which messages are divided into a series of packets before they are sent. Each packet is then transmitted individually. Once all the packets arrive at the destination, they are recompiled into the original message.
⇒ See also CDPD; CELL RELAY; CIRCUIT SWITCHING; FRAME RELAY; NETWORK; SVC; TCP/IP; WIDE-AREA NETWORK; X.25.

pad character *n.* a character used to fill empty space. Many applications have fields that must be a particular length. If all the allotted characters are not used, the program must fill in the remaining ones with pad characters.
⇒ See also DATABASE; FIELD; NULL CHARACTER.

padding *n.* filling in unused space.
⇒ See also PAD CHARACTER.

page *n.* **1.** a fixed amount of data. **2.** in word processing, a page of text. **3.** in virtual memory systems, a fixed number of bytes recognized by the operating system. **4.** WEB PAGE. —*v.t., v.i.* **5.** to display one page or screenful of (a document) at a time. **6.** to copy a page of (data) from main memory to a mass storage device, or vice versa.
⇒ See also FPM RAM; MAIN MEMORY; PAGING; SEGMENT; SWAP; VIRTUAL MEMORY.

page break *n.* the end of a page of text. In word processing, the user enters special codes, called *hard page breaks* or *forced page breaks*, that cause the printer to advance to the next page. Otherwise, the word processor begins a new page after a page has been filled; this is called a *soft page break*.

⇒ See also HARD; SOFT; WORD PROCESSING.

Page Description Language *n.* a language for describing the layout and contents of a printed page. *Abbr.:* PDL

⇒ See also LASER PRINTER; OBJECT ORIENTED; PCL; POSTSCRIPT.

Page Down key *n.* a key that is standard on PC and Macintosh keyboards. Its meaning differs from one program to another, but it usually moves the cursor down a set number of lines.

⇒ See also KEYBOARD.

page eject *n.* FORM FEED.

page fault *n.* an interrupt that occurs when a program requests data not currently in virtual memory. The interrupt triggers the operating system to retrieve the data from a storage device and load it into RAM.

⇒ See also INVALID PAGE FAULT; MMU; PAGING; VIRTUAL MEMORY.

page fault error *n.* INVALID PAGE FAULT.

page layout program *n.* a program enabling the user to format pages of text and graphics.

⇒ See also DESKTOP PUBLISHING; KERNING; TEXT WRAP; WORD PROCESSING.

page-mode memory *n.* a type of memory that works by eliminating the need for a row address if data is located in the row previously accessed.

page preview *n.* See under PREVIEWING.

page printer *n.* a printer that processes an entire page at one time. All laser and ink-jet printers are page printers.

⇒ See also LASER PRINTER; PAGE DESCRIPTION LANGUAGE (PDL); PRINTER.

pages per minute *n.* See PPM.

Page Up key *n.* a standard key on PC and Macintosh keyboards. Its meaning differs from one program to another, but it usually scrolls the document up one screenful.

⇒ See also KEYBOARD.

page-white display *n.* a special type of LCD display screen that uses supertwist technology to produce a high contrast between the foreground and background.

⇒ See also FLAT-PANEL DISPLAY; LCD; SUPERTWIST.

pagination *n.* **1.** the numbering of pages in a document. **2.** the division of a document into pages.

⇒ See also ORPHAN; WIDOW; WORD PROCESSING.

paging *n.* a technique used by virtual memory operating systems to help ensure that needed data is available as quickly as possible. When a program needs a page that is not in main memory, the operating system copies the required page into memory and copies another page back to the disk. One says that the operating system *pages* the data. Each time a page is needed that is not currently in memory, a *page fault* occurs.

⇒ See also DEMAND PAGING; MAIN MEMORY; OPERATING SYSTEM; PAGE; PAGE FAULT; SEGMENT; SWAP; THRASH; VIRTUAL MEMORY.

paint program *n.* a graphics program that enables the user to draw pictures on the display screen that are represented as bit maps (bit-mapped graphics).

⇒ See also ADOBE PHOTOSHOP; BIT-MAPPED GRAPHICS; DRAW PROGRAM; GRAPHICS; MARQUEE; VECTOR GRAPHICS.

PAL 1. Phase Alternating Line: the dominant television standard in Europe. PAL delivers 625 lines at 50 half-frames per second. **2.** Programmable Array Logic: a type of Programmable Logic Device (PLD).

⇒ See also COMMON INTERMEDIATE FORMAT; NTSC; QCIF; VIDEO ADAPTER.

palette *n.* **1.** in computer graphics, the set of available colors. For a given application, the palette may be only a subset of all the colors that can be physically displayed. **2.** in paint and illustration programs, a collection of symbols that represent drawing tools. For example, a simple palette might contain a paintbrush, a pencil, and an eraser.

⇒ See also DRAW PROGRAM; EGA; GRAPHICS; PAINT PROGRAM; VIDEO ADAPTER.

palmtop *n.* a small computer that literally fits in the palm. Compared with full-size computers, palmtops are severely limited. Those that use a pen rather than a keyboard for input are often called *hand-held computers* or *PDAs*.

⇒ See also HAND-HELD COMPUTER; NOTEBOOK COMPUTER; PDA; PORTABLE; WINDOWS CE.

Pantone Matching System *n.* a popular color matching system used by the printing industry to print spot colors. *Abbr.:* PMS

⇒ See also CMYK; COLOR MANAGEMENT SYSTEM (CMS); PROCESS COLORS; SPOT COLOR.

PAP Password Authentication Protocol: the most basic form of authentication, in which a user's name and password are transmitted over a network and compared with a table of name–password pairs.

⇒ See also AUTHENTICATION; CHAP.

paper feed *n.* the mechanism or method that moves paper through a printer.

⇒ See also PRINTER; TRACTOR FEED.

paperless office *n.* the idealized office in which paper is absent because all information is stored and transferred electronically.

⇒ See also DOCUMENT MANAGEMENT; FAX MACHINE; OPTICAL CHARACTER RECOGNITION; WORKGROUP COMPUTING.

paper-white display *n.* a high-quality monochrome monitor that displays characters in black against a white background. Such monitors are popular for desktop publishing.

⇒ See also DISPLAY SCREEN; MONITOR.

parallel *adj.* referring to processes that occur simultaneously. *Parallel* means that the printer or other device is capable of receiving more than one bit at a time (that is, it receives several bits *in parallel*).

⇒ See also PARALLEL PORT; PORT; PRINTER; SERIAL.

parallel computing *n.* PARALLEL PROCESSING.

parallel interface *n.* a channel capable of transferring more than one bit simultaneously.

⇒ See also CENTRONICS INTERFACE; CHANNEL; PARALLEL; PARALLEL PORT; SERIAL PORT.

parallel port *n.* a parallel interface for connecting an external device such as a printer. Most personal computers have both a parallel port and at least one serial port.

⇒ See also CENTRONICS INTERFACE; ECP; EPP; IrDA; LOCALTALK; PARALLEL; PORT; SCSI; SERIAL PORT; USB.

parallel processing *n.* the simultaneous use of more than one CPU to execute a program. Single-CPU computers can process data in a parallel way when they are connected in a network.

⇒ See also CLUSTERING; CPU; DISTRIBUTED PROCESSING; HIGH PERFORMANCE COMPUTING; MPP; MULTITASKING; NUMA; SUPERSCALAR.

parameter *n.* **1.** a characteristic used to customize a program, such as filenames, page lengths, and font specifications. **2.** (in programming) ARGUMENT.

parameter RAM *n.* See PRAM.

parent directory *n.* the directory (or folder) above another directory (or folder). The lower directory is called a subdirectory. In DOS and UNIX systems, the parent directory is identified by two dots (..).

⇒ See also DIRECTORY; ROOT DIRECTORY.

parity *n.* the quality of being either odd or even. The fact that all numbers have a parity is commonly used in data communications to ensure the validity of data.

⇒ See also PARITY CHECKING.

parity bit *n.* See under PARITY CHECKING.

parity checking *n.* in communications, the use of *parity bits* to check that data has been transmitted accurately. The parity bit is added to every data unit that is transmitted. The parity bit for each unit is set so that all bytes have either an odd number or an even number of set bits. Parity checking is used not only in communications but also in the testing of memory storage devices.

⇒ See also CCITT; COMMUNICATIONS; COMMUNICATIONS PROTOCOL; MNP; MODEM.

park *v.t.* to lock the *read/write head* of (a hard

disk drive) in a safe position so that the disk will not be damaged while the drive is being moved.

⇒ See also DISK DRIVE; HEAD; HEAD CRASH.

parse *v.t.* to divide (language) into small components that can be analyzed. Compilers must parse source code to be able to translate it into object code. Similarly, any application that processes complex commands must be able to parse the commands.

⇒ See also COMPILE; COMPILER; SEMANTICS.

partition *v.t.* **1.** to divide (memory or mass storage) into isolated sections. In DOS systems, each partition of a disk will behave like a separate disk drive. —*n.* **2.** a section of main memory or mass storage that has been reserved for a particular application.

⇒ See also CLUSTER; DISK DRIVE; FDISK; FILE ALLOCATION TABLE; Finder; MBR; SLACK SPACE.

Pascal (pa skal′), *n.* a high-level programming language developed in the late 1960s. Pascal is best known for its affinity to structured programming techniques. Despite its success in academia, it has had only modest success in the business world. [named after Blaise Pascal, a 17th-century mathematician who constructed one of the first adding machines]

⇒ See also BORLAND INTERNATIONAL; DELPHI; HIGH-LEVEL LANGUAGE; MODULA-2; PROGRAMMING LANGUAGE.

passive backplane *n.* See under BACKPLANE.

passive-matrix display *n.* a type of flat-panel display consisting of a grid of horizontal and vertical wires. At the intersection of each grid is an LCD element that constitutes a single pixel, either letting light through or blocking it.

⇒ See also ACTIVE-MATRIX DISPLAY; CSTN; DSTN; FLAT-PANEL DISPLAY; LCD; PIXEL; TFT.

password *n.* a secret series of characters that enables a user to access a file, computer, or program. The password helps ensure that unauthorized users do not access the computer. In addition, data files and programs may require a password.

⇒ See also ACCESS CODE; AUTHENTICATION; KEY; LOG ON; SECURITY.

Password Authentication Protocol *n.* See PAP.

paste *v.t.* to copy (an object) from a buffer or clipboard to a file. In word processing, blocks of text can be cut (removed) from a file and placed in a temporary buffer. The material can then be pasted somewhere else. It is also possible to cut an object from one application and paste it into another.

⇒ See also BUFFER; CLIPBOARD; COPY; CUT; EMBEDDED OBJECT; LINK; OLE.

patch *n.* a temporary fix to a program bug. A patch is an actual piece of object code that is inserted into an executable program.

⇒ See also BUG; EXECUTABLE FILE; OBJECT CODE.

path *n.* **1.** in DOS and Windows systems, a list of directories where the operating system looks for executable files if it is unable to find the file in the working directory. **2.** PATHNAME.

⇒ See also DIRECTORY; DOS; EXECUTABLE FILE; PATHNAME; WORKING DIRECTORY.

pathname *n.* a sequence of symbols and names that identifies a file. The operating system finds the directory containing a particular file by following the specified path.

⇒ See also DIRECTORY; FILENAME; ROOT DIRECTORY; UNC; WORKING DIRECTORY.

pattern recognition *n.* an important field of computer science concerned with recognizing patterns, particularly visual and sound patterns. It is central to optical character recognition (OCR), voice recognition, and handwriting recognition.

⇒ See also HANDWRITING RECOGNITION; OPTICAL CHARACTER RECOGNITION; VOICE RECOGNITION.

Pause key *n.* a key used to temporarily halt the display of data.

⇒ See also SCROLL.

PBX private branch exchange: a private telephone network used within a company. PBX users share outside lines for external telephone calls.

⇒ See also CENTREX; POTS; TELEMATICS.

PC 1. personal computer or IBM PC. The first personal computer produced by IBM was called the

PC; increasingly, the term came to mean IBM or IBM-compatible personal computers. In recent years, the term *PC* has been applied to any personal computer based on an Intel or Intel-compatible microprocessor. **2.** printed circuit.

⇒ See also CLONE; COMPAQ; COMPATIBLE; DELL COMPUTER; EXPANSION BUS; IBM; IBM PC; LOCAL BUS; MACINTOSH COMPUTER; OPERATING SYSTEM; PERSONAL COMPUTER; PRINTED CIRCUIT BOARD; VIDEO STANDARDS.

PC/AT See under AT.

PCB PRINTED CIRCUIT BOARD.

PC card *n.* a computer device packaged in a small card about the size of a credit card and conforming to the PCMCIA standard.

⇒ See also CARDBUS; PCMCIA; ZV PORT.

PC-DOS *n.* the name IBM uses to market its version of the DOS operating system.

⇒ See also DOS.

PC fax *n.* FAX MODEM.

PCI Peripheral Component Interconnect: a local bus standard developed by Intel Corporation. PCI is a 64-bit bus, though it is usually implemented as a 32-bit bus. It can run at clock speeds of 33 or 66 MHz.

⇒ See also AGP; BUS; BUS MASTERING; CONTROLLER; EXPANSION BUS; I2O; INDUSTRY STANDARD ARCHITECTURE (ISA) BUS; INTEL; LOCAL BUS; NUBUS.

PCL Printer Control Language: the page description language (PDL) developed by Hewlett-Packard and used in many of its laser and ink-jet printers.

⇒ See also HP; HP-COMPATIBLE PRINTER; HPGL; INTELLIFONT; LASER PRINTER; PAGE DESCRIPTION LANGUAGE (PDL); POSTSCRIPT; SCALABLE FONT.

PCM Pulse Code Modulation: a sampling technique for digitizing analog signals, especially audio signals.

⇒ See also ADPCM; DIGITIZE; MODULATE; SAMPLING; TDM.

PCMCIA Personal Computer Memory Card International Association: an organization that has developed a standard for PC cards. Originally designed for adding memory to portable computers, the PCMCIA standard is now suitable for many types of devices. There are three types of PCM-CIA cards. Type I cards are used primarily for adding more ROM or RAM to a computer. Type II cards are often used for modem and fax modem cards. Type III cards can hold portable disk drives.

⇒ See also CardBus; Device Bay; hot plugging; IEEE 1394; plug-and-play; USB; ZV Port.

PCS Personal Communications Service: the U.S. Federal Communications Commission (FCC) term used to describe a set of digital cellular technologies being deployed in the U.S.

⇒ See also CDMA; cellular; GSM; TDMA.

PC/TV a combination of a personal computer and television.

⇒ See also television board; WebTV.

PCX a graphics file format for graphics programs running on PCs.

⇒ See also bit-mapped graphics; BMP; graphics file formats; TIFF.

PDA personal digital assistant: a hand-held device that combines computing, telephone/fax, and networking features. Most PDAs are pen-based, using a stylus rather than a keyboard for input.

⇒ See also Apple Computer; EPOC; hand-held computer; handwriting recognition; HPC; palmtop; voice recognition; Windows CE.

PDF Portable Document Format: a file format developed by Adobe Systems. PDF captures formatting information from desktop publishing applications, making it possible to send formatted documents and have them appear on the recipient's monitor or printer as they were intended.

⇒ See also Acrobat; file format.

PDL page description language.

peer-to-peer architecture *n.* a type of network in which each workstation has equivalent capabilities and responsibilities.

⇒ See also client/server architecture; local-area network.

pel pixel.

pen computer *n.* a computer that utilizes an electronic pen (called a *stylus*) rather than a keyboard for input. Pen computers generally require special operating systems that support handwriting recognition.

⇒ See also HAND-HELD COMPUTER; HANDWRITING RECOGNITION; PALMTOP; PDA.

Pentium 2 *n.* PENTIUM II.

Pentium II *n.* Intel's Pentium chip that builds on the design of the Pentium Pro. Current versions run at speeds of from 233 to 450 MHz.

⇒ See also DESCHUTES; INTEL MICROPROCESSORS; PENTIUM MICROPROCESSOR; PENTIUM PRO; SLOT 1.

Pentium microprocessor *n.* a 32-bit microprocessor introduced by Intel in 1993. Though still in production, it has been superseded by the Pentium Pro and Pentium II microprocessors.

⇒ See also AMD; CYRIX; DESCHUTES; INTEL MICROPROCESSORS; K6; MERCED; MICROPROCESSOR; PENTIUM II; PENTIUM PRO; SOCKET 7; TILLAMOOK; TRITON.

Pentium MMX *n.* See MMX.

Pentium Pro *n.* Intel's sixth-generation microprocessor (P6). The Pentium Pro can perform at nearly twice the speed of previous Pentium microprocessors.

⇒ See also DIB; INTEL MICROPROCESSORS; MICROPROCESSOR; PENTIUM II; PENTIUM MICROPROCESSOR; SOCKET 8.

peripheral *n.* PERIPHERAL DEVICE.

Peripheral Component Interconnect *n.* See PCI.

peripheral device *n.* any external device attached to a computer. Examples include printers, disk drives, monitors, keyboards, and mice.

⇒ See also CONTROLLER; DEVICE; EXTERNAL BUS.

Perl Practical Extraction and Report Language: a programming language developed by Larry Wall, especially designed for processing text.

⇒ See also AWK; CGI; INTERPRETER; TCL.

Permanent Virtual Circuit *n.* See PVC.

persistent cookie *n.* Another name for *cookie*, so called because cookies typically stay in a user's browser for long periods of time.

persistent URL *n.* See PURL.

Personal Communications Service *n.* See PCS.

personal computer *n.* a small, relatively inexpensive computer designed for an individual user. One of the first personal computers was the Apple II, introduced in 1977 by Apple Computer. The IBM PC, introduced in 1981, quickly became the personal computer of choice. Other companies adjusted to IBM's dominance by building IBM clones. Today, the world of personal computers is basically divided between Apple Macintoshes and PCs. The principal characteristics of personal computers are that they are single-user systems and are based on microprocessors.

⇒ See also AMIGA; CLONE; COMPUTER; HOME COMPUTER; MACINTOSH COMPUTER; MICROPROCESSOR; PC; WORKSTATION.

Personal Computer Memory Card International Association *n.* See PCMCIA.

Personal Digital Assistant *n.* See PDA.

personal finance manager *n.* a simple accounting program that helps individuals manage their finances.

⇒ See also ACCOUNTING SOFTWARE.

personal information manager *n.* See PIM.

petabyte *n.* 2^{50} (1,125,899,906,842,624) bytes. A petabyte is equal to 1,024 terabytes.

⇒ See also EXABYTE; GIGABYTE; TERABYTE.

PFE INVALID PAGE FAULT.

PGA 1. pin grid array: a type of chip package in which the connecting pins are located on the bottom in concentric squares. **2.** Professional Graphics Adapter: a video standard developed by IBM that supports 640 by 480 resolution.

⇒ See also CHIP; DIP; SIP.

PgDn key *n.* PAGE DOWN KEY.

PGP PRETTY GOOD PRIVACY.

PgUp key *n.* PAGE UP KEY.

phase change disk *n.* a type of rewritable optical disk that employs the phase change recording method. The disk drive writes data with a laser that changes spots on the disk between amorphous and crystalline states. An optical head reads data by detecting the difference in reflected light from amorphous and crystalline spots. A medium-intensity pulse can then restore the original crystalline structure.

⇒ See also MAGNETO-OPTICAL (MO) DRIVE; OPTICAL DISK; SOLID INK-JET PRINTER; WORM.

phase-change printer *n.* SOLID INK-JET PRINTER.

Phoenix BIOS *n.* a common version of the PC BIOS developed by Phoenix Corporation.

⇒ See also BIOS; CLONE.

phosphor pitch *n.* DOT PITCH.

PhotoCD *n.* a file format for storing digital photographs developed by Eastman Kodak Co.

⇒ See also PHOTO ILLUSTRATION.

photo illustration *n.* a type of computer art that begins with a digitized photograph. Using special image-enhancement software, an artist can then apply a variety of special effects.

⇒ See also IMAGE ENHANCEMENT; PhotoCD.

photo scanner *n.* a type of high-resolution optical scanner designed for scanning photographs.

⇒ See also IMAGE ENHANCEMENT; IMAGE PROCESSING; OPTICAL SCANNER; SNAPSHOT PRINTER.

Photoshop *n.* ADOBE PHOTOSHOP.

phreaking *n.* using a computer or other device to trick a phone system. Phreaking is used to make free calls or to have calls charged to a different account.

⇒ See also CRACK; HACKER.

physical *adj.* pertaining to hardware. For example, *physical memory* refers to the actual RAM chips installed in a computer. A *physical data structure* refers to the actual organization of data on a storage device.

⇒ See also FRAGMENTATION; HARDWARE; LOGICAL; SOFTWARE; VIRTUAL MEMORY.

PIC Lotus Picture File: the graphics file format used to represent graphics generated by Lotus 1-2-3.

⇒ See also GRAPHICS; GRAPHICS FILE FORMATS; LOTUS 1-2-3.

pica *n.* in typesetting, a unit of measurement equal to 1/6 of an inch, or 12 points.

⇒ See also POINT.

PICT file format *n.* a file format developed by

Apple Computer in 1984. PICT files are encoded in QuickDraw commands and can hold both object-oriented images and bit-mapped images.

⇒ See also GRAPHICS; GRAPHICS FILE FORMATS; MACINTOSH COMPUTER; OBJECT ORIENTED; QUICKDRAW.

pie chart *n.* a type of presentation graphic in which percentage values are represented as proportionally sized slices of a pie.

⇒ See also PRESENTATION GRAPHICS.

PIF *n.* program information file: a type of file that holds information about how Windows should run a non-Windows application. These instructions can include the amount of memory to use, the path to the executable file, and what type of window to use.

⇒ See also DOS; EXECUTABLE FILE; WINDOWS.

PIM (*usually pronounced as separate letters*), *n.* personal information manager: a type of software application designed to help users organize random bits of information. Most PIMs are used to enter various kinds of textual notes—reminders, lists, dates—and to link this information in useful ways. Many PIMs also include calendar, scheduling, and calculator programs.

⇒ See also CALCULATOR; CALENDAR; CONTACT MANAGER; SCHEDULER.

pin *n.* **1.** in dot-matrix printers, the device that presses on the ink ribbon to make dots on the paper. Dot-matrix printers can have anywhere from 9 to 24 pins. A 24-pin printer can produce letter-quality print. **2.** a male lead on a connector. **3.** one of an array of thin metal feet (pins) on the underside of silicon chips that enables them to be attached to a circuit board.

⇒ See also CHIP; CONNECTOR; DOT-MATRIX PRINTER; LETTER QUALITY (LQ); NEAR LETTER QUALITY; PINOUT; PRINTER.

pincushion distortion *n.* a common type of distortion in CRT monitors in which horizontal and vertical lines bend inward toward the center of the display. The opposite of pincushion distortion is *barrel distortion*, in which horizontal and vertical lines bend outward toward the edge of the display. A third type of distortion, called *trap-*

ezoid distortion, occurs when vertical lines are straight but not parallel with one another.

⇒ See also CRT; DEGAUSS; DISPLAY SCREEN; MONITOR.

pincushioning *n.* See under PINCUSHION DISTORTION.

PINE (pīn), *n.* pine is not elm (or Program for Internet News and E-Mail): a character-based e-mail client for UNIX systems. Developed at the University of Washington, PINE replaces an older e-mail program called *elm.*

⇒ See also E-MAIL CLIENT.

pin feed *n.* TRACTOR FEED.

PING Packet Internet Groper: a utility to determine whether a specific IP address is accessible. It works by sending a packet to the specified address and waiting for a reply.

⇒ See also HOP; ICMP; IP ADDRESS; SMURF; TRACEROUTE.

pin grid array *n.* See PGA.

pinout *n.* a diagram or table that describes the purpose of each pin in a chip or connector, or each wire in a cable.

⇒ See also CHIP; CONNECTOR; PIN.

PIO Programmed Input/Output: a method of transferring data between two devices that uses the computer's main processor as part of the data path.

⇒ See also ATA; DATA TRANSFER RATE.

pipe *n.* a temporary software connection between two programs or commands. Sometimes it is useful to use the output from one command as the input for a second command, without passing the data through the keyboard or display screen. Pipes were invented for these situations.

⇒ See also INPUT; OUTPUT.

pipeline *n.* See under PIPELINING.

pipeline burst *n.* See under PIPELINE BURST CACHE.

pipeline burst cache *n.* a type of memory cache built into many DRAM controller and chipset designs. Pipeline burst caches use two techniques—a burst mode that pre-accesses memory contents before they are requested, and pipelining, so that one memory value can be accessed in the cache at the same time that another memory value is accessed in DRAM.

⇒ See also BEDO DRAM; BURST MODE; CACHE; DRAM; PIPELINING; SDRAM; WAIT STATE.

pipeline processing *n.* See under PIPELINING.

pipelining *n.* **1.** a technique used in advanced microprocessors where the microprocessor begins executing a second instruction before the first has been completed. When a segment of the pipeline completes an operation, it passes the result to the next segment and fetches the next operation from the preceding segment. The final results of each instruction emerge at the end of the pipeline in rapid succession. **2.** a similar technique used in DRAM, in which the memory loads the requested memory contents into a small cache composed of SRAM and then immediately begins accessing the next memory contents.

⇒ See also INTEL MICROPROCESSORS; MICROPROCESSOR; PIPELINE BURST CACHE; RISC; SUPERSCALAR.

piracy *n.* SOFTWARE PIRACY.

pitch *n.* **1.** (for fixed-pitch fonts) the number of characters printed per inch. Pitch is one characteristic of a monospaced font. Common pitch values are 10 and 12. **2.** in graphics, *dot pitch* refers to the spacing between pixels on a monitor. The smaller the dot pitch, the sharper the image.

⇒ See also CPI; DOT PITCH; FIXED PITCH; FONT; MONITOR; PROPORTIONAL SPACING.

pixel *n.* Picture Element: a single point in a graphic image. Graphics monitors display pictures by dividing the display screen into thousands (or millions) of pixels, arranged in rows and columns. The pixels are so close together that they appear connected. The quality of a display system largely depends on its resolution, how many pixels it can display, and how many bits are used to represent each pixel.

⇒ See also ALPHA CHANNEL; CONVERGENCE; GRAPHICS; GRAY SCALING; MONITOR; RESOLUTION; TRUE COLOR.

PKI public-key infrastructure: a system of digital certificates, Certificate Authorities, and other registration authorities that verify and authenticate the validity of each party involved in an Internet transaction.

⇒ See also CERTIFICATE AUTHORITY; ELECTRONIC COMMERCE.

PKZIP *n.* a widely used file compression method. Files that have been compressed using PKWARE are said to be *zipped*. Decompressing them is called *unzipping*.

⇒ See also DATA COMPRESSION; SHAREWARE; TAR; ZIP.

plain text *n.* **1.** textual data in ASCII format. Plain text is supported by nearly every application on every machine, regardless of operating system. It is quite limited, however, because it cannot contain any formatting commands. **2.** (in cryptography) any message that is not encrypted.

⇒ See also ASCII FILE; CIPHER TEXT; ENCRYPTION.

plasma display *n.* a type of flat-panel display that works by sandwiching an ionized gas between two wired panels. In one panel the wires are in vertical rows, and in the other they are in horizontal rows. The two panels form a grid. An individual pixel can then be charged by passing a current through the appropriate x-coordinate and y-coordinate wires. When the gas is charged, it glows a bright orange. Plasma displays are not often used today.

⇒ See also FLAT-PANEL DISPLAY; PIXEL.

platform *n.* the underlying hardware or software for a system. For example, the platform might be an Intel 80486 processor running DOS Version 6.0. Once the platform has been defined, software developers can produce appropriate software and managers can purchase appropriate hardware and applications. The term *cross-platform* refers to applications, formats, or devices that work on different platforms.

⇒ See also ENVIRONMENT; PPCP; SDK.

platter *n.* a round magnetic plate that constitutes part of a hard disk. Hard disks typically contain up to a dozen platters. Most platters require two read/write heads, one for each side.

⇒ See also HARD DISK.

PLD Programmable Logic Device: an integrated circuit that can be programmed in a laboratory to perform complex functions. A PLD consists of arrays of AND and OR gates. A system designer implements a logic design with a device programmer that blows fuses on the PLD to control gate operation.
⇒ See also CHIP; INTEGRATED CIRCUIT; PROM.

plot *v.t.* to produce (an image) by drawing lines. A computer can be programmed to plot images on a display screen or on paper.
⇒ See also PLOTTER.

plotter *n.* a device that draws pictures on paper based on commands from a computer. Plotters draw lines using a pen and can produce continuous lines. In general, plotters are considerably more expensive than printers. They are used in engineering applications, where precision is mandatory.
⇒ See also CAD; PRINTER.

plug *n.* a connector used to link devices.
⇒ See also CONNECTOR.

plug-and-play *adj.* denoting a computer system's ability to configure expansion boards and other devices automatically. Since the introduction of the NuBus, the Apple Macintosh has been a plug-and-play computer. The Plug and Play (PnP) specification has made PCs more plug-and-play.
⇒ See also HOT PLUGGING; IEEE 1394; PnP; SCAM.

plug-compatible *adj.* able to replace another product without any alterations. Two devices are plug-compatible if either one can be plugged into the same interface. The term is sometimes used to describe software modules that interface with an application in the same way.
⇒ See also COMPATIBLE; EXPANSION BOARD.

plug-in *n.* a hardware or software module that adds a specific feature or service to a larger system.
⇒ See also COMPONENT SOFTWARE; MODULAR ARCHITECTURE; SHOCKWAVE.

PMS PANTONE MATCHING SYSTEM (PMS).

PNG (ping), *n.* Portable Network Graphics: a new

bit-mapped graphics format similar to GIF. In contrast to GIF, PNG is completely patent- and license-free.

⇒ See also BIT-MAPPED GRAPHICS; GIF; LZW.

PnP Plug and Play: a technology developed by Microsoft and Intel that supports plug-and-play installation.

⇒ See also BIOS; ESCD; EXPANSION BOARD; PLUG-AND-PLAY; SCAM.

point *v.i.* **1.** to move the pointer on a display screen to select an item. Graphical user interfaces are often called *point-and-click* interfaces because a user typically points to an object on the screen and then clicks a button on the mouse. —*n.* **2.** in typography, 1/72 of an inch used to measure the height of characters. The height of the characters is one characteristic of fonts.

⇒ See also FONT; GRAPHICAL USER INTERFACE; LEADING; MOUSE; POINTER; SCALABLE FONT.

PointCast *n.* a company founded in 1992 to deliver news and other information over Internet connections.

⇒ See also CDF; PUSH; WEBCASTING.

pointer *n.* **1.** in graphical user interfaces, a small arrow or other symbol on the display screen that moves as the mouse is moved. Commands and options are selected by positioning the tip of the arrow over the desired choice and clicking a mouse button. **2.** in programming, a special type of variable that holds a memory address (that is, it *points* to a memory location).

⇒ See also ADDRESS; GRAPHICAL USER INTERFACE; I-BEAM POINTER; VARIABLE.

pointing device *n.* a device with which a user can control the movement of the pointer to select items on a display screen. Examples include mice, trackballs, joysticks, touchpads, and light pens.

⇒ See also INPUT DEVICE; JOYSTICK; LIGHT PEN; MOUSE; POINTER; POINTING STICK; PUCK; TOUCHPAD; TRACKBALL.

pointing stick *n.* a pointing device first developed by IBM for its notebook computers. It consists of a miniature joystick, usually with a rubber eraser-head tip, positioned somewhere between the keys on the keyboard.

⇒ See also JOYSTICK; POINTING DEVICE; TRACKBALL.

Point of Presence *n.* See POP.

Point-to-Point Protocol *n.* See PPP.

Point-to-Point Tunneling Protocol *n.* See PPTP.

polling *n.* making continual requests for data from another device. For example, modems that support polling can call another system and request data.

⇒ See also MODEM.

polyline *n.* in computer graphics, a continuous line composed of one or more line segments.

⇒ See also DRAW PROGRAM.

polymorphism *n.* in object-oriented programming, a programming language's ability to process objects differently, depending on their data type or class. For example, given a base class *shape*, polymorphism enables the programmer to define different *circumference* methods for any number of derived classes, such as circles and triangles. Polymorphism is considered to be a requirement of any true object-oriented programming language (OOPL).

⇒ See also CLASS; DATA TYPE; OBJECT-ORIENTED PROGRAMMING; OVERLOADING.

POP or **pop 1.** Post Office Protocol: a protocol used to retrieve e-mail from a mail server. The first version, called *POP2*, became a standard in the mid-1980s and requires SMTP to send messages. The newer version, *POP3*, can be used with or without SMTP. **2.** Point of Presence: a telephone number that gives a user dial-up access. Internet service providers (ISPs) generally provide many POPs so that users can make a local call to gain Internet access.

⇒ See also DIAL-UP ACCESS; DIAL-UP NETWORKING; E-MAIL; IMAP; SMTP; SNMP.

pop *v.t.* to pull (an item) off a stack of items. Although originally coined to describe manipulation of data stacks, the term is often used in connection with popping a display window so that it is the topmost window.

⇒ See also POP-UP WINDOW; PUSH; WINDOW.

POP3 See under POP.

pop-up menu *n.* a menu that appears temporarily when the user clicks the mouse button on a selection.

⇒ See also MENU.

pop-up utility *n.* a program installed to be memory resident. When the hot key is pressed, the pop-up utility appears, regardless of which application is currently running.

⇒ See also HOT KEY; MEMORY RESIDENT; TSR.

pop-up window *n.* a window that suddenly appears when a user selects an option with a mouse or presses a special function key. Usually, the pop-up window contains a menu of commands and stays on the screen only until one of the commands is selected.

⇒ See also GRAPHICAL USER INTERFACE; PULL-DOWN MENU; WINDOW.

port *n.* **1.** an interface on a computer to which a device can be connected. Internally, there are several ports for connecting disk drives, display screens, and keyboards. Externally, there are ports for connecting modems, printers, mice, and other peripheral devices. **2.** in TCP/IP and UDP networks, an endpoint to a logical connection. The port number identifies the type of port. —*v.t.* **3.** to move (a program) from one type of computer to another. Sections that are machine dependent are rewritten, and the program is recompiled on the new computer.

⇒ See also CENTRONICS INTERFACE; COM; COMPILE; CONNECTOR; INTERFACE; MACHINE DEPENDENT; PARALLEL PORT; PORT REPLICATOR; PORTABLE; PS/2 PORT; SERIAL PORT.

portable *adj.* **1.** (of hardware) small and lightweight. Portable computers include notebook and subnotebook computers, hand-held computers, palmtops, and PDAs. **2.** (of software) having the ability to run on a variety of computers.

⇒ See also DOCKING STATION; HAND-HELD COMPUTER; MACHINE INDEPENDENT; NOTEBOOK COMPUTER; PALMTOP; PDA; POSIX; SUBNOTEBOOK COMPUTER.

Portable Document Format *n.* See PDF.

Portable Network Graphics *n.* See PNG.

portrait *adj.* referring to a vertical orientation of the paper. A page with portrait orientation, typical for letters and other text documents, is taller than it is wide. Orientation is also a characteristic of monitors.
⇒ See also LANDSCAPE; MONITOR; PRINTER.

port replicator *n.* a device containing common PC ports, such as serial and parallel ports, that plugs into a notebook computer.
⇒ See also DOCKING STATION; NOTEBOOK COMPUTER; PORT.

port-switching hub *n.* SWITCHING HUB.

POSIX (pŏ′siks, -ziks), *n.* Portable Operating System Interface for UNIX: a set of IEEE and ISO standards that define an interface between programs and operating systems.
⇒ See also PORTABLE; UNIX; WINDOWS NT.

POST or **post** power-on self test: a series of diagnostic tests that run automatically when a computer is turned on. Usually the POST tests the RAM, the keyboard, and the disk drives.
⇒ See also BIOS; BOOT; POWER UP.

post *v.t.* **1.** to publish (a message) in an on-line forum or newsgroup. —*n.* **2.** a message published in an on-line forum or newsgroup.
⇒ See also FORUM; USENET.

Post Office Protocol *n.* See POP.

PostScript *n.* a page description language (PDL) developed by Adobe Systems. PostScript is primarily a language for printing documents on laser printers. It is the standard for desktop publishing because it is supported by *imagesetters*, the very-high-resolution printers used to produce camera-ready copy. PostScript is an object-oriented language, meaning that it treats images, including fonts, as collections of geometrical objects rather than as bit maps. There are three basic versions of PostScript: Level 1, Level 2, and PostScript 3.
⇒ See also DESKTOP PUBLISHING; EPS; ISP; LASER PRINTER; OBJECT-ORIENTED GRAPHICS; PAGE DESCRIPTION LANGUAGE (PDL).

PostScript 3 *n.* See under POSTSCRIPT.

POTS plain old telephone service: the standard telephone service that most homes use. The main distinctions between POTS and non-POTS services are speed and bandwidth.

⇒ See also ADSL; COMMUNICATIONS; DSVD; IAC; ISDN; K56FLEX; PBX; PSTN; X2; xDSL.

PowerBuilder n. one of the leading client/server development environments. PowerBuilder supports all the leading platforms.

⇒ See also CLIENT/SERVER ARCHITECTURE; INTEGRATED DEVELOPMENT ENVIRONMENT; SYBASE.

power down v.i. to turn a computer or other machine off.

⇒ See also POWER UP; SHUT DOWN.

power management n. the directing of power to different components of a system in an efficient manner. Power management is especially important for portable devices that rely on battery power.

⇒ See also ACPI; APM; BATTERY PACK.

power-on self test n. See POST.

PowerPC n. a RISC-based computer architecture developed jointly by IBM, Apple Computer, and Motorola Corporation. The name is derived from IBM's name for the architecture, *Performance Optimization With Enhanced RISC*. There are already a number of different operating systems that run on PowerPC-based computers, including the Macintosh operating system (System 7.5 and higher), Windows NT, and OS/2.

⇒ See also BEOS; CHRP; INTEL MICROPROCESSORS; MACINTOSH COMPUTER; MICROPROCESSOR; MOTOROLA MICROPROCESSORS; PPCP; RISC.

PowerPC Platform n. See PPCP.

power supply n. the component that supplies power to a computer. Most personal computers can be plugged into standard electrical outlets. The power supply then pulls the required amount of electricity and converts the AC current to DC current. It also regulates the voltage to eliminate spikes and surges.

⇒ See also UPS; VOLTAGE REGULATOR; VRM.

power up v.i. to turn a computer or other machine on.

⇒ See also POST; POWER DOWN.

power user n. a sophisticated and experienced user of personal computers.

⇒ See also USER.

PPCP PowerPC Platform: a computer hardware specification that allows a computer to run multiple operating systems.

⇒ See also CHRP; PLATFORM; POWERPC; RISC.

ppm pages per minute: the speed of certain types of printers, particularly laser and ink-jet printers.

⇒ See also GPPM; LASER PRINTER; PRINTER.

PPP Point-to-Point Protocol: a method of connecting a computer to the Internet. PPP is more stable than the older SLIP protocol.

⇒ See also INTERNET; PPTP; PROTOCOL; SLIP.

PPTP Point-to-Point Tunneling Protocol: a technology for creating *Virtual Private Networks (VPNs)*, developed jointly by Microsoft Corporation, U.S. Robotics, and several remote-access vendor companies. A VPN is a private network of computers that uses the public Internet to connect some nodes. The Point-to-Point Tunneling Protocol (PPTP) is used to ensure that messages transmitted from one VPN node to another are secure.

⇒ See also L2TP; LAYER TWO FORWARDING; PPP; TUNNELING; VPN; WINDOWS NT.

PRAM (pē′ram′), n. parameter RAM: (on Macintosh computers) a small portion of RAM used to store information about the way the system is configured.

⇒ See also CONFIGURE; CONTROL PANEL; MACINTOSH COMPUTER; MEMORY; RAM.

precedence n. a characteristic of operators that indicates when they will be evaluated when they appear in complex expressions. Operators with high precedence are evaluated before operators with low precedence.

⇒ See also EXPRESSION; OPERAND; OPERATOR.

precision n. (of floating-point numbers) the number of bits used to hold the fractional part. A double-precision floating-point number uses twice as many bits as a single-precision value, so it can represent fractional quantities much more exactly.

⇒ See also DOUBLE PRECISION; FLOATING-POINT NUMBER.

preemptive multitasking *n.* a type of multitasking in which the operating system parcels out CPU time slices to each program.

prepress service bureau *n.* SERVICE BUREAU.

presentation graphics *n.* a type of business software that enables users to create highly stylized images for slide shows and reports, such as charts and graphs. Also called **business graphics.**

⇒ See also BAR CHART; GRAPHICS; LINE GRAPH; PIE CHART; SCATTER DIAGRAM; SPREADSHEET.

Pretty Good Privacy *n.* a technique for encrypting messages. It is one of the most common ways to protect messages on the Internet because it is effective, easy to use, and free.

⇒ See also CRYPTOGRAPHY; PUBLIC-KEY ENCRYPTION; RSA.

previewing *n.* in word processing, formatting a document for the printer but then displaying it on the display screen instead of printing it. Previewing shows exactly how the document will appear when printed.

⇒ See also GREEKING; THUMBNAIL; WORD PROCESSING; WYSIWYG.

primary cache *n.* L1 CACHE.

primary key *n.* a field in a database upon which records can be sorted, which—unlike other key fields in that database, upon which records can also be sorted—holds a unique, nonduplicable value for each record.

primary storage *n.* a somewhat dated term for *main memory.* Mass storage devices, such as disk drives and tapes, are sometimes called *secondary storage.*

⇒ See also MAIN MEMORY; MASS STORAGE.

printed circuit board *n.* a thin plate on which chips and other electronic components are placed. Computers consist of one or more boards, often called *cards* or *adapters.*

⇒ See also BACKPLANE; CHIP; CONTROLLER; DAUGHTERCARD; EXPANSION BOARD; EXPANSION SLOT;

FORM FACTOR; LOCAL-AREA NETWORK; MOTHERBOARD; VIDEO ADAPTER.

printer *n.* a device that prints text or illustrations on paper. There are many different types of printers.

⇒ See also BILEVEL PRINTER; DAISY-WHEEL PRINTER; DOT-MATRIX PRINTER; DRAFT QUALITY; FONT; GRAPHICS; HOST-BASED PRINTER; HP; IMPACT PRINTER; INK-JET PRINTER; LASER PRINTER; LCD; LCD PRINTER; LED; LETTER QUALITY (LQ); LINE PRINTER; MFP; NEAR LETTER QUALITY; PAGE PRINTER.

Printer Control Language *n.* See PCL.

printer driver *n.* a program that controls a printer.

⇒ See also DRIVER.

printer engine *n.* the main component of a printer that actually performs the printing. The printer engine determines how fast and at what resolution the printer can print.

⇒ See also PRINTER.

print merge *n.* MAIL MERGE.

printout *n.* a printed version of text or data. Also called **hard copy**.

Print Screen key *n.* a key on most PCs. In DOS, pressing this key causes the computer to send whatever images and text are currently on the display screen to the printer. Some graphical user interfaces, including Windows, use this key to obtain screen captures.

⇒ See also CAPTURE; HARD COPY.

print server *n.* See under SERVER.

print spooling *n.* See under SPOOLING.

procedure *n.* **1.** a section of a program that performs a specific task; a routine, subroutine, or function. **2.** an ordered set of tasks for performing some action.

⇒ See also FUNCTION; ROUTINE.

process *n.* **1.** an executing program. The term is used loosely as a synonym of *task*. —*v.t.* **2.** to perform some useful operations on (data).

⇒ See also DAEMON; TASK.

process colors *n.pl.* the CMYK color model used in offset printing.

⇒ See also CMYK; COLOR SEPARATION; OFFSET PRINT-ING.

processor *n.* MICROPROCESSOR.

⇒ See also CPU.

processor unit *n.* CENTRAL PROCESSING UNIT.

Prodigy *n.* an online service developed jointly by IBM and Sears.

⇒ See also ONLINE SERVICE.

program *n.* **1.** an organized list of instructions that, when executed, causes the computer to be-have in a predetermined manner. A program is like a recipe. It contains a list of ingredients (called *variables*) and a list of directions (called *statements*) that tell the computer what to do with the variables. The variables can represent numeric data, text, or graphical images. —*v.t.* **2.** to write programs for (a computer).

⇒ See also ALGORITHM; ASSEMBLER; ASSEMBLY LAN-GUAGE; CASE; CODE; COMPILER; EXECUTABLE FILE; FLOW CONTROL; HIGH-LEVEL LANGUAGE; INSTRUCTION; INTERPRETER; LANGUAGE; LOW-LEVEL LANGUAGE; MA-CHINE LANGUAGE; MODULE; PROGRAMMING LANGUAGE; PSEUDOCODE; SOFTWARE.

Programmable Logic Device *n.* See PLD.

programmable read-only memory *n.* See PROM.

programmer *n.* **1.** an individual who writes programs. **2.** a device that writes a program onto a PROM chip.

⇒ See also HACKER; PROGRAM; PROM; SOFTWARE EN-GINEER.

programming language *n.* a vocabulary and set of grammatical rules for instructing a com-puter to perform specific tasks. The term *pro-gramming language* usually refers to high-level languages. Each language has a unique set of keywords (words that it understands) and a spe-cial syntax for organizing program instructions. The choice of which language to use depends on the type of computer the program is to run on, what sort of program it is, and the expertise of the programmer.

⇒ See also ADA; ASSEMBLY LANGUAGE; AWK; BASIC; C; C++; COBOL; COMPILER; FLOW CONTROL; FOR-

TRAN; FOURTH-GENERATION LANGUAGE; HIGH-LEVEL
LANGUAGE; INTERPRETER; JAVA; LANGUAGE; LISP; LOW-
LEVEL LANGUAGE; MACHINE LANGUAGE; MODULA-2; OB-
JECT-ORIENTED PROGRAMMING; PASCAL; PROLOG; TCL;
VBSCRIPT; VISUAL BASIC.

Progress Software *n.* a leading software company in the DBMS field. Although Progress Software has its own DBMS system, it also provides
tools to develop applications that can interact
with any DBMS.
⇒ See also DATABASE MANAGEMENT SYSTEM.

Prolog *n.* Programming Logic: a high-level programming language based on defining and then
solving logical formulas. Prolog is used for artificial intelligence applications, particularly expert
systems.
⇒ See also ARTIFICIAL INTELLIGENCE; EXPERT SYSTEM;
LISP; PROGRAMMING LANGUAGE.

PROM (prom), *n.* programmable read-only memory: a memory chip on which data can be written
only once. PROMs retain their contents when the
computer is turned off. The difference between a
PROM and a ROM is that a PROM is manufac-
tured as blank memory, whereas a ROM is programmed during the manufacturing process. The
process of programming a PROM is sometimes
called *burning* the PROM.
⇒ See also EEPROM; EPROM; MAIN MEMORY; MEM-
ORY; PLD; ROM.

prompt *n.* a symbol on a display screen indicating that the computer is waiting for input.
⇒ See also TIME-OUT.

property *n.* a characteristic of an object. In
many programming languages, the term is used
to describe attributes associated with a data
structure.
⇒ See also ATTRIBUTE.

proportional font *n.* a font in which different
characters have different *pitches* (widths). Also
called **proportional-pitch font.**
⇒ See also FIXED PITCH; FONT; PITCH; PROPORTIONAL
SPACING.

proportional pitch *adj.* proportionally spaced.
See under PROPORTIONAL SPACING.

proportional spacing n. the use of different widths for different characters. In a proportionally spaced font, the letter *i* is narrower than the letter *q*, and the letter *m* is wider. Most books, magazines, and newspapers use a proportionally spaced font.

⇒ See also CPI; FIXED PITCH; FONT; MONOSPACING; PITCH.

proprietary adj. privately owned and controlled. A proprietary design or technique is one that is owned by a company; it implies that the company has not divulged specifications. Consumers prefer open and standardized architectures, which allow them to mix and match products from different manufacturers.

⇒ See also ARCHITECTURE; OPEN ARCHITECTURE; STANDARD.

protected mode n. a type of memory utilization available on Intel 80286 and later-model microprocessors. In protected mode, these processors provide the following features: **protection** (each program is allocated a section of memory, so it is protected from interference), **extended memory, virtual memory,** and **multitasking.**

⇒ See also DOS; EXTENDED MEMORY; INTEL MICROPROCESSORS; MICROSOFT WINDOWS; MULTITASKING; OS/2; UNIX; VIRTUAL MEMORY.

protocol n. an agreed-upon format for transmitting data between two devices. There are a variety of standard protocols from which programmers can choose. From a user's point of view, the computer or device must support the right protocols to communicate with other computers.

⇒ See also CCITT; COMMUNICATIONS; COMMUNICATIONS PROTOCOL; CONNECTIONLESS; HANDSHAKING; MODEM; PROTOCOL STACK.

protocol stack n. a set of network protocol layers that work together. The OSI Reference Model that defines seven protocol layers is often called a stack, as is the set of TCP/IP protocols that define communication over the Internet. The term *stack* also refers to the actual software that processes the protocols.

⇒ See also NETWORK INTERFACE CARD; OSI; PROTOCOL; TCP/IP; WINSOCK.

proxy *n.* See under PROXY SERVER.

proxy server *n.* a server that sits between a client application, such as a Web browser, and a real server. It intercepts all requests to the real server to see if it can fulfill the requests itself. If not, it forwards the request to the real server.
⇒ See also FIREWALL; SERVER; SOCKS; WEB SERVER.

Prt Scr key *n.* PRINT SCREEN KEY.

PS/2 port *n.* a type of port developed by IBM for connecting a mouse or keyboard to a PC.
⇒ See also PORT; SERIAL MOUSE; SERIAL PORT.

pseudocode *n.* an outline of a program, written in a form that can easily be converted into real programming statements.
⇒ See also ALGORITHM; BUBBLE SORT; CODE; PROGRAM.

PSTN Public Switched Telephone Network: the international telephone system based on copper wires carrying analog voice data. Telephone service carried by the PSTN is often called POTS.
⇒ See also CIRCUIT SWITCHING; POTS.

public carrier *n.* any of the government-regulated organizations that provide telecommunications services to the public. These include AT&T, MCI, and Western Union.
⇒ See also E-MAIL.

public-domain software *n.* any program that is not copyrighted. Public-domain software is free and can be used without restrictions.
⇒ See also FREEWARE; SHAREWARE.

public key *n.* See under PUBLIC-KEY ENCRYPTION.

public-key encryption *n.* a cryptographic system that uses two keys—a *public key* known to everyone and a *private* or *secret key* known only to the recipient of the message. Public-key systems, such as Pretty Good Privacy (PGP), are becoming popular for transmitting information via the Internet. This kind of encryption is also called *asymmetric encryption* because it uses two keys instead of one key *symmetric encryption*).
⇒ See also CERTIFICATE AUTHORITY; CRYPTOGRAPHY; DIGITAL CERTIFICATE; DIGITAL ENVELOPE; ENCRYPTION; LDAP; PRETTY GOOD PRIVACY; RSA; S/MIME; SYMMETRIC-KEY CRYPTOGRAPHY.

public-key infrastructure *n*. See PKI.

puck *n*. CURSOR (def. 2).
⇒ See also POINTING DEVICE.

pull *v.t.* to request (data) from another program or computer. The World Wide Web is based on pull technologies, where a page is not delivered until a browser requests it. Increasingly, however, information services are harnessing the Internet to broadcast information using push technologies.
⇒ See also PUSH.

pull-down menu *n*. a menu of commands or options that appears when an item is selected with a mouse. The item selected is generally at the top of the display screen, and the menu appears just below it.
⇒ See also COMMAND; MENU; OPTION; POP-UP WINDOW.

pulse code modulation *n*. See PCM.

punctuation *n*. (in programming languages) special characters that serve to separate words and phrases. Unlike human language punctuation, which is often optional, computer punctuation is strictly required.
⇒ See also SPECIAL CHARACTER.

purge *v.t.* to remove (old and unneeded data) systematically and permanently. It is often possible to regain deleted objects by *undeleting* them, but purged objects are gone forever.
⇒ See also DELETE; RECYCLE BIN.

PURL persistent URL: a type of URL that acts as an intermediary for a real URL. When a user enters a PURL, the browser sends the page request to a PURL server, which then returns the real URL of the page. Once a PURL is established, it never needs to change.
⇒ See also URL.

push *v.t.* **1.** in client/server applications, to send (data) to a client without the client's requesting it. Broadcast media are push technologies because they send information out regardless of whether anyone is tuned in. Increasingly, companies are using the Internet to deliver information push-style. **2.** in programming, to place (a data item) onto a stack.

⇒ See also CDF; POINTCAST; POP; PULL; WEBCAST-ING.

push-button *n.* a button in a dialog box. See under BUTTON.

⇒ See also DIALOG BOX.

PVC permanent virtual circuit: a virtual circuit that is permanently available. PVCs are more efficient than SVCs for connections between hosts that communicate frequently.

⇒ See also FRAME RELAY; SVC; VIRTUAL CIRCUIT.

Q q

QBASIC *n.* an interpreter for the BASIC programming language, at one time provided by Microsoft with the DOS operating system.
⇒ See also BASIC; GW-BASIC.

QBE QUERY BY EXAMPLE.

QCIF *n.* Quarter Common Intermediate Format: a videoconferencing format that specifies data rates of 30 frames per second (fps), with each frame containing 144 lines and 176 pixels per line. This is one fourth the resolution of Full CIF. QCIF support is required by the ITU H.261 videoconferencing standard.
⇒ See also COMMON INTERMEDIATE FORMAT; NTSC; PAL; VIDEOCONFERENCING.

QIC (kwik), *n.* quarter-inch cartridge: a standard for magnetic tape drives. QIC tapes are among the most popular tapes used for backing up personal computers. They are divided into two general classes: full-size (also called *data-cartridge*) and minicartridge.
⇒ See also MASS STORAGE; TAPE; TRAVAN.

QoS Quality of Service: a networking term that specifies a guaranteed throughput level.
⇒ See also ATM; CIR; LATENCY; RSVP.

QTVR QUICKTIME VR.

quad-speed CD-ROM drive *n.* a CD-ROM drive designed to run four times as fast as original models.
⇒ See also CD-ROM PLAYER.

Quality of Service *n.* See QoS.

quarter-inch cartridge *n.* See QIC.

query *n.* **1.** a request for information matching certain criteria from a database. —*v.t.* **2.** to make a request for information from (a database).
⇒ See also DATABASE MANAGEMENT SYSTEM; FIELD; QUERY BY EXAMPLE; QUERY LANGUAGE; RECORD.

query by example *n.* in database management systems, a method of forming queries in which the database program displays a blank record with a space for each field. A user can then enter conditions for each field.

⇒ See also DATABASE MANAGEMENT SYSTEM; FIELD; QUERY; QUERY LANGUAGE; RECORD.

query language *n.* a specialized language for requesting information from a database.

⇒ See also DATABASE MANAGEMENT SYSTEM; QUERY; SQL.

queue *v.t.* **1.** to line up (jobs) for a computer or device. For example, the operating system (or a print spooler) queues documents to be printed by placing them in a special area called a *print buffer* or *print queue.* —*n.* **2.** a group of jobs waiting to be executed. **3.** in programming, a data structure in which elements are removed in the same order in which they were entered. This is often referred to as FIFO (first in, first out). In contrast, a *stack* is a data structure in which elements are removed in the reverse order from which they were entered. This is referred to as LIFO (last in, first out).

⇒ See also BUFFER; DATA STRUCTURE; JOB; OPERATING SYSTEM; SPOOLING.

QuickDraw *n.* the underlying graphics display system for Apple Macintosh computers. The QuickDraw system enables programs to create and manipulate graphical objects.

⇒ See also GRAPHICS; MACINTOSH COMPUTER; PIXEL; POSTSCRIPT.

QuickTime *n.* a video and animation system developed by Apple Computer. QuickTime is built into the Macintosh operating system and is used by most Mac applications that include video or animation. PCs with appropriate software can also run files in QuickTime format.

⇒ See also ANIMATION; AVI; CINEPAK; CODEC; INDEO; MPEG; MULTIMEDIA; QUICKTIME VR.

QuickTime Virtual Reality *n.* QUICKTIME VR.

QuickTime VR *n.* an enhanced version of the QuickTime standard developed by Apple for displaying multimedia content. This enhanced version allows a user to move through a three-dimensional scene.

⇒ See also QUICKTIME; VIRTUAL REALITY; VRML.

quit *v.t.* to exit (a program) in an orderly way.
⇒ See also ABORT.

QWERTY keyboard (kwûr′tē, kwer′-), *n.* a standard English computer or typewriter keyboard layout. The name derives from the first six characters on the top alphabetic line of the keyboard.
⇒ See also DVORAK KEYBOARD; KEYBOARD.

R r

RAD *n.* RAPID APPLICATION DEVELOPMENT.

radio buttons *n.pl.* in graphical user interfaces, groups of buttons, of which only one can be on at a time.
⇒ See also BUTTON; CHECK BOX; GRAPHICAL USER INTERFACE; SELECT.

RADIUS *n.* Remote Authentication Dial-In User Service: an authentication and accounting system used by many Internet service providers (ISPs).
⇒ See also AUTHENTICATION; DIAL-UP ACCESS; ISP.

ragged *adj.* in text processing, not aligned along a margin, esp. the right margin.
⇒ See also FLUSH; JUSTIFY.

RAID *n.* Redundant Array of Independent (or Inexpensive) Disks: a category of disk subsystems that employ two or more drives in combination for fault tolerance and performance, used frequently on servers.
⇒ See also DISK DRIVE; DISK MIRRORING; DISK STRIPING; FAULT TOLERANCE.

RAM (ram), *n.* random-access memory: a type of computer memory that can be accessed randomly; that is, any byte of memory can be accessed without touching adjacent bytes. RAM is the most common type of memory found in computers and other devices.
⇒ See also DYNAMIC RAM; MAIN MEMORY; MEMORY; NVRAM; ROM; SRAM; TAG RAM; VRAM; WRAM.

Rambus memory *n.* See RDRAM.

RAM cache *n.* **1.** L2 CACHE. **2.** on Apple Macintosh computers, a disk cache.
⇒ See also CACHE; DISK CACHE; L2 CACHE.

RAMDAC (ram′dak′), *n.* Random Access Memory Digital-to-Analog Converter: a chip on video adapter cards that converts digitally encoded images into analog signals that can be displayed by a monitor.
⇒ See also DAC; MONITOR; VIDEO ADAPTER; VIDEO MEMORY.

RAM disk or **drive** *n.* RAM that has been configured to simulate a disk drive. Faster than hard disk drives, RAM disks are useful for applications that require frequent disk access.

⇒ See also DISK; EXTENDED MEMORY; RAM.

RAM resident *n.* MEMORY RESIDENT.

random access *n.* the ability to access data at random. Disks are effectively random-access media; tape drives are not. A random-access data file enables users to read or write information anywhere in the file.

⇒ See also ACCESS; RAM; SEQUENTIAL ACCESS.

random-access memory *n.* See RAM.

range *n.* in spreadsheet applications, one or more contiguous cells. For example, a range could be an entire row or column, or multiple rows or columns.

⇒ See also CELL; EXPRESSION; FUNCTION; SPREADSHEET.

rapid application development *n.* a programming system that enables programmers to build working programs quickly. Among other things, RAD systems provide tools to help build graphical user interfaces.

⇒ See also DELPHI; PROGRAMMING LANGUAGE; VISUAL BASIC.

RAS Remote Access Services: a feature built into Windows NT that enables users to log into an NT-based LAN using a modem, X.25 connection, or WAN link.

⇒ See also DIAL-UP NETWORKING; REMOTE ACCESS; REMOTE CONTROL; WINDOWS NT.

raster *n.* the rectangular area in which images are displayed on a monitor or LCD display.

⇒ See also AUTOSIZING; BIT-MAPPED GRAPHICS; DISPLAY SCREEN; MONITOR; RASTER IMAGE PROCESSOR; RESOLUTION.

raster graphics *n.* BIT-MAPPED GRAPHICS.

raster image processor *n.* a hardware-software combination that converts a vector image into a bit-mapped image, often for printing.

⇒ See also BIT MAP; POSTSCRIPT; RASTER; VECTOR GRAPHICS.

raw data *n.* information that has not been organized, formatted, or analyzed.

⇒ See also DATA.

ray tracing *n.* in computer graphics, an advanced technique for adding realism to an image.
⇒ See also 3-D GRAPHICS; GRAPHICS; TEXTURE.

RDBMS relational database management system: a type of database management system (DBMS) that stores data in the form of related tables. Relational databases are powerful because they require few assumptions about how data is related or how it will be extracted from the database. As a result, the same data can be viewed in many different ways.
⇒ See also BORLAND INTERNATIONAL; DATABASE; DATABASE MANAGEMENT SYSTEM; DB2; FLAT-FILE DATABASE; MULTIDIMENSIONAL DBMS; NORMALIZATION; QUERY; REFERENTIAL INTEGRITY; SQL SERVER.

RDRAM *n.* Rambus DRAM: a type of memory (DRAM) developed by Rambus, Inc. RDRAM can transfer data at up to 600 MHz, much faster than SDRAM.
⇒ See also DRAM; EDO DRAM; MEMORY; SDRAM; VIDEO MEMORY.

read *v.t.* **1.** to copy (data) to a place where it can be used by a program. The term is commonly used to describe copying data from a storage medium, such as a disk, to main memory. —*n.* **2.** the act of reading: *A fast disk drive performs 100 reads per second.*
⇒ See also ACCESS.

readme file *n.* a small text file that comes with many software packages and contains information not included in other documentation.
⇒ See also DOCUMENTATION.

read-only *adj.* capable of being displayed, but not modified or deleted. All operating systems allow users to protect disks, files, and directories with a *read-only attribute* that prevents other users from modifying them.
⇒ See also ATTRIBUTE; CD-ROM; READ/WRITE; ROM.

read-only memory *n.* See ROM.

read/write *adj.* capable of being displayed (read) and modified (written to). Most disks, files, and directories are read/write, but operating systems also allow users to prevent other users from modifying them.

⇒ See also READ-ONLY.

read/write head *n.* HEAD.

real address *n.* ABSOLUTE ADDRESS.

RealAudio *n.* the de facto standard for streaming audio data over the World Wide Web. A RealAudio player or plug-in program is needed to hear a RealAudio sound file.

⇒ See also REALVIDEO; STREAMING.

real mode *n.* an execution mode supported by the Intel 80286 and later processors. In real mode, these processors imitate the Intel 8088 and 8086 microprocessors, although they run much faster.

⇒ See also DOS; INTEL MICROPROCESSORS; MICRO-SOFT WINDOWS; MULTITASKING; OS/2; PROTECTED MODE.

real time *adj.* describing immediate response by a computer system. Most general-purpose operating systems are not real-time because they can take a few seconds, or even minutes, to react to input. *Real time* can also refer to events simulated by a computer at the same speed that they would occur in real life.

⇒ See also ISOCHRONOUS; OPERATING SYSTEM; OS/9.

real-time clock *n.* a clock that keeps track of the time even when the computer is turned off.

⇒ See also CLOCK SPEED.

Real Time Streaming Protocol *n.* See RTSP.

Real-Time Transport Protocol *n.* See RTP.

RealVideo *n.* a streaming technology for transmitting live video over the Internet.

⇒ See also IP MULTICAST; REALAUDIO; STREAMING.

reboot *v.t., v.i.* to restart (a computer), as by pressing the Alt, Control, and Delete keys simultaneously or by turning the computer off and then on again. On Macs, the user reboots by selecting the "Restart" option from the Special menu or pushing the reset button.

⇒ See also BOOT.

recalculation *n.* in spreadsheet programs, the computing of the values of cells in a spreadsheet. Recalculation is necessary whenever a formula is changed or new data is entered into one or more cells.

⇒ See also AUTOMATIC RECALCULATION; BACKGROUND; CELL; FORMULA; SPREADSHEET.

record n. **1.** in database management systems, a complete set of information. Records are composed of *fields*, each of which contains one item of information. A set of records constitutes a *file*. **2.** in some programming languages, a special data structure. Generally, a record is a combination of other data objects.

⇒ See also DATA STRUCTURE; DATA TYPE; DATABASE; DATABASE MANAGEMENT SYSTEM; FIELD; FILE.

record locking n. See under LOCK.

recursion n. a programming method in which a routine calls itself.

⇒ See also PROGRAM; PROGRAMMING LANGUAGE.

Recycle Bin n. an icon on the Windows 95 and Windows 98 desktops that represents a directory where deleted files are temporarily stored.

⇒ See also DELETE.

Red Book n. the standard for audio CDs, developed by Philips and Sony.

⇒ See also CD-ROM; COMPACT DISC; GREEN BOOK; ORANGE BOOK; WHITE BOOK.

red-green-blue monitor n. RGB MONITOR.

redirection n. the diversion of input and output to files and devices other than the default I/O devices (usually the keyboard and screen respectively).

⇒ See also DEFAULT; DEVICE; FILE; I/O; OPERATING SYSTEM; SHELL; UNIX.

redlining n. in word processing, the marking of text that has been edited, as with a change in font or color, to enable the next person in the editorial process to track changes.

⇒ See also WORD PROCESSING.

reduced instruction set computer n. See RISC.

Redundant Array of Independent Disks n. See RAID.

referential integrity n. a feature of relational database management systems (RDBMSs) that prevents users or applications from entering inconsistent data.

⇒ See also KEY; NORMALIZATION; RDBMS.

refresh *v.t.* **1.** generally, to update (something) with new data. For example, some Web browsers have a refresh button that updates the currently displayed Web pages. **2.** to recharge (a device) with power or information. For example, *dynamic RAM* needs to be refreshed thousands of times per second. Similarly, display monitors must be refreshed many times per second. The faster this refresh rate, the less the monitor flickers.

⇒ See also DYNAMIC RAM; INTERLACING; MONITOR; SCREEN FLICKER.

refresh rate *n.* See under REFRESH.

register *n.* **1.** a special high-speed storage area within the CPU. All data must be represented in a register before it can be processed. —*v.i., v.t.* **2.** to notify the manufacturer after purchasing (a product). Registering a product is often a prerequisite to receiving customer support, and it is one of the ways that software producers control software piracy.

⇒ See also CPU; MICROPROCESSOR; SOFTWARE PIRACY.

Registry *n.* a database used by the Windows operating system (Windows 95, 98, and NT) to store configuration information.

⇒ See also CONFIGURATION; WINDOWS 95.

relational database *n.* See RDBMS.

relational expression *n.* RELATIONAL OPERATOR.

relational operator *n.* an operator that compares two values. For example, the expression x < 5 means *x is less than 5*. This expression will have a value of TRUE if the variable x is less than 5; otherwise the value will be FALSE.

⇒ See also BOOLEAN LOGIC; EXPRESSION; OPERATOR.

relative address *n.* an address specified by indicating its distance from another address, called the *base address*.

⇒ See also ABSOLUTE ADDRESS; ADDRESS; BASE ADDRESS; CELL; MEMORY; OFFSET.

relative cell reference *n.* in spreadsheet applications, a reference to a cell or group of cells by indicating how far away it is from some other cell. For example, the cell reference "C2" points to the cell in the third column and second row. If this reference is inserted in cell A1, the program can translate it to "2 columns right and 1 row down."

⇒ See also ABSOLUTE CELL REFERENCE; CELL; SPREAD-SHEET.

remote *adj.* in networks, referring to files, devices, and other resources that are not connected directly to a workstation.

⇒ See also LOCAL; LOCAL-AREA NETWORK; NETWORK; REMOTE ACCESS; REMOTE CONTROL SOFTWARE; WORKSTATION.

remote access *n.* the ability to log onto a network from a distant location either by telephone or by an internetwork connection. The remote computer becomes a full-fledged host on the network.

⇒ See also RAS; REMOTE; REMOTE CONTROL.

remote control *n.* a program's ability to control a computer system from a remote location. Only keystrokes and screen updates are transmitted between the two machines as all processing takes place in the controlled computer.

⇒ See also HOST; LOCAL; RAS; REMOTE; REMOTE ACCESS; REMOTE CONTROL SOFTWARE.

remote control software *n.* software, installed in both machines, that allows a user at a local computer to have control of a remote computer via modem or other connection.

⇒ See also HOST; REMOTE CONTROL.

remote procedure call *n.* See RPC.

removable cartridge *n.* REMOVABLE HARD DISK.

removable drive *n.* REMOVABLE HARD DISK.

removable hard disk *n.* a type of disk drive system in which hard disks are enclosed in plastic or metal cartridges so that they can be inserted into and removed from an accessible drive bay like floppy disks.

⇒ See also CARTRIDGE; DISK; DISK PACK; HARD DISK; JAZ DRIVE; MASS STORAGE.

render *v.t.* to create (a computer graphics image) from a file containing descriptions of the objects in a scene.

⇒ See also 3-D GRAPHICS; 3-D SOFTWARE; CAD/
CAM; MODELING; RAY TRACING; TEXTURE.

repaginate *v.i.* to recalculate page breaks. Most
systems automatically repaginate whenever a
document is modified.

⇒ See also ORPHAN; PAGE BREAK; WIDOW.

repeater *n.* a network device used to regenerate
or replicate a signal. Repeaters are used to regenerate signals distorted by transmission loss.

⇒ See also 10BASET; BRIDGE; HUB; ROUTER.

replace *v.t.* to insert (a new object) in place of
an existing object.

⇒ See also SEARCH AND REPLACE.

replication *n.* the process of creating and managing duplicate versions of a database. Replication enables many users to work with their own
local copy of a database but have the database
updated as if they were working on a single, cen-
tralized database.

⇒ See also DATABASE; LOTUS NOTES.

report *n.* a formatted and organized presentation
of data.

⇒ See also REPORT WRITER; RPG.

report generator *n.* REPORT WRITER.

report writer *n.* a program, usually part of a
database management system, that extracts information from one or more files and presents the
information in a specified format.

⇒ See also DATABASE MANAGEMENT SYSTEM; FIELD;
RECORD; REPORT; RPG.

Request for Comments *n.* See RFC.

reserved word *n.* a special word reserved by a
programming language or by a program. Reserved words cannot be used as variable names.

⇒ See also KEYWORD; VARIABLE.

reset button *n.* a button or switch that is used
to reset the computer. The computer will enter its
start-up procedure as if the power had been
turned off and then on again. Generally, the reset
button is used only when a program error has
caused the computer to hang.

⇒ See also BOOT; HANG; REBOOT.

resident *adj.* **1.** permanently available to a user, as a font in a printer's ROM or software on a CD-ROM. **2.** of a computer program, currently in RAM.

resident font *n.* a font built into the hardware of a printer. Additional fonts can be added by inserting font cartridges or downloading soft fonts.
⇒ See also DOWNLOAD; FONT; FONT CARTRIDGE; PRINTER; SOFT FONT.

resize *v.t.* SIZE.

resolution *n.* the sharpness and clarity of an image. The term is most often used to describe the potential performance of given monitors and printers, and the achieved fineness of bit-mapped graphic images. Printers, monitors, scanners, and other I/O devices are often classified as *high resolution, medium resolution,* or *low resolution.*
⇒ See also BIT MAP; DPI; MONITOR; OPTICAL RESOLUTION; PIXEL; PRINTER; RASTER; VIDEO ADAPTER.

resolution enhancement *n.* a collection of techniques used in many laser printers to enable the printer to print at a higher resolution than normal.
⇒ See also LASER PRINTER; PRINTER ENGINE; RESOLUTION.

resource *n.* **1.** generally, any item that can be used, such as memory or a disk drive. **2.** in an operating system, a routine or data available to a program.

Resource Reservation Setup Protocol *n.* See RSVP.

restore *v.t.* in graphical user interfaces, to return (a window) to its original size.
⇒ See also GRAPHICAL USER INTERFACE; SIZE; WINDOW; ZOOM.

return *n.* a special code that marks the end of a line.
⇒ See also CARRIAGE RETURN; HARD RETURN; RETURN KEY; SOFT RETURN.

Return key *n.* a key marked *Return* or *Enter:* in text entry, this key moves the cursor (or insertion point) to the beginning of the next line. During other program activity, pressing the Return key may signal that the program's requests for information from the user have been responded to, thus returning control to the program. In word-processing programs, pressing the Return key inserts a hard return into a document.

⇒ See also CURSOR; ENTER KEY; HARD RETURN; INSERTION POINT; KEYBOARD; PROMPT.

reverse engineering *n.* the process of recreating a software or hardware design by analyzing a final product.

⇒ See also SOFTWARE ENGINEER.

reverse video *n.* a display method that causes a portion of the display to appear like a negative of the regular display. If the display screen normally displays light images against a dark background, *reverse video mode* will cause it to display dark images against a light background.

⇒ See also BACKGROUND; DISPLAY SCREEN; FOREGROUND.

RFC Request for Comments: a series of notes about the Internet. An RFC can be submitted by anyone. If it gains enough interest, it may evolve into an Internet standard.

⇒ See also IETF; INTERNET ARCHITECTURE BOARD.

RGB monitor *n.* red, green, blue monitor: a monitor that requires separate signals for each of the three colors. This differs from color televisions, in which all the colors are mixed together. Almost all color computer monitors are RGB monitors.

⇒ See also COLOR MONITOR; COMPOSITE VIDEO; CONVERGENCE; MASK PITCH; MONITOR; S-VIDEO.

rich text format *n.* a standard developed by Microsoft Corporation for specifying formatting of documents. *Abbr.:* RTF

⇒ See also HTML; SGML; WORLD WIDE WEB.

right justify *v.t.* to align (text) along the right margin.

ring network *n.* a local-area network (LAN) whose topology is a ring; all of the nodes are connected in a closed loop.

⇒ See also BUS NETWORK; LOCAL-AREA NETWORK; TOKEN-RING NETWORK; TOPOLOGY.

RIP (rip) *n.* **1.** RASTER IMAGE PROCESSOR **2.** ROUTING INFORMATION PROTOCOL.

RISC (risk), *n.* reduced instruction set computer: a type of microprocessor that recognizes a relatively limited number of instructions. One advantage of RISC computers is that they can execute their instructions very fast. Another advantage is that RISC chips require fewer transistors.

⇒ See also ALPHA PROCESSOR; CISC; CPU; INSTRUCTION; MICROPROCESSOR; SPARC.

RJ-11 Registered Jack-11: a four- or six-wire modular connector used primarily to connect telephone equipment in the United States.

⇒ See also MODEM; RJ-45.

RJ-45 Registered Jack-45: an eight-wire modular connector used commonly to connect computers to local-area networks (LANs), especially Ethernets.

⇒ See also 10BASET; CONNECTOR; RJ-11.

RJ45 See RJ-45.

RLL run length limited: an encoding scheme used to store data on newer PC hard disks. RLL produces fast data access times and increases a disk's storage capacity over the older MFM encoding.

⇒ See also DISK DRIVE; MFM.

RMI a set of protocols being developed by Sun's JavaSoft division that enables Java objects to communicate remotely with other Java objects.

⇒ See also CORBA; DCOM; JAVA.

RMON remote monitoring: a network management protocol that allows network information to be gathered from a single workstation.

⇒ See also NETWORK MANAGEMENT; SNMP.

robot *n.* **1.** a device that can move and respond to sensory input. **2.** a program that runs automatically on a networked computer, without human intervention.

⇒ See also ROBOTICS; SPIDER.

robotics *n.* the field of computer science and engineering concerned with creating robots, devices that can move and react to sensory input. Robotics is one branch of artificial intelligence.

⇒ See also ARTIFICIAL INTELLIGENCE; CAM; CYBERNETICS.

ROM (rom), *n.* read-only memory: computer

memory on which data have been prerecorded. ROM retains its contents even when the computer is turned off; it is nonvolatile. Most personal computers contain a small amount of ROM that stores critical low-level programs. ROM is used extensively in calculators and peripheral devices such as laser printers.

⇒ See also BIOS; BOOT; EEPROM; FIRMWARE; MEMORY; PROM; RAM.

roman adj. referring to fonts with characters whose ascending and descending parts are straight up and down rather than slanted.

⇒ See also FONT; ITALIC.

ROM-BIOS n. See BIOS.

root directory n. the top directory in a file system. The root directory is provided by the operating system and has a special name; for example, in DOS systems the root directory is given the name of the backslash character (\).

⇒ See also DIRECTORY; FILE MANAGEMENT SYSTEM; HIERARCHICAL.

router n. a device that connects two or more networks. Routers are similar to the bridges that connect LANs but provide additional functionality, such as the ability to filter messages and forward them to different places. The Internet uses routers to forward packets from one host to another.

⇒ See also 3COM; BGP; BRIDGE; BROUTER; GATEWAY; HOP; INTERNETWORKING; IP SPOOFING; IP SWITCHING; OSPF; PACKET; REPEATER; ROUTING; ROUTING INFORMATION PROTOCOL; ROUTING SWITCH.

routine n. a section of a program that performs a particular task. Also called **procedure, function, subroutine.**

⇒ See also FUNCTION; MODULE; PROGRAM.

routing n. in internetworking, the process of moving a packet of data from source to destination. Routing is a key feature of the Internet. Part of this process involves analyzing a *routing table* to determine the best path.

⇒ See also BGP; BRIDGING; CIDR; IP ADDRESS; IP SWITCHING; OSPF; PACKET; ROUTER; ROUTING INFORMATION PROTOCOL; ROUTING SWITCH.

Routing Information Protocol *n.* a protocol defined by RFC 1058 that specifies how routers exchange routing table information. *Abbr.:* RIP
⇒ See also OSPF; ROUTER; ROUTING.

routing switch *n.* a switch that also performs routing operations. Routing switches perform many of the layer 3 (Network layer) functions usually reserved for routers.
⇒ See also IP SWITCHING; ROUTER; ROUTING; SWITCH.

RPC remote procedure call: a type of protocol that allows a program on one computer to execute a program on another computer.
⇒ See also API; CORBA; MIDDLEWARE; PROTOCOL; REMOTE.

RPG 1. Report Program Generator: a programming language developed by IBM in the mid-1960s for developing business applications, especially generating reports from data. The newest version, RPG 400, is still widely used on AS/400 systems. **2.** role-playing game: a computer game in which one or more players adopt a role and act it out.
⇒ See also REPORT; REPORT WRITER.

RS-232C or RS-232 recommended standard-232C: a standard interface approved by the Electronic Industries Association (EIA) for connecting serial devices. In 1987, the EIA released a new version of the standard and changed the name to *EIA-232-D*. And in 1991, they issued a new version of the standard called *EIA/TIA-232-E*.
⇒ See also CONNECTOR; DTE; ELECTRONIC INDUSTRIES ASSOCIATION (EIA); INTERFACE; MODEM; RS-422 AND RS-423; SERIAL PORT.

RS-422 and RS-423 standard interfaces approved by the Electronic Industries Association (EIA) for connecting serial devices. RS-422 supports multipoint connections whereas RS-423 supports only point-to-point connections.
⇒ See also COMMUNICATIONS; CONNECTOR; ELECTRONIC INDUSTRIES ASSOCIATION (EIA); INTERFACE; MODEM; PORT; RS-232C; RS-485.

RS-485 an Electronic Industries Association (EIA) standard for multipoint serial communications. It supports several types of connectors.

⇒ See also ELECTRONIC INDUSTRIES ASSOCIATION (EIA); RS-422 AND RS-423.

RSA a public-key encryption technology developed by RSA Data Security, Inc. The abbreviation stands for Rivest, Shamir, and Adelman, the inventors. The RSA algorithm is the de facto standard for industrial-strength encryption, especially for data sent over the Internet, but software containing it is not generally exportable from the U.S.

⇒ See also ENCRYPTION; PRETTY GOOD PRIVACY; PUBLIC-KEY ENCRYPTION; S/MIME; SECURITY.

RSVP Resource Reservation Setup Protocol: an Internet protocol being developed to enable the Internet to support specified Qualities-of-Service (QoSs). RSVP is a chief component of a new type of Internet, known broadly as an *integrated services Internet*. The idea is to enhance the Internet to support transmission of real-time data.

⇒ See also QoS.

RTF RICH TEXT FORMAT.

RTP Real-Time Transport Protocol: an Internet protocol for transmitting real-time data such as audio and video. It provides mechanisms for the sending and receiving of applications to support streaming data.

⇒ See also RTSP; STREAMING; UDP; VIDEOCONFERENCING.

RTSP Real-Time Streaming Protocol: a proposed standard for controlling streaming data over the Internet.

⇒ See also BROADCAST; H.323; MULTICAST; Net-Show; RTP; STREAMING.

rule *n.* **1.** in word processing and desktop publishing, a straight line that separates columns of text or illustrations. **2.** in expert systems, a conditional statement that tells the system how to react to a particular situation.

⇒ See also EXPERT SYSTEM.

ruler *n.* in word processing, a line running across the display screen. It measures the printed-page layout, as measured on paper, in points, picas, inches, or centimeters, and is useful for setting margins and tabs. It is also used in graphics programs.

⇒ See also DESKTOP PUBLISHING; MARGINS; PAGE LAYOUT PROGRAM.

run *v.t.* **1.** to execute (a program). —*v.i.* **2.** to operate. For example, a device that is *running* is one that is turned on and operating properly.

⇒ See also LAUNCH; RUNTIME.

run length limited *n.* See RLL.

running head *n.* HEADER (def. 1).

runtime *adj.* occurring while a program is executing.

⇒ See also COMPILE; LIBRARY; RUN; RUNTIME ERROR; RUNTIME VERSION.

runtime error *n.* an error that occurs during the execution of a program. Runtime errors indicate bugs in the program or operating system, or hardware failures.

⇒ See also BOMB; BUG; COMPILER; CRASH; FATAL ERROR; GPF; RUNTIME.

runtime version *n.* a limited version of one program that enables a user to run programs written in a high-level language but not necessarily to write them. To run a program written in Visual Basic, for example, the runtime version of Visual Basic is needed.

⇒ See also RUNTIME; SOFTWARE LICENSING.

S s

SAA System Application Architecture: a set of architecture standards developed by IBM for program, user, and communications interfaces on various IBM platforms.
⇒ See also CUA; STANDARD; USER INTERFACE.

sampling *n.* a technique used to capture continuous phenomena, whereby periodic snapshots are taken. Music CDs are produced by sampling live sound at frequent intervals and then digitizing each sample. The term sampling is also used to describe a similar process in digital photography.
⇒ See also ADPCM; ANALOG; DIGITAL; DIGITAL CAMERA; DIGITIZE; PCM.

sans serif (san′ser′if, sans′-), *n.* a category of typefaces that do not use *serifs*, small lines at the ends of characters. Popular sans serif fonts include Helvetica, Avant Garde, Arial, and Geneva.
⇒ See also FONT.

SAP 1. Service Advertising Protocol: a NetWare protocol used to identify the services and addresses of servers attached to the network. **2.** Secondary Audio Program: an NTSC audio channel used for auxiliary transmission in television broadcasting, such as foreign language dialog or teletext. **3.** (*SAP America, Inc., Lester, PA*) the U.S. branch of the German software company SAP AG.
⇒ See also NETWARE; NTSC.

save *v.t., v.i.* to copy (data) from a temporary area to a more permanent storage medium. For example, in word processing, in order to record modifications made to a file, the file must be saved. To do this, the word processor copies the contents of its working buffer back to the file on the disk, replacing the previous version of the file.
⇒ See also AUTOSAVE; CLOSE.

scalability *n.* the quality of being scalable.

scalable *adj.* **1.** referring to how well a hardware or software system can adapt to increased demands. **2.** referring to anything whose size can be changed.

⇒ See also ARCHITECTURE; SCALABLE FONT.

scalable font *n.* a font represented in an object-oriented graphics language such as PostScript or TrueType. The representation of the font defines the shape of each character (the typeface) but not the size. A scalable font system can produce well-formed characters at any size.

⇒ See also FONT; INTELLIFONT; OUTLINE FONT; POST-SCRIPT; TRUETYPE; TYPEFACE; VECTOR GRAPHICS.

scale *v.t.* to change the size of (an object) while maintaining its shape. Most graphics software, particularly vector-based packages, allow users to scale objects freely.

⇒ See also GRAPHICS; SCALABLE FONT; VECTOR GRAPH-ICS.

SCAM *n.* SCSI Configuration Automatically: a subset of the PnP specification that provides plug-and-play support for SCSI devices.

⇒ See also PLUG-AND-PLAY; PNP; SCSI.

scan *v.t.* to digitize (an image) by passing it through an optical scanner.

⇒ See also OPTICAL SCANNER.

ScanDisk *n.* a DOS and Windows utility that finds different types of errors on hard disks and is able to correct some of them.

⇒ See also CLUSTER; DEFRAG; HARD DISK.

scanner *n.* OPTICAL SCANNER.

scatter diagram *n.* a type of diagram used to show the relationship between data items that have two numeric properties, one represented along the *x*-axis and the other along the *y*-axis. Each item is then represented by a single point. Scatter diagrams are used frequently by computer publications to compare categories of hardware and software products. One axis represents price, while the other represents performance.

⇒ See also PRESENTATION GRAPHICS.

scheduler *n.* **1.** a software product designed to help a group of colleagues schedule meetings and other appointments. The scheduler program allows members of a group to view one anothers' calendars. **2.** in operating systems, a program that coordinates the use of shared resources, such as a printer.

⇒ See also CALENDAR; GROUPWARE; OPERATING SYSTEM; WORKGROUP COMPUTING.

scientific notation *n.* a format for representing real (floating-point) numbers. Instead of writing the full number, it represents values as a number between 1 and 10 multiplied by 10 to some power. The 10 is often replaced by an *e*. Most programming languages, and many numeric applications, use scientific notation.

⇒ See also FLOATING-POINT NUMBER.

scissoring *n.* CLIPPING. See under CLIP.

Scrapbook *n.* in Macintosh environments, a desk accessory (DA) that enables users to store objects for future use. It retains its contents when the computer is turned off.

⇒ See also CLIPBOARD; DESK ACCESSORY (DA).

screen *n.* **1.** DISPLAY SCREEN. **2.** in offset printing, a mesh used to create halftones. See under HALFTONE.

screen capture *n.* the act of copying what is currently displayed on a screen to a file or printer.

⇒ See also CAPTURE; PRINT SCREEN KEY.

screen dump *n.* SCREEN CAPTURE.

screen flicker *n.* the phenomenon whereby a display screen appears to flicker. This phenomenon may occur if the image on the screen is refreshed too slowly, so that the phosphors in the screen cease glowing between refreshes.

⇒ See also INTERLACING; MONITOR; REFRESH.

screen font *n.* a font designed especially for a display screen. Typically, display fonts are bitmapped and must be specially designed to compensate for the relatively low resolution of display screens.

⇒ See also FONT; RESOLUTION.

screen resolution *n.* See under RESOLUTION.

screen saver *n.* a small program that takes over the display screen if there are no keystrokes or mouse movements for a specified duration. Screen savers were originally developed to prevent *ghosting*, the permanent etching of a pattern on a display screen. Modern display screens do not suffer so much from this problem. Today, therefore, screen savers are mostly an adornment.

⇒ See also DISPLAY SCREEN; MONITOR.

screen shot *n.* SCREEN CAPTURE.

script *n.* a list of commands that can be executed without user interaction. A *script language* is a simple programming language in which scripts can be written. Apple Computer uses the term *script* to refer to programs written in its Hyper-Card or AppleScript language.

⇒ See also APPLESCRIPT; BATCH FILE; HYPERCARD; JAVASCRIPT; MACRO.

scroll *v.i.* to view more data than fits in a display window. When a user scrolls down, each new line appears at the bottom of the screen and all the other lines move up one row, so that the top line disappears. The term *vertical scrolling* refers to the ability to scroll up or down. *Horizontal scrolling* means that the image moves sideways.

⇒ See also PAGE; SCROLL BAR.

scroll bar *n.* a bar that appears on the side or bottom of a window to control which part of a list or document is currently in the window's frame. Typically, a scroll bar has arrows at either end, and a *scroll box* (or *elevator*) that moves from one end to the other to reflect position in the document. Clicking on the arrows causes the document to scroll in the indicated direction.

⇒ See also CLICK; DRAG; GRAPHICAL USER INTERFACE; WINDOW.

scroll box *n.* See under SCROLL BAR.

Scroll Lock key *n.* a key on PC and enhanced Macintosh keyboards that controls the way the cursor control keys work for some programs.

⇒ See also CURSOR CONTROL KEYS; SCROLL.

SCSI (skuz'ē), *n.* Small Computer System Interface: a parallel interface standard used by Apple Macintosh computers, PCs, and many UNIX systems for attaching peripheral devices to computers. SCSI interfaces provide for faster data transmission rates (up to 80 megabytes per second) than standard serial and parallel ports. In addition, many devices can be attached to a single SCSI port.

⇒ See also BUS; DAISY CHAIN; FIBRE CHANNEL; INTERFACE; PORT.

SDH Synchronous Digital Hierarchy: an international standard for synchronous data transmission over fiber optic cables.

⇒ See also FIBER OPTICS; OC; SONET.

SDK software development kit: a programming package that enables a programmer to develop applications for a specific platform. Typically, an SDK includes one or more APIs, programming tools, and documentation.

⇒ See also API; JDK; PLATFORM.

SDLC Synchronous Data Link Control: a protocol used in IBM's SNA networks.

⇒ See also HDLC; SNA.

SDRAM *n.* Synchronous DRAM: a new type of DRAM that can run at much higher clock speeds than conventional memory. SDRAM actually synchronizes itself with the computer's bus and is capable of running about three times faster than conventional FPM RAM, and about twice as fast as EDO DRAM and BEDO DRAM.

⇒ See also BEDO DRAM; DDR-SDRAM; DRAM; EDO DRAM; MDRAM; PIPELINE BURST CACHE; RDRAM; SGRAM; SLDRAM; WAIT STATE.

SDRAM II *n.* DDR-SDRAM.

SDSL symmetric digital subscriber line: a new technology that allows more data to be sent over existing copper telephone lines (POTS). SDSL is called symmetric because, unlike ADSL, it supports the same data rate in both directions.

⇒ See also ADSL; ISDN; xDSL.

search and replace *n.* a feature supported by most word processors that lets a user replace a character string (a series of characters) with another string wherever the first string appears in the document.

⇒ See also CHARACTER STRING; WORD PROCESSING.

search engine *n.* a program that searches one or more documents, as on the World Wide Web, for specified keywords and returns a list of locations where those keywords were found. Although *search engine* designates a general type of program, such as one that enables a user to find information in an electronic book, the term is most often used to refer to such Internet services as Alta Vista and Excite.

⇒ See also ALTA VISTA; EXCITE; HOTBOT; INFOSEEK; JUGHEAD; LYCOS; META TAG; OPEN TEXT; SPIDER; VERONICA; WEBCRAWLER; YAHOO!.

secondary cache *n.* L2 CACHE.

secondary storage *n.* MASS STORAGE.

sector *n.* the smallest unit that can be accessed on a disk. When a disk undergoes a low-level format, it is divided into tracks and sectors. The tracks are concentric circles around the disk, and the sectors are segments within each circle. The operating system and disk drive keep tabs on where information is stored on the disk by noting its track and sector number.

⇒ See also BAD SECTOR; DISK; FORMAT; INTERLEAVE; TRACK.

Secure Electronic Transactions *n.* See SET.

Secure HTTP *n.* See S-HTTP.

Secure Socket Layer *n.* See SSL.

security *n.* any of several techniques for ensuring that data stored in a computer cannot be read or compromised, usually involving data encryption and passwords.

⇒ See also ACCESS CONTROL; AUDIT TRAIL; AUTHENTICATION; AUTHORIZATION; BIOMETRICS; CLIPPER CHIP; CRYPTOGRAPHY; ENCRYPTION; FIREWALL; KERBEROS; NETWORK MANAGEMENT; PASSWORD; RSA; SNIFFER; SSL.

seek time *n.* the time a program or device takes to locate a particular piece of data. For disk drives, the terms *seek time* and *access time* are often used interchangeably. Technically speaking, however, the access time is often longer than the seek time because it includes a brief latency period until disk rotation brings the desired sector under the read-write head.

⇒ See also ACCESS TIME; DISK DRIVE.

segment *n.* **1.** in networks, a section of a network that is bounded by bridges, routers, hubs, or switches. Dividing an Ethernet into multiple segments is one of the most common ways of increasing bandwidth on the LAN. If segmented correctly, most network traffic will remain within a single segment. Hubs and switches are used to connect each segment to the rest of the LAN. **2.** in virtual memory systems, a variable-sized portion of data that is swapped in and out of main memory. **3.** in graphics, a piece of a polyline.

⇒ See also MAIN MEMORY; PAGE; SWAP; SWITCHING HUB; VIRTUAL MEMORY.

select *v.t.* to choose (an object) so that it can be manipulated in some way. To select an object, such as an icon or file, the user moves the pointer to the object and clicks a mouse button. In many applications, blocks of text are selected by positioning the pointer at an end-point of the block and then dragging it over the block.

⇒ See also BLOCK; CHOOSE; DRAG; GRAPHICAL USER INTERFACE; HIGHLIGHT; ICON; MARQUEE; POINTER.

semantics *n.* the meaning of an instruction or command. If a user enters a legal command that does not make sense in the current context, that is a semantic error. If the command is misspelled, or has the wrong parameters, that is a syntax error.

⇒ See also PARSE; PROGRAMMING LANGUAGE; SYNTAX.

semaphore *n.* a hardware or software flag. In multitasking systems, a semaphore is a variable with a value that indicates the status of a common resource. It is used to lock a resource that is being used.

⇒ See also FLAG; INTERPROCESS COMMUNICATION (IPC); MULTITASKING.

semiconductor *n.* a material that is neither a good conductor of electricity (like copper) nor a good insulator (like rubber). The most common semiconductor materials are silicon and germanium. Computer chips, both for CPU and memory, are composed of semiconductor materials.

⇒ See also CHIP; CMOS; INTEGRATED CIRCUIT; NEC; TEXAS INSTRUMENTS; TRANSISTOR.

sequential access *n.* reading or writing data records in sequential order—that is, one after another. Some programming languages and operating systems distinguish between sequential-access data files and random-access data files, allowing a choice between the two types. Devices can also be classified as sequential access or random access. For example, a tape drive is a sequential-access device and a disk drive is a random-access device.

⇒ See also ISAM; RANDOM ACCESS.

serial *adj.* one by one. *Serial data transfer* refers to transmitting data one bit at a time.

⇒ See also COMMUNICATIONS; PARALLEL; SERIAL PORT.

serial interface *n.* SERIAL PORT.

Serial Line Internet Protocol *n.* See SLIP.

serial mouse *n.* a mouse that connects to a computer via a serial port.

⇒ See also MOUSE; PORT; PS/2 PORT; SERIAL; SERIAL PORT.

serial port *n.* a port that can be used for serial communication, in which only one bit is transmitted at a time.

⇒ See also ACCESS.BUS; COMMUNICATIONS; GEOPORT; IEEE 1394; INTERFACE; PARALLEL PORT; PORT; PS/2 PORT; RS-232C; RS-422 AND RS-423; UART; USB.

serif *n.* a small decorative line added as embellishment to the basic form of a character. The most common serif typeface is Times Roman.

⇒ See also FONT; SANS SERIF; TYPEFACE.

server *n.* a computer or device on a network that manages network resources. For example, a *file server* is a computer and storage device dedicated to storing files. A *network server* is a computer that manages network traffic. A *print server* is a computer that manages one or more printers, allowing access from the rest of the network.

⇒ See also CLIENT; CLIENT/SERVER ARCHITECTURE; DEC; LOAD BALANCING; LOCAL-AREA NETWORK; NETWORK; PROXY SERVER; SERVER MIRRORING; SERVER-SIDE; SGI; SUN MICROSYSTEMS; VIRTUAL SERVER.

server mirroring *n.* utilizing a backup server that duplicates all the processes and transactions of the primary server. Server mirroring is an expensive but effective strategy for achieving fault tolerance.

⇒ See also DISK MIRRORING; FAULT TOLERANCE; SERVER.

server-side *adj.* occurring on the server side of a client/server system. For example, on the World Wide Web, CGI scripts are server-side applications because they run on the Web server rather than in the browser.

⇒ See also CLIENT-SIDE; CLIENT/SERVER ARCHITECTURE; SERVER; SSI.

Server-Side Include *n.* See SSI.

service *n.* **1.** CUSTOMER SUPPORT. **2.** ONLINE SERVICE.

Service Advertising Protocol *n.* See SAP.

service bureau *n.* a company that provides a variety of desktop publishing services. In addition to providing high-resolution output with imagesetters, many service bureaus also offer scanning services.

⇒ See also DESKTOP PUBLISHING; IMAGESETTER; LINOTRONIC; OFFSET PRINTING; POSTSCRIPT.

Service Profile Identifier *n.* See SPID.

service provider *n.* INTERNET SERVICE PROVIDER.

servlet *n.* an applet that runs on a server. The term usually refers to a Java applet that runs within a Web server environment.

⇒ See also APPLET; CGI.

SET *n.* Secure Electronic Transaction: a standard intended to enable secure credit card transactions on the Internet.

⇒ See also ELECTRONIC COMMERCE.

setup *v.t.* **1.** to install and configure (hardware or software). Most Windows applications come with a program called SETUP.EXE or INSTALL.EXE, which installs the software on the computer's hard disk. —*n.* **2.** the configuration of hardware or software.

⇒ See also CONFIGURATION.

SGI Silicon Graphics Incorporated: a company based in Mountain View, California, that provides computer hardware and software.

⇒ See also ANIMATION; DEC; IBM; OPENGL; SERVER; SUN MICROSYSTEMS; VIDEO EDITING; WORKSTATION.

SGML Standard Generalized Markup Language: a system for organizing and tagging elements of a document. SGML specifies the rules for tagging elements. These tags can then be interpreted to format elements in different ways. SGML is used widely to manage large documents that are revised frequently and need to be printed in different formats.

⇒ See also HTML; HYPERTEXT; ISO; RICH TEXT FORMAT; TAG; WORLD WIDE WEB; XML.

SGRAM *n.* Synchronous Graphic Random Access Memory: a type of DRAM used increasingly on video adapters and graphics accelerators.

⇒ See also DRAM; GRAPHICS ACCELERATOR; SDRAM; VIDEO ADAPTER; VIDEO MEMORY; VRAM; WRAM.

shadowing *n.* a technique used to increase a computer's speed by using RAM in place of slower ROM. On PCs all code to control hardware devices is normally executed from a ROM chip called the *BIOS ROM.* However, many manufacturers configure their PCs to copy the BIOS code into RAM when the computer boots. The RAM used to hold the BIOS code is called *shadow RAM.*

⇒ See also BIOS; BOOT; MAIN MEMORY; RAM; ROM.

shared Ethernet *n.* the traditional type of Ethernet, in which all hosts are connected to the same bus and compete with one another for bandwidth.

⇒ See also ETHERNET; SWITCHED ETHERNET.

shareware *n.* software that, although copyrighted, is usually distributed free of charge. The author requests that users pay a small fee if they like the program and use it regularly.

⇒ See also BULLETIN BOARD SYSTEM; FREEWARE; ONLINE SERVICE; PUBLIC-DOMAIN SOFTWARE; SOFTWARE LICENSING; SOFTWARE PIRACY; WAREZ.

sheet feeder *n.* a mechanism that holds a stack of paper and feeds each sheet into a printer, fax machine, or scanner one at a time.

⇒ See also DOT-MATRIX PRINTER; FAX MACHINE; LASER PRINTER; OPTICAL SCANNER; PRINTER.

shell *n.* **1.** Also called **user interface.** the outermost layer of a program. **2.** Also called **command shell.** the command processor interface. The command processor is the program that executes operating system commands directly in response to user input.

⇒ See also COMMAND DRIVEN; COMMAND LANGUAGE; COMMAND PROCESSOR; INTERFACE; MENU DRIVEN; OPERATING ENVIRONMENT; OPERATING SYSTEM; UNIX; USER INTERFACE.

shift clicking *n.* clicking a mouse button while holding the Shift key down. In Microsoft Windows and Macintosh systems, shift clicking enables the user to select multiple items.

⇒ See also CLICK; GRAPHICAL USER INTERFACE; MACINTOSH COMPUTER; MICROSOFT WINDOWS; MOUSE; SELECT.

Shift key *n.* a key on computer keyboards. When combined with alphabetic keys, the Shift key causes the system to output a capital letter. The Shift key can also be combined with other keys to produce program-dependent results.

⇒ See also ALT KEY; CONTROL KEY; KEYBOARD.

Shockwave *n.* a technology developed by Macromedia, Inc., that enables Web pages to include multimedia objects. Shockwave supports audio, animation, and video.

⇒ See also ACTIVEX CONTROL; MULTIMEDIA; PLUG-IN.

shortcut *n.* in Windows 95 and Windows 98, a special type of file that points to another file or device. A user can place shortcuts on the desktop to conveniently access files that may be stored deep in the directory structure.

⇒ See also ALIAS; DESKTOP; LINK; SHORTCUT KEY.

shortcut key *n.* a special key combination that causes a specific command to be executed. Typically, shortcut keys combine the Ctrl or Alt keys with some other keys.

⇒ See also ALT KEY; COMMAND; CONTROL KEY; SHORTCUT.

shtml See under SSI.

S-HTTP an extension to the HTTP protocol to support sending data securely over the World Wide Web. Not all Web browsers and servers support S-HTTP.

⇒ See also HTTP; SSL.

shut down *v.t., v.i.* **1.** to turn (a device's) power off. **2.** in Windows 95 and Windows 98, to turn (a computer) off by selecting **Start→Shut**

Down...
⇒ See also POWER DOWN.

SIG (sig) *n.* special interest group: a group of users interested in a particular subject who discuss the subject at meetings or via an online service. Online SIGs are sometimes called *forums*.
⇒ See also BULLETIN BOARD SYSTEM; FORUM; ONLINE SERVICE.

sign *n.* a symbol that identifies a number as being either positive or negative. A positive sign is +; a negative sign is -. These two signs are also used to indicate addition and subtraction, respectively.
⇒ See also OPERATOR.

Silicon Graphics *n.* See SGI.

Silicon Valley *n.* a nickname for the region south of San Francisco that contains an unusually high concentration of computer companies. Silicon is the most common semiconductor material used to produce chips.
⇒ See also CHIP; SEMICONDUCTOR.

SIMM (sim), *n.* single in-line memory module: a small circuit board that can hold a group of memory chips. Unlike memory chips, SIMMs are measured in bytes rather than bits.
⇒ See also CHIP; DIMM; RAM.

Simple Mail Transfer Protocol *n.* See SMTP.

Simple Network Management Protocol *n.* See SNMP.

simplex *adj.* referring to transmission in only one direction. Simplex refers to *one-way* communications where one party is the transmitter and the other is the receiver. An example is a radio broadcast.
⇒ See also FULL DUPLEX; HALF DUPLEX.

simulation *n.* the process of imitating a real phenomenon with a set of mathematical formulas. Advanced computer programs can simulate weather conditions, chemical reactions, atomic reactions, even biological processes.

single-density disk *n.* a low-density floppy disk. All modern floppies are double-density or high-density.
⇒ See also FLOPPY DISK.

single in-line memory module *n.* See SIMM.

single in-line package *n.* See SIP.

single-sided disk *n.* a floppy disk with only one side prepared for storing data. All modern floppies are double-sided.
⇒ See also FLOPPY DISK.

SIP (sip) *n.* single in-line package: a type of housing for electronic components in which the connecting pins protrude from one side. Also called **Single In-line Pin Package (SIPP).**
⇒ See also DIP; PGA.

site *n.* WEB SITE.

680x0 See under MOTOROLA MICROPROCESSORS.

16-bit *adj.* referring to the number of bits that can be processed or transmitted in parallel, or the number of bits used for a single element in a data format. The term is often applied to microprocessors, buses, graphics devices, operating systems, applications, and expansion boards.
⇒ See also 32-BIT; BIT; BUS.

size *v.t.* to set the dimensions of (an object).
⇒ See also GRAPHICAL USER INTERFACE; SCALE; WINDOW.

slack space *n.* the unused space in a disk cluster. The DOS and Windows file systems use fixed-size clusters. Even if the actual data being stored require less storage than the cluster size, an entire cluster is reserved for the file.
⇒ See also CLUSTER; FAT32; FILE ALLOCATION TABLE; PARTITION.

slate PC *n.* a class of notebook computer that accepts input from an electronic pen rather than from a keyboard. Typically, slate PCs can decipher clearly written block letters and translate them into their ASCII equivalents.
⇒ See also HAND-HELD COMPUTER; HANDWRITING RECOGNITION; NOTEBOOK COMPUTER; PDA; PEN COMPUTER.

slave *n.* any device that is controlled by another device, called the *master.*
⇒ See also MASTER/SLAVE.

SLDRAM *n.* SyncLink DRAM: a new type of memory being developed by a consortium of computer manufacturers. SLDRAM is competing with Rambus memory (RDRAM).

⇒ See also BEDO DRAM; DRAM; EDO DRAM; FPM RAM; RDRAM; SDRAM.

sleep mode *n.* an energy-saving mode of operation in which all unnecessary components are shut down. Many battery-operated devices, such as notebook computers, support a sleep mode.

⇒ See also GREEN PC.

slimline model *n.* a small desktop model computer.

⇒ See also DESKTOP MODEL COMPUTER.

SLIP *n.* Serial Line Internet Protocol: a method of connecting to the Internet via telephone line. SLIP is an older protocol than PPP.

⇒ See also INTERNET; ISP; PPP; PROTOCOL.

slot *n.* an opening in a computer in which to insert a printed circuit board. Also called **expansion slot**.

⇒ See also BAY; CARTRIDGE; CHASSIS; EXPANSION BOARD; EXPANSION SLOT; PRINTED CIRCUIT BOARD.

Slot 1 *n.* the form factor for Intel's Pentium II processors. The Slot 1 package replaces the Socket 7 and Socket 8 form factors.

⇒ See also FORM FACTOR; PENTIUM II; SOCKET 7.

small computer system interface *n.* See SCSI.

Smalltalk *n.* an object-oriented operating system and programming language. It was the first object-oriented programming language, although it never achieved the commercial success of other languages such as C + + and Java.

⇒ See also C++; JAVA; OBJECT ORIENTED; OBJECT-ORIENTED PROGRAMMING.

SMART (smärt), *n.* Self-Monitoring, Analysis and Reporting Technology: an open standard for developing disk drives and software systems that automatically monitor a disk drive's health and report potential problems.

⇒ See also CRASH; DISK DRIVE; HARD DISK; MTBF.

smart battery *n.* See under BATTERY PACK.

smart card *n.* a small electronic device about the size of a credit card that contains an integrated circuit (IC). Such devices are sometimes called *Integrated Circuit Cards (ICCs)*. Smart cards are used for a variety of purposes, including storing medical records, storing digital cash, and generating network IDs.

⇒ See also CHALLENGE-RESPONSE; DIGITAL CASH; TOKEN.

Smartdrive *n.* a disk-caching system provided by Microsoft with later versions of DOS and used with Windows 3.1. Starting with Windows 95, Smartdrive was replaced by *VCACHE*.

⇒ See also DISK CACHE; VCACHE.

smart terminal *n.* a terminal that has some processing capabilities. Smart terminals have built-in logic for performing simple display operations, such as blinking and boldface.

⇒ See also DUMB TERMINAL; INTELLIGENT TERMINAL; TERMINAL.

SMB Server Message Block: a message format used by DOS and Windows to share files, directories and devices. NetBIOS is based on the SMB format, and many network products use SMB.

⇒ See also NETBIOS.

SMDS Switched Multimegabit Data Services: a high-speed switched data communications service offered by telephone companies that enables organizations to connect geographically separate local-area networks (LANs) into a single wide-area network (WAN).

⇒ See also CSU/DSU; WIDE-AREA NETWORK.

SMIL Synchronized Multimedia Integration Language: a new markup language now being developed. It would enable Web developers to divide multimedia content into separate files and streams (audio, video, text, and images), send them to a user's computer, and then have them displayed together as if they were a single multimedia stream. SMIL is based on the eXtensible Markup Language (XML).

⇒ See also MULTIMEDIA; RTSP; STREAMING; XML.

smiley *n.* EMOTICON.

S/MIME *n.* Secure/MIME: a new version of the MIME protocol that supports encryption of messages. S/MIME is based on RSA's public-key encryption technology.

⇒ See also MIME; PUBLIC-KEY ENCRYPTION; RSA.

smoothing *n.* a technique used by some printers to make curves look smoother. Most printers that support smoothing implement it by reducing the size of the dots that make up a curved line.

⇒ See also ANTIALIASING; JAGGIES; LASER PRINTER.

SMP 1. Symmetric Multiprocessing: a computer architecture that provides fast performance by making multiple CPUs work together as peers. **2.** Simple Management Protocol: another name for SNMP2. See under SNMP.

⇒ See also BeOS; MPP; MULTIPROCESSING; MULTITHREADING; NUMA; SNMP; SOLARIS.

SMS Systems Management Server: a set of tools from Microsoft that assists network administrators in managing PCs connected to a local-area network (LAN).

⇒ See also NET PC; NETWORK COMPUTER; SYSTEM MANAGEMENT; SYSTEMS ADMINISTRATOR.

SMTP Simple Mail Transfer Protocol: a protocol for sending e-mail messages between servers. The messages can then be retrieved with an e-mail client using either POP or IMAP. In addition, SMTP is generally used to send messages from a mail client to a mail server.

⇒ See also POP.

smurf *n.* a type of network security breach in which a network connected to the Internet is swamped with replies to ICMP echo (PING) requests. Smurfing is a *Denial of Service attack*—it doesn't try to steal information, but instead tries to disable a computer or network.

⇒ See also CRACK; IP SPOOFING; PING.

SNA Systems Network Architecture: a set of network protocols originally designed for IBM's mainframe computers. SNA now also supports peer-to-peer networks of workstations.

⇒ See also MAINFRAME; NETWORK; SDLC; VTAM.

snailmail or **snail mail** *n.* normal postal mail, where an actual physical letter or package is delivered. The term is a retronym; that is, it did not exist until electronic mail (e-mail) became so prevalent that there was a requirement to differentiate the two.

⇒ See also E-MAIL.

snapshot printer *n.* a color printer designed to print photographic-quality snapshots.

⇒ See also COLOR PRINTER; DIGITAL PHOTOGRAPHY; PHOTO SCANNER.

sniffer *n.* a program and/or device that monitors data traveling over a network. Sniffers can be used both for legitimate network management functions and for stealing information from a network.

⇒ See also HACKER; NETWORK MANAGEMENT; SECURITY.

SNMP Simple Network Management Protocol: a set of protocols for managing complex networks. SNMP 1 reports only whether a device is functioning properly. The industry has attempted to define a new set of protocols called *SNMP 2* that would provide additional information. However, network managers have turned to a related technology called *RMON* that provides more detailed information about network usage.

⇒ See also LOCAL-AREA NETWORK; MIB; NETWORK; NETWORK MANAGEMENT; RMON.

socket *n.* **1.** in UNIX and some other operating systems, a software object that connects an application to a network protocol. The programmer need only manipulate the socket and can rely on the operating system to transport messages across the network. **2.** a receptacle into which a plug can be inserted. **3.** a receptacle for a microprocessor or other hardware component.

⇒ See also SOCKET 8; SOCKET 7; TCP/IP; WINSOCK.

Socket 7 *n.* the form factor for fifth-generation CPU chips from Intel, Cyrix, and AMD. All Pentium chips, except Intel's Pentium Pro (Socket 8) and Pentium II (Slot 1), conform to the Socket 7 specifications.

⇒ See also FORM FACTOR; K6; PENTIUM MICROPROCESSOR; SLOT 1; SOCKET 8; ZERO INSERTION FORCE (ZIF) SOCKET.

Socket 8 *n.* the form factor for Intel's Pentium Pro microprocessors.

⇒ See also PENTIUM PRO; SOCKET; SOCKET 7; ZERO INSERTION FORCE (ZIF) SOCKET.

SOCKS *n.* a protocol for handling TCP traffic

through a proxy server. It provides a simple firewall because it checks incoming and outgoing packets and hides the IP addresses of client applications.

⇒ See also PROXY SERVER; TCP.

soft *adj.* in computer science, describing things that are intangible. For example, you cannot touch *software*. *Soft* is also used to describe things that are easily changed or impermanent.

⇒ See also HARD; HARDWARE; SOFTWARE.

soft font *n.* a font that is copied from a computer's disk to a printer's memory. Soft fonts require a lot of disk space and printer memory. Also called **downloadable font**.

⇒ See also DOWNLOAD; FONT; FONT CARTRIDGE; LASER PRINTER; RESIDENT FONT.

soft hyphen *n.* DISCRETIONARY HYPHEN.

soft return *n.* a set of special codes inserted into a document to cause the display screen, printer, or other output device to advance to the next line if necessary. Soft returns are inserted automatically by some word processors as part of their word wrap capability.

⇒ See also HARD RETURN; MARGINS; WORD WRAP.

software *n.* computer instructions and associated data. Software is often divided into two categories: systems software and applications software.

⇒ See also APPLICATION; BLOATWARE; DATA; FIRMWARE; HARDWARE; PROGRAM; SYSTEMS SOFTWARE; VAPORWARE.

software development kit *n.* See SDK.

software engineer *n.* a programmer. The term implies that the individual is more involved with design and management than with actual coding.

⇒ See also PROGRAMMER; SOFTWARE ENGINEERING.

software engineering *n.* the computer science discipline concerned with developing large applications. Software engineering covers not only the technical aspects of building software systems but also management issues, such as directing programming teams, and budgeting.

⇒ See also COMPUTER SCIENCE; FUNCTIONAL SPECIFICATION; SOFTWARE ENGINEER; UML.

software licensing *n.* allowing an individual or group to use a piece of software. Nearly all applications are licensed rather than sold. Some licenses are based on the number of machines on which the licensed program can run, whereas others are based on the number of users that can use the program.

⇒ See also APPLICATION; COPY PROTECTION; EULA; SHAREWARE.

software modem *n.* a modem implemented entirely in software. Software modems rely on the computer's processor to modulate and demodulate signals.

⇒ See also HOST-BASED MODEM; MODEM.

software piracy *n.* the unauthorized copying of software. Most retail programs are licensed for use at just one computer site or for use by only one user at any time. Originally, companies tried to stop software piracy by copy-protecting their software. Most software now requires some sort of registration, which may discourage piracy.

⇒ See also COPY PROTECTION; DIGITAL WATERMARK; REGISTER; SHAREWARE; SOFTWARE; WAREZ.

SOHO (sō′hō), *n.* Small Office/Home Office: the fastest-growing market for computer hardware and software. SOHO products are specifically designed to meet the needs of professionals who work at home or in small offices.

⇒ See also MFP.

Solaris *n.* a UNIX-based operating environment developed by Sun Microsystems. Originally developed to run on Sun's SPARC workstations, Solaris now runs on many workstations from other vendors.

⇒ See also SMP; SUN MICROSYSTEMS; UNIX; X-WINDOW.

solid ink-jet printer *n.* a type of color printer that works by melting wax-based inks and then spraying them on paper. Solid ink-jet printers produce vivid colors and can print on nearly any surface, but they are relatively slow and expensive.

⇒ See also COLOR PRINTER; INK-JET PRINTER; PHASE CHANGE DISK.

SOM System Object Model: an architecture developed by IBM that allows binary code to be shared by different applications. It serves the same purpose as Microsoft's competing COM standard.

⇒ See also COMPONENT OBJECT MODEL; CORBA; DSOM.

SONET Synchronous Optical Network: a standard for connecting fiber-optic transmission systems. SONET is now an ANSI standard.

⇒ See also BROADBAND ISDN (B-ISDN); FIBER OPTICS; OC; SDH; T-1 CARRIER; T-3 CARRIER.

sound card *n.* an expansion board that enables a computer to output sounds through speakers connected to the board, to record sound input from a microphone connected to the computer, and to manipulate sound stored on a disk.

⇒ See also 3-D AUDIO; CD-ROM; MIDI; MULTIMEDIA; WAVE TABLE SYNTHESIS.

source *n.* a place from which data is taken. The place from which the data is moved is called the *source*, whereas the place it is moved to is called the *destination* or *target*. The source and destination can be files, directories, or devices.

⇒ See also COPY; DESTINATION.

source code *n.* program instructions in their original form. A programmer writes a program in a particular programming language. This form of the program is called the *source program* or, more generically, the *source code*. To execute the program, it must be translated into machine language.

⇒ See also ASSEMBLER; CODE; COMPILER; EDITOR; MACHINE LANGUAGE; OBJECT CODE; PROGRAM; PROGRAMMING LANGUAGE.

spam *n.* **1.** electronic junk mail or junk newsgroup postings. Spam is generally e-mail advertising for some product sent to a mailing list or newsgroup. In addition to wasting people's time with unwanted e-mail, spam also eats up a lot of network bandwidth. —*v.t.*, *v.i.* **2.** to send spam (to). [term derives from a comedy routine on *Monty Python's Flying Circus*, a British TV series]

⇒ See also E-MAIL; MODERATED NEWSGROUP.

SPARC *n.* Scalable Processor Architecture: a RISC technology developed by Sun Microsystems. The term *SPARC®* itself is a trademark of SPARC International, an independent organization that licenses the term to Sun.
⇒ See also RISC; SUN MICROSYSTEMS; WORKSTATION.

SPEC *n.* **1.** Standard Performance Evaluation Corporation: a nonprofit corporation set up by computer and microprocessor vendors to create a standard set of benchmark tests. **2.** Also **spec.** a functional or other specification.
⇒ See also BENCHMARK; FLOPS; MIPS.

special character *n.* a character that is not a letter, number, symbol, or punctuation mark. Control characters, for example, are special characters, as are special formatting characters such as paragraph marks.
⇒ See also CONTROL CHARACTER; PUNCTUATION.

special interest group *n.* See SIG.

speech recognition *n.* VOICE RECOGNITION.

speech synthesis *n.* computerized production of sound that resembles human speech. Speech synthesis systems can read text files and output them in a very intelligible, if somewhat dull, voice.
⇒ See also VOICE RECOGNITION.

spell checker *n.* a program that checks the spelling of words in a text document. Many word processors come with a built-in spell checker, but stand-alone utilities can be purchased.
⇒ See also WORD PROCESSING.

spelling checker *n.* SPELL CHECKER.

SPID Service Profile Identifier: a number that identifies a specific ISDN line. Part of the ISDN initialization procedure is to configure the terminal adapter to use this SPID.
⇒ See also ISDN; TERMINAL ADAPTER.

spider *n.* a program that automatically retrieves Web pages. Spiders are used to feed pages to search engines. Also called **webcrawler.**
⇒ See also ALTA VISTA; ROBOT; SEARCH ENGINE.

spline *n.* in computer graphics, a smooth curve that passes through two or more points. Splines are generated with mathematical formulas.

⇒ See also BÉZIER CURVE; NURBS.

split screen *n.* division of the display screen into separate parts, each of which displays a different document, or different parts of the same document.

⇒ See also WINDOW.

spoof *v.t.*, *v.i.* to fool or trick (hardware or software). IP spoofing, for example, involves trickery that makes a message appear as if it came from an authorized IP address. Spoofing is also used as a network management technique to reduce traffic. Routers and other network devices can be programmed to *spoof* replies from distant nodes. Rather than sending the packets to the remote nodes and waiting for a reply, the devices generate their own *spoofed* replies.

⇒ See also IP SPOOFING; NETWORK MANAGEMENT.

spool *v.i.* See under SPOOLING.

spooler *n.* a program that controls spooling. Most operating systems come with one or more spoolers. In addition, some applications include spoolers.

⇒ See also QUEUE; SPOOLING.

spooling *n.* simultaneous peripheral operations on-line: the loading of jobs into a buffer, a special area in memory or on a disk where a device can access them when it is ready. In print spooling, documents are loaded into a buffer and the printer pulls them off the buffer at its own rate. Spooling also lets the user place a number of print jobs on a queue.

⇒ See also BACKGROUND; BUFFER; QUEUE.

spot color *n.* a method of specifying and printing colors in which each color is printed with its own ink. Spot color printing is effective when the printed matter contains only one to three different colors, but it becomes prohibitively expensive for more colors.

⇒ See also COLOR SEPARATION; PANTONE MATCHING SYSTEM (PMS); PROCESS COLORS.

spreadsheet *n.* a table of values arranged in rows and columns. Each value can have a predefined relationship to the other values. If one value is changed, other values may need to be changed as well. *Spreadsheet applications* (sometimes referred to as *spreadsheets*) are computer programs that let the user create and manipulate spreadsheets electronically. Most spreadsheet applications are *multidimensional,* meaning that the user can link one spreadsheet to another.

⇒ See also BORLAND INTERNATIONAL; CELL; EXCEL; FORMULA; LABEL; LOTUS 1-2-3; RECALCULATION; THREE-DIMENSIONAL SPREADSHEET; VISICALC.

sprite *n.* a graphic image that can move within a larger graphic. Animation software that supports sprites enables the designer to develop independent animated images that can then be combined in a larger animation.

⇒ See also ANIMATION.

SPX Sequenced Packet Exchange: a transport layer protocol used in Novell NetWare networks. The SPX layer sits on top of the IPX layer. SPX is used primarily by client/server applications.

⇒ See also IPX; NETWARE; TCP.

SQL (sē′kwəl *or as separate letters*), *n.* structured query language: a standardized query language for requesting information from a database. SQL has been the favorite query language for database management systems running on minicomputers and mainframes. Increasingly, however, SQL is being supported by PC database systems because it supports distributed databases.

⇒ See also DATABASE MANAGEMENT SYSTEM; DISTRIBUTED DATABASE; JDBC; ORACLE; QUERY; QUERY LANGUAGE; SQL SERVER.

SQL server *n.* generically, any database management system (DBMS) that can respond to queries from client machines formatted in the SQL language. When capitalized, the term generally refers to either of two database management products from Sybase and Microsoft.

⇒ See also RDBMS; SQL; SYBASE.

SRAM (es′ram′), *n.* static random access memory: a type of memory that is generally faster than the more common DRAM (dynamic RAM). The term *static* is derived from the fact that it does not need to be refreshed like dynamic RAM.

⇒ See also ACCESS TIME; CACHE; CYCLE TIME; DYNAMIC RAM; NVRAM; RAM.

SSI server-side include: a type of HTML comment that directs the Web server to dynamically generate data for the Web page whenever it is requested. The basic format for SSIs is:

    < !—#command tag = 'value'... >

where #command can be any of various commands supported by the Web server. SSIs can also be used to execute programs and insert the results. They therefore represent a powerful tool for Web developers.

⇒ See also DYNAMIC HTML; HTML; SERVER-SIDE.

SSL Secure Sockets Layer: a protocol developed by Netscape for transmitting private documents via the Internet. SSL works by using a private key to encrypt data that is transferred over the SSL connection.

⇒ See also DIGITAL CERTIFICATE; DIGITAL SIGNATURE; IETF; IPSEC; S-HTTP; SECURITY; X.509.

ST-412 interface n. ST-506 INTERFACE.

ST-506 interface n. an old standard interface for hard disks. Newer standards, such as enhanced IDE and SCSI, support faster data transfer rates.

⇒ See also HARD DISK; IDE INTERFACE; INTERFACE; MFM; RLL; SCSI.

stack n. **1.** in programming, a special type of data structure in which items are removed in the reverse order from that in which they are added, so the most recently added item is the first one removed. This is also called *last-in, first-out (LIFO)*. Adding an item to a stack is called *pushing*. Removing an item from a stack is called *popping*. **2.** in networking, short for *protocol stack*. **3.** in Apple Computer's HyperCard software system, a collection of cards.

⇒ See also DATA STRUCTURE; HEAP.

standalone adj. referring to a device that is self-contained, or one that does not require any other devices to function. For example, a fax machine is a standalone device. A printer, on the other hand, is not a standalone device because it requires a computer to feed it data.

standard *n.* a definition or format that has been approved by a recognized standards organization or is accepted as a de facto standard by the industry. Standards exist for programming languages, operating systems, data formats, communications protocols, and electrical interfaces.
⇒ See also ACM; ANSI; ARCHITECTURE; CCITT; COMPATIBLE; DE FACTO STANDARD; ELECTRONIC INDUSTRIES ASSOCIATION (EIA); IEEE; IETF; INTERNET SOCIETY; ISO; ITU; OPEN ARCHITECTURE; SAA; VESA.

Standard Generalized Markup Language *n.* See SGML.

standard input *n.* the place from which input comes unless the user specifies a different input device. The standard input device is usually the keyboard.
⇒ See also INPUT.

standard output *n.* the place where output goes unless the user specifies a different output device. The standard output device is usually the display screen.
⇒ See also OUTPUT.

standby power system LINE-INTERACTIVE UPS.

star network *n.* a local-area network (LAN) that uses a star topology in which all nodes are connected to a central point.
⇒ See also 10BaseT; BUS NETWORK; HUB; LOCAL-AREA NETWORK; TOPOLOGY.

start bit *n.* in asynchronous communications, the bit that signals the receiver that data is coming. Every byte of data is preceded by a start bit and followed by a stop bit.
⇒ See also ASYNCHRONOUS; BIT; BYTE.

start-stop transmission *n.* asynchronous communication, which distinguishes between noise and valid data by placing a *start bit* and a *stop bit* at the beginning and end of each piece of data.

startup disk *n.* BOOTABLE DISKETTE.

stateless *adj.* having no information about what occurred previously. Most modern applications *maintain state*, which means they remember what the user was doing last time he or she interacted with the application. The World Wide Web, on the other hand, is intrinsically stateless.

⇒ See also COOKIE; HTTP; ISAPI; NSAPI.

statement *n.* an instruction written in a high-level language. A statement directs the computer to perform a specified action. A single statement in a high-level language can represent several machine-language instructions.

⇒ See also EXPRESSION; PROGRAMMING LANGUAGE.

static RAM *n.* See SRAM.

static variable *n.* a variable that retains the same data throughout the execution of a program.

⇒ See also DYNAMIC VARIABLE; VARIABLE.

station *n.* WORKSTATION.

STN supertwist nematic. See under SUPERTWIST.

stop bit *n.* in asynchronous communications, a bit that indicates that a byte has just been transmitted. Every byte of data is preceded by a start bit and followed by a stop bit.

⇒ See also ASYNCHRONOUS; BIT; BYTE.

storage *n.* **1.** the capacity of a device to hold and retain data. **2.** MASS STORAGE.

⇒ See also HSM; STORAGE DEVICE.

storage device *n.* a device capable of storing data. The term usually refers to mass storage devices, such as disk and tape drives.

⇒ See also DISK DRIVE; HSM; MASS STORAGE; STORAGE; TAPE DRIVE.

store *v.t.* **1.** to copy (data) from a CPU to memory, or from memory to a mass storage device. —*n.* **2.** a storage device.

⇒ See also SAVE.

stored procedure *n.* in database management systems (DBMSs), an operation that is stored with the database server. Typically, stored procedures are written in SQL. They are especially important for client/server database systems because storing the procedure on the server side means that it is available to all clients. When the procedure is modified, all clients automatically get the new version.

⇒ See also DATABASE MANAGEMENT SYSTEM; SQL.

streamer *n.* TAPE.

streaming *n.* a technique for transferring data such that it can be processed as a steady and continuous stream. Streaming technologies are becoming increasingly important because most users do not have fast enough access to download large multimedia files quickly. With streaming, the client browser or plug-in can start displaying the data before the entire file has been transmitted.
⇒ See also ActiveMovie; H.324; MULTIMEDIA; NetShow; RealAudio; RealVideo; RTP; RTSP; SMIL.

strikeout *n.* a method of marking text by drawing a horizontal line through the characters. Many word processors support edit modes in which deleted sections are displayed with strikeouts.
⇒ See also WORKGROUP COMPUTING.

strikethrough *n.* STRIKEOUT.

string *n.* CHARACTER STRING.

Structured Query Language *n.* See SQL.

stub *n.* a routine that does nothing other than declare itself and the parameters it accepts. Stubs are used commonly as placeholders for routines that still need to be developed.
⇒ See also DECLARE; ROUTINE.

style *n.* in word processing, a named set of formatting parameters. By applying the style name to a section of text, many formatting properties may be changed at once.
⇒ See also FORMAT; STYLE SHEET.

style sheet *n.* in word processing and desktop publishing, a file or form that defines the layout of a document, such as the page size, margins, and fonts. Also called **template**.
⇒ See also CSS; DESKTOP PUBLISHING; FONT; LAYOUT; MARGINS; STYLE; WORD PROCESSING.

stylus *n.* a pointing and drawing device shaped like a pen. It is used with a digitizing tablet or touch screen.
⇒ See also DIGITIZING TABLET; TOUCH SCREEN.

subdirectory *n.* a directory below another directory. Every directory except the root directory is a subdirectory.

⇒ See also DIRECTORY; FOLDER; ROOT DIRECTORY.

subnet *n.* a portion of a network that shares a common address component. On TCP/IP networks, subnets are defined as all devices whose IP addresses have the same prefix. Dividing a network into subnets is useful for both security and performance reasons.

⇒ See also IP ADDRESS; SUBNET MASK.

subnet mask *n.* a mask used to determine what subnet an IP address belongs to. An IP address has two components, the network address and the host address. Subnetting divides the host address further into two or more subnets by reserving a part of the host address to identify the particular subnet. The subnet mask indicates which bits in the host address are used for subnetting: all the bits in the network-address part and the subnetting part are set to 1.

⇒ See also MASK; SUBNET.

subnotebook computer *n.* a portable computer that is slightly lighter and smaller than a full-sized notebook computer.

⇒ See also HAND-HELD COMPUTER; NOTEBOOK COMPUTER; PORTABLE.

subroutine *n.* ROUTINE.

subscript *n.* **1.** in programming, a symbol or number used to identify an element in an array. Usually, it is placed in brackets following the array name. For example, AR[5] identifies element number 5 in an array called AR. **2.** in word processing, a character that appears slightly below the line, as in this example: H_2O.

⇒ See also ARRAY; SUPERSCRIPT; WORD PROCESSING.

Sun Microsystems *n.* a company that builds computer hardware and software. The firm is best known for developing workstations and operating environments for UNIX, and for developing the Java programming language.

⇒ See also DEC; IBM; JAVA; JAVASOFT; MICROSOFT; NETSCAPE; NETWORK COMPUTER; SERVER; SGI; SOLARIS; SPARC; UNIX; WORKSTATION.

supercomputer *n.* the fastest type of computer, used for applications that require immense

amounts of mathematical calculations. A supercomputer executes a few programs as fast as possible, whereas a mainframe uses its power to execute many programs concurrently.
⇒ See also COMPUTER; HIGH PERFORMANCE COMPUT-
ING; HIPPI; MAINFRAME.

supercomputing *n.* HIGH PERFORMANCE COMPUT-
ING.

SuperDisk *n.* a disk storage technology that supports very high-density diskettes. A SuperDisk
diskette can have 2,490 tracks. This higher density translates into 120 MB capacity per diskette.
⇒ See also FLOPPY DISK; HIFD; ZIP DRIVE.

SuperDrive *n.* another name for the *FDHD*
(floppy disk, high density) disk drive. The Super-
Drive can read and write to all Macintosh disk
sizes as well as the two PC 3½-inch disk sizes.
⇒ See also FDHD; FLOPPY DISK; MACINTOSH COM-
PUTER.

super-programmer *n.* WIZARD (def. 2).

superscalar *adj.* referring to microprocessor architectures that enable more than one instruction
to be executed per clock cycle.
⇒ See also CLOCK SPEED; INSTRUCTION; MICROPROCES-
SOR; PARALLEL PROCESSING; PIPELINING.

superscript *n.* a symbol or character that appears slightly above a line, such as a footnote
number.
⇒ See also SUBSCRIPT; WORD PROCESSING.

supertwist *n.* a technique for improving LCD
display screens by increasing the helicity of their
liquid crystals. In general, the more twists, the
higher the contrast, and double-twist (or *dual supertwist*) and triple-twist displays are common.
Supertwist displays are also called supertwist nematic (STN) displays.
⇒ See also BACKGROUND; BACKLIGHTING; CSTN;
DSTN; FLAT-PANEL DISPLAY; LCD; NOTEBOOK COM-
PUTER.

Super VGA *n.* See SVGA.

Super-Video *n.* See S-VIDEO.

support *v.t.* **1.** to have (a specific functionality).
For example, a word processor that *supports*
graphics is one that has a graphics component.

—*n.* **2.** the assistance that a vendor offers to customers.

⇒ See also CUSTOMER SUPPORT.

surf *v.t.*, *v.i.* to move from place to place on (the Internet or Web) searching for topics of interest. The term generally describes an undirected type of Web browsing as opposed to searching for specific information.

⇒ See also BROWSE; LURK; WORLD WIDE WEB.

surge protector *n.* a device that protects a power supply and communications lines from electrical surges. All computers come with some built-in surge protection, but this separate device offers added protection. Also called **surge suppressor.**

⇒ See also UPS.

surround sound *n.* DOLBY DIGITAL.

SVC switched virtual circuit: a temporary virtual circuit that is set up and used only as long as data is being transmitted.

⇒ See also PACKET SWITCHING; PVC; VIRTUAL CIRCUIT.

SVGA Super VGA: a set of graphics standards designed to offer greater resolution than VGA. There are several varieties of SVGA, each providing a different resolution. All SVGA standards support a palette of 16 million colors.

⇒ See also 8514/A; PALETTE; RESOLUTION; VESA; VGA; VIDEO STANDARDS.

S-Video *n.* Super-Video: a technology for transmitting video signals over a cable by dividing the video information into two separate signals: one for color (*chrominance*), and the other for brightness (*luminance*). Most digital video devices, such as digital cameras, produce video in RGB format. The images look best, therefore, when output on a computer monitor. When output on a television, however, they look better in S-Video format than in composite format.

⇒ See also COMPOSITE VIDEO; NTSC; RGB MONITOR; VIDEO.

swap *v.i.* **1.** to replace pages or segments of data in memory. Swapping enables a computer to execute programs and manipulate data files larger than main memory. The operating system copies as much data as needed into main memory and leaves the rest on the disk. When the operating system needs data from the disk, it exchanges a portion of data in main memory with a portion of data on the disk. **2.** in UNIX systems, to move entire processes in and out of main memory.

⇒ See also DEMAND PAGING; MAIN MEMORY; MEMORY; OPERATING SYSTEM; PAGE; PAGING; PROCESS; SEGMENT; THRASH; UNIX; VIRTUAL MEMORY.

swap file *n.* a file used by the operating system for swapping.

⇒ See also SWAP.

switch *n.* **1.** in networks, a device that forwards packets between LAN segments. LANs that use switches to join segments are called *switched LANs*. **2.** a small lever or button. The switches on the back of printers and on expansion boards are called DIP switches. **3.** OPTION; PARAMETER.

⇒ See also 3COM; DIP SWITCH; ROUTING SWITCH; SWITCHED ETHERNET; TOGGLE.

switched Ethernet *n.* an Ethernet LAN that uses switches to connect individual hosts or segments. Switched Ethernets are becoming very popular because they are an effective and convenient way to extend the bandwidth of existing Ethernets.

⇒ See also 100BASE-T; ETHERNET; SHARED ETHERNET; SWITCH; SWITCHING HUB.

switched virtual circuit *n.* See SVC.

switching hub *n.* a special type of network hub that forwards packets to the appropriate port based on the packet's address. Because switching hubs forward each packet only to the required port, they provide much better performance than conventional hubs.

⇒ See also HUB; LOCAL-AREA NETWORK; SEGMENT; SWITCHED ETHERNET.

Sybase *n.* a software company. Its DBMS products are branded with the Sybase name, whereas its client/server products, chiefly PowerBuilder, are branded with the name *PowerSoft*.

⇒ See also INFORMIX; ORACLE; POWERBUILDER; SQL SERVER.

symmetric digital subscriber line *n*. See SDSL.

symmetric encryption *n*. a type of encryption where the same key is used to encrypt and decrypt the message. This differs from asymmetric (or public-key) encryption.

⇒ See also ENCRYPTION.

symmetric-key cryptography *n*. an encryption system in which the sender and receiver of a message share a single key that is used to encrypt and decrypt the message. Contrast this with public-key cryptology, which utilizes a public key to encrypt messages and a private key to decrypt them.

⇒ See also CRYPTOGRAPHY; DES; KEY; PUBLIC-KEY ENCRYPTION.

Symmetric Multiprocessing *n*. See SMP.

synchronous *adj*. occurring at regular intervals. Communication within a computer is usually synchronous and is governed by the microprocessor clock.

⇒ See also ASYNCHRONOUS; BISYNC; BUS; CLOCK SPEED; ISOCHRONOUS.

Synchronous Digital Hierarchy *n*. See SDH.

synchronous DRAM *n*. See SDRAM.

Synchronous Optical Network *n*. See SONET.

SyncLink memory *n*. See SLDRAM.

syntax *n*. the spelling and grammar of a programming language. Each program defines its own syntactical rules that control which words the computer understands, which combinations of words are meaningful, and what punctuation is necessary.

⇒ See also LANGUAGE; SEMANTICS.

sysadmin *n*. SYSTEM ADMINISTRATOR.

sysop (sis/op′), *n*. system operator: an individual who manages a bulletin board system (BBS), online service, or special interest group (SIG).

⇒ See also BULLETIN BOARD SYSTEM; NETWORK; SIG.

System *n*. System File: an essential program that runs whenever a Macintosh is started up. The System provides information to all other applications that run on a Macintosh.

⇒ See also FINDER; MACOS; MACINTOSH COMPUTER; OPERATING SYSTEM.

system *n.* **1.** a combination of components working together. For example, a *computer system* includes both hardware and software. A *Windows system* is a personal computer running the Windows operating system. **2.** COMPUTER SYSTEM. **3.** OPERATING SYSTEM **4.** an organization or methodology.

⇒ See also COMPUTER SYSTEM; EMBEDDED SYSTEM; OPERATING SYSTEM; SYSTEM MANAGEMENT.

system administrator *n.* an individual responsible for maintaining a multi-user computer system, often including a local-area network (LAN). Also called **systems administrator, sysadmin.**

⇒ See also MIS; SYSTEM MANAGEMENT.

System Application Architecture *n.* See SAA.

system board *n.* MOTHERBOARD.

system call *n.* the invocation of an operating system routine.

⇒ See also INVOKE; OPERATING SYSTEM; ROUTINE.

System folder *n.* a standard folder on Macintoshes that contains the System and Finder programs, as well as other resources needed by the operating system.

⇒ See also FINDER; FOLDER; MACINTOSH COMPUTER; SYSTEM.

system management *n.* the general area of Information Technology (IT) that concerns configuring and managing computer resources, especially network resources.

⇒ See also IS; IT; MIS; SMS; SYSTEM; SYSTEM ADMINISTRATOR.

System Object Model *n.* See SOM.

system prompt *n.* See under PROMPT.

systems administrator *n.* SYSTEM ADMINISTRATOR.

systems analyst *n.* a programmer or consultant who designs and manages the development of business applications. Typically, systems analysts are more involved in design issues than in day-to-day coding.

⇒ See also PROGRAMMER; SYSTEMS INTEGRATOR.

systems integrator *n.* an individual or company that specializes in building complete computer systems by putting together components from different vendors.

⇒ See also PROGRAMMER; SYSTEMS ANALYST.

Systems Management Server *n.* See SMS.

Systems Network Architecture *n.* See SNA.

system software *n.* SYSTEMS SOFTWARE.

systems software *n.* the operating system and all utility programs that manage computer resources at a low level. Software is generally divided into systems software and applications software. Systems software includes compilers, loaders, linkers, and debuggers.

⇒ See also APPLICATION; END USER; SOFTWARE; UTILITY.

system unit *n.* the main part of a personal computer. The system unit includes the chassis, microprocessor, main memory, bus, and ports but does not generally include the keyboard or monitor, or any peripheral devices other than disk drives.

⇒ See also CHASSIS; MAIN MEMORY; MICROPROCESSOR; PORT.

T t

T-1 carrier *n.* a dedicated phone connection supporting data rates of 1.544 Mbps. Most telephone companies sell individual channels, known as *fractional T-1* access. T-1 lines are a popular option for businesses connecting to the Internet and for Internet Service Providers (ISPs) connecting to the Internet backbone.
⇒ See also CARRIER; CSU/DSU; FRACTIONAL T-1; ISP; LEASED LINE; OC; SONET; T-3 CARRIER; TDM.

T-3 carrier *n.* a dedicated phone connection supporting data rates of about 43 Mbps. T-3 lines are used mainly by Internet Service Providers (ISPs) connecting to the Internet backbone and for the backbone itself.
⇒ See also BACKBONE; CARRIER; CSU/DSU; ISP; LEASED LINE; OC; SONET; T-1 CARRIER; TDM.

TA TERMINAL ADAPTER.

tab character *n.* a special character that can be inserted into a text document. Most word processors move the cursor or insertion point to the next tab stop, and most printers move the print head to the next tab stop as well.
⇒ See also TAB KEY; TAB STOP.

Tab key *n.* a key on computer keyboards that inserts a tab character or moves the insertion point to the next tab stop. Spreadsheet and database management applications usually respond to the Tab key by moving the cursor to the next field or cell. In dialog boxes and menus, pressing the Tab key highlights the next button or option.
⇒ See also CELL; CURSOR; FIELD; INSERTION POINT; TAB CHARACTER; TAB STOP.

table *n.* data arranged in rows and columns, such as a spreadsheet. In relational database management systems, all information is stored in the form of tables.
⇒ See also DATABASE MANAGEMENT SYSTEM; RDBMS; SPREADSHEET.

tablet *n.* DIGITIZING TABLET.

tab stop *n.* a stop point for tabbing. In word processing, each line generally contains a number of tab stops placed at regular intervals. When the Tab key is pressed, the cursor or insertion point jumps to the next tab stop.

⇒ See also TAB CHARACTER; TAB KEY.

tag *n.* **1.** a command inserted in a document that specifies how the document, or a portion of the document, should be formatted. Tags are used by all format specifications that store documents as text files. This includes SGML, XML, and HTML, although the tags in SGML and XML do not directly specify formatting, but indicate the content or structure of what is tagged. —*v.t.* **2.** to mark a section of (a document) with a formatting command.

⇒ See also FORMAT; HTML; META TAG; SGML; XML.

Tagged Image File Format *n.* See TIFF.

tag RAM *n.* the area in an L2 cache that identifies which data from main memory is currently stored in each *cache line.* The actual data is stored in a different part of the cache, called the *data store.* The values stored in the tag RAM determine whether a cache lookup results in a *hit* or a *miss.*

⇒ See also CACHE; L2 CACHE; RAM.

tape *n.* a magnetically coated strip of plastic on which data can be encoded. Storing data on tapes is considerably cheaper than storing data on disks. Tapes also have large storage capacities. Tapes are sequential-access media, and because they are so slow, they are generally used only for long-term storage and backup. They are also used for transporting large amounts of data.

⇒ See also 3480, 3490; BACKUP; DAT; DISK DRIVE; DLT; HELICAL-SCAN CARTRIDGE; MASS STORAGE; QIC; SEQUENTIAL ACCESS; TRAVAN.

tape drive *n.* a device, like a tape recorder, that reads data from and writes it onto a tape. Data capacities and transfer speeds of tape drives vary considerably. They are sequential-access devices, which makes them too slow for general-purpose storage. Therefore, they are used for making backups.

⇒ See also BACKUP; DLT; SEQUENTIAL ACCESS; TAPE; TRAVAN.

TAPI Telephony Application Programming Interface: an API for connecting a PC running Windows to telephone services.

⇒ See also API; TELEPHONY; TSAPI.

tar *n.* **1.** tape archive: a UNIX utility that combines a group of files into a single file. The resulting file has a .TAR extension. Frequently, a tar file is compressed with the *compress* or *gzip* commands to create a file with a .TAR.GZ or .TAR.Z extension. —*v.t.* **2.** to combine (files) with the **tar** command.

⇒ See also PKZIP.

target *n.* a file, device, or any type of location to which data is moved or copied. The computer copies from the source to the target (or destination).

⇒ See also SOURCE.

task *n.* the combination of a program being executed and bookkeeping information used by the operating system. The task is like an envelope for the program. The terms *task* and *process* are often used interchangeably, although some operating systems make a distinction between the two.

⇒ See also JOB; MULTITASKING; MULTITHREADING; OPERATING SYSTEM.

taskbar *n.* in Windows 95 and 98, a graphical list of active applications. If the application window is minimized, it can be restored by clicking on its button in the taskbar. By default, the taskbar appears on the bottom of the screen.

task switching *n.* the ability of operating systems or operating environments to enable a user to switch from one program to another without quitting the spot in the first program.

⇒ See also DOS; MULTITASKING; OPERATING ENVIRONMENT; OPERATING SYSTEM.

Tcl (tik′əl *or as separate letters*), *n.* tool command language: a powerful interpreted programming language. Tcl can be easily extended through the addition of custom libraries. It is used for prototyping applications as well as for developing CGI scripts.

⇒ See also INTERPRETER; PERL; PROGRAMMING LANGUAGE.

TCO Total Cost of Ownership: a popular buzzword representing how much it actually costs to own a PC. Most estimates place the TCO at about three to four times the actual purchase cost of the PC.

⇒ See also NETWORK COMPUTER; UPGRADE; ZAW.

TCP Transmission Control Protocol: one of the main protocols in TCP/IP networks. TCP enables two hosts to establish a connection and exchange streams of data. TCP guarantees delivery of data in order.

⇒ See also IP; SOCKS; SPX; TCP/IP.

TCP/IP Transmission Control Protocol/Internet Protocol: the suite of communications protocols used to connect hosts on the Internet. TCP/IP is built into the UNIX operating system and is the fundamental standard of the Internet.

⇒ See also INTERNET; IP; IP ADDRESS; PACKET SWITCHING; PROTOCOL; SOCKET; TCP; UDP.

TDM Time Division Multiplexing: a type of multiplexing that combines data streams by assigning each stream a different time slot in a set. TDM repeatedly transmits a fixed sequence of time slots over a single transmission channel.

⇒ See also CDMA; FDM; LEASED LINE; MODULATE; MULTIPLEX; PCM; T-1 CARRIER; T-3 CARRIER; TDMA; WDM.

TDMA Time Division Multiple Access: a technology for delivering digital wireless service using time-division multiplexing (TDM). TDMA works by dividing a radio frequency into time slots and then allocating slots to multiple calls. In this way, a single frequency can support multiple, simultaneous data channels.

⇒ See also CDMA; CELLULAR; GSM; PCS; TDM.

teamware *n.* GROUPWARE.

tear-off menu *n.* a pop-up menu that can be moved around the screen like a window.

⇒ See also MENU.

technical support *n.* CUSTOMER SUPPORT.

telecommunications *n.* all types of long-distance data transmission, from voice to video.

⇒ See also COMMUNICATIONS; ITU; TELEMATICS; TELEPHONY.

telecommuting *n.* working at home on a computer and transmitting data and documents to a central office via telephone lines.
⇒ See also E-MAIL; NETWORK; WORKGROUP COMPUTING.

teleconference *v.i.* to hold a conference via a telephone or network connection.
⇒ See also MULTICAST; NetMeeting; VIDEOCONFERENCING; WHITEBOARD; WORKGROUP COMPUTING.

telecopy *v.t.* to send (a document) from one place to another via a fax machine.
⇒ See also FAX MACHINE.

telematics *n.* the broad industry related to using computers in concert with telecommunications systems. This includes dial-up service to the Internet as well as all types of networks that rely on a telecommunications system to transport data.
⇒ See also PBX; TELECOMMUNICATIONS; TELEPHONY.

Telnet *n.* one of the largest public data networks (PDNs) in the United States, owned by U.S. Sprint Communications Corporation.
⇒ See also ONLINE SERVICE; WIDE-AREA NETWORK.

telephony *n.* the science of translating sound into electrical signals, transmitting them, and then converting them back to sound. The term is used frequently to refer to computer hardware and software that perform functions traditionally performed by telephone equipment, such as voice mail.
⇒ See also CTI; DTMF; INTERNET TELEPHONY; MODEM; TAPI; TELECOMMUNICATIONS; TELEMATICS; TSAPI.

Telephony API *n.* See TAPI.

Telephony Server API *n.* See TSAPI.

television board *n.* an expansion board that enables a computer monitor to function as a television screen. Most television boards support windowed as well as full-screen viewing.
⇒ See also EXPANSION BOARD; NTSC; PC/TV.

Telnet *n.* a terminal emulation protocol for TCP/IP networks such as the Internet. The Telnet client runs on a PC and connects it to a server on the network. Telnet is a common way to control Web servers remotely.

⇒ See also HOST; INTERNET; TERMINAL EMULATION.

template *n.* **1.** Also called **keyboard template.** a plastic or paper diagram placed on a keyboard to indicate the meanings of different keys, esp. the function keys, for a particular program. **2.** a sheet of plastic with menus and command boxes drawn on it that is placed on top of a digitizing tablet. Commands are selected by pressing the digitizing tablet's pen against a command box or by positioning the cursor over a box and pressing one of the cursor keys. **3.** in spreadsheet and database applications, a blank form that shows which fields exist, their locations, and their length. **4.** (in some word processing applications) STYLE SHEET. **5.** (in DOS) COMMAND BUFFER.

⇒ See also BOILERPLATE; COMMAND BUFFER; CURSOR; DIGITIZING TABLET.

10Base-2 *n.* one of several adaptations of the Ethernet standard for local-area networks (LANs). The 10Base-2 standard uses 50 ohm coaxial cable with maximum lengths of 185 meters. This cable is thinner and more flexible than that used for the 10Base-5 standard. The 10Base-2 system operates at 10 Mbps and uses baseband transmission methods. Also called **Thin Net.**

⇒ See also 10BASE5; 10BASET; BASEBAND TRANSMISSION; BNC CONNECTOR; COAXIAL CABLE; ETHERNET.

10Base-5 *n.* the original cabling standard for Ethernet that uses coaxial cables. The name derives from the fact that the maximum data transfer speed is 10 Mbps, it uses baseband transmission, and the maximum length of cables is 500 meters. Also called **thick Ethernet, ThickNet.**

10Base-T *n.* one of several adaptations of the Ethernet standard for local-area networks (LANs). The 10Base-T standard uses a twisted-pair cable with maximum lengths of 100 meters. The cable is thinner and more flexible than that used for the 10Base-2 or 10Base-5 standards.

⇒ See also 100BASE-T; 10BASE-2; 10BASE5; ETHERNET; HUB; REPEATER; RJ-45; STAR NETWORK; TWISTED-PAIR CABLE.

terabyte n. **1.** 2^{40} (1,099,511,627,776) bytes. This is approximately 1 trillion bytes. **2.** 10^{12} (1,000,000,000,000) bytes.
⇒ See also EXABYTE; GIGABYTE; MEGABYTE; PETABYTE.

terminal n. **1.** a device that enables a user to communicate with a computer. Generally, a terminal is a combination of keyboard and display screen. **2.** in networking, a personal computer or workstation connected to a mainframe. The personal computer usually runs terminal emulation software.
⇒ See also CONSOLE; DISPLAY SCREEN; DUMB TERMINAL; EMULATION; HLLAPI; INTELLIGENT TERMINAL; KEYBOARD; MONITOR; NETWORK; SMART TERMINAL.

terminal adapter n. a device that connects a computer to an external digital communications line, such as an ISDN line. A terminal adapter is analogous to a modem (which is used for analog lines).
⇒ See also ISDN; MODEM; SPID.

terminal emulation n. making a computer respond like a particular type of terminal. Terminal emulation programs allow users to access a mainframe computer or bulletin board service with a personal computer.
⇒ See also BULLETIN BOARD SYSTEM; EMULATION; MAINFRAME; TELNET; TERMINAL.

terminate and stay resident n. See TSR.

TeX (tek), n. a typesetting language that provides complete control over formatting. Most people who use TeX, however, utilize one of several macro packages that provide an easier interface.
⇒ See also LaTeX; MuTeX.

Texas Instruments n. a large electronics company. In 1958, a TI researcher demonstrated the first integrated circuit (IC), and in 1967, TI introduced the first hand-held calculator. Today, its core business is in producing semiconductors.
⇒ See also DLP; INTEGRATED CIRCUIT; SEMICONDUCTOR; TEXAS INSTRUMENTS GRAPHICS ARCHITECTURE (TIGA); TI 34010.

Texas Instruments Graphics Architecture (TIGA) n. a high-resolution graphics specification designed by Texas Instruments. TIGA does not specify a particular resolution or number of colors. Instead, it defines an interface between software and graphics processors.

⇒ See also 8514/A; GRAPHICS; SVGA; TEXAS INSTRUMENTS; TI 34010; VESA; VIDEO STANDARDS; XGA.

text *n.* words, sentences, and paragraphs. *Text processing* refers to the ability to manipulate information consisting only of printable ASCII characters and intended to be readable. Typically, the term *text* refers to text stored as text files, usually documents. Objects that are *not* text include graphics, numbers, and machine code.

⇒ See also ASCII.

text editor *n.* EDITOR.

text file *n.* a file that holds text. The term *text file* is often used as a synonym for *ASCII file*, a file in which characters are represented simply by their ASCII codes.

⇒ See also ASCII; FILE; TEXT.

text flow *n.* TEXT WRAP.

text mode *n.* a video mode in which a display screen is divided into rows and columns of boxes. Each box can contain one character. Also called **character mode.**

⇒ See also CHARACTER BASED; GRAPHICS BASED; GRAPHICS MODE; VIDEO MODE; VIDEO STANDARDS.

texture *n.* in 3-D graphics, the digital representation of the surface of an object. In addition to two-dimensional qualities, such as color and brightness, a texture is also encoded with three-dimensional properties, such as how transparent and reflective the object is. Once a texture has been defined, it can be wrapped around any three-dimensional object. This is called *texture mapping.* Well-defined textures are very important for rendering realistic 3-D images. However, they also require a lot of memory.

⇒ See also 3-D GRAPHICS; 3-D SOFTWARE; AGP; MODELING; RAY TRACING; RENDER.

texture mapping *n.* See under TEXTURE.

text wrap *n.* a feature supported by many word processors that enables a user to surround a picture or diagram with text. The text wraps around the graphic. Also called **text flow.**

⇒ See also WORD PROCESSING.

TFT thin film transistor: the basis for a type of LCD flat-panel display screen in which each pixel is controlled by from one to four transistors. The TFT technology provides the best performance of all the flat-panel techniques, but it is also the most expensive.

⇒ See also ACTIVE-MATRIX DISPLAY; CSTN; FLAT-PANEL DISPLAY; LCD.

TFTP Trivial File Transfer Protocol: a simple form of the file transfer protocol (FTP). It is often used by servers to boot diskless workstations, X-terminals, and routers.

⇒ See also FTP.

The Open Group *n.* an international consortium of computer and software manufacturers and users dedicated to advancing multivendor technologies. The Open Group was formed in 1996 by merging two previously independent groups— the *Open Software Foundation (OSF)* and *X/Open Company Ltd.*

⇒ See also DCE; OPEN ARCHITECTURE.

thermal printer *n.* a type of printer that produces images by electrically heating pins in contact with special heat-sensitive paper. Thermal printers are inexpensive; they are used in most printing calculators and many fax machines.

⇒ See also FAX MACHINE; PRINTER.

thin client *n.* in client/server applications, a client designed to be especially small so that the bulk of the data processing occurs on the server. The term *thin client* usually refers to software, but it is used for hardware designed to run thin-client software. A thin client is a network computer without a hard disk drive, whereas a fat client includes a disk drive.

⇒ See also CLIENT; CLIENT/SERVER ARCHITECTURE; JAVA; NC; NETWORK COMPUTER; WinFrame.

thin film transistor *n.* See TFT.

ThinNet *n.* See 10BASE2.

1394 short for *IEEE 1394.*

3480, 3490 the IBM designation for families of half-inch magnetic tape drives typically used on mainframes and AS/400s.

⇒ See also BACKUP; TAPE.

32-bit *adj.* referring to the number of bits processed or transmitted in parallel, or the number of bits used for a single element in a data format. The term is often applied to microprocessors (indicating the width of the registers), buses (indicating the number of data wires), graphics devices (indicating the number of bits used to represent a pixel), operating systems (indicating the number of bits used to represent memory addresses), and applications (indicating how a program is compiled).

⇒ See also 16-BIT; BIT; BUS; REGISTER.

thrash *v.i.* (of virtual memory operating systems) to spend too much time moving data in and out of virtual memory (swapping pages) rather than executing programs. A computer is often thrashing when an application stops responding but the disk drive light keeps blinking on and off.

⇒ See also PAGING; SWAP; VIRTUAL MEMORY.

thread *n.* **1.** in on-line discussions, a series of messages that have been posted as replies to one another. A single forum or conference typically contains many threads covering different subjects. **2.** in programming, a part of a program that can execute independently of other parts. Operating systems that support multithreading enable programmers to design programs whose parts can execute concurrently.

⇒ See also FORUM; MULTITHREADING; ONLINE SERVICE.

3COM *n.* one of the largest networking companies in the world. The name is derived from the prefixes of three terms—com(puter), com(munication), and com(patibility).

⇒ See also CISCO SYSTEMS; HUB; ROUTER; SWITCH.

3-D audio *n.* a technique for giving more depth to traditional stereo sound. Typically, 3-D audio is produced by placing a device in a room with stereo speakers. The device analyzes the sound coming from the speakers and sends feedback to the sound system so that it can readjust the sound. 3-D audio devices are particularly popular for improving computer audio where the speakers

tend to be small and close together.
⇒ See also MULTIMEDIA; SOUND CARD.

3-D graphics n. the field of computer graphics concerned with generating and displaying 2-D images of three-dimensional objects. Whereas pixels in a two-dimensional graphic have the properties of position, color, and brightness, 3-D pixels include a depth property.
⇒ See also 3-D SOFTWARE; ANIMATION; GRAPHICS; GRAPHICS ACCELERATOR; RAY TRACING; RENDER; TEXTURE; Z-BUFFER.

three-dimensional spreadsheet n. a spreadsheet program that allows the user to arrange data as a stack of identically-formatted tables.
⇒ See also SPREADSHEET.

3DO a technology that supports photo-realistic graphics, full-motion video, and CD-quality sound.
⇒ See also EXPANSION BOARD; MULTIMEDIA.

3-D software n. the category of software that represents three-dimensional objects on a computer. This includes CAD/CAM, computer games, and animation packages.
⇒ See also 3-D GRAPHICS; ANIMATION; DIRECT3D; MODELING; NURBS; OPENGL; RENDER; TEXTURE.

3-D sound n. 3-D AUDIO.

3-D spreadsheet n. THREE-DIMENSIONAL SPREADSHEET.

386 short for the *Intel 80386 microprocessor*.
⇒ See also INTEL MICROPROCESSORS.

386DX See under INTEL MICROPROCESSORS.

386SX short for the *Intel 80386SX microprocessor*.
⇒ See also INTEL MICROPROCESSORS.

three-tier adj. referring to a special type of client/server architecture consisting of three well-defined and separate processes, each running on a different platform. The first tier is the user interface, which runs on the user's computer (the *client*). Next are the functional modules that actually process data. This middle tier runs on a server and is often called the *application server*. The third tier is a database-management system (DBMS) that stores the data required by the middle tier. This tier runs on a second server called the *database server*. The three-tier design has many advantages over traditional two-tier or single-tier designs.

⇒ See also CLIENT/SERVER ARCHITECTURE; LOAD BALANCING; MIDDLEWARE; TP MONITOR; TWO-TIER.

throughput *n.* the amount of data transferred from one place to another or processed in a specified amount of time. Typically, throughputs are measured in FLOPS, MIPS, Kbps, Mbps, and Gbps.

⇒ See also DISK DRIVE; ISOCHRONOUS; NETWORK.

thumbnail *n.* a miniature display of a page to be printed. Thumbnails make it possible to see the layout of many pages on the screen at once.

⇒ See also DESKTOP PUBLISHING; GREEKING; LAYOUT.

thunk *v.i.* **1.** in PCs, to convert a 16-bit memory address to a 32-bit address, and vice versa. Windows 95 supports a thunk mechanism to enable 32-bit programs to call 16-bit DLLs. This is called a *flat thunk*. On the other hand, 16-bit applications running under Windows 3.x and Windows for Workgroups cannot use 32-bit DLLs unless the 32-bit addresses are converted to 16-bit addresses. This is the function of Win32s and is called a *universal thunk*. —*n.* **2.** the operation of converting between a segmented memory address space and a flat address space.

⇒ See also ADDRESS SPACE; WIN32S.

TI TEXAS INSTRUMENTS.

TI 34010 *n.* a video standard from Texas Instruments that supports a resolution of 1,024 by 768 pixels.

⇒ See also TEXAS INSTRUMENTS GRAPHICS ARCHITECTURE (TIGA); VIDEO STANDARDS.

TIF *n.* See under TIFF.

TIFF (tif) *n.* tagged image file format: one of the most widely supported file formats for storing bitmapped images on personal computers. TIFF graphics can be any resolution, and they can be black and white, gray-scaled, or color. Files in TIFF format often end with a .TIF extension.

⇒ See also BIT MAP; GRAPHICS; GRAPHICS FILE FORMATS; GRAY SCALING.

TIGA *n.* TEXAS INSTRUMENTS GRAPHICS ARCHITECTURE.

tiled windows *n.pl.* windows arranged so that they do not overlap one another.
⇒ See also CASCADING WINDOWS; OVERLAID WINDOWS; WINDOW.

Tillamook *n.* the codename for a low-power version of the Pentium microprocessor designed especially for portable devices.
⇒ See also PENTIUM MICROPROCESSOR.

Time Division Multiple Access *n.* See TDMA.

Time Division Multiplexing *n.* See TDM.

time-out *n.* a signal generated by a program or device that has waited a certain length of time for some input but has not received it.
⇒ See also INTERRUPT.

time sharing *n.* the concurrent use of a computer by more than one user. Almost all mainframes and minicomputers are time-sharing systems, but most personal computers and workstations are not.
⇒ See also MAINFRAME; MINICOMPUTER; MULTITASKING; MULTI-USER.

title bar *n.* a bar on top of a window that contains the name of the file or application. In many graphical user interfaces, a user moves (drags) a window by grabbing the title bar.
⇒ See also DRAG; WINDOW.

TLD top-level domain: the suffix attached to Internet domain names. There are a limited number of predefined suffixes, and each one represents a top-level domain. Current top-level domains include: com (commercial businesses); gov (government agencies); and edu (educational institutions).
⇒ See also DOMAIN NAME; IP ADDRESS.

TNEF (tē'nef), *n.* Transport Neutral Encapsulation Format: a proprietary format used by the Microsoft Exchange and Outlook e-mail clients when sending messages in rich text format (RTF). Because of the proprietary nature of TNEF encoding, most non-Microsoft e-mail clients cannot decifer such a message, which usually appears as an attached file named *WINMAIL.DAT*.
⇒ See also E-MAIL CLIENT; RICH TEXT FORMAT.

toggle *v.t.* to switch (a parameter) from one setting to another. A *toggle switch* is a switch that has just two positions: pressing it once turns it on; pressing it again turns it off. On computer keyboards, the Caps Lock key is a toggle switch. Toggle switches exist in software too. For example, a check box in a dialog box is a toggle switch.

⇒ See also DIP SWITCH; KEYBOARD; SWITCH.

token *n.* **1.** in programming languages, a single element of a programming language, such as a keyword, an operator, or a punctuation mark. **2.** in networking, a special series of bits that travels around a token-ring network. As the token circulates, computers attached to the network can capture it. The token acts like a ticket, enabling its owner to send a message across the network. **3.** in security systems, a small device the size of a credit card that displays a constantly changing ID code. A user first enters a password and then the card displays an ID that can be used to log into a network.

⇒ See also KEYWORD; OPERATOR; PROGRAMMING LANGUAGE; SMART CARD; TOKEN BUS NETWORK; TOKEN-RING NETWORK.

token bus network *n.* a type of local-area network (LAN) that has a bus topology and uses a token-passing mechanism to regulate traffic on the bus.

⇒ See also BUS NETWORK; IEEE 802 STANDARDS; LOCAL-AREA NETWORK; TOKEN; TOKEN-RING NETWORK; TOPOLOGY.

Token Ring *n.* See under TOKEN-RING NETWORK.

token-ring network *n.* **1.** a type of computer network in which all the computers are arranged (schematically) in a circle. A *token*, which is a special bit pattern, travels around the circle. To send a message, a computer catches the token, attaches a message to it, and then lets it continue to travel around the network. **2.** (*caps.*) the PC network protocol developed by IBM. The Token-Ring specification has been standardized as the IEEE 802.5 standard.

⇒ See also ARCNET; IEEE; IEEE 802 STANDARDS; LOCAL-AREA NETWORK; NETWORK; TOKEN; TOKEN BUS NETWORK.

toner *n.* a special type of ink used by copy machines and laser printers. Toner consists of a dry, powdery substance that can be electrically charged so that it adheres to a drum, plate, or piece of paper charged with the opposite polarity.

⇒ See also LASER PRINTER.

Top-Level Domain *n.* See TLD.

topology *n.* the shape of a local-area network (LAN) or other communications system. There are three principal topologies used in LANs. In a *bus topology*, all devices are connected to a central cable, called the *bus* or *backbone.* In a *ring topology*, all devices are connected to one another in the shape of a closed loop, so that each device is connected directly to two other devices. In a *star topology*, all devices are connected to a central *hub.*

⇒ See also BUS NETWORK; ETHERNET; LOCAL-AREA NETWORK.

TOPS *n.* transparent operating system: a type of local-area network that can combine Macintosh computers, PCs, and Sun workstations on the same network. TOPS uses the Macintosh computer's built-in AppleTalk protocol. It is a peer-to-peer network.

⇒ See also APPLETALK; LOCAL-AREA NETWORK; PEER-TO-PEER ARCHITECTURE; SUN MICROSYSTEMS.

Total Cost of Ownership *n.* See TCO.

touchpad *n.* a small touch-sensitive pad used as a pointing device on some portable computers.

⇒ See also DIGITIZING TABLET; POINTING DEVICE.

touch screen *n.* a type of display screen that has a touch-sensitive transparent panel covering the screen.

⇒ See also DISPLAY SCREEN; KIOSK; LIGHT PEN; MOUSE; POINT.

touch tablet *n.* DIGITIZING TABLET.

tower model *n.* a computer in which the power supply, motherboard, and mass storage devices are stacked on top of one another in a case.

⇒ See also CHASSIS; DESKTOP MODEL COMPUTER.

TPI tracks per inch: the density of tracks on a disk. For example, high-density 3.5-inch diskettes are formatted with 135 TPI. Hard disks have TPIs in the thousands.

⇒ See also DISK; TRACK.

TP monitor *n.* transaction processing monitor: a program that monitors a transaction as it passes from one stage in a process to another. TP monitors are especially important in three-tier architectures that employ load balancing because a transaction may be forwarded to any of several servers.

⇒ See also CICS; LOAD BALANCING; MIDDLEWARE; THREE-TIER; TRANSACTION PROCESSING.

traceroute *n.* a utility that traces a packet from a computer to an Internet host, showing how many hops the packet requires to reach the host and how long each hop takes.

⇒ See also HOP; PACKET; PING.

track *n.* an annular region on a disk where data can be written. A typical floppy disk has 80 (double-density) or 160 (high-density) tracks. The operating system remembers where information is stored by noting its track and sector numbers. The density of tracks (how close together they are) is measured in terms of tracks per inch (TPI).

⇒ See also CYLINDER; FORMAT; HARD DISK; INTER-LEAVE; SECTOR.

trackball *n.* a pointing device. Essentially, a trackball is a mouse lying on its back. To move the pointer, the ball is rotated with a finger or the palm. There are usually one to three buttons next to the ball, which are used like mouse buttons. The trackball is stationary, so not much space is required to use it.

⇒ See also MOUSE; POINTING DEVICE.

tracks per inch *n.* See TPI.

tractor feed *n.* a method of feeding paper through an impact printer. Tractor-feed printers have two sprocketed wheels on either side of the printer that fit into holes in the paper. As the wheels revolve, the paper is pulled through the printer.

⇒ See also FRICTION FEED; IMPACT PRINTER.

traffic *n.* the load on a communications device or system. One of the principal jobs of a system administrator is to monitor traffic levels and take appropriate actions when traffic becomes heavy.

⇒ See also LOAD.

transaction processing *n.* a type of computer processing in which the computer responds to requests individually. ATMs for banks are an example of transaction processing. The opposite of transaction processing is batch processing.

⇒ See also BATCH PROCESSING; CICS; TP MONITOR; TWO-PHASE COMMIT.

transceiver *n.* transmitter-receiver: a device that both transmits and receives analog or digital signals. The term is used most frequently to describe the component in local-area networks (LANs) that actually applies signals onto the network wire and detects signals passing through the wire.

⇒ See also LOCAL-AREA NETWORK; NETWORK; NETWORK INTERFACE CARD.

transfer rate *n.* DATA TRANSFER RATE.

transistor *n.* a device composed of semiconductor material that amplifies a signal or opens or closes a circuit. Invented in 1947 at Bell Labs, transistors have become the key ingredient of all digital circuits, including computers. Today's microprocessors contain tens of millions of microscopic transistors. Prior to the invention of transistors, digital circuits were composed of vacuum tubes.

⇒ See also CHIP; INTEGRATED CIRCUIT; MOORE'S LAW; SEMICONDUCTOR.

Transmission Control Protocol/Internet Protocol *n.* See TCP/IP.

transparent *adj.* in computer software, referring to complex action (such as converting data from one format to another) that takes place without any visible effect on the user. Transparency is usually considered to be a good characteristic.

transportable *n.* a large portable computer (over 15 pounds). Also called **luggable**.

⇒ See also LAPTOP COMPUTER; NOTEBOOK COMPUTER; PORTABLE.

trap *n.* an interrupt signal initiated by a software program.

trapezoid distortion *n.* See under PINCUSHION DISTORTION.

Travan *n.* a magnetic tape technology that allows for higher data densities. Travan tape drives can read and write older QIC tapes as well as the newer high-capacity Travan tapes.
⇒ See also QIC; TAPE; TAPE DRIVE.

tree structure *n.* a type of data structure in which each element is attached to one or more elements directly *beneath* it. The connections between elements are called branches. Trees are often called *inverted trees* because they are normally drawn with the *root* at the top. The elements at the very bottom of an inverted tree (that is, those that have no elements below them) are called *leaves*. Inverted trees are used to represent hierarchical file structures.
⇒ See also BINARY TREE; BRANCH; DATA STRUCTURE; DIRECTORY; HIERARCHICAL; LEAF.

Triton *n.* the Intel 430 family of Pentium chipsets. The first in the family, the 430FX, is called the *Triton*; the 430 HX is called *Triton 2.* The VX model is sometimes called *Triton-2* or *Triton-3.*
⇒ See also CHIPSET; INTEL MICROPROCESSORS; PENTIUM MICROPROCESSOR.

Trivial File Transfer Protocol *n.* See TFTP.

Trojan horse *n.* a destructive program that masquerades as a benign application. Unlike viruses, Trojan horses do not replicate themselves.
⇒ See also VIRUS.

true color *adj.* referring to any graphics device or software that uses at least 24 bits to represent each dot or pixel. Using 24 bits means that more than 16 million unique colors can be represented.
⇒ See also COLOR DEPTH.

TrueType *n.* an outline font technology developed jointly by Microsoft and Apple. Anyone using Windows or Macintosh operating systems can create documents using TrueType fonts.
⇒ See also FONT; OUTLINE FONT; POSTSCRIPT.

truncate *v.t.* to cut off the end of. Usually, the term is used to describe a type of rounding of floating-point numbers. For example, if there is too little space to print or store a long floating-point number, a program may truncate the number by lopping off the decimal digits that do not fit. Truncation always rounds toward zero: 1.199 truncated to two digits yields 1.1.

⇒ See also FLOATING-POINT NUMBER.

trust hierarchy *n.* PUBLIC-KEY INFRASTRUCTURE (PKI).

TSAPI Telephony Server API: an API developed by Novell and AT&T that enables programmers to build telephony and CTI applications. TSAPI runs on NetWare applications, whereas TAPI has been implemented for the Windows operating system. Another difference is that TSAPI is strictly a server API, whereas TAPI can be used for client- and server-based applications.

⇒ See also API; TAPI; TELEPHONY.

TSR terminate and stay resident: a DOS program that can be memory resident (remaining in memory at all times) regardless of whether it is currently running. Calendars, calculators, spell checkers, thesauruses, and notepads are often set up as TSRs so that they can be instantly accessed from within another program. TSRs are sometimes called *pop-up programs* because they can pop up in applications.

⇒ See also HOT KEY; LOW MEMORY; MEMORY RESIDENT; MULTITASKING; OPERATING SYSTEM.

TTL 1. transistor-transistor logic: a common type of digital circuit in which the output is derived from two transistors. The term is commonly used to describe any system based on digital circuitry, as in *TTL monitor.* **2.** Time to Live: a field in the Internet Protocol (IP) that specifies how many more hops a packet can travel before being discarded or returned.

⇒ See also HOP; IP; SEMICONDUCTOR; TTL MONITOR.

TTL monitor *n.* a computer display, mostly obsolete, that accepts digital inputs rather than analog ones.

⇒ See also ANALOG MONITOR; DIGITAL MONITOR; MDA; TTL.

tunneling *n.* a technology that enables one network to send its data via another network's connections. Tunneling works by encapsulating a network protocol within packets carried by the second network.

⇒ See also L2TP; LAYER TWO FORWARDING; PPTP; VPN.

turnkey system *n.* a computer system that has been customized for a particular application. Turnkey systems include all the hardware and software necessary for the application.

⇒ See also OEM; VAR.

TWAIN (twān), *n.* Technology [or Toolkit] Without An Interesting Name: a de facto interface standard for scanners. Nearly all scanners come with a TWAIN driver, which makes them compatible with any TWAIN-supporting software.

⇒ See also DRIVER; OPTICAL SCANNER.

tweak *v.t., v.i.* to make small changes that fine-tune (a piece of software or hardware). Tweaking sometimes refers to changing the values of underlying variables slightly to make the results of a program coincide with desired results.

⇒ See also DEBUG.

tweening *n.* in-betweening: the process of generating intermediate frames between two images to give the appearance that the first image evolves smoothly into the second image. Tweening is a key process in all types of animation.

⇒ See also ANIMATION.

TWIP *n.* twentieth of a point: a typographical measurement.

⇒ See also POINT.

twisted-pair cable *n.* a type of cable that consists of two independently insulated wires twisted around each other. One wire carries the signal while the other wire is grounded and absorbs signal interference. Twisted-pair cable is used by older telephone networks and is the least expensive type of local-area network (LAN) cable.

⇒ See also 10BASE-T; CDDI; COAXIAL CABLE; FIBER OPTICS; LOCAL-AREA NETWORK.

286 short for the *Intel 80286 microprocessor.*

⇒ See also INTEL MICROPROCESSORS.

two-phase commit *n.* a feature of transaction processing systems that enables databases to be returned to the pre-transaction state if some error condition occurs. A single transaction can update many different databases. The two-phase commit strategy is designed to ensure that either all the databases are updated or none of them, so that the databases remain synchronized.

⇒ See also DISTRIBUTED DATABASE; TRANSACTION PROCESSING.

two-tier *adj.* referring to client/server architectures in which the user interface runs on the client and the database is stored on the server. The actual application logic can run on either the client or the server.

⇒ See also CLIENT/SERVER ARCHITECTURE; THREE-TIER.

Tymnet (tīm′net′), *n.* one of the largest public data networks (PDNs) in the United States, owned by MCI.

⇒ See also NETWORK; TELENET.

type *v.i., v.t.* **1.** to enter (characters) by pressing keys on the keyboard. **2.** in DOS, OS/2, and many other operating systems, the TYPE command causes a file to appear on the display screen. —*n.* **3.** DATA TYPE.

typeface *n.* a design for a set of characters. Popular typefaces include Times Roman, Helvetica, and Courier. The typeface is one aspect of a font.

⇒ See also FONT; FONT FAMILY; SERIF; SANS SERIF.

typesetter *n.* IMAGESETTER.

U u

UART (yōō′ärt′), *n.* universal asynchronous receiver-transmitter: a computer component that handles asynchronous serial communication. Every computer contains a UART to manage the serial ports, and all internal modems have their own UART.
⇒ See also ASYNCHRONOUS; DTE; SERIAL PORT.

UDMA ULTRA DMA.

UDP User Datagram Protocol: a connectionless protocol that, like TCP, runs on top of IP networks. UDP/IP provides very few error recovery services, offering instead a direct way to send and receive individual datagrams over an IP network. It is used primarily for broadcasting messages over a network.
⇒ See also CONNECTIONLESS; IP; IPX; RTP; TCP/IP.

UDP/IP See under UDP.

UIDE Ultra IDE: See ATA-3.

ULSI ultra large scale integration: referring to technology that places more than about one million circuit elements on a single chip. The Intel 486 and Pentium microprocessors use ULSI technology.
⇒ See also CHIP; PENTIUM MICROPROCESSOR.

Ultra2 SCSI *n.* a type of SCSI interface that uses an 8-bit bus and supports data rates of 40 MBps.

Ultra ATA *n.* the newest version of the AT Attachment (ATA) standard, which supports burst mode data transfer rates of 33.3 MBps.
⇒ See also ATA; ULTRA DMA.

Ultra DMA *n.* a protocol developed by Quantum Corporation and Intel that supports burst mode data transfer rates of 33.3 MBps, which is twice as fast as the previous disk drive standard for PCs and is necessary to take advantage of Ultra ATA disk drives. The official name for the protocol is Ultra DMA/33. Also called **UDMA; UDMA/33; DMA mode 33.**
⇒ See also ULTRA ATA.

ultra large scale integration *n.* See ULSI.

Ultra SCSI *n.* a type of SCSI interface that uses an 8-bit bus and supports data rates of 20 MBps.

UML Unified Modeling Language: a general-purpose notational language for specifying and visualizing complex software, esp. large, object-oriented projects.
⇒ See also OBJECT-ORIENTED PROGRAMMING; SOFTWARE ENGINEERING.

UNC Universal Naming Convention *or* Uniform Naming Convention: a PC format for specifying the location of resources on a local-area network (LAN). UNC uses the following format:
\\server-name\shared-resource-pathname
⇒ See also DIRECTORY SERVICE; PATHNAME; RESOURCE.

underflow *n.* the condition that occurs when a computer attempts to represent a number that is too small for it (that is, a number too close to zero).
⇒ See also FLOATING-POINT NUMBER; OVERFLOW ERROR.

undo *v.t.* to reverse (a command) and return to a previous state.
⇒ See also COMMAND.

undocumented *adj.* referring to features that are not described in the official documentation of a product, as features that were useful to the programmers developing the product but were deemed unnecessary to end users.
⇒ See also DOCUMENTATION.

Unicode *n.* a standard for representing characters as integers that uses 16 bits, which means that it can represent more than 65,000 unique characters: necessary for languages such as Chinese and Japanese. Many analysts believe that as the software industry becomes increasingly global, Unicode will eventually supplant ASCII as the standard character coding format.
⇒ See also ASCII; CHARACTER; CHARACTER SET; NTFS.

Unified Modeling Language *n.* See UML.
Uniform Naming Convention *n.* See UNC.
Uniform Resource Identifier *n.* See URI.
Uniform Resource Locator *n.* See URL.

uninterruptible power supply *n.* See UPS.

universal asynchronous receiver-transmitter *n.* See UART.

Universal Naming Convention *n.* See UNC.

Universal Serial Bus *n.* See USB.

UNIX (yōō′niks), *n.* a widely-used multi-user, multitasking operating system. Developed at Bell Labs in the early 1970s, it was one of the first operating systems to be written in a high-level programming language.

⇒ See also A/UX; AIX; BSDI; C; DAEMON; FREE-BSD; GNU; LINUX; MULTITASKING; NFS; OPERATING SYSTEM; OS/2; POSIX; SOLARIS; SUN MICROSYSTEMS; VMS.

Unix-to-Unix Copy *n.* See UUCP.

unpack *v.t.* to convert (a packed file) into its original form. A packed file is a file that has been compressed to take up less storage area.

⇒ See also DATA COMPRESSION.

Unshielded Twisted Pair *n.* See UTP.

upgrade *n.* a new version of a software or hardware product designed to replace an older version of the same product, often sold at a discount to owners of the older version.

⇒ See also ESD; TCO.

upload *v.t.* to transmit (data) from a computer to a bulletin board service, mainframe, or network.

⇒ See also BULLETIN BOARD SYSTEM; DOWNLOAD; NETWORK; ONLINE SERVICE.

uppercase *adj.* referring to capital letters.

⇒ See also CAPS LOCK KEY; CASE SENSITIVE; LOWERCASE.

upper memory *n.* HIGH MEMORY.

UPS uninterruptible power supply: a power supply that can maintain power temporarily in the event of a power outage. This enables the user to save data and shut down the computer safely.

⇒ See also POWER SUPPLY.

upward compatible *adj.* referring to software that runs not only on the computer for which it was designed but also on newer and more powerful models. Also called **forward compatible**.

⇒ See also BACKWARD COMPATIBLE; COMPATIBLE; DOS.

URI Uniform Resource Identifier: the generic term for all types of names and addresses that refer to objects on the World Wide Web. A URL is one kind of URI.
⇒ See also URL.

URL Uniform Resource Locator: the global address of documents and other resources on the World Wide Web. The first part of the address indicates what protocol to use, and the second part specifies the location of the resource.
⇒ See also ADDRESS; INTERNET; PURL; URI; WORLD WIDE WEB.

USB Universal Serial Bus: an external bus standard that supports data transfer rates of 12 Mbps (12 million bits per second). A single USB port can be used to connect up to 127 peripheral devices, such as mice, modems, and keyboards.
⇒ See also BUS; DEVICE BAY; HOT PLUGGING; IEEE 1394; PARALLEL PORT; PCMCIA; SERIAL PORT.

USENET *n.* a worldwide discussion system that contains more than 14,000 forums, called newsgroups.
⇒ See also BULLETIN BOARD SYSTEM; FORUM; INTERNET; NNTP.

user *n.* an individual who uses a computer.
⇒ See also APPLICATION; END USER.

User Datagram Protocol *n.* See UDP.

user-friendly *adj.* referring to anything that makes it easier for people to use a computer, as a menu-driven program or an on-line help system.
⇒ See also GRAPHICAL USER INTERFACE.

user group *n.* a group of individuals with common interests in some aspect of computers.
⇒ See also SIG.

user interface *n.* the set of commands or menus through which a user communicates with a program. A *command-driven interface* is one in which the user enters commands. A *menu-driven interface* is one in which the user selects command choices from various menus displayed on the screen.
⇒ See also COMMAND DRIVEN; CUA; FUNCTIONAL

SPECIFICATION; GRAPHICAL USER INTERFACE; LOOK-AND-FEEL; SAA; XEROX.

username *n.* a name used to gain access to a computer system.

⇒ See also AUTHENTICATION; BULLETIN BOARD SYSTEM; MULTI-USER; ONLINE SERVICE; PASSWORD.

utility *n.* a program that performs a very specific task, usually related to managing system resources such as disk drives, printers, etc.

⇒ See also APPLICATION; TSR.

UTP Unshielded Twisted Pair: a type of cable that consists of two unshielded wires twisted around each other that is used extensively for local-area networks (LANs).

⇒ See also CDDI; COAXIAL CABLE; ETHERNET; FIBER OPTICS; LOCAL-AREA NETWORK.

UUCP UNIX-to-UNIX Copy: a UNIX utility and protocol that enables one computer to send files to another.

⇒ See also FTP; UNIX.

Uudecode *n.* See under UUENCODE.

Uuencode *n.* a set of algorithms for converting files on any platform into a series of 7-bit ASCII characters that can be transmitted over the Internet: esp. popular for sending e-mail attachments. Files are Uudecoded at the receiving end.

⇒ See also BINHEX; E-MAIL; MIME.

V v

V.22 (vē′dot twen′tē tōō′), *n.* the CCITT *V.22* communications standard.
⇒ See also CCITT.

V.22bis (vē′dot twen′tē tōō′bis′), *n.* the CCITT *V.22bis* communications standard.
⇒ See also CCITT.

V.32 (vē′dot thûr′tē tōō′), *n.* the CCITT *V.32* communications standard.
⇒ See also CCITT.

V.34 (vē′dot thûr′tē fôr′), *n.* the CCITT *V.34* communications standard.
⇒ See also CCITT.

V.35 (vē′dot thûr′tē fīv′), an ITU standard for high-speed synchronous data exchange that is used by most routers and DSUs that connect to T-1 carriers in the U.S.
⇒ See also CSU/DSU; ITU.

V.42 (vē′dot fôr′tē tōō′), *n.* the CCITT *V.42* communications standard.
⇒ See also CCITT.

V.90 (vē′dot nīn′tē) *n.* a standard for 56 Kbps modems that resolved the battle between the two competing 56 Kbps technologies—X2 from 3COM and K56flex from Rockwell Semiconductor.
⇒ See also K56FLEX; MODEM; X2.

value-added reseller *n.* See VAR.

vanilla *adj.* without added features: *a vanilla PC.*
⇒ See also FEATURE.

vaporware *n.* a sarcastic term used to designate software and hardware products that have been announced and advertised but are not yet available or may never become available.
⇒ See also BLOATWARE; SOFTWARE.

VAR (*pronounced as separate letters*), *n.* value-added reseller: a company that integrates hardware and software from multiple sources and sells them as a single package to customers.
⇒ See also OEM.

variable *n.* a symbol or name that stands for a value, as x and y in the expression $x + y$.

⇒ See also CHARACTER STRING; CONSTANT; DATA; DATA TYPE; EXPRESSION; LITERAL.

variable-length *adj.* referring to anything whose length can vary: *a variable-length field in a database.*

⇒ See also DATABASE MANAGEMENT SYSTEM; FIELD; FIXED LENGTH; RECORD.

variable-length record *n.* a record that has at least one variable-length field. The length of the entire record, therefore, varies according to what data are placed in the variable-length field.

⇒ See also FIELD; FIXED LENGTH; RECORD; VARIABLE LENGTH.

VAX *n.* Virtual Address eXtension: Digital Equipment Corporation's successor to its PDP-11 line of minicomputers, featuring an operating system, VMS, that supports virtual memory.

⇒ See also DEC; MINICOMPUTER; VMS.

VB VISUAL BASIC.

vBNS very high-speed Backbone Network Service: an experimental wide-area network backbone, sponsored by the National Science Foundation (NSF) and implemented by MCI, that is designed to serve as a platform for testing new, high-speed Internet technologies and protocols.

⇒ See also BACKBONE; I2; INTERNET; NGI INITIATIVE.

VBScript *n.* Visual Basic Scripting Edition: a scripting language, developed by Microsoft and supported by Microsoft's Internet Explorer Web browser, that is based on the Visual Basic programming language but is much simpler.

⇒ See also INTERNET EXPLORER; JAVASCRIPT; JSCRIPT; VISUAL BASIC.

VBX Visual Basic custom control: a reusable software component designed for use in many different applications.

⇒ See also COMPONENT; CONTROL; DLL; OCX; VISUAL BASIC.

VCACHE *n.* the 32-bit disk cache system in Windows 95/98 that replaced the Smartdrive system used in older versions of Windows.

⇒ See also CDFS; DISK CACHE; SMARTDRIVE.

VCPI Virtual Control Program Interface: a specification for managing memory beyond the first

megabyte on PCs with 80386 or later processors.
⇒ See also EXTENDED MEMORY; XMS.

VDT video display terminal. See under MONITOR.

VDT radiation *n.* the radiation emitted by video display terminals.
⇒ See also ELF EMISSION; MONITOR.

VDU visual display unit: an obsolete term for a display monitor.
⇒ See also CRT; MONITOR.

vector *n.* **1.** in computer programming, a one-dimensional array or a pointer. **2.** in computer graphics, a line that is defined by its start and end point.
⇒ See also ARRAY; VECTOR GRAPHICS.

vector font *n.* SCALABLE FONT.

vector graphics *n.* software and hardware that use geometrical expressions to represent images. Also called **object-oriented graphics.**
⇒ See also AUTOTRACING; BÉZIER CURVE; BIT MAP; BIT-MAPPED GRAPHICS; DRAW PROGRAM; GRAPHICS; GRAPHICS FILE FORMATS.

Veronica *n.* a search engine for Gopher sites.
⇒ See also GOPHER; JUGHEAD; SEARCH ENGINE.

VersaModule Eurocard bus *n.* VME BUS.

vertical frequency *n.* See under REFRESH.

vertical justification *n.* a feature supported by some word processors and desktop publishing systems in which the system automatically adjusts the vertical space between lines (the leading) so that columns and pages have an even top and bottom margin. Also called **feathering**.
⇒ See also JUSTIFICATION; LEADING; WORD PROCESSING.

vertical refresh rate *n.* See under REFRESH.

vertical scrolling *n.* See under SCROLL.

very large-scale integration *n.* See VLSI.

VESA Video Electronics Standards Association: a consortium of video adapter and monitor manufacturers whose goal is to standardize video protocols.
⇒ See also DDC; SVGA; VL-BUS.

VESA Local Bus *n.* VL-BUS.

VFAT Virtual File Allocation Table: the 32-bit file

system used in Windows for Workgroups and Windows 95/98.

⇒ See also FILE ALLOCATION TABLE; FILE MANAGEMENT SYSTEM; WINDOWS 95.

VGA video graphics array: a graphics display system developed by IBM that has become one of the de facto standards for PCs.

⇒ See also SVGA; VIDEO ADAPTER; ZV PORT.

VGA Plus *n.* See under SVGA.

video *adj.* **1.** referring to recording, manipulating, and displaying moving images, esp. in a format that can be presented on a television. **2.** referring to displaying images and text on a computer monitor. —*n.* **3.** a recording produced with a video recorder (camcorder) or some similar device.

⇒ See also DVI; INDEO; QUICKTIME; REALVIDEO; S-VIDEO; SHOCKWAVE; VIDEO CAPTURE; VIDEO EDITING; VIDEO FOR WINDOWS; VIDEO OVERLAY; VIDEO STANDARDS; VIDEOCONFERENCING.

video accelerator *n.* GRAPHICS ACCELERATOR.

video adapter *n.* a board that plugs into a personal computer to give it display capabilities. Most modern video adapters contain memory, so that the computer's RAM is not used for storing displays. In addition, most adapters have their own graphics coprocessor for performing graphics calculations. These adapters are often called *graphics accelerators.* Also called **video card, video board, video display board, graphics card, graphics adapter.**

⇒ See also 8514/A; ADAPTER; COLOR DEPTH; DDC; DIRECTDRAW; GRAPHICS ACCELERATOR; MDRAM; MONITOR; PAL; RAMDAC; SGRAM; VIDEO MEMORY; VIDEO MODE; VIDEO STANDARDS; VRAM; WRAM.

video capture *n.* the conversion of analog video signals, such as those generated by a video camera, into a digital format that is then stored on a computer's mass storage device.

⇒ See also DIGITAL VIDEO; VIDEO EDITING.

video card *n.* VIDEO ADAPTER.

videoconferencing *n.* conducting a conference between two or more participants at different sites by using computer networks to transmit audio and video data.

⇒ See also APPLICATION SHARING; COMMON INTERMEDIATE FORMAT; CU-SeeMe; DISTANCE LEARNING; H. 323; H.324; QCIF; RTP; TELECONFERENCE; WORKGROUP COMPUTING.

video display board *n.* VIDEO ADAPTER.

video editing *n.* the process of manipulating video images by cutting segments (trimming), resequencing clips, and adding transitions and other special effects.

⇒ See also DIGITAL VIDEO; MPEG; SGI; VIDEO CAPTURE.

Video Electronics Standards Association *n.* See VESA.

Video for Windows *n.* a format developed by Microsoft Corporation for storing video and audio information.

⇒ See also CODEC; MPEG; QUICKTIME.

Video Graphics Array *n.* See VGA.

video memory *n.* RAM installed on a video adapter. The amount of video memory dictates the maximum resolution and color depth available.

⇒ See also BIT MAP; GRAPHICS ACCELERATOR; MAIN MEMORY; RAMDAC; RDRAM; SGRAM; VIDEO ADAPTER; VRAM; WRAM.

video mode *n.* the setting of a video adapter. Most video adapters can run in either *text mode* or *graphics mode*.

⇒ See also GRAPHICS MODE; TEXT MODE; VIDEO ADAPTER.

Video-on-Demand *n.* See VoD.

video overlay *n.* the placement of a full-motion video window on the display screen.

⇒ See also NTSC; VIDEO ADAPTER.

video RAM *n.* See VRAM.

video standard *n.* any of the standards that defines the resolution and colors for displays on a monitor.

⇒ See also 8514/A; MCGA; MDA; SVGA; TI 34010; VGA; VIDEO ADAPTER; XGA.

view *n.* in database management systems, a particular way of looking at the records in a database. A single database can support numerous different views. Typically, a view arranges the records in some order and makes only certain fields visible.

⇒ See also DATABASE; DATABASE MANAGEMENT SYSTEM; FIELD.

viewer *n.* a utility program that enables the user to read a file.

⇒ See also FILE MANAGEMENT SYSTEM; FORMAT; SHELL.

virtual *adj.* not real; referring to something that behaves in some ways like the object in question, but without physical reality: *virtual memory*.

⇒ See also VIRTUAL MACHINE; VIRTUAL MEMORY; VIRTUAL SERVER; VLAN.

virtual circuit *n.* a permanent or temporary connection between two devices that acts as though it is a direct physical connection: used to describe certain connections between two hosts in a packet-switching network.

⇒ See also PACKET SWITCHING; PVC; SVC.

Virtual Control Program Interface *n.* See VCPI.

virtual desktop *n.* **1.** a feature supported by some notebook computers that enables them to display images on an external monitor at a higher resolution than is supported by the built-in flat-panel display. **2.** a feature supported by some video adapters that enables them to provide a desktop larger than what is actually displayed. The user scrolls the display to see hidden areas.

⇒ See also FLAT-PANEL DISPLAY; NOTEBOOK COMPUTER.

virtual device driver *n.* in Windows systems, a special type of device driver that has direct access to the operating system. In Windows 95, virtual device drivers are often called *VxDs* because the filenames end with the .vxd extension.

⇒ See also DRIVER.

virtual disk *n.* RAM DISK.

Virtual File Allocation Table *n.* See VFAT.

virtual LAN *n.* See VLAN.

virtual machine *n.* **1.** a self-contained operating environment that behaves as if it is a separate computer. **2.** a specification for a computing system that can then be instantiated by many different kinds of hardware or software.

⇒ See also Java; JIT; OPERATING ENVIRONMENT; VIRTUAL.

virtual memory *n.* a conceptual view of memory supported by some operating systems, as UNIX, in conjunction with the hardware in order to increase the amount of instructions and data that can be stored. When the program is actually executed, the virtual addresses are converted into real memory addresses.

⇒ See also ADDRESS SPACE; MAIN MEMORY; MEMORY; MMU; OPERATING SYSTEM; PAGE; PAGE FAULT; PAGING; SWAP; THRASH; VIRTUAL.

Virtual Memory System *n.* See VMS.

virtual private network *n.* See VPN.

virtual reality *n.* **1.** an artificial environment created with computer hardware and software and presented to the user in such a way that it appears and feels like a real environment. To "enter" a virtual reality, a user dons special gloves, earphones, and goggles, all of which receive their input from the computer system. **2.** any virtual world represented in a computer as a text-based or graphical representation.

⇒ See also AVATAR; CYBERSPACE; HMD; MUD; QuickTime VR; VIRTUAL; VRML.

Virtual Reality Modeling Language *n.* See VRML.

virtual server *n.* a server, usually a Web server, that shares computer resources with other virtual servers.

⇒ See also SERVER; VIRTUAL; WEB SERVER.

virus *n.* a program or piece of code that is loaded onto a computer without the user's knowledge and runs against the user's wishes. Most viruses can also replicate themselves and are capable of using all available memory and bringing the entire system to a halt.

⇒ See also ANTIVIRUS PROGRAM; ARPANET; BOOTABLE DISKETTE; DATA RECOVERY; HACKER; MACRO VIRUS; MBR; NETWORK; Trojan horse.

VisiCalc *n.* the first electronic spreadsheet application, introduced in the late 1970s.

⇒ See also LOTUS 1-2-3; SPREADSHEET.

Visual Basic *n.* a programming language and environment developed by Microsoft. Based on the BASIC language, Visual Basic was one of the first products to provide a graphical programming environment and a paint metaphor for developing user interfaces.

⇒ See also BASIC; DAO; DELPHI; JET; MICROSOFT; PROGRAMMING LANGUAGE; RAPID APPLICATION DEVELOPMENT; VBSCRIPT; VBX.

Visual Basic custom control *n.* See VBX.

Visual Basic Scripting Edition *n.* VBSCRIPT.

Visual C++ *n.* an application development tool, developed by Microsoft for C++ programmers, that supports object-oriented programming of 32-bit Windows applications.

⇒ See also C; C++; IDE; MFC; OBJECT-ORIENTED PROGRAMMING.

visual display unit *n.* See VDU.

VLAN virtual LAN: a network of computers that behave as if they were connected to the same wire even though they may actually be physically located on different segments of a LAN.

⇒ See also LOCAL-AREA NETWORK; VIRTUAL.

VLB VESA LOCAL-BUS.

VL-Bus VESA Local-Bus: a local bus architecture created by the Video Electronics Standards Association (VESA).

⇒ See also EXPANSION BUS; LOCAL BUS; PCI.

VLSI very large-scale integration: the process of placing hundreds of thousands of electronic components on a single chip.

⇒ See also CHIP; INTEGRATED CIRCUIT; ULSI.

VM VIRTUAL MACHINE.

VME See under VME BUS.

VME bus *n.* Versa Module Eurocard bus: a 32-bit bus developed by Motorola, Signetics, Mostek, and Thompson CSF that is widely used in industrial, commercial, and military applications.

⇒ See also BACKPLANE; BUS.

VMS Virtual Memory System: a multi-user, multitasking, virtual memory operating system that runs on DEC's VAX and Alpha lines of minicomputers and workstations.

⇒ See also MULTI-USER; MULTITASKING; OPERATING SYSTEM; UNIX; VAX; VIRTUAL MEMORY.

VoD Video-on-Demand: an umbrella term for a wide set of technologies and companies whose common goal is to enable individuals to select videos from a central server for viewing on a television or computer screen.

⇒ See also VIDEO.

VOI Voice over the Internet: See INTERNET TELEPHONY.

voice mail n. a voice message held on a central server for later retrieval.

⇒ See also E-MAIL.

Voice over the Internet n. INTERNET TELEPHONY.

voice recognition n. the field of computer science that deals with designing computer systems that can recognize spoken words.

⇒ See also ARTIFICIAL INTELLIGENCE; NATURAL LANGUAGE.

VOIP Voice Over IP: See INTERNET TELEPHONY.

volatile memory n. memory, as most RAM, that loses its contents when the power is turned off.

⇒ See also MEMORY; RAM; ROM.

voltage regulator n. a small device or circuit that regulates the voltage fed to the microprocessor.

⇒ See also HEAT SINK; MICROPROCESSOR; MOTHERBOARD; POWER SUPPLY; VRM.

voltage regulator module n. See VRM.

volume n. a fixed unit of disk or tape storage.

⇒ See also DISK; MASS STORAGE.

volume label n. in DOS systems, the name of a volume, as a disk or tape.

⇒ See also DISK; LABEL; VOLUME.

VON Voice on the Net: a coalition of Internet telephony software producers whose main goal is to ensure that the telephone companies do not succeed in their bid to outlaw Internet telephony.

VPN virtual private network: a network that is

constructed by using public links, as the Internet, to connect nodes.

⇒ See also L2TP; LAYER TWO FORWARDING; PPTP; TUNNELING.

VRAM (vē′ram′), *n.* video RAM: special-purpose memory used by video adapters.

⇒ See also GRAPHICS; GRAPHICS ACCELERATOR; MDRAM; MEMORY; MONITOR; PROCESSOR; RAM; VIDEO MEMORY.

VRM voltage regulator module: a small module that installs on a motherboard to regulate the voltage to the microprocessor.

⇒ See also POWER SUPPLY; VOLTAGE REGULATOR.

VRML (vûr′məl), *n.* Virtual Reality Modeling Language: a specification for displaying three-dimensional objects on the World Wide Web.

⇒ See also BROWSER; CYBERSPACE; HTML; MODELING; QUICKTIME VR; VIRTUAL REALITY; WORLD WIDE WEB.

VSAM (vē′sam) *n.* Virtual Sequential Access Method: a file management system used on IBM mainframes that speeds up access to data by using an inverted index of all records added to each file.

⇒ See also FILE MANAGEMENT SYSTEM; LEGACY APPLICATION; MAINFRAME; MVS.

VTAM (vē′tam) *n.* Virtual Telecommunications Access Method: the software component that controls communications in Systems Network Architecture (SNA) networks.

⇒ See also SNA; TOKEN-RING NETWORK.

VxD See under VIRTUAL DEVICE DRIVER.

W w

W3C World Wide Web Consortium: an international consortium of companies involved with the Internet and the Web whose purpose is to develop open standards so that the Web evolves in a single direction rather than being splintered among competing factions.
⇒ See also HTML; HTTP; WORLD WIDE WEB.

WAIS (wās) *n.* Wide Area Information Server: a program for retrieving documents on the Internet.
⇒ See also GOPHER; INTERNET.

wait state *n.* a period during which a CPU or bus lies idle to enable a component that functions at a slower speed to catch up.
⇒ See also BURST MODE; CACHE; CLOCK SPEED; FPM RAM; INTERLEAVE; LATENCY; PIPELINE BURST CACHE; SDRAM.

WAN (wan *or pronounced as initials*), *n.* WIDE-AREA NETWORK.

warez (wârz, wârs) *n.* commercial software that has been pirated and made available to the public via a BBS or the Internet.
⇒ See also COPY PROTECTION; FREEWARE; SHAREWARE; SOFTWARE PIRACY.

warm boot *n.* the process of resetting a computer that is already turned on: sometimes necessary when a program encounters an error from which it cannot recover.
⇒ See also BOOT; COLD BOOT.

WAV (wāv) *n.* the format for storing sound in files, developed jointly by Microsoft and IBM.
⇒ See also AU; MULTIMEDIA.

Wavelength Division Multiplexing *n.* See WDM.

wavetable *n.* the stored samples for WAVE TABLE SYNTHESIS.

wave table synthesis *n.* a technique that stores digital samples of sound from various instruments, which can then be combined, edited, and enhanced to reproduce sound defined by a digital input signal.
⇒ See also MIDI; SOUND CARD.

WDM Wavelength Division Multiplexing: a type of multiplexing developed for use on optical fiber that modulates each of several data streams onto a different part of the light spectrum.
⇒ See also FDM; FIBER OPTICS; MULTIPLEX; TDM.

Web *n.* WORLD WIDE WEB.

Web browser *n.* BROWSER.

webcasting *n.* the use of the World Wide Web to broadcast information.
⇒ See also BROADCAST; PointCast; PUSH.

webCrawler *n.* a popular Web search engine run by America Online.
⇒ See also ALTA VISTA; EXCITE; INFOSEEK; LYCOS; OPEN TEXT; SEARCH ENGINE.

webcrawler *n.* SPIDER.

Webmaster *n.* an individual who manages a Web site, performing tasks such as creating and updating Web pages, monitoring traffic through the site, etc.
⇒ See also CGI; WEB PAGE; WEB SITE.

Web page *n.* a document on the World Wide Web.
⇒ See also DOM; HOME PAGE; URL; WEB SERVER; WEBMASTER; WORLD WIDE WEB.

Web server *n.* a computer that delivers Web pages to machines that request them.
⇒ See also APACHE WEB SERVER; IIS; PROXY SERVER; SERVER; VIRTUAL SERVER; WEB PAGE; WEB SITE; WORLD WIDE WEB.

Web site *n.* a coherent collection of one or more pages (URLs) on the World Wide Web, usually under a single domain or username.
⇒ See also E-ZINE; HOME PAGE; WEB SERVER; WEBMASTER; WORLD WIDE WEB.

WebTV *n.* a category of products and technologies that enable users to surf the Web on a TV. WebTV products make a connection to the Internet via telephone service.
⇒ See also CABLE MODEM; OS/9; PC/TV; WORLD WIDE WEB.

what-you-see-is-what-you-get *adj.* WYSIWYG.

whiteboard *n.* **1.** an area on a display screen on

which multiple users can write or draw: a principal component of teleconferencing applications. **2.** a large, smooth, glossy sheet of white plastic used in offices for making presentations with markers.

⇒ See also APPLICATION SHARING; TELECONFERENCE.

White Book *n.* the specification covering the video CD format.

⇒ See also YELLOW BOOK.

whitespace *n.* all characters that appear as blanks on a display screen or printer, such as the space character and the tab character.

⇒ See also NULL CHARACTER.

whois (hoo´iz´), *n.* an Internet utility that returns information about a domain name or IP address.

⇒ See also DOMAIN NAME; FINGER; IP ADDRESS.

Wide Area Information Server *n.* See WAIS.

wide-area network *n.* a computer network that spans a relatively large geographical area usu. consisting of two or more local-area networks (LANs).

⇒ See also BRIDGE; INTERNET; INTERNETWORKING; LOCAL-AREA NETWORK; MAN; NETWORK; PACKET SWITCHING; SMDS.

wide SCSI *n.* See under SCSI.

widow *n.* **1.** in word processing, the last line of a paragraph that appears as the first line of a page. **2.** the last line of a paragraph that is much shorter than all the other lines in the paragraph.

⇒ See also ORPHAN; PAGINATION; WORD PROCESSING.

wildcard character *n.* a special symbol that stands for one or more characters, used for identifying files and directories, and enabling the user to select multiple files with a single specification, as the asterisk (*) in UNIX.

⇒ See also FILENAME.

Win32 *n.* the Windows API for developing 32-bit applications.

⇒ See also API; WIN32s; WINDOWS; WINDOWS 95; WINDOWS NT.

Win32s *n.* WIN32 subset: a software package that can be added to Windows 3.1 and Windows for Workgroups systems to give them the ability to run some 32-bit applications.

⇒ See also THUNK; WIN32; WINDOWS.

Win95 *n.* WINDOWS 95.

Winchester disk drive *n.* HARD DISK DRIVE.

⇒ See also DISK DRIVE; HARD DISK.

window *n.* **1.** an enclosed, rectangular area on a display screen. Most modern operating systems and applications have graphical user interfaces that allow the user to divide the display into several windows. Within each window, it is possible to run a different program or display different data. **2.** a logical view of a file.

⇒ See also DIALOG BOX; GRAPHICAL USER INTERFACE; ICON; MDI; MICROSOFT WINDOWS.

Windows *n.* MICROSOFT WINDOWS.

⇒ See also MICROSOFT; WIN32s; WINDOWS 98; WINDOWS CE; WINFRAME; WINTEL.

Windows 95 *n.* a major release of the Microsoft Windows operating system released in 1995.

⇒ See also DIAL-UP NETWORKING; MICROSOFT WINDOWS; OSR 2; REGISTRY; VFAT; WIN32; WINDOWS 98; WINDOWS CE; WINDOWS NT.

Windows 98 *n.* the successor to Windows 95, released in mid-1998.

⇒ See also INTERNET EXPLORER; WINDOWS; WINDOWS 95; WINDOWS NT.

Windows CE *n.* a version of the Windows operating system designed for small devices such as personal digital assistants (PDAs).

⇒ See also HAND-HELD COMPUTER; HPC; PALMTOP; PDA; WINDOWS.

Windows DNA *n.* Windows Distributed (Inter) Net Applications Architecture: a marketing name for a collection of Microsoft technologies that enables the Windows platform to work with the Internet.

⇒ See also ACTIVEX; COM; DYNAMIC HTML.

Windows Internet Naming Service *n.* See WINS.

Windows Metafile Format *n.* See WMF.

Windows NT *n.* a 32-bit operating system that supports preemptive multitasking.

⇒ See also MICROSOFT WINDOWS; MULTITASKING; OPERATING SYSTEM; WINDOWS TERMINAL; WINFRAME.

Windows terminal *n.* a terminal that is connected to a Windows NT server through a network and that sends the user's input (keystrokes and mouse movements) to the server and displays the results on the display screen but does not process or store data.

⇒ See also DUMB TERMINAL; NC; NET PC; NETWORK COMPUTER; WINDOWS NT; WINFRAME.

WinFrame *n.* a technology developed by Citrix Systems that turns Windows NT into a multi-user operating system.

⇒ See also THIN CLIENT; WINDOWS; WINDOWS NT; WINDOWS TERMINAL; X-WINDOW.

WINMAIL.DAT *n.* See under TNEF.

WINS *n.* Windows Internet Naming Service: a Windows system that determines the IP address associated with a particular network computer.

⇒ See also DHCP; DNS; IP ADDRESS.

Winsock (win′sok′) *n.* Windows Socket: an Application Programming Interface (API) for developing Windows programs that can communicate with other machines via the TCP/IP protocol.

⇒ See also API; MTU; PROTOCOL STACK; SOCKET; TCP/IP.

Wintel (win′tel) *adj. Informal.* of or designating a computer that uses an Intel microprocessor and any of the Windows operating systems.

⇒ See also INTEL; INTEL MICROPROCESSORS; MICROSOFT; WINDOWS.

wireless modem *n.* a modem that accesses a private wireless data network or a wireless telephone system, such as the CDPD system.

⇒ See also CDPD; MODEM.

wizard *n.* **1.** a utility within an application that assists in the use of the application to perform a particular task. **2.** Also called **super-programmer.** an outstanding programmer. **3.** the system administrator for a chat room or MUD.

⇒ See also UTILITY.

WMF *n.* Windows Metafile Format: a graphics file format used to exchange graphics information between Microsoft Windows applications.

⇒ See also GRAPHICS; GRAPHICS FILE FORMATS.

Wolfpack *n.* the codename for Microsoft's clustering solution, Microsoft Cluster Server (MSCS).

⇒ See also CLUSTERING; MSCS; WINDOWS NT.

word *n.* **1.** in word processing, any group of characters separated by spaces or punctuation on both sides. **2.** in programming, the natural data size, such as 32 bits, that can be handled by a computer processor. **3.** MICROSOFT WORD.

⇒ See also BIT; BYTE; CPU.

WordPerfect *n.* one of the most popular word processors for PCs and Apple Macintoshes.

⇒ See also WORD PROCESSING.

word processing *n.* the use of a computer to create, edit, and print documents.

⇒ See also COPY; CUT; DELETE; DESKTOP PUBLISHING; EDITOR; FONT; FOOTER; GRAPHICS; HEADER; HYPHENATION; INSERT; JUSTIFY; LAYOUT; MACRO.

word processor *n.* a program or computer that enables the user to perform word processing functions.

⇒ See also WORD PROCESSING.

word wrap *n.* in word processing, a feature that causes the word processor to force all text to fit within the defined margins by moving automatically to the next line, observing appropriate word breaks, when the right margin is reached. The user is not required to insert hard returns manually within a paragraph of continuous text.

⇒ See also HARD RETURN; HYPHENATION; MARGINS; SOFT RETURN; WORD PROCESSING.

workflow *n.* the defined series of tasks within an organization to produce a final outcome. Sophisticated workgroup computing applications allow the user to define different workflows for different types of jobs.

⇒ See also WORKGROUP COMPUTING.

workgroup *n.* a collection of individuals working together on a task.

workgroup computing *n.* the connection to a network by all the individuals in a workgroup that allows them to send e-mail to one another, share data files, and schedule meetings.

⇒ See also E-MAIL; GROUPWARE; TELECONFERENCE; WORKFLOW; WORKGROUP.

workgroup productivity package *n.* a software package that includes e-mail, calendar programs, scheduling programs, and other utilities that promote communication between users on a local-area network.
⇒ See also CALENDAR; E-MAIL; LOCAL-AREA NETWORK; SCHEDULER; WORKGROUP COMPUTING.

working directory *n.* the directory in which one is currently working.
⇒ See also DIRECTORY; PATHNAME; ROOT DIRECTORY.

worksheet *n.* SPREADSHEET.

workstation *n.* **1.** a type of computer used for engineering applications (CAD/CAM), desktop publishing, software development, and other types of applications that require a moderate amount of computing power and relatively high-quality graphics capabilities. **2.** in networking, any computer connected to a local-area network.
⇒ See also CAD/CAM; COMPUTER; DESKTOP PUBLISHING; DISKLESS WORKSTATION; GRAPHICS; LOCAL-AREA NETWORK; NETWORK; NETWORK COMPUTER; PERSONAL COMPUTER; SGI; UNIX.

World Wide Web *n.* the system of Internet servers that delivers documents formatted in a language called HTML (HyperText Markup Language). It supports links to other documents, as well as graphics, audio, and video files.
⇒ See also BROWSER; CERN; CGI; HTML; HTTP; HYPERMEDIA; HYPERTEXT; INTERNET; MOSAIC; SURF; W3C; WEB SITE; WEBTV.

WORM *n.* write once, read many (times): an optical disk technology that allows the user to write data onto a disk only once. After that, the data are permanent and can be read any number of times.
⇒ See also CD-ROM; ERASABLE OPTICAL DISK; MASS STORAGE; OPTICAL DISK; PHASE CHANGE DISK.

WRAM *n.* Windows RAM: a type of RAM developed by Samsung Electronics that supports two ports, enabling a video adapter to fetch the contents of memory for display at the same time that new bytes are being written.

⇒ See also RAM; SGRAM; VIDEO ADAPTER; VIDEO MEMORY; VRAM.

write *v.t.* to copy (data) from main memory to a storage device, such as a disk.
⇒ See also ACCESS; READ; WRITE-BACK CACHE.

write-back cache *n.* a caching method in which modifications to data in the cache are not copied to the cache source until the cache line is replaced by an unrelated one. Also called **copy-back cache.**
⇒ See also CACHE; WRITE.

write once/read many *n.* See WORM.

write-protect *v.t.* to mark (a file or disk) so that the contents cannot be modified or deleted.
⇒ See also FLOPPY DISK; LOCK.

write-through cache *n.* a cache in which modifications to cached data are simultaneously written to main memory.

WWW *n.* WORLD WIDE WEB.

WYSIWYG (wiz′ē wig′) *adj.* What You See Is What You Get: referring to an application that shows on the screen exactly what will appear when the document is printed.
⇒ See also COLOR MATCHING; DESKTOP PUBLISHING; FONT; POSTSCRIPT; RESOLUTION; WORD PROCESSING; WYSIWYP.

WYSIWYP (wiz′ē wip′) *adj.* What You See Is What You Print: referring to the ability of a computer system to print colors exactly as they appear on a monitor.
⇒ See also COLOR MANAGEMENT SYSTEM (CMS); COLOR MATCHING; WYSIWYG.

X x

X2 a technology developed by U.S. Robotics (now 3COM) for delivering data rates up to 56 Kbps over analog telephone lines.
⇒ See also K56FLEX; MODEM; V.90.

X.25 (eks′dot twen′tē fīv′) *n.* a popular standard for packet-switching networks.
⇒ See also CCITT; PACKET SWITCHING.

X.400 (eks′dot fôr′hun′drid) *n.* an ISO and ITU standard for addressing and transporting e-mail messages.
⇒ See also CCITT; E-MAIL ADDRESS; X.500.

X.500 (eks′dot fīv′hun′drid) *n.* an ISO and ITU standard that defines how global directories should be structured.
⇒ See also ACTIVE DIRECTORY; CCITT; DIRECTORY SERVICE; ITU; NDS; X.400.

X.509 (eks′dot fīv′ō nīn′) *n.* the most widely used standard for defining digital certificates.
⇒ See also DIGITAL CERTIFICATE; SSL.

x86 (eks′dot ā′tē siks′) *n.* See under INTEL MICROPROCESSORS.

xDSL the collective term for all types of digital subscriber lines, which use sophisticated modulation schemes to jam data through copper wires.
⇒ See also ADSL; ISDN; POTS; SDSL.

Xenix (zē′niks) *n.* a version of UNIX that runs on PCs.
⇒ See also OPERATING SYSTEM; UNIX.

Xerox (zēr′oks) *n.* a company that is best known for its photocopiers. Xerox Corporation also has conducted pioneering work on user interfaces and document management. Modern GUIs trace their inspiration to Xerox's Palo Alto Research Center.
⇒ See also GRAPHICAL USER INTERFACE; LASER PRINTER; USER INTERFACE.

XGA extended graphics array: a high-resolution graphics standard introduced by IBM in 1990.
⇒ See also 8514/A; INTERLACING; RESOLUTION; SVGA; VGA; VIDEO STANDARDS.

x-height *n.* in typography, the height of a lower-case *x* in a specific font. Also called **body height.**

⇒ See also ASCENDER; BASELINE; DESCENDER; TYPEFACE.

XML eXtensible Markup Language: a pared-down, simplified version of SGML, designed especially for Web documents, that enables designers to create their own customized tags to provide functionality not available with HTML.

⇒ See also DOM; HTML; SGML; TAG.

Xmodem *n.* one of the most popular non-Internet file transfer protocols.

⇒ See also COMMUNICATIONS PROTOCOL; COMMUNICATIONS SOFTWARE; KERMIT; MODEM; PROTOCOL; YMODEM; ZMODEM.

XMS Extended Memory Specification: a procedure for using extended memory and DOS's high memory area, a 64K block just above 1 MB.

⇒ See also EXPANDED MEMORY; EXTENDED MEMORY; HIGH MEMORY AREA.

XOR operator *n.* exclusive OR operator: a Boolean operator that returns a value of TRUE only if just one of its operands is TRUE.

⇒ See also BOOLEAN OPERATOR.

XT form factor *n.* BABY AT.

X-Window *n.* a windowing and graphics system developed at the Massachusetts Institute of Technology (MIT), which has placed the X-Window source code in the public domain, making it a particularly attractive system for UNIX vendors.

⇒ See also GRAPHICAL USER INTERFACE; PUBLIC-DOMAIN SOFTWARE; SOLARIS; UNIX.

Y y

Y2K Year 2000 Problem.

Yahoo! Yet Another Hierarchical Officious Oracle: a World Wide Web directory started by David Filo and Jerry Yang at Stanford University. It is the leading Web portal (the starting location for Web activities).
⇒ See also Alta Vista; Excite; HotBot; Infoseek; Lycos; Magellan.

Y/C video *n.* See under S-Video.

Year 2000 problem *n.* the pervasive problem caused by the fact that many applications are designed to assume that all years begin with '19'. Also called **millennium bug, Y2K problem.**
⇒ See also accounting software.

Yellow Book *n.* the specification for CD-ROMs and CD-ROM/XA.
⇒ See also CD-ROM; CD-ROM/XA; Green Book; Orange Book; Red Book; White Book.

Ymodem *n.* an asynchronous communications protocol that extends Xmodem by increasing the number of bytes transferred between acknowledgments and by supporting batch file transfers.
⇒ See also batch processing; communications protocol; Xmodem; Zmodem.

yottabyte *n.* 2^{80} bytes, which is approximately 10^{24} (1,000,000,000,000,000,000,000,000) bytes. A yottabyte is equal to 1,024 zettabytes. [*yotta* is the second-to-last letter of the Latin alphabet and it sounds like the Greek letter *iota*]
⇒ See also exabyte; zettabyte.

Z z

ZAW *n.* Zero Administration for Windows: a collection of utilities developed by Microsoft that enables administrators to centrally manage and update software on PCs connected to a LAN.
⇒ See also NET PC; NETWORK COMPUTER; TCO.

Z-buffer *n.* an area in graphics memory reserved for storing the Z-axis value of each pixel.
⇒ See also 3-D GRAPHICS; Z-BUFFERING.

Z-buffering *n.* an algorithm used in 3-D graphics to determine which objects, or parts of objects, are visible and which are hidden behind other objects.
⇒ See also 3-D GRAPHICS; Z-BUFFER.

Zero Administration for Windows *n.* See ZAW.

Zero Insertion Force (ZIF) socket *n.* a chip socket that allows the user to insert and remove a chip without special tools.
⇒ See also CHIP.

zero wait state *adj.* referring to systems that have no *wait states*—that is, they allow the microprocessor to run at its maximum speed without waiting for the memory chips.
⇒ See also WAIT STATE.

zettabyte *n.* 2^{70} bytes, which is approximately 10^{21} (1,000,000,000,000,000,000,000) bytes. A zettabyte is equal to 1,024 exabytes. [*zetta* is the last letter of the Latin alphabet]
⇒ See also EXABYTE; YOTTABYTE.

ZIF socket *n.* ZERO INSERTION FORCE (ZIF) SOCKET.

zine *n.* E-ZINE.

ZIP (zip) *n.* a popular data compression format. Files that have been compressed with the ZIP format are called *ZIP files* and usually end with a .*zip* extension.
⇒ See also ARC; DATA COMPRESSION; LZW.

Zip drive *n.* a high-capacity floppy disk drive developed by Iomega Corporation. Zip disks are slightly larger than conventional floppy disks and can hold 100 MB of data. New generations of Zip drives and disks hold more.

⇒ See also FLOPPY DISK; FLOPPY DRIVE; HiFD; SuperDisk.

Zmodem *n.* an asynchronous communications protocol that provides faster data transfer rates and better error detection than Xmodem.

⇒ See also COMMUNICATIONS PROTOCOL; KERMIT; XMODEM; YMODEM.

zoom *v.i.* in graphical user interfaces, to make a window larger. Many applications also provide a zoom feature, which enlarges the view of an object, such as a portion of text, enabling you to see more detail.

⇒ See also BOX; GRAPHICAL USER INTERFACE; MAXIMIZE.

zoomed video *n.* See under ZV PORT.

ZV Port *n.* zoomed video port: a port that enables data to be transferred directly from a PC card to a VGA controller.

⇒ See also BUS; LAPTOP COMPUTER; NOTEBOOK COMPUTER; PC CARD; PCMCIA; VGA.